ISSN 1681-4789

2004 EDITION

Eurostat yearbook 2004

The statistical guide to Europe

Data 1992-2002

1

EUROPEAN
COMMISSION

eurostat

THEME 1
General
statistics

·········Immediate access to harmonised statistical data

Internet

Essentials on Community statistical news

★ Euro indicators: more than 100 indicators on the euro zone; harmonised, comparable, and free of charge.

★ About Eurostat: what it does and how it works.

★ Products and databases: a detailed description of what Eurostat has to offer.

★ Indicators on the European Union: convergence criteria; euro yield curve and further main indicators on the European Union at your disposal.

★ Press releases: direct access to all Eurostat press releases.

For further information, visit us on the Internet: **www.europa.eu.int/comm/eurostat/**

Europe Direct is a service to help you find answers to your questions about the European Union

New freephone number:
00 800 6 7 8 9 10 11

Cataloguing data can be found at the end of this publication.

A great deal of additional information on Eurostat is available on the Internet:
http://www.europa.eu.int/comm/eurostat/

Office for Official Publications of the European Communities, 2004

ISBN 92-894-4963-2
ISSN 1681-4789

EUROSTAT

L-2920 Luxembourg — Tel. (352) 43 01-1 — Telex COMEUR LU 3423

Eurostat is the Statistical Office of the European Communities. Its task is to provide the European Union with statistics, at a European level, that allow comparisons to be made between countries and regions. Eurostat consolidates and harmonises the data collected by the Member States.

To ensure that the vast quantity of accessible data is made widely available and to help each user make proper use of the information, Eurostat has set up a publications and services programme.

This programme makes a clear distinction between general and specialist users and particular collections have been developed for these different groups. The collections *Press releases*, *Statistics in focus*, *Panorama of the European Union*, *Pocketbooks* and *Catalogues* are aimed at general users. They give immediate key information through analyses, tables, graphs and maps.

The collections *Methods and nomenclatures* and *Detailed tables* suit the needs of the specialist who is prepared to spend more time analysing and using very detailed information and tables.

As part of the new programme, Eurostat has developed its web site. It includes a broad range of online information on Eurostat products and services, newsletters, catalogues, online publications and indicators on the euro zone.

Eurostat

ACKNOWLEDGEMENTS

The authors of the Eurostat yearbook 2004 would like to thank all those who were involved in its preparation. The Yearbook could be published thanks to the assistance and support of the following colleagues:

EUROSTAT, THE STATISTICAL OFFICE OF THE EUROPEAN COMMUNITIES

Unit A5: Information and dissemination
M. Copers, V. Guillemet, A. Johansson-Augier, G. Kyi, M. Radulescu,
with the assistance and support of the following Eurostat directorates:

Directorate B: Statistical methodologies and tools
B1 Coordination of methods (M. Hahn, M. Léonard, M. Mietzner, L. Sproge, H. Strandell)
B2 IT management — Information systems (V. Dreux)
B4 Reference databases (D. Groenez, M. Loos, S. Paganoni, A. Pasqui, O. Stembert)
B5 Research (S. Frank, G. Strack)

Directorate C: Economic and monetary statistics
C2 Economic accounts (J.-P. Arnotte, R. Barcellan, I. Kuhnert)
C3 Public finance and taxation (G. Amerini, P. Borges, G. Thouvenin)
C4 Balance of payments (L. Biedma, D. Comini, P. Passerini)
C5 Prices (L. Viglino)

Directorate D: Single market, employment and social statistics
D1 Labour market (A. Franco Lopez, W. Grünewald, A. Paternoster, A. Persenaire)
D2 Living conditions and social protection (G. Abramovici, I. Dennis, A. Melis, J. Piirto)
D3 Business (P. Feuvrier, M. Hult)
D4 Energy and transport (A. Gikas, H. Strelow)
D5 Education and culture (B. Andrén, E. Kailis, K. Nestler)
D6 Health and food safety (B. De Norre, D. Dupre, A. Karjalainen)
D7 Information society and services (M. Lumio, H.-W. Schmidt)

Directorate E: Agriculture, fisheries, Structural Funds and environment statistics
E1 Structural statistics, agriculture (K. Duchateau)
E2 Agricultural product statistics (G. Mahon)
E3 Fisheries, rural development and forestry (P. Boday, D. Cross)
E4 Structural Funds (T. Carlquist)
E5 Environment and sustainable development (C. Garland, J. Klein, P. Wolff)

Directorate F: External relations statistics
F1 Demography, migration (F. Bovagnet, D. Thorogood)
F2 International trade (A. Berthomieu, C. Corsini)

EFTA *(R. Ragnarson)*
Geonomenclature *(E. Jouangrand)*

TRANSLATION
Directorate-General for Translation of the European Commission, Luxembourg

OFFICE FOR OFFICIAL PUBLICATIONS OF THE EUROPEAN COMMUNITIES

Contents

The Eurostat yearbook as a combined product

The Eurostat yearbook 2004 is a combined product consisting of a book and a CD-ROM. The CD-ROM contains the complete statistical information of the Eurostat yearbook 2004, a selection of which is presented in the book.

The CD-ROM is in three languages (English, French, German). It contains the following:

- The PDF files of the paper version.
- More than 1 000 statistical tables and graphs. All data can be easily extracted from the tables. The graphs can be generated dynamically according to the wishes of the reader.
- All the statistical background information about 'In the spotlight: sustainable development'.
- Links to the Eurostat Internet site to find more information, for example on further publications or on more up-to-date data. On its website, Eurostat provides access to a range of statistical information that can be consulted online or downloaded free of charge.

The Eurostat yearbook is easy to use

- Introductory texts for each section explain the main features and the relevance of the information presented and give an idea of what other data on the subject Eurostat has on offer.
- A glossary clarifies the statistical terms and concepts used.
- The abbreviations and acronyms used are spelled out on the bookmark to the yearbook.

Date of data extraction

The statistical data presented in this yearbook were extracted on 10 May 2004 and represent the data availability at that time.

Order and coding of countries

The order of the EU Member States used in the Eurostat yearbook is their order of protocol. It follows the alphabetical order of the countries' short names in their respective native languages.

Generally, the countries are identified in the Eurostat yearbook 2004 by using the shortest official designation. If codes are used, these are the two-digit ISO codes, except for Greece and the United Kingdom for which EL and UK, respectively, are used.

A complete list of ISO codes can be found at:
http://www.iso.org/iso/en/prods-services/iso3166ma/index.html

Symbols and codes in the tables

-    "Not applicable" or "real zero" or "zero by default"
- 0   Less than half of the unit used
- :   not available
- p   Provisional value
- e   Estimated value
- s   Eurostat estimate
- r   Revised value
- f   Forecast
- u   Unreliable or uncertain data (see explanatory texts)
- :u Extremely unreliable data
- :c Confidential
- :n Not significant
- b   Break in series (see explanatory texts)
- i   see footnote

€ zone stands for Euro-zone. "€ zone", which is not an official symbol, is used for practical reasons.

Statisticians for Europe

1

Eurostat, your key to European statistics

Comparable information about Europe has a name: Eurostat

'Eurostat' is the synonym for a high-quality information service providing statistical data about, and for, the European Union. Using our data means having a finger on the pulse of current developments in Europe: we report the background figures and facts needed to understand these developments.

The Eurostat yearbook: compiled for everyone with an interest in Europe

The Eurostat yearbook opens the door to Eurostat's information service by providing an overview of the spectrum of data we offer. It shows how benchmark figures have developed during the last 10 years in the European Union, the euro-zone and the EU Member States. To facilitate international comparison, some tables include the comparable data for other countries, for example the United States of America.

Introductory texts for each section give an idea of what data Eurostat has on the subject and what the relevance of this information is. We understand the yearbook not to be a mere collection of tables, but a 'portal' to European statistics. We hope it will make you curious about the data Eurostat has on offer.

How to get the data you want

An address for your list of favourites: http://www.europa.eu.int/comm/eurostat

Eurostat offers a wide range of statistical information on its website that you can consult online or download free of charge:

— data, accessible as soon as it is available;
— all of Eurostat's news releases;
— the *Statistics in Focus* series that provides up-to-date summaries of the main results of statistical surveys, studies and analysis;
— all Eurostat publications in PDF format. The background to specific topics is provided in our *Panorama* publications which contain thoroughly elaborated analysis, tables, graphs and maps;
— catalogues;
— working papers and studies (methodological work and reports on data quality; one-off studies and their results; documents drafted by partners such as national statistical institutes or universities);
— methods and nomenclatures, accessible in PDF format or via RAMON, Eurostat's classification server.

1

Eurostat's indicators: long-term or short-term — but always relevant

Long-term indicators

— The 'Structural indicators' help to assess the longer-term progress in the policy domains of employment, innovation and research, economic reform, social cohesion, and the environment as well as the general economic background. They are recognised as being most relevant for political discussion. All Structural indicators are presented in the Eurostat yearbook and are identified with a specific icon (✎).

— Many more predefined tables on different areas of life, work, the economy and the environment in the EU.

Short-term indicators

The 'Euro-Indicators' provide a collection of the latest data which are helpful for a short-term evaluation of the economic situation in the euro zone and in the European Union. The Euro-Indicators are updated daily. Their publication is announced in the 'Release' calendar.

Eurostat's service for journalists

Statistics make news. They are essential background to many news stories, features and in-depth analysis. The printed press as well as radio and TV programmes use our data intensively. Eurostat's Press Office puts out user-friendly news releases on a key selection of data covering the EU, the euro zone, the Member States and their partners. About 150 press releases are published each year, of which nearly 120 are on the monthly or quarterly Euro-Indicators. The Press Office also coordinates interviews and press conferences on important statistical results and events. Eurostat's Media Support helps professional journalists to find data on all kinds of topics.

All Eurostat news releases are available free of charge on the web at 11 a.m. on the day they are released.

Journalists can contact the Media Support if they need further information on our news releases or other data (tel. (352) 43 01-33408, fax (352) 43 01-35349, e-mail: eurostat-mediasupport@cec.eu.int).

Why Eurostat data?

Equal information for a democratic society

Being informed is the first step to actively participating in a democratic Europe. Europeans demand a high-quality information service providing impartial, reliable and comparable statistical data. They want to access them easily and without exemption: no key information must be withheld; all citizens and enterprises must have equal and complete access to it. Eurostat and its partners in the European statistical system open the door and guarantee this equal and comprehensive information on social, economic and environmental developments in Europe. It is up to you to use it!

Impartiality and objectivity: two pillars of trust

Access to reliable and high-quality statistics becomes evermore important in the information society in which we live, and trust in the source an immeasurable value. Eurostat's trustworthiness is enshrined by law. Article 285(2) of the EC Treaty says: 'The production of Community statistics shall conform to impartiality, reliability, objectivity, scientific independence, cost-effectiveness and statistical confidentiality; it shall not entail excessive burdens on economic operators.' These are not abstract words for us: they are the leading principle for our day-to-day work.

Comparability through harmonisation

It is easier to understand each other if one knows about the other's conditions of life and work. What is true for the relationship between individuals is also true for society as a whole. Comparisons, however, require comparable statistics that, in turn, demand the use of a common 'statistical language'.

The common language has to embrace concepts, methods and definitions, as well as technical standards and infrastructures. This is what statisticians call harmonisation. It is what the European statistical system is all about. And it is Eurostat's primary *raison d'être*.

The European statistical system

The European statistical system comprises Eurostat and the statistical offices, ministries, agencies and central banks that collect official statistics in the EU Member States, Iceland, Liechtenstein and Norway. The statistical authorities in the Member States collect, verify and analyse national data and send them to Eurostat. Eurostat consolidates the data and ensures their comparability. The European statistical system concentrates on EU policy areas. But, with the extension of EU policies, harmonisation has extended to nearly all statistical fields.

The European statistical system is a network in which Eurostat's role is to lead the way in the harmonisation of statistics in close cooperation with the national statistical authorities. At the heart of the European statistical system is the Statistical Programme Committee, which brings together the heads of Member States' national statistical offices and is chaired by Eurostat. The Statistical Programme Committee discusses joint actions and programmes to be carried out to meet EU information requirements. It agrees a five-year programme, which is implemented by the national authorities and monitored by Eurostat.

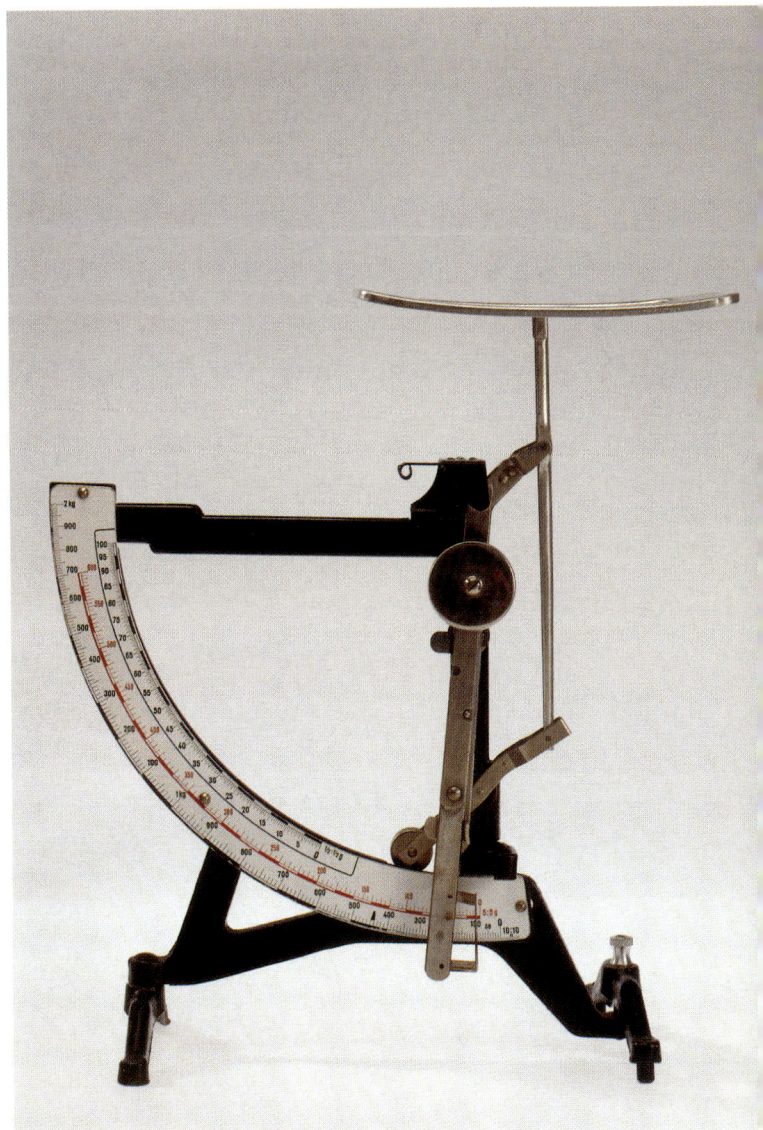

1

A matter of disposition: an attractive and relevant data assortment

Data become information when they become interesting. As a matter of disposition, Eurostat has an open ear for what people are interested in.

The statistical programme of the European statistical system does not 'fall out of the blue'. What we report on has been decided through a well-defined political process at the European level in which the EU Member States are deeply involved. Most surveys and data collections are based on European regulations that are legally binding on the national level. A central question during the political and legal discussions that lead to European statistical regulations is: 'To whom and why are the data of interest?' Every statistical regulation has to pass a critical test.

On the other hand, the European statistical programme is constantly revised. In view of the principle of cost-efficiency, the production of data that have been rendered less relevant by new developments will be modified or even discontinued. As a result, the statistical programme is kept lean and modern.

Our data are worth looking at.

Eurostat's Structural indicators

Eurostat's Structural indicators: high-quality statistics for competent governance in Europe

At the Lisbon European Council in spring 2000, the European Union set itself the following strategic goal for the next decade: to become the most competitive and dynamic knowledge-based economy in the world capable of sustainable economic growth with more and better jobs and greater social cohesion.

The Council acknowledged the need to regularly discuss and assess progress made in achieving this goal on the basis of commonly agreed Structural indicators. To this end, it invited the European Commission to draw up an annual spring report on progress on the basis of Structural indicators relating to employment, innovation and research, economic reform, social cohesion and the general economic background, as well as, since 2002, the environment.

For the first time in 2004, the Commission has presented a shortlist of 14 Structural indicators which were covered in the statistical annex to its 2004 spring report to the European Council. This shortlist has been agreed with the Council. Its concise layout makes it easier to present policy messages and the Member States' positions towards the key Lisbon targets. In keeping with the recent streamlining of procedures in the wider context of the Lisbon strategy, it is foreseen to keep this list stable for three years.

To ensure that the public has access to the detailed database of Structural indicators, which continues to play an important role in the EU's policy process, Eurostat disseminates the full set of Structural indicators on its Structural indicators website (http://www.europa.eu.int/comm/eurostat/structuralindicators). Time series are presented for EU-25 and EU-15, EUR-12, the EU Member States, the EEA/EFTA countries, Japan, the United States and the candidate countries.

The 2004 complete set of Structural indicators is listed below. The indicators of the shortlist are marked in bold. All Structural indicators are presented in the Eurostat yearbook. They are marked with the following icon ( ) which appears next to the title of the respective tables.

1

List of Structural indicators

General economic background

GDP per capita in PPS
Real GDP growth rate
Labour productivity per person employed
Labour productivity per hour worked
Employment growth (*)
Inflation rate
Unit labour cost growth
Public balance
General government debt

Employment

Employment rate (*)
Employment rate of older workers (*)
Average exit age from the labour force (*)
Gender pay gap in unadjusted form
Tax rate on low-wage earners: tax wedge on labour cost
Tax rate on low-wage earners: unemployment trap
Lifelong learning (*)
Serious accidents at work (*)
Fatal accidents at work (*)
Unemployment rate (*)

Innovation and research

Spending on human resources
Total R & D expenditure
R & D expenditure by source of funds: industry, government, abroad
Level of Internet access: households and enterprises
Science and technology graduates (*)
Patents, EPO
Patents, USPTO
Venture capital investments: early stage, expansion and replacement
ICT expenditure: IT expenditure
ICT expenditure: telecommunications expenditure
E-commerce: percentage of enterprises' total turnover from e-commerce
Youth education attainment level (*)

Economic reform

Comparative price levels
Price convergence between EU Member States
Price of telecommunications: local calls, national calls, and calls to the United States
Electricity prices: industrial users and households
Gas prices: industrial users and households

Market share of the largest generator in the electricity market
Market share of the incumbent in fixed telecommunications: local calls, long-distance calls and international calls
Market share of the leading operator in mobile telecommunication
Public procurement
Sectoral and ad hoc State aid
Convergence in bank lending rates: loans to households for house purchases, loans to non-financial corporations up to one year, and loans to non-financial corporations over one year
Trade integration of goods, services
Foreign direct investment intensity
Business investment
Business demography: birth rate of enterprises
Business demography: survival rate of enterprises
Business demography: death rate of enterprises

Social cohesion

Inequality of income distribution (income quintile share ratio)
At-risk-of-poverty rate before social transfers (*)
At-risk-of-poverty rate after social transfers (*)
At-persistent-risk-of-poverty rate (*)
Dispersion of regional employment rates (*)
Early school-leavers (*)
Long-term unemployment rate (*)
Children aged 0–17 living in jobless households
People aged 18–59 living in jobless households (*)

Environment

Greenhouse gas emissions
Energy intensity of the economy
Volume of freight transport relative to GDP
Volume of passenger transport relative to GDP
Modal split of freight transport
Modal split of passenger transport: percentage share of cars
Population exposure to air pollution by ozone and by particulate matter
Municipal waste collected, landfilled or incinerated
Share of renewable energy (including indicative targets)
Fish stocks in European marine waters
Protected areas for biodiversity: habitats directive
Protected areas for biodiversity: birds directive

(*) Indicators disaggregated by gender.

The European Union in the global context

Get an idea of the EU's position in the world

Eurostat's data allow comparison between the EU and other parts of the world. They help in analysing its relation to other countries and economic zones. To locate the EU's position in the world, this section presents a statistical selection on the following:

— the EU population and its development relative to the world population;
— some economic indicators;
— the expenditure on information technology and telecommunication as well as the percentage of citizens who have Internet access at home;
— how much energy is being used to produce the GDP in different countries. The indicator 'energy intensity of the economy' gives the answer. Other environmental indicators are available.

The world population from 1960 to 2002
Mid-year population in million persons

	1960	1965	1970	1975	1980	1985	1990	1995	2000	2001	2002
World	3 039.7	3 346.2	3 708.1	4 087.3	4 454.3	4 850.4	5 275.9	5 686.0	6 079.0	6 154.3	6 228.6
More developed countries, of which:	910.4	961.6	1 003.2	1 044.9	1 080.8	1 111.5	1 143.0	1 171.8	1 192.0	1 195.7	1 199.1
EU-25	378.0	395.1	406.9	418.4	427.0	432.6	439.5	447.1	452.0	452.4	453.1
Japan	94.1	98.9	104.3	111.6	116.8	120.8	123.5	125.3	126.7	126.9	127.1
United States	180.7	194.3	205.1	216.0	227.7	238.5	250.1	266.6	282.3	285.0	287.7
Russian federation	119.6	126.5	130.2	134.3	139.0	144.0	148.1	148.1	146.0	145.5	145.0
Less developed countries, of which:	2 129.3	2 384.6	2 704.4	3 042.5	3 373.5	3 739.0	4 132.9	4 514.2	4 887.0	4 958.7	5 029.5
China	650.7	715.5	820.4	917.9	984.7	1 054.7	1 138.9	1 206.0	1 262.5	1 271.1	1 279.2
India	445.9	495.7	555.0	620.5	687.0	762.4	841.7	922.1	1 002.7	1 018.5	1 034.2
Nigeria	39.9	45.0	51.1	58.9	69.6	79.9	92.6	107.4	123.4	127.1	130.5
Brazil	71.7	83.1	95.7	108.8	123.0	137.3	151.1	163.5	175.6	177.8	179.9

Source (excluding EU-25): US Bureau of the Census, International database.

1

Shares in the world population from 1960 to 2002
Mid-year population; in %

	1960	1965	1970	1975	1980	1985	1990	1995	2000	2001	2002
World	100	100	100	100	100	100	100	100	100	100	100
More developed countries, of which:	30	29	27	26	24	23	22	21	20	19	19
EU-25	12	12	11	10	10	9	8	8	7	7	7
Japan	3	3	3	3	3	2	2	2	2	2	2
United States	6	6	6	5	5	5	5	5	5	5	5
Russian Federation	4	4	4	3	3	3	3	3	2	2	2
Less developed countries, of which:	70	71	73	74	76	77	78	79	80	81	81
China	21	21	22	22	22	22	22	21	21	21	21
India	15	15	15	15	15	16	16	16	16	17	17
Nigeria	1	1	1	1	2	2	2	2	2	2	2
Brazil	2	2	3	3	3	3	3	3	3	3	3

Source (excluding EU-25): US Bureau of the Census, International database.

Share in the world's population
In %

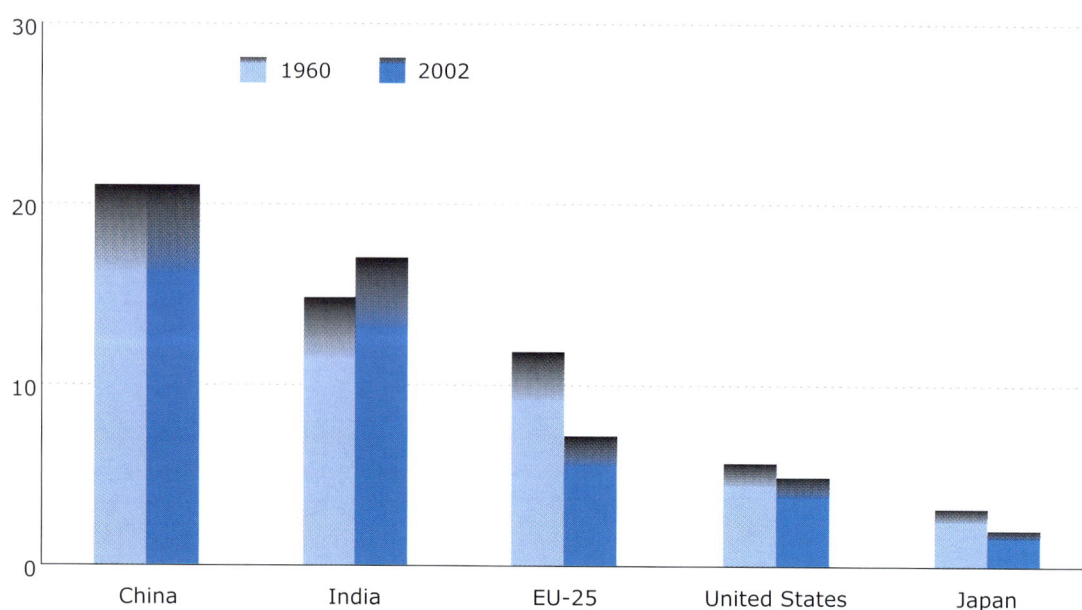

Source (excluding EU-25): US Bureau of the Census, International database.

Share in the world population 1960
In %

- 30 More developed countries
- 70 Less developed countries

- More developed countries
- Less developed countries

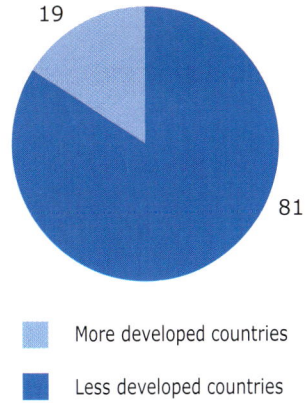

Source (excluding EU-25): US Bureau of the Census, International database.

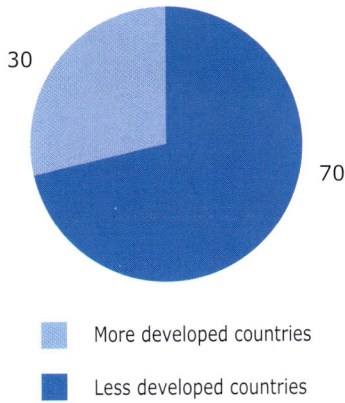

Share in the world population 2002
In %

- 19
- 81

- More developed countries
- Less developed countries

Source (excluding EU-25): US Bureau of the Census, International database.

Total population change in the world and the EU-15
Change to the preceding year in %

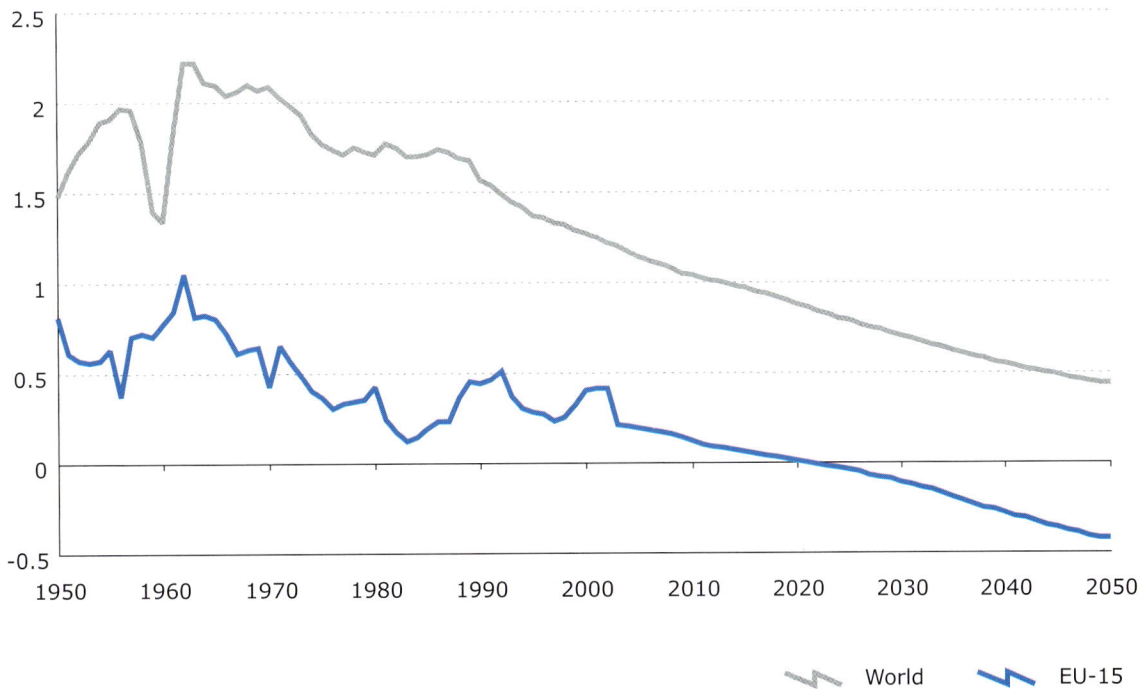

World   EU-15

Includes forecast.

1

Gross domestic product per capita in purchasing power standards (PPS)
EU-15 = 100

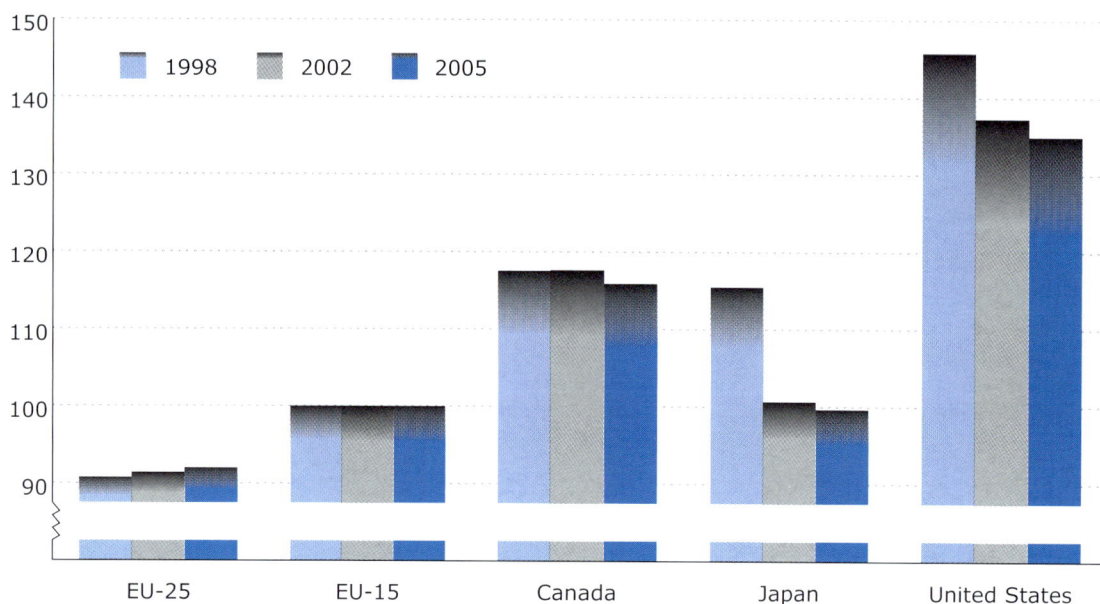

Legend: 1998, 2002, 2005

Categories: EU-25, EU-15, Canada, Japan, United States

2005: forecast; 2002 Canada, Japan, United States: forecast.

The gross domestic product is an indicator for a nation's economic situation. It reflects the total value of all goods and services produced less the value of goods and services used for intermediate consumption in their production. Expressing GDP in purchasing power standards eliminates differences in price levels between countries, and calculation on a per head basis allows the comparison of economies significantly different in absolute size.

Growth rate of the gross domestic product
Percentage change to the previous year; GDP at constant prices (1995)

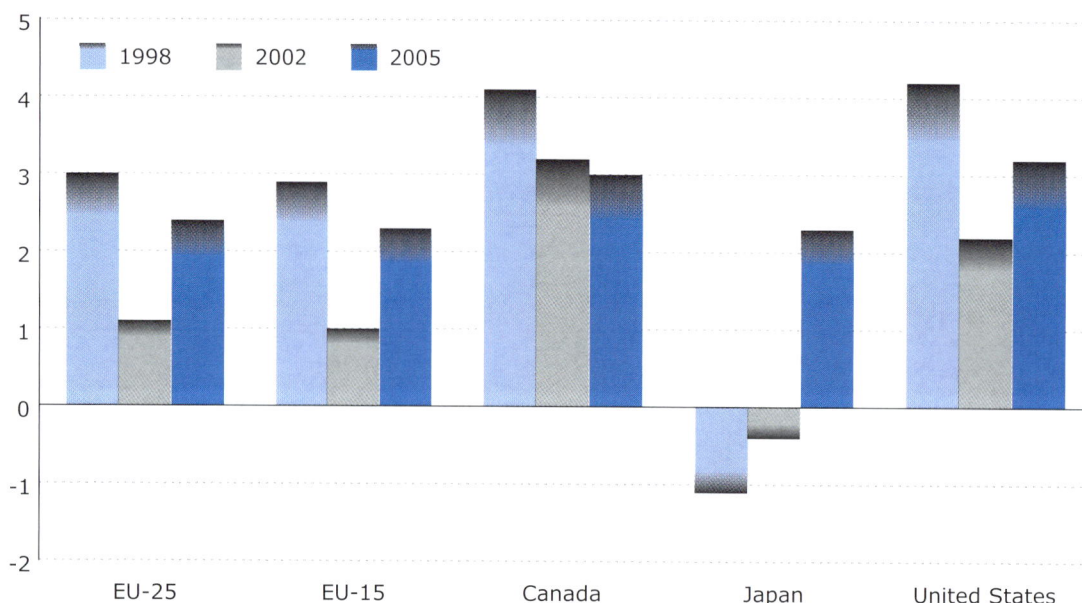

Legend: 1998, 2002, 2005

Categories: EU-25, EU-15, Canada, Japan, United States

2005: forecast.

Gross domestic product (GDP) is a measure for the economic activity. It is defined as the value of all goods and services produced less the value of any goods or services used in their creation. The calculation of the annual growth rate of GDP at constant prices is intended to allow comparisons of the dynamics of economic development both over time and between economies of different sizes. The growth rate is calculated from figures at constant prices since these give volume movements only, i.e. price movements will not inflate the growth rate.

1

General government consolidated gross debt
In % of GDP

Legend: 1998, 2001, 2003

Categories: EU-25, EU-15, Canada, Japan, United States

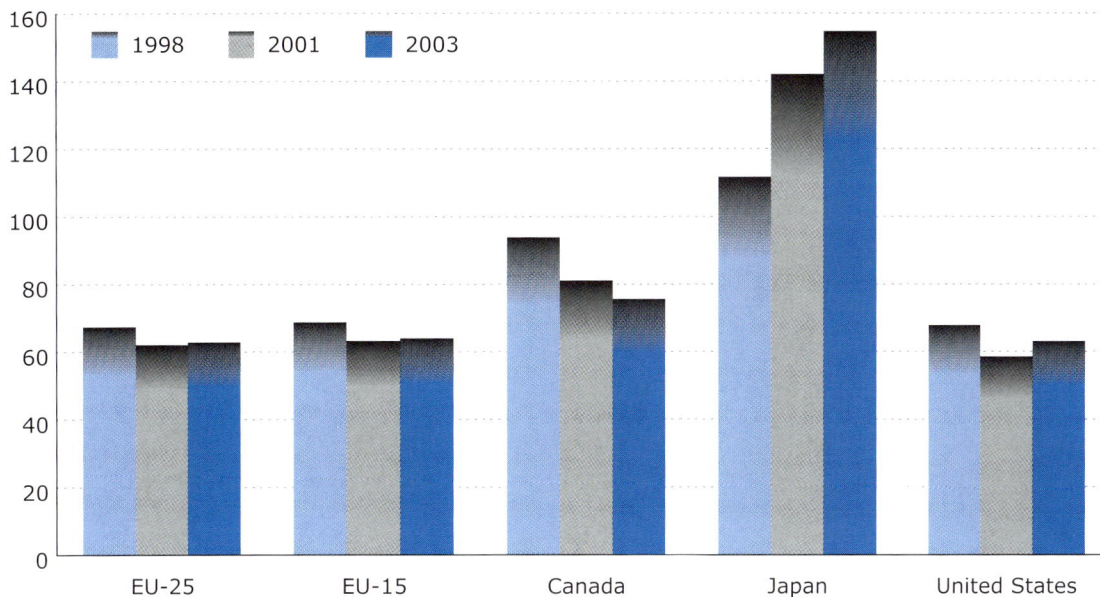

The general government sector comprises the subsectors of central government, State government, local government and social security funds. GDP used as a denominator is the gross domestic product at current market prices. Debt is valued at nominal (face) value, and foreign currency debt is converted into national currency using end-year market exchange rates (though special rules apply to contracts). The national data for the general government sector are consolidated between the subsectors. Basic data are expressed in national currency, converted into euro using end-year exchange rates for the euro provided by the European Central Bank. Data are compiled on an accrual basis.

Labour productivity
GDP in purchasing power standards (PPS) per person employed relative to EU-15 (= 100)

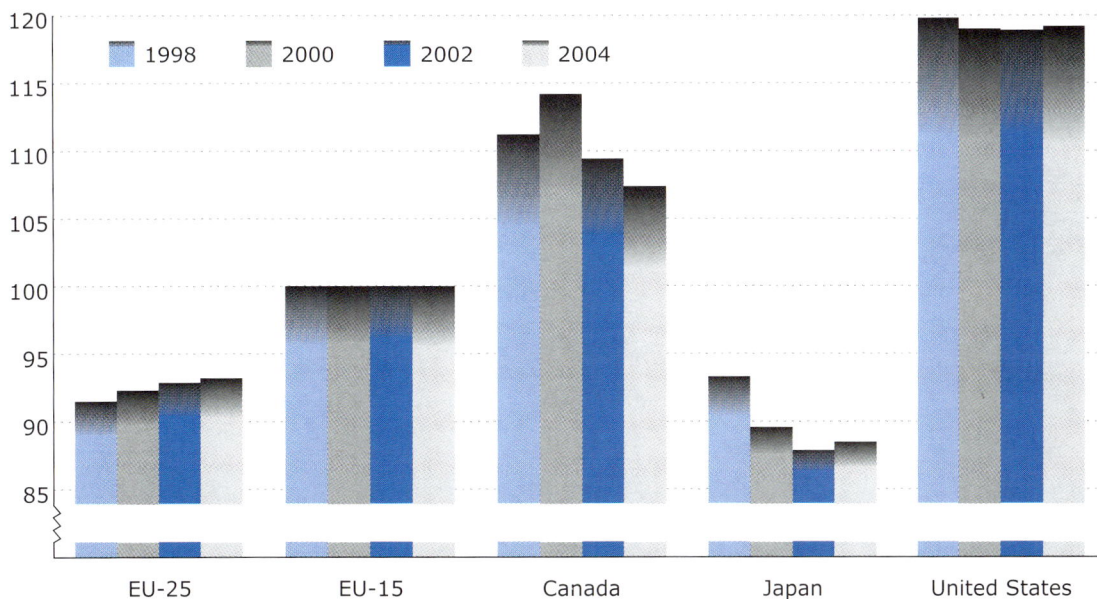

Legend: 1998, 2000, 2002, 2004

Categories: EU-25, EU-15, Canada, Japan, United States

Includes forecasts.

Gross domestic product (GDP) is a measure for the economic activity. It is defined as the value of all goods and services produced less the value of any goods or services used in their production. GDP per person employed gives an overall impression of the productivity of national economies expressed in relation to the European Union (EU-15) average. If the index of a country is higher than 100, this country's level of GDP per person employed is higher than the EU average and vice versa. Basic figures are expressed in PPS, i.e. a common currency that eliminates the differences in price levels between countries allowing meaningful volume comparisons of GDP between countries. Please note that 'persons employed' does not distinguish between full-time and part-time employment.

1

Tax rate on low-wage earners
Tax rate on labour cost in %

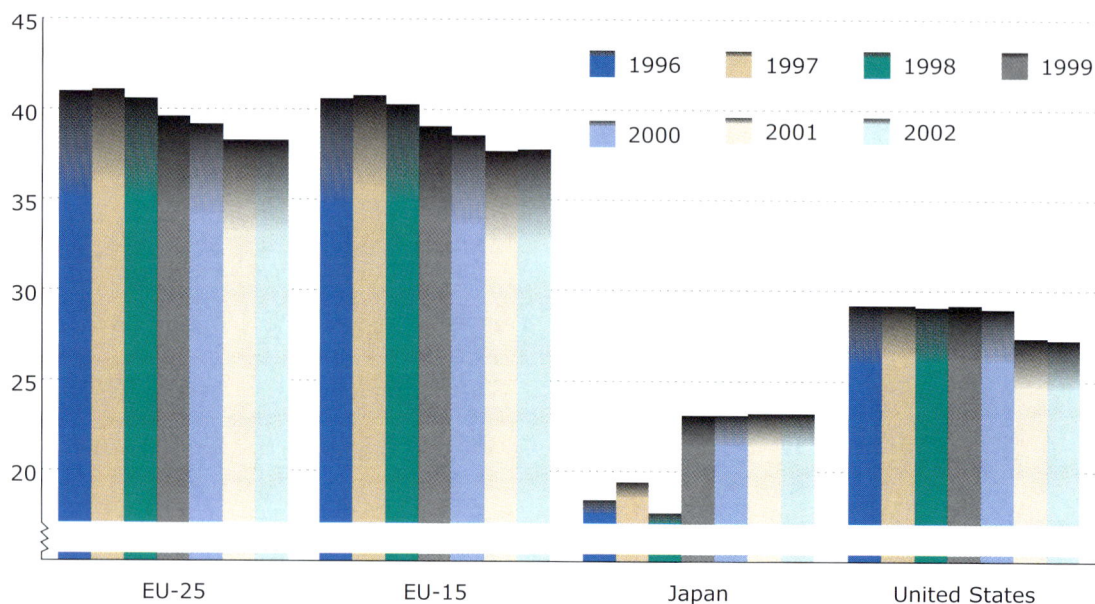

	1996	1997	1998	1999
	2000	2001	2002	

EU-25   EU-15   Japan   United States

The tax wedge on labour cost calculates the income tax on gross earnings plus the employee's and employer's social security contributions, and then expresses this sum in % of the total labour cost for this low-wage earner.

Total unemployment rate
In %

EU-25   EU-15   Japan   United States

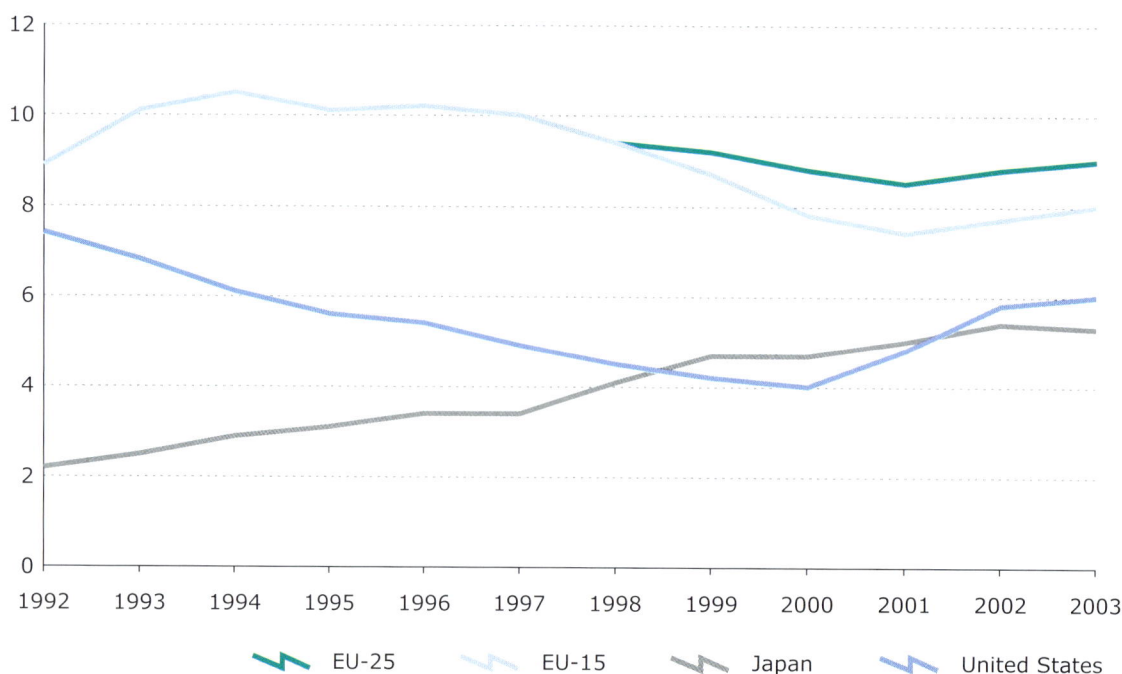

Unemployment rates represent unemployed persons as a percentage of the labour force. The labour force is the total number of people employed and unemployed. Unemployed persons comprise persons aged 15 to 74 who were: a. without work during the reference week, b. currently available for work, i.e. were available for paid employment or self-employment before the end of the two weeks following the reference week, c. actively seeking work, i.e. had taken specific steps in the four weeks period ending with the reference week to seek paid employment or self-employment or who found a job to start later, i.e. within a period of, at most, three months.

Foreign direct investment intensity
In %

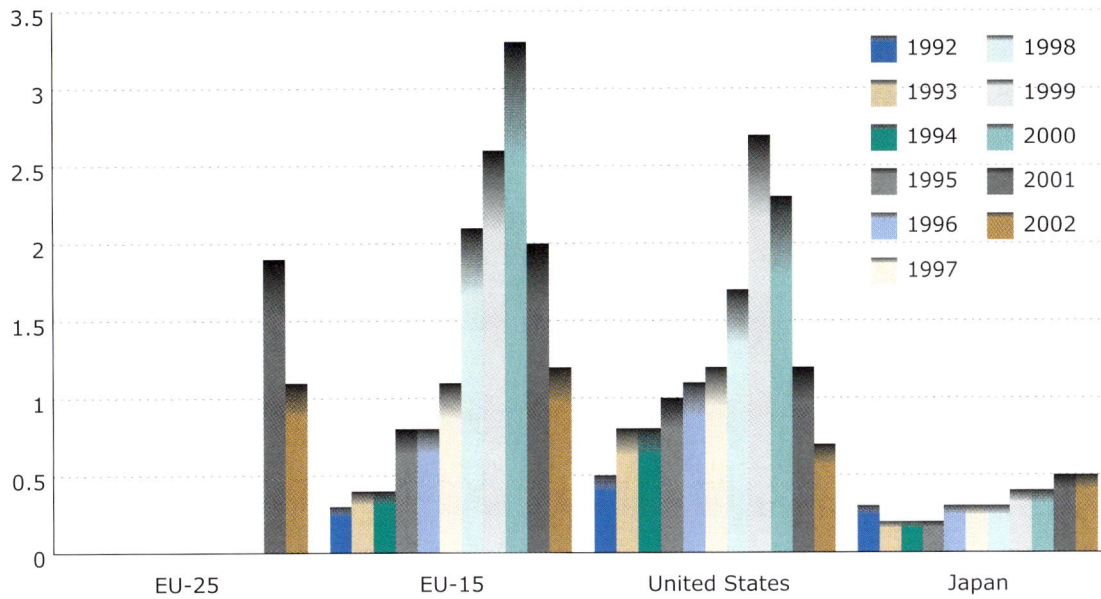

Average of inward and outward foreign direct investment (FDI) flows divided by gross domestic product (GDP). The index measures the intensity of investment integration within the international economy. The direct investment refers to the international investment made by a resident entity (direct investor) to acquire a lasting interest in an entity operating in an economy other than that of the investor (direct investment enterprise). Direct investment involves both the initial transactions between the two entities and all subsequent capital transactions between them and among affiliated enterprises, both incorporated and unincorporated.

Expenditure on information technology
In % of GDP

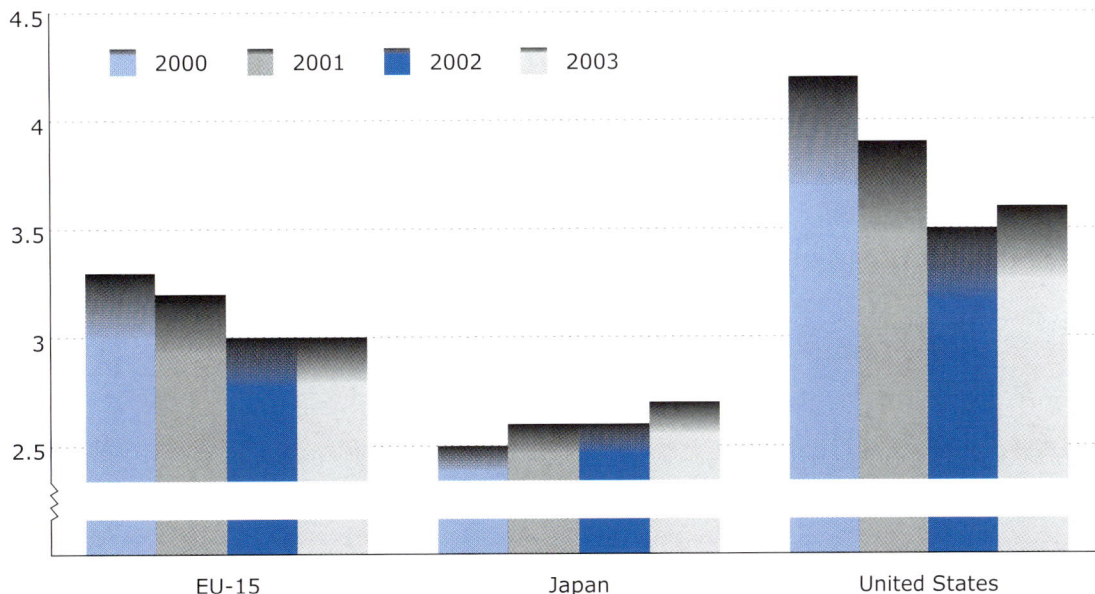

Expenditure on IT (information technology) hardware, equipment, software and other services as a percentage of GDP.

1

Exports to EU countries
Share in total national exports (fob); in %

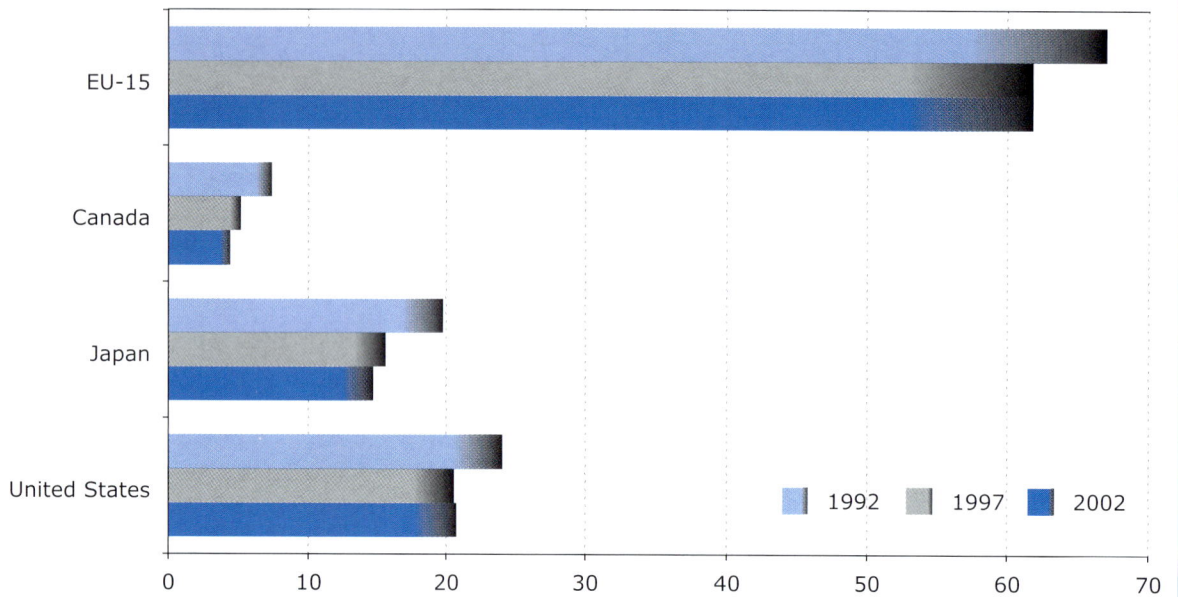

Legend: 1992 | 1997 | 2002

Source: Eurostat, national sources, United Nations.

The graph shows the part of intra-EU exports of declaring countries expressed in value compared to their total exports.

Imports from EU countries
Share in total national imports (cif); in %

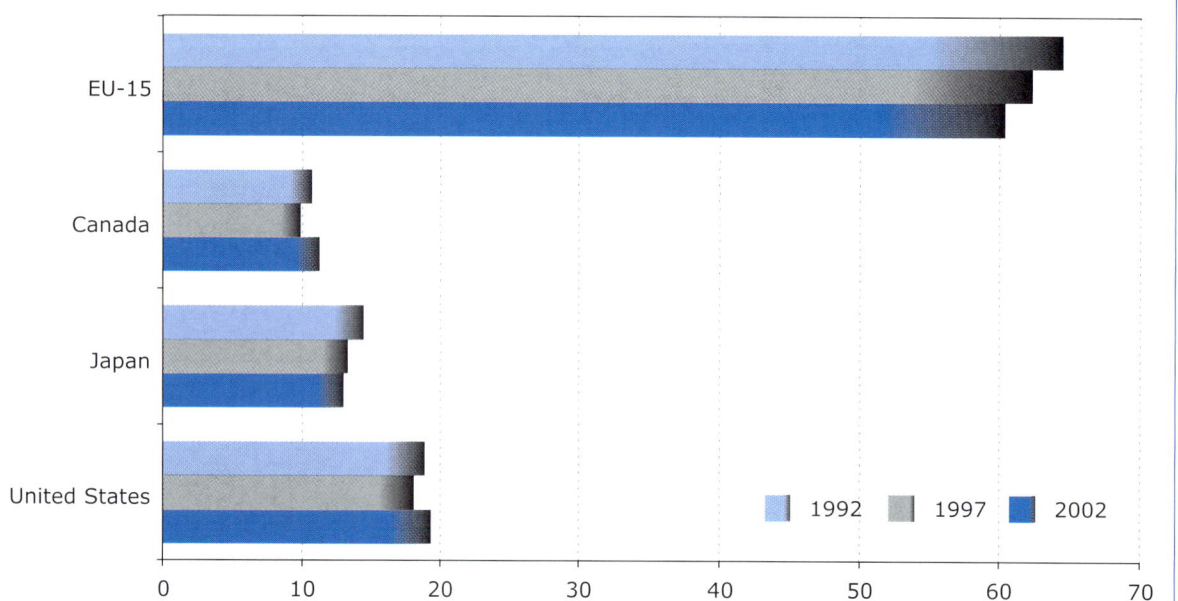

Legend: 1992 | 1997 | 2002

Source: Eurostat, national sources, UN.

The graph shows the part of intra-EU imports of declaring countries expressed in value compared to their total imports.

Extra-EU exports — Main trading partners
In 1 000 million ECU/EUR

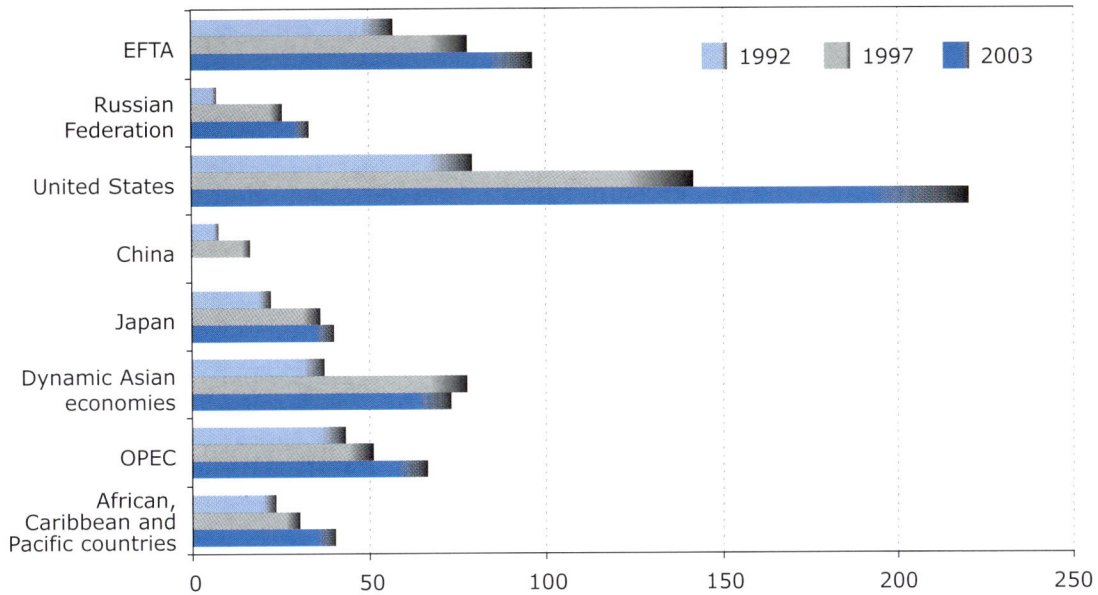

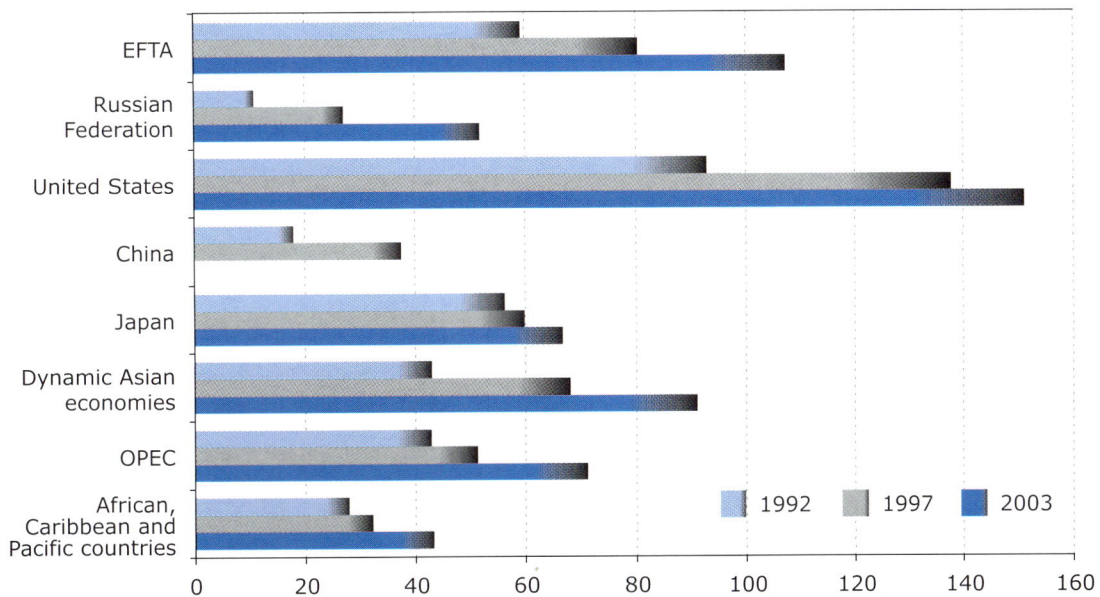

Legend: 1992 | 1997 | 2003

Categories: EFTA, Russian Federation, United States, China, Japan, Dynamic Asian economies, OPEC, African, Caribbean and Pacific countries

X-axis: 0, 50, 100, 150, 200, 250

Extra-EU exports represent the value of the Union's exports to the main third countries. Values are fob (free on board), i.e. the costs of transport and insurance outside the declaring country are not taken into account.

Extra-EU imports — Main trading partners
In 1 000 million ECU/EUR

Categories: EFTA, Russian Federation, United States, China, Japan, Dynamic Asian economies, OPEC, African, Caribbean and Pacific countries

Legend: 1992 | 1997 | 2003

X-axis: 0, 20, 40, 60, 80, 100, 120, 140, 160

Extra-EU imports show the value of the Union's imports from the main third countries. Values are cif (cost, insurance, freight), i.e. the costs of transport and insurance within the borders of the declaring country are included.

1

Energy intensity of the economy
Kgoe per 1 000 EUR

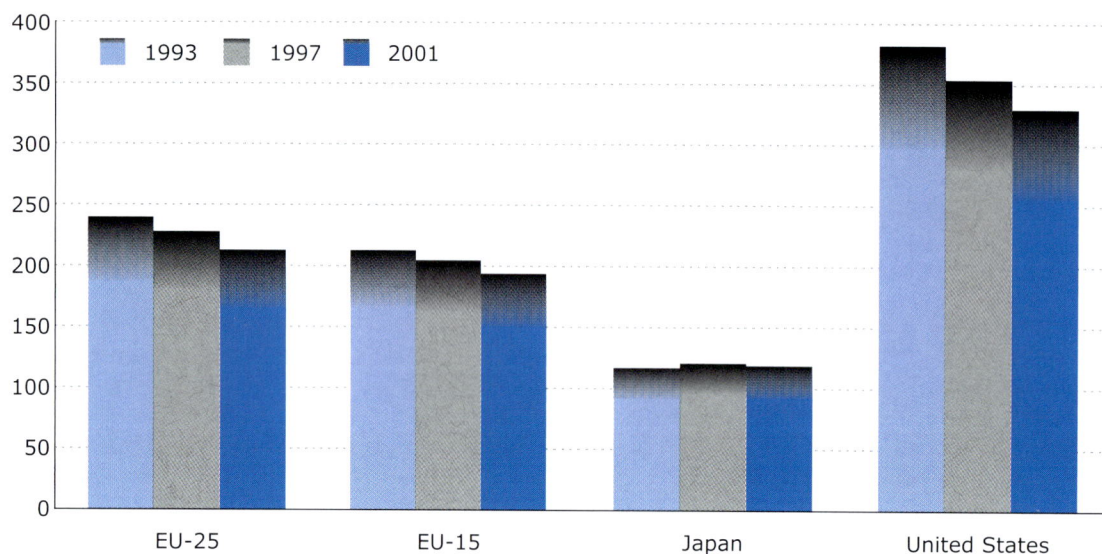

Legend: 1993 | 1997 | 2001

Categories: EU-25, EU-15, Japan, United States

2001 EU-25, EU-15: provisional data.

This indicator is the ratio between the gross inland consumption of energy and the gross domestic product (GDP) for a given calendar year. It measures the energy consumption of an economy and its overall energy efficiency. The gross inland consumption of energy is calculated as the sum of the gross inland consumption of five energy types: coal, electricity, oil, natural gas and renewable energy sources. The GDP figures are taken at constant prices to avoid the impact of the inflation, base year 1995 (ESA 95). The energy intensity ratio is determined by dividing the gross inland consumption by the GDP. Since gross inland consumption is measured in kgoe (kilogram of oil equivalent) and GDP in 1 000 EUR, this ratio is measured in kgoe per 1 000 EUR.

Greenhouse gas emissions
1990=100

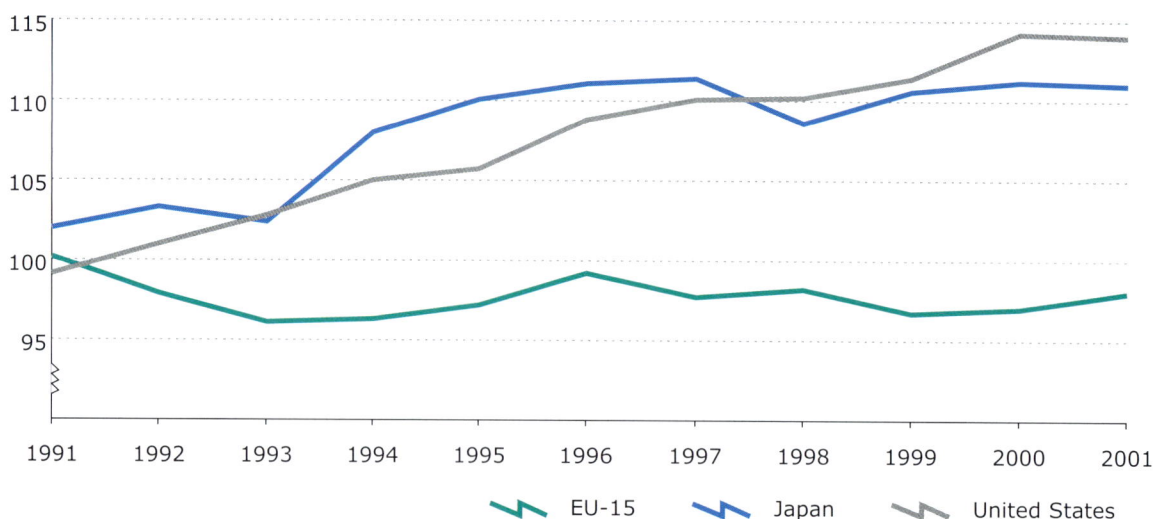

EU-15 | Japan | United States

Under the Kyoto Protocol, the EU has agreed to an 8 % reduction in its greenhouse gas emissions by 2008–12, compared to the base year 1990. The reductions for each of the EU-15 countries have been agreed under the so-called EU burden-sharing agreement, which allows some countries to increase emissions, provided these are offset by reductions in other Member States. The ACCs have chosen other reduction targets and other base years, as allowed under the protocol. These and the 'burden-sharing' targets for 2008–12 are shown in the table as figures for 2010. Emissions of the six greenhouse gases covered by the protocol are weighted by their global warming potentials (GWPs) and aggregated to give total emissions in CO_2 equivalents. The total emissions are presented as indices, with the base year = 100.

In the spotlight: sustainable development

Sustainable development (SD) is a complex concept which accentuates the need for 'better', rather than just 'more'. Ever since Gro Harlem Brundtland first defined sustainable development as development that 'meets the needs of the present without compromising the ability of future generations to meet their own needs' [1] it has been criticised for its vagueness. However, sustainable development is not a fixed objective, but rather an evolving process that will move us in the 'right' direction. The challenge lies in making the concept operational.

While we do not know precisely the recipe for achieving sustainability we do know what is unsustainable. Therefore, the pursuit of sustainability is not so much a journey towards sustainability but rather away from unsustainability. Supranational organisations such as the European Union have an important role to play in creating a policy framework that is conducive to SD.

It was with this in mind that the European Council adopted a strategy for sustainable development at Gothenburg in 2001 [2], which was subsequently completed by the adoption of an external dimension — the role the EU intends to play to promote global sustainable development — at the Seville European Council [3]. The strategy has been further extended by the EU commitments at the World Summit on Sustainable Development in Johannesburg in autumn 2002. The EU strategy adopts an integrated and holistic approach to policy-making that seeks to strike the 'right' balance between the economic, social and environmental dimensions. To keep a tight focus, the strategy limits itself to a number of key trends that pose a serious threat to our future well-being.

While SD is perceived to have three dimensions — economic, social and environmental — we can also identify a number of issues or themes which cut across these dimensions. It is, in fact, these themes that the sustainable development indicators (SDIs) set out to measure. The advantage of such an approach is that, rather than individually measuring economic, social or environmental issues, the indicators often capture elements of two or three of the dimensions.

This strategy has been divided into 10 policy themes: 'Economic development', 'Poverty and social exclusion', 'Ageing society', 'Public health', 'Climate change and energy', 'Production and consumption patterns', 'Management of natural resources', 'Transport', 'Good governance' and 'Global partnership'. For each theme, one, or sometimes two, headline SDIs have been identified, covering the essence or the most important aspect of the theme. This spotlight chapter presents only the trends in the headline indicators,

---

[1] Report of the World Commission on Environment and Development (Brundtland report, 1987).
[2] Commission communication COM(2001) 264 final.
[3] Commission communication COM(2002) 82 final.

1

while basing its analysis on the trends in both the indicators themselves and on other, complementary, policy indicators. This larger set of more detailed indicators is either presented in other chapters of the yearbook or included on the CD-ROM attached to the yearbook (^{4}).

Although many of the SDIs have been constructed from existing data collections or indicators, statistics for sustainable development will constitute a challenge for official statistics, as it will require both looking at or even collecting some new data and also combining these data in a different way in order to measure the trade-offs and the interlinkages between the various SD dimensions.

Economic development — Striving for structural reforms and new dynamism

The Lisbon process lays down the ambition that the EU should have the world's most competitive and knowledge-based economy by 2010. The agenda underlines the need for economic growth, innovation and the pursuit of structural reforms to raise Europe's growth potential. Simultaneously, it recognises the need for social cohesion and environmental protection.

The headline indicator, GDP per capita growth (^{5}), measures the dynamism of the economy and its ability to deliver general welfare to its population. It represents the core socioeconomic element in the overall set of SDIs, influencing also the themes 'Poverty and social exclusion', 'Ageing society', 'Public health' and 'Production and consumption patterns'. Increasing GDP per capita generally increases consumption, with knock-on effects on the themes 'Climate change and energy', 'Management of natural resources' and 'Transport', as well as on 'Global partnership'.

In EU-15, GDP per capita has increased steadily over the last 10 years, although in recent years economic growth has been weaker than the target of 3 % (^{6}). In the new Member States, GDP per capita growth has been considerably higher than in EU-15, although from a lower level.

Further assessment of the sustainability of macroeconomic developments looks at investments, competitiveness, and employment.

GDP per capita at constant prices
2000 = 100

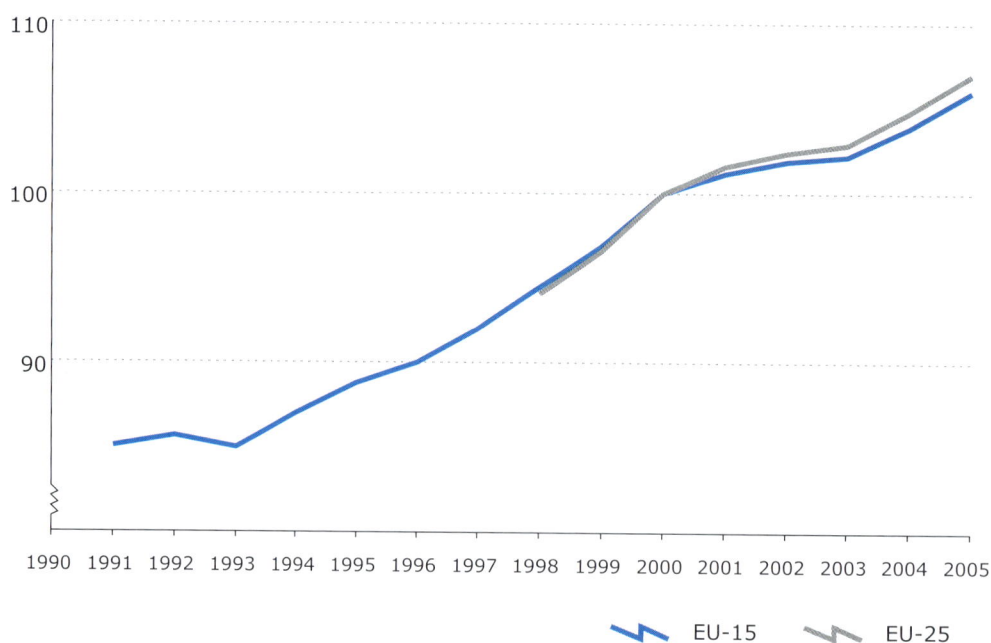

(^{4}) The list of SDIs and the work of the SDI Task Force are accessible at http://forum.europa.eu.int/Public/irc/dsis/susdevind/home.
(^{5}) Gross domestic product (GDP) is defined as the value of all goods and services produced less the value of any goods or services used in their creation. The indicator refers to the growth rate of GDP per inhabitant at constant (market) prices.
(^{6}) See 'GDP growth in the EU' on the attached CD-ROM.

Population at risk of poverty in EU-15
In %

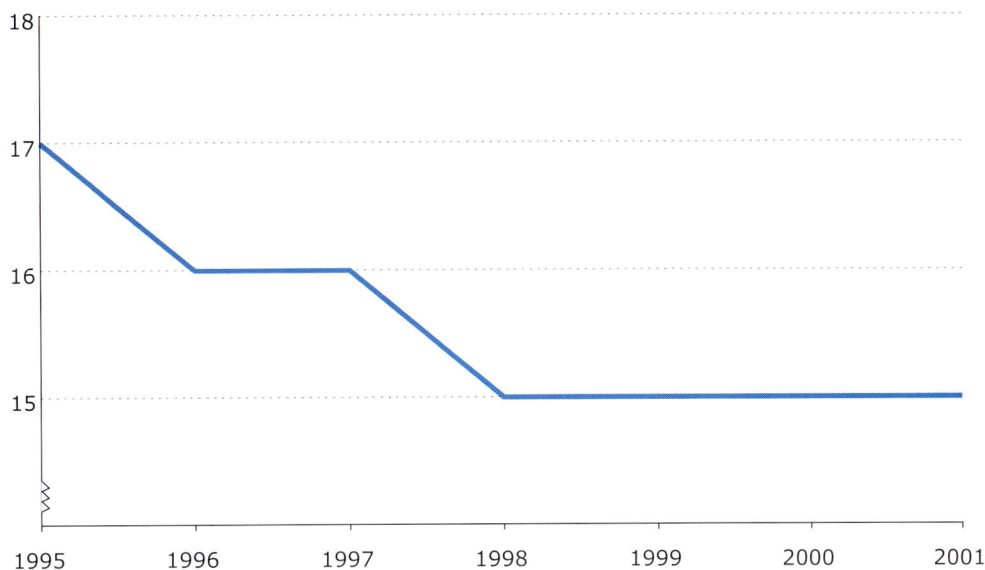

These topics also influence long-term developments in socioeconomic conditions, technological developments and shifts to more sustainable production and consumption.

Poverty and social exclusion — Towards stronger cohesion

Poverty and social exclusion have high social costs and lead to a waste of human capacity. Tackling these problems is central to the sustainable development of present and future generations. Therefore, one of the objectives of the SD strategy is to make a decisive impact on the eradication of poverty.

The headline indicator, population at risk of poverty ([7]), monitors this target and also contributes to the assessment of the situation in the themes 'Ageing society', 'Public health' and 'Production and consumption patterns'. The percentage of the population at risk of poverty in EU-15 fell slightly during the 1990s, but, since 1998, has remained at around 15 %.

Further assessment of poverty and social exclusion looks at monetary poverty, access to the labour market, and other aspects of social exclusion. These also affect the overall state of health, the income of persons aged over 65, and levels of consumption.

Ageing society — Highlighting needs for renewal of the economy

The ageing society is a complex socioeconomic issue that affects not only retired persons, but also the whole workforce and economy. The objective of the SD strategy is to address the demographic challenge and to ensure the adequacy of pension systems as well as healthcare and childcare systems while maintaining the sustainability of public finances and intergenerational solidarity.

The headline indicator, current and projected old-age dependency ratio ([8]), indicates the potential increasing financial burden in terms of pensions and costs of elderly care systems, if measures such as the structural reform of labour and pensions, later withdrawal from the

---

([7]) The indicator is defined as the share of persons with an equivalised total net income (after social transfers) below 60 % of the national median income.

([8]) The old-age dependency ratio is the ratio of the number of elderly persons of an age when they are generally economically inactive (aged 65 and over or aged 60 and over depending on the context) to the number of persons of working age (from 15 to 64 or from 20 to 59 depending on the context).

1

Current and projected old-age dependency ratio in EU-15
In %

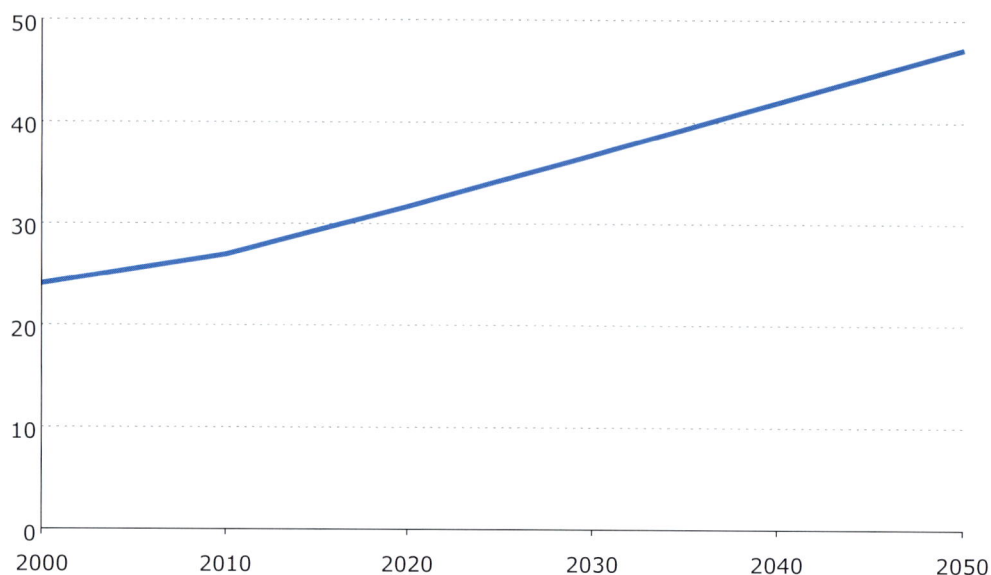

labour market, flexible employment, immigration, better labour productivity and technological developments are not taken. This indicator is also particularly linked to developments in the themes 'Economic development', 'Poverty and social exclusion', and 'Public health', as well as 'Production and consumption patterns'.

On current trends, the dependency ratio in the EU will almost double in 50 years from 24.1 % to 47.2 %. The most drastic changes will take place in Ireland — where the ratio could be multiplied by 2.5 from 17.4 % to 43.6 % — followed by Italy and Spain, where this ratio could increase by 2.3 and 2.1 respectively by 2050.

A complementary analysis looks at pension adequacy, demographic changes, and financial stability that describe welfare conditions, but also influence the production and consumption of goods and services.

Public health — Poorly known welfare factor

A healthy population is traditionally considered crucial for the well-being of society, and also as an important driver of economic prosperity. The main concerns of the EU sustainable development strategy and the EU health strategy relate to the overall health of citizens, outbreaks of infectious diseases and resistance to antibiotics, mainte-nance of food safety and quality, chemicals management and also for health and the environment (with particular reference to children), inequalities and the effectiveness of health systems, mental health, and communicable diseases.

The proxy headline indicator, life expectancy at birth, shows the number of years a person may be expected to live if subjected throughout their lives to the current mortality conditions. This indicator will be replaced by an indicator on disability-free life expectancy which is still under development. Both indicators reflect long-term socioeconomic and environmental conditions which are described first of all in the themes 'Economic development', 'Poverty and social exclusion', 'Ageing society' and 'Management of natural resources'.

Between 1995 and 2001, life expectancy at birth increased by almost two years. However, the situations of men and women differ by almost 10 years and the gap is even larger in the new Member States.

Further assessments focus on human health protection and lifestyles, food safety and quality, chemicals management, and health risks due to environmental conditions. These issues tend to reflect developments in socioeconomic conditions, but also reflect environmental conditions and how nature is used.

Life expectancy at birth in EU-15
Years

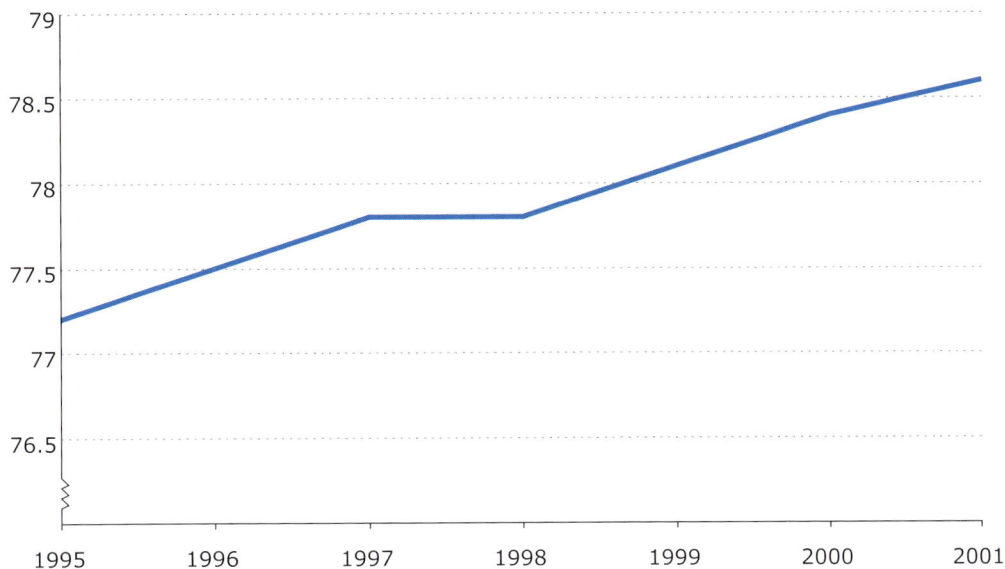

Climate change and energy — Limiting global warming

Man-made impact on the climate is primarily due to emissions of the six main greenhouse gases (GHGs), largely arising from industry and energy, but also from transport, agriculture, and waste management. The objectives of the SD strategy are to meet the Kyoto commitment ([9]) and to increase the use of clean energy.

The indicator measuring GHG emissions versus the Kyoto target ([10]) shows that the reductions made by EU-15 in the early 1990s have been eroded by rising emissions since 2000. The current upward emission trend threatens both the fulfilment of the Kyoto target and the continuous reduction path of 1 % a year. The targets and reference years for the new Member States largely differ from one another and do not fa-

cilitate a similar distance-to-target assessment for EU-25.

The second headline indicator, gross inland energy consumption ([11]), demonstrates that the upward trend in energy consumption is dominated by an increase in the use of fossil fuels ([12]). The uptake of renewable energy has been sluggish as it still accounts for only 6 % of primary energy and 15.7 % of electricity, while the targets set for 2010 are 12 and 22 % respectively ([13]).

Several of the other themes, such as 'Economic development', 'Production and consumption patterns', 'Transport', 'Management of natural resources' and 'Global partnership', contribute to climate change. Global warming may require costly changes in infrastructure, cultivation practices, human health protection, and ecosystem functions.

---

[9] The EU ratified the Kyoto Protocol in 2002. The EU target of a reduction in GHG emissions by 8 % compared with 1990 levels should be achieved by 2008–12. The EU SD strategy has set a further objective of an average 1 % per year reduction over 1990 levels up to 2020.

[10] Emissions of the six greenhouse gases covered by the protocol are weighted by their global warming potentials and aggregated to give total emissions in CO_2 equivalents. The total emissions are presented as indices, with 1990 = 100.

[11] Gross inland energy consumption is the quantity of energy consumed within the borders of a country/zone.

[12] See data on the CD-ROM.

[13] See data on the CD-ROM.

1

Greenhouse gas emissions versus Kyoto target for EU-15
1990 = 100

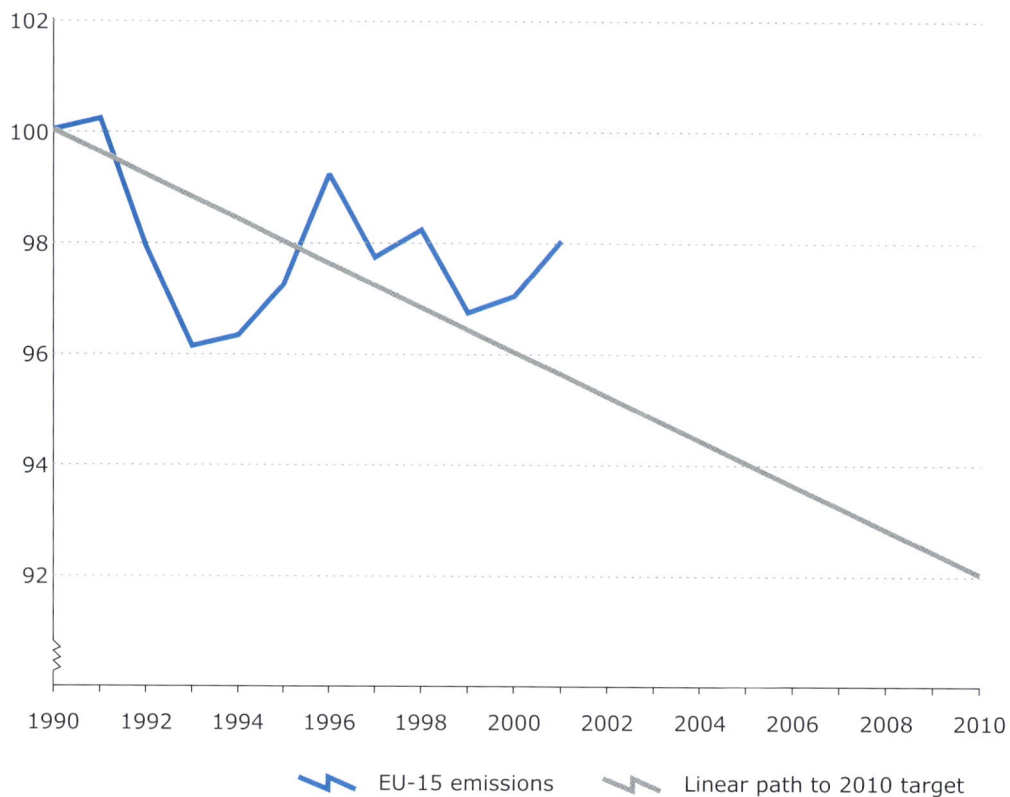

EU-15 emissions   Linear path to 2010 target

1

An example for material consumtion (see next page).

Gross inland energy consumption
Million toe

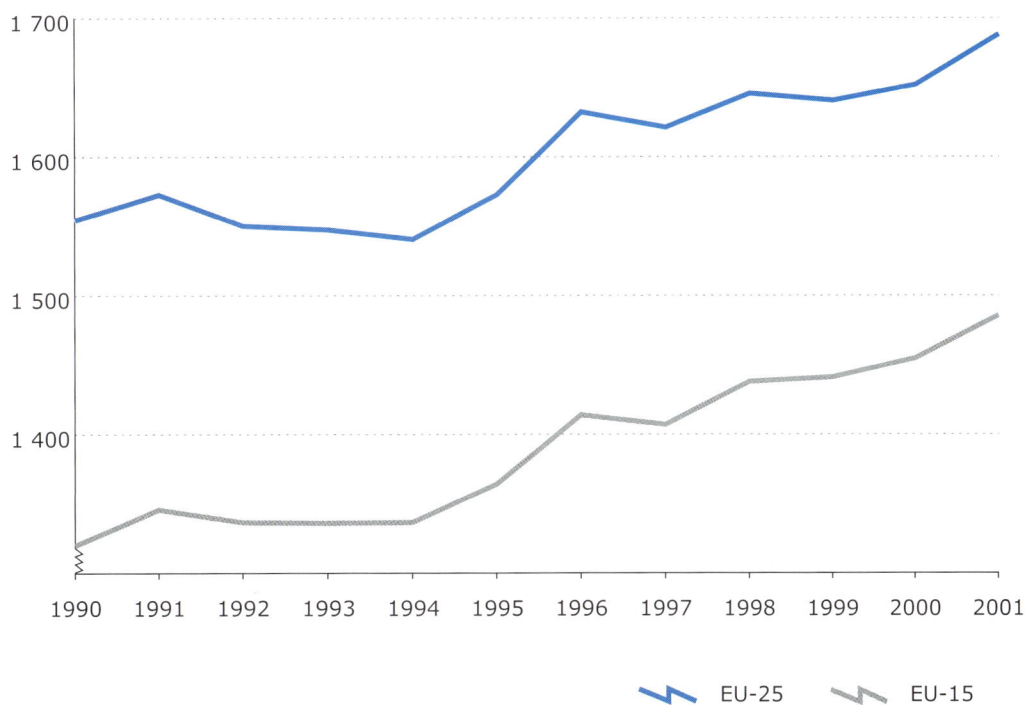

Domestic material consumption versus GDP at constant prices in the EU-15
1995 = 100

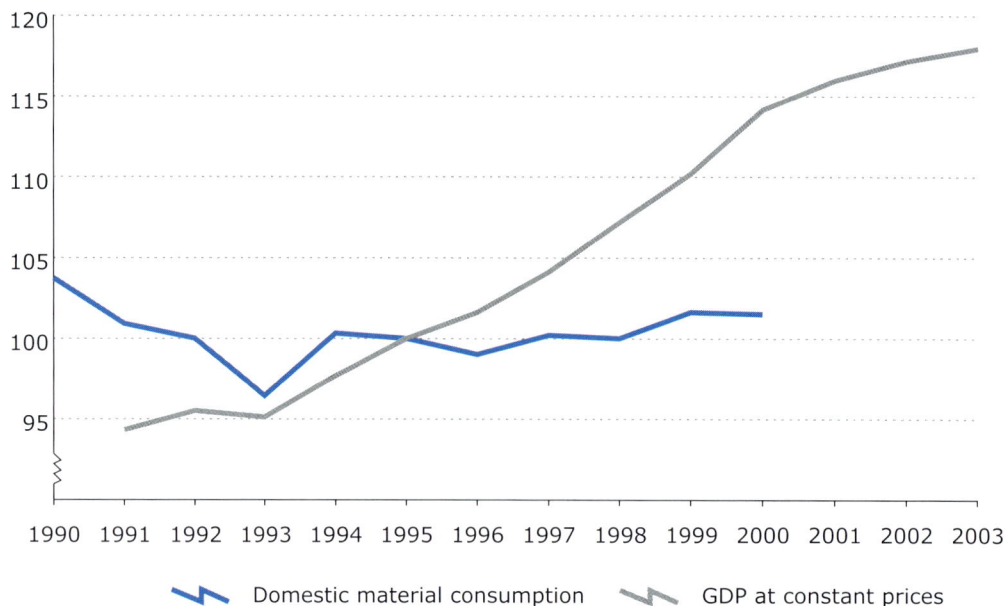

Legend: Domestic material consumption — GDP at constant prices

Production and consumption patterns — A new path to an eco-efficient economy

The goal of sustainable production and consumption is to decouple resource use and generation of environmental pollution from GDP growth. This is possible through more efficient use of natural resources so creating more from less and by requiring the main actors, such as enterprises, public authorities and consumers, to contribute to the changes.

The current headline indicator, domestic material consumption (DMC) ([14]) versus GDP, is intended to represent the amounts of material consumed by EU countries, although there are some methodological shortcomings. This indicator is closely interlinked to developments in the themes 'Economic development', 'Climate change and energy', 'Management of natural resources', 'Transport' and 'Global partnership'.

DMC decreased during the period 1990–93 due to the weakness of economic growth in the EU and the restructuring of east German industries, but since then has stabilised while GDP has steadily increased. This indicator indicates a relative, but not absolute, decoupling of environmental pressures and economic growth, reflecting the relative decline in manufacturing and the rise of services in the EU economy. However, the indicator does not include the consumption of natural resources used to produce goods imported from non-EU countries.

Further analysis of eco-efficiency, consumption patterns, agriculture, and corporate social responsibility describe the contributions of various sectors and stakeholders, but also highlight interactions between the internal and external dimensions of sustainable development.

Management of natural resources — Halting the decline of biodiversity

The destruction and fragmentation of ecosystems usually take place as a consequence of land-use changes, agriculture, forestry, transport infrastructure, and urbanisation. Other threats arise due to changing environmental conditions, overexploitation of resources, and pollution. These factors impair or exceed the carrying capacity of ecosystems and can lead to considerable economic and social losses due to diminished possibilities of benefiting from nature.

([14]) The indicator domestic material consumption presents the quantity of material consumed by EU countries. DMC equals domestic material input (DMI — i.e. domestic extraction plus extra-EU imports) minus extra-EU exports.

1

Population of wild birds in the EU — Farmland species
1990 = 100

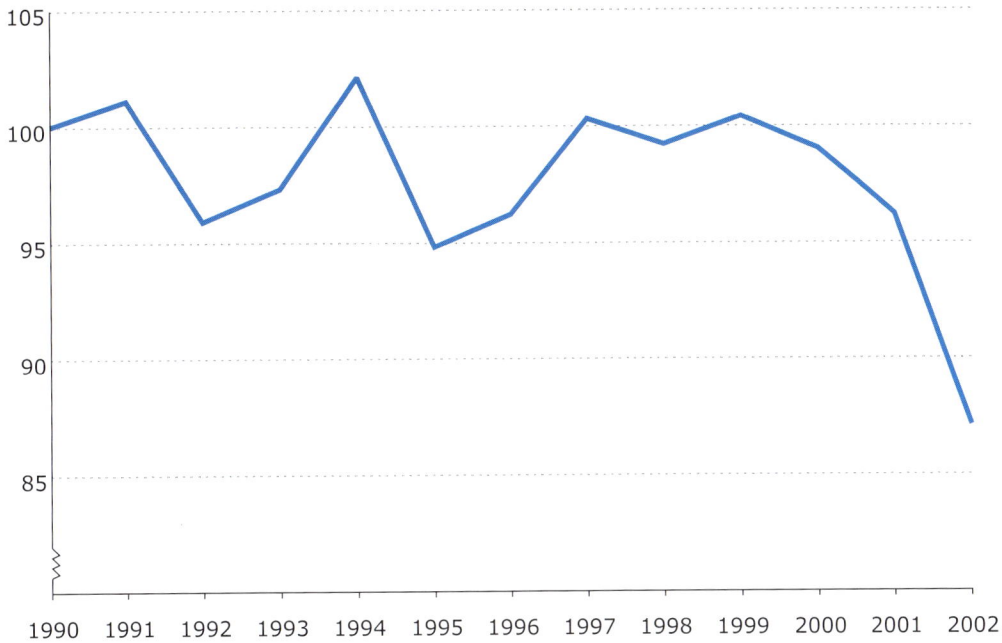

Sources: Royal Society for the Protection of Birds, European Bird Census Council and Birdlife International.

Fish catches outside the SBL in the north-east Atlantic
In %

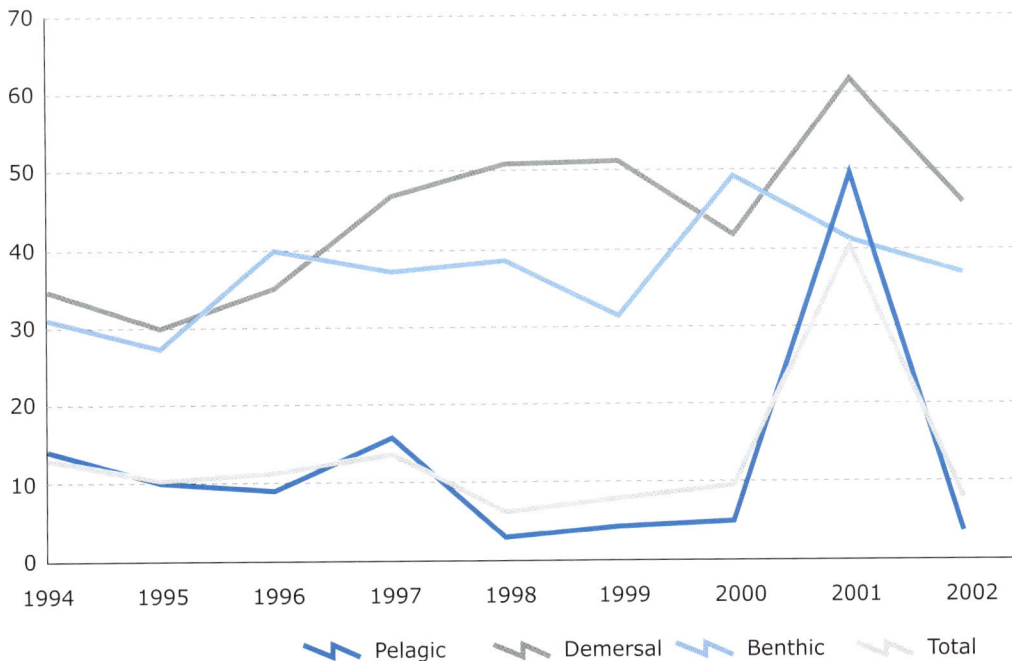

Pelagic   Demersal   Benthic   Total

Source: European Commission, Fisheries DG.

Industrial: O for all years.

1

The EU sustainability target is to halt the decline in the loss of biodiversity by 2010. As it is difficult to measure biodiversity with a single indicator, statisticians have suggested using the population of wild birds ([15]) as the headline indicator for the terrestrial environment. The basic idea behind this choice is that the population of birds may contribute to measuring the degree of environmental health and the sustainability of human activities. This indicator shows a deterioration in ecological conditions for farmland breeding birds.

The EU has also set a target for the protection of fish resources: to halt the decline in fish stocks by 2015. The second headline indicator for the management of natural resources, fish catches taken from stocks that are considered to be outside the safe biological limit (SBL) ([16]), shows that 8 % of catches in the north-east Atlantic were outside the SBL in 2002 and thus not sustainable.

Changes in terrestrial and aquatic ecosystems are due to complex socioeconomic and environmental developments and are therefore closely related to the themes 'Economic development', 'Climate change and energy', 'Production and consumption patterns', 'Transport' and 'Global partnership'.

Transport — Striving for decoupling and restructuring

Transport has an important role in access to community services and healthy economic development in both rural and urban areas. Nevertheless, transport growth is a major contributor to congestion, air pollution, noise, and ecosystem fragmentation, leading to an impairment of human health and the state of the environment.

Final energy consumption by transport in EU-15 versus GDP at constant prices
1995 = 100

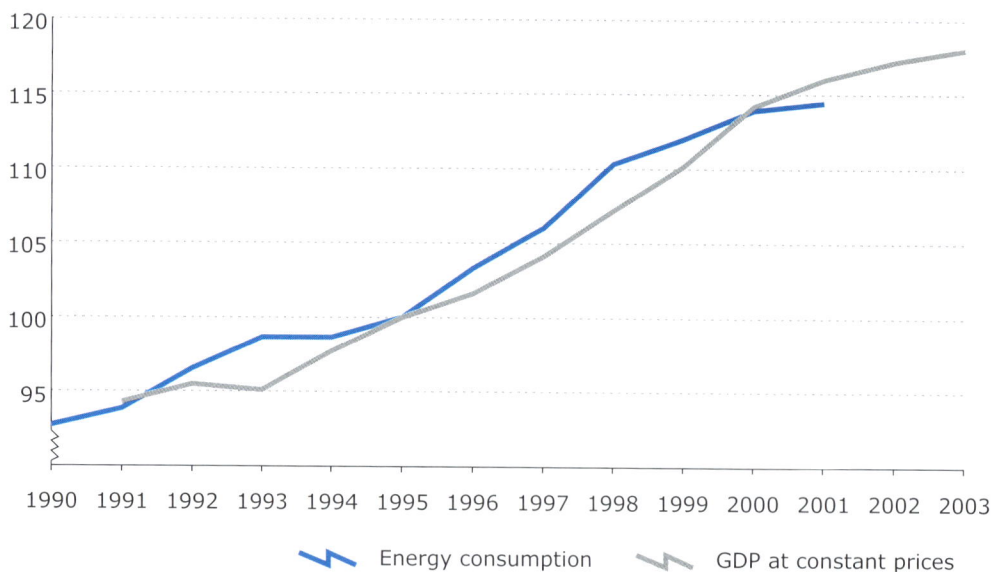

Energy consumption   GDP at constant prices

([15]) The indicator is defined as the index of the wild bird population for 23 selected farmland species measured over 11 countries of the EU (Belgium, Denmark, Germany, Spain, France, Ireland, Italy, the Netherlands, Austria, Sweden and the United Kingdom). This indicator has been prepared by the Royal Society for the Protection of Birds, the European Bird Census Council and Birdlife International and is currently under scrutiny by Eurostat. Time series on the population of woodland and wetland birds are also maintained, but still need some further methodological improvements.
([16]) This indicator relates to the catches of a number of stocks that have been assessed to be outside safe biological limits. In general terms, it is considered that a stock is within safe biological limits if its current biomass is above the value corresponding to a precautionary approach advocated by the International Council for the Exploration of the Sea (ICES).

Significant decoupling of transport growth from GDP growth is an essential goal of the SD strategy. Due to its economic and material implications, it is interlinked with the themes 'Economic development', 'Climate change and energy', 'Production and consumption patterns' and 'Management of natural resources'.

It is currently difficult to construct a robust indicator showing transport growth, which ideally would show vehicle-kilometres versus GDP. The proxy indicator, energy consumption by transport ([17]) versus GDP, indirectly shows the increase in the volume of transport, and illustrates that, despite the increase in the fuel efficiency of new vehicles, energy use by transport has increased by 14.4 % in EU-15 since 1995 when the GDP rose by 16.0 %. These figures show that no significant decoupling has been achieved.

Further analyses relate to transport growth and the environmental impact of transport that are linked to improved mobility and changes in socioeconomic, environmental and health conditions.

Good governance — Emphasis on citizens and policy coherence

Modern, open and citizen-oriented institutions are considered essential for the European Union. Improving policy coherence, better information, widespread participation, and strong leadership are proposals for EU sustainable development.

The headline indicator, citizens' confidence in EU institutions ([18]), is taken from the standard Eurobarometer opinion poll organised twice a year by the European Commission. Over the last five years, citizens' confidence in the EU institutions has increased by between 5 and 10 %.

Policy coherence and participation are essential preconditions for the advancement of sustainable development in the EU.

Citizens' confidence in EU institutions
In %

- European Parliament
- Council of Ministers
- European Commission

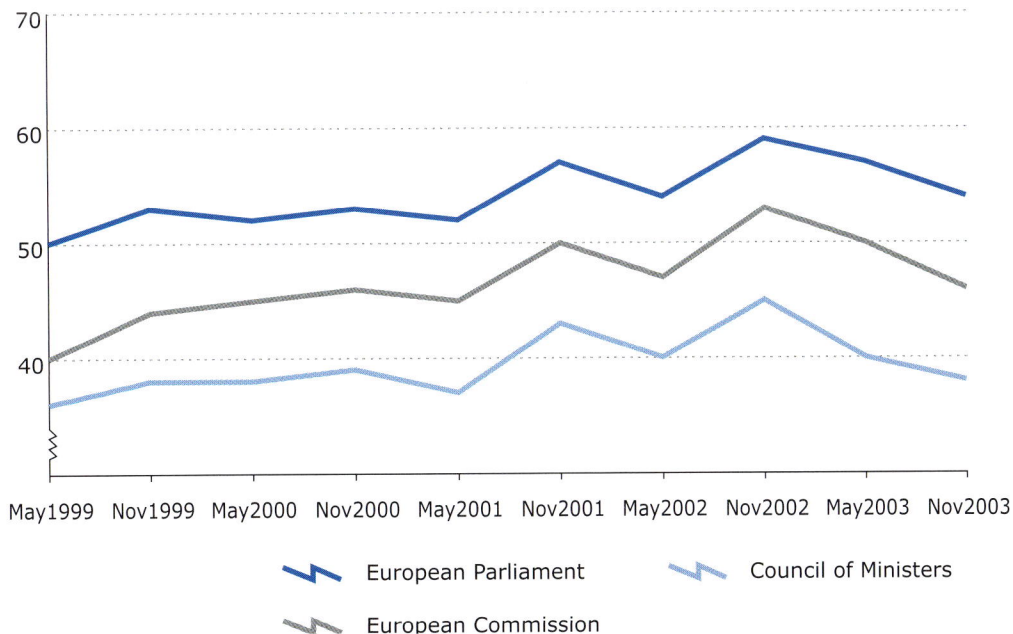

([17]) The indicator is expressed as the energy consumption by all transport modes, i.e. rail, road, air, inland navigation (final energy consumption) and marine bunkers.
([18]) The indicator is defined as the share of the population who tend to trust the European Parliament, the European Commission and the Council of Ministers.

1

Global partnership — Towards new modes of cooperation

The interdependencies and interactions between countries have considerably increased over the last two decades. At the Millennium Summit in 2000, the EU together with other nations acknowledged their global responsibility for concerted actions leading towards a better world. The EU is committed to take a leading role in the pursuit of global sustainable development.

This theme refers to six priorities ([19]), of which the headline objective for the priority 'financing sustainable development' is to help developing countries to receive the necessary financing for the attainment of the millennium development goals. The EU objective is to reach the United Nations goal of 0.7 % of gross national income (GNI) for official development assistance

(ODA). Member States lagging behind this goal are requested to increase their ODA by 2006 to at least 0.33 % so that collectively an EU average of 0.39 % is reached by 2006. In 2002, the EU average was 0.35 % and well above the average of 0.23 % in the donor countries. Nevertheless, the majority of EU countries were still below the 0.39 % target.

Further analyses focus on globalisation of trade, financing for development, and resource management. These are interwoven, especially with the themes 'Economic development' and 'Production and consumption patterns'. Furthermore, the tighter interdependencies between the EU and developing countries also set new requirements to ensure that current trends in the loss of environmental resources will be effectively reversed at national and global levels by 2015.

Official development assistance per Gross national income
In %

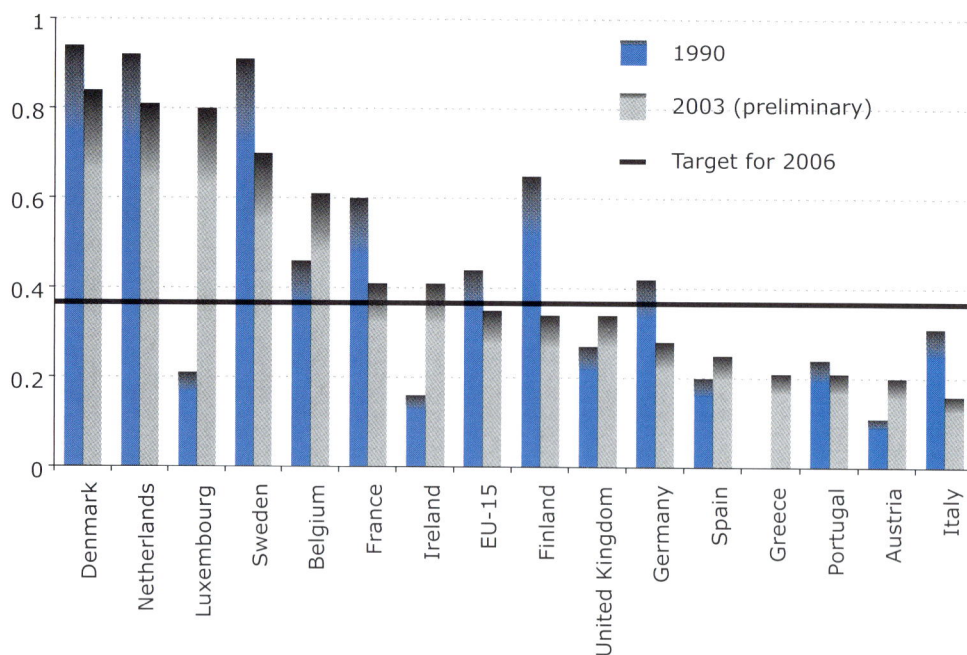

([19]) The six priorities are: harnessing globalisation, fighting poverty and promoting social development, sustainable management of natural resources and environmental resources, coherence of EU policies, better governance at all levels, and financing sustainable development.

People in Europe

2

The EU population

Eurostat data

Eurostat provides a wide range of data on:

— Population by sex and age on 1 January of each year
— Population by marital status
— Population structure indicators on 1 January
— Changes of population (absolute numbers and crude rates)
— Population at regional level (NUTS 2 and NUTS 3 levels)
— Projections

2

Demographic data

Eurostat produces a large range of demographic data both at national and regional levels. The information on population, births, deaths and nuptiality is collected each year from 37 European countries and allows the production of a large number of demographic indicators calculated by Eurostat on a comparable basis. Every three years, demographic projections (for the years up to 2070) are also produced by Eurostat.

This information is used by the European institutions and governments for a number of important policies notably in the social and economic fields. For instance, the past and future evolutions of the population structure, fertility behaviours and increasing life expectancy are very much needed for governing and planning social policies such as retirement schemes. Another example is the use of regional population data for the calculation of GDP per capita for the allocation of structural funds. It is also used by the educational world, the research institutes and the media.

The EU-15 population

During the last 50 years, the population of the EU-15 has grown from 295 to almost 380 million. In 1953, the EU's population exceeded 300 million. Thereafter it took 10, 13 and 22 years, respectively, to increase by 25 million inhabitants. Thus, population growth began to slow during the last two to three decades.

2002 fits fairly well in this latter general trend. Although during the second half of the 1990s lower levels were recorded, the latest increase is much smaller than those observed during the 1960s (on average 2.5 million a year).

Total population
At 1 January; in 1 000

	1994	1995	1996	1997	1998	1999	2000	2001	2002	2003
EU-25	445 624.2	446 808.1	447 862.7	448 894.5	449 759.1	450 677.5	451 841.2	453 316.2(b)	453 023.7(b)	454 552.3(b)
EU-15	370 421.1	371 605.4	372 715.2	373 799.7	374 719.9	375 719.5	376 956.3	378 529.1	378 354.2(b)	380 351.4(e)
Euro-zone	298 186.4	299 073.1	299 923.1	300 775	301 487.8	302 160.5	303 141.5	304 434.3	304 936.8(b)	306 698.2(e)
Belgium	10 100.6	10 130.6	10 143	10 170.2	10 192.3	10 213.8	10 239.1	10 263.4	10 309.7	10 355.8
Czech Republic	10 334	10 333.2	10 321.3	10 309.1	10 299.1	10 289.6	10 278.1	10 266.5	10 206.4(b)	10 203.3
Denmark	5 196.6	5 215.7	5 251	5 275.1	5 294.9	5 313.6	5 330	5 349.2	5 368.4	5 383.5
Germany	81 338.1	81 538.6	81 817.5	82 012.2	82 057.4	82 037	82 163.5	82 259.5	82 440.3	82 536.7(e)
Estonia	1477	1 448.1	1 425.2	1 406	1 393.1	1 379.2	1 372.1	1 367	1 361.2	1356
Greece	10 511	10 595.1	10 673.7	10 744.6	10 808.3	10 861.4	10 903.7	10 931.1	10 988.0(b)	11 018.4(e)
Spain	39 218.8	39 305.4	39 383.1	39 467.8	39 570.9	39 724.4	39 960.7	40 376.4	4 0850.5	41 550.6(p)
France	57 565	57 752.5	57 936	58 116	58 299	58 496.6	58 748.7	59 042.7	5 9342.1	59 630.1(p)
Ireland	3 583.2	3 597.6	3 620.1	3 652.2	3 694	3 734.9	3 776.6	3826.2	3 899.9(b)	3 963.6
Italy	57 138.5	57 268.6	57 333	57 461	57 563.4	57 612.6	57 679.9	57 844	56 993.7(b)	57 321.0(e)
Cyprus	632.9	645.4	656.3	666.3	675.2	682.9	690.5	697.5	705.5	715.1
Latvia	2 540.9	2 500.6	2 469.5	2 444.9	2 420.8	2 399.2	2 381.7	2 364.3	2 345.8	2 331.5
Lithuania	3 671.3	3643	3 615.2	3 588	3 562.3	3 536.4	3 512.1	3 487	3 475.6	3 462.6
Luxembourg	400.2	405.7	411.6	416.9	422.1	427.4	433.6	439	444.1	448.3
Hungary	10 350	10 336.7	10 321.2	10 301.2	10 279.7	10 253.4	10 221.6	10 200.3	10 174.9	10 142.4
Malta	366.4	369.5	371.2	374	376.5	378.5	388.8	391.4	394.6	397.3
Netherlands	15 341.6	15 424.1	15 493.9	15 567.1	15 654.2	15 760.2	1 5864	15 987.1	16 105.3	16 192.6
Austria	7 928.7	7 943.5	7953.1	7 965	7 971.1	7 982.5	8 002.2	8 020.9	8 038.9	8 067.3
Poland	38 504.7	38 580.6	38 609.4	38 639.3	38 660	38 667	38 653.6	38 644.2	38 632.5	38 218.5(b)
Portugal	9 982.8	10 012.8	10 041.4	10 069.8	10 107.9	10 150.1	10 198.2	10 262.9	10 329.3	10 407.5
Slovenia	1 989.4	1 989.5	1 990.3	1 987	1 984.9	1 978.3	1 987.8	1 990.1	1 994	1 995
Slovakia	5 336.5	5 356.2	5 367.8	5 378.9	5 387.7	5 393.4	5 398.7	5 378.8(b)	5 379	5 379.2
Finland	5 077.9	5 098.8	5 116.8	5 132.3	5 147.3	5 159.6	5 171.3	5 181.1	5 194.9	5 206.3
Sweden	8 745.1	8 816.4	8 837.5	8 844.5	8 847.6	8 854.3	8 861.4	8 882.8	8 909.1	8 940.8
United Kingdom	58 292.9	58 500.2	58 703.7	58 905.1	59 089.6	59 391.1	59 623.4	59 862.8	59 139.9(b)	59 328.9(e)
Iceland	265.1	267	268	269.9	272.4	275.7	279	283.4	286.6	288.5
Liechtenstein	30.3	30.6	30.9	31.1	31.3	32	32.4	32.9	33.5	33.9
Norway	4 324.8	4 348.4	4370	4 392.7	4 417.6	4 445.3	4 478.5	4 503.4	4 524.1	4 552.3
Canada	29 076.9	29 437	29 789	30 110.7	30 425.3	:	:	:	:	:
Japan	125 033.5	125 570	125 503.8	124 645.2	126 109.7	126 056.8	126 550	126 771.7	:	:
United States	259 159	261 687	264 162.2	266 490.1	269 106.3	271 626	275 562.7	278 058.9	:	:

The inhabitants of a given area on 1 January of the year in question (or, in some cases, on 31 December of the previous year). The population is based on data from the most recent census adjusted by the components of population change produced since the last census, or based on population registers.

The EU-25 population

During the last 40 years, the population of the 25 countries of today's EU has grown from 378 million (1960) to over 453 million (2002). During the last three decades, the population growth has slowed down. The EU-25 population is expected to have grown by 0.3 % in 2003, which is again a modest rise.

In 2003, Germany had the largest population within the 25 countries that today form the EU with more than 18 % of the total, followed by France, the United Kingdom and Italy with roughly 13 % each. These four countries together comprise 57 % of the total population of today's European Union. The new Member States represent almost 16 % of the total population (74.2 million).

The EU-25 population
In million persons

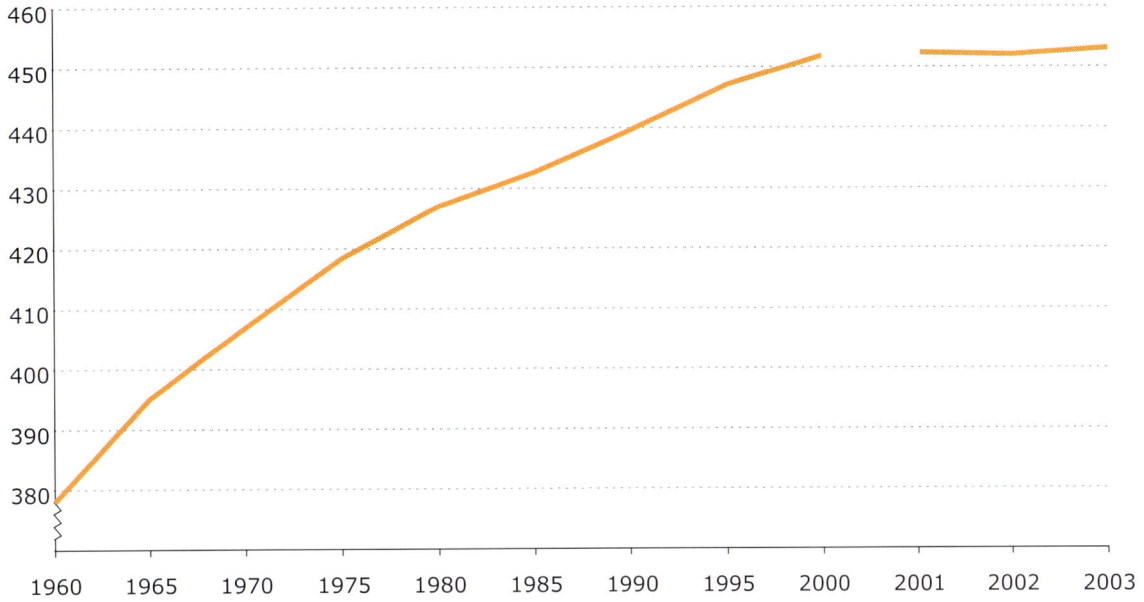

Growth of the EU-25 population
Per 1 000 inhabitants

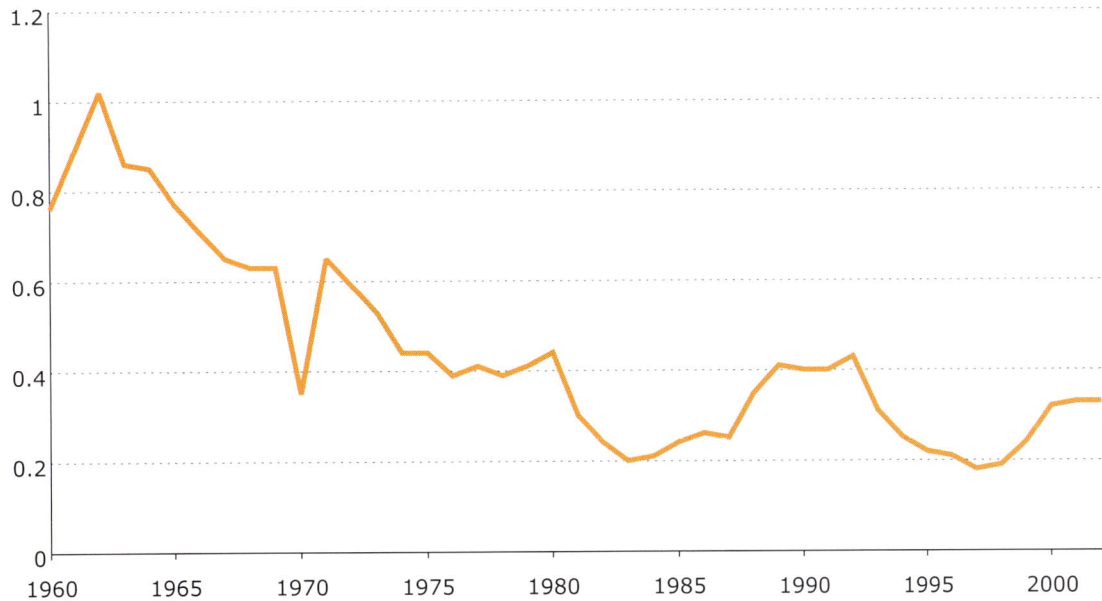

Population in the EU-15 by age classes
Share of total population in %

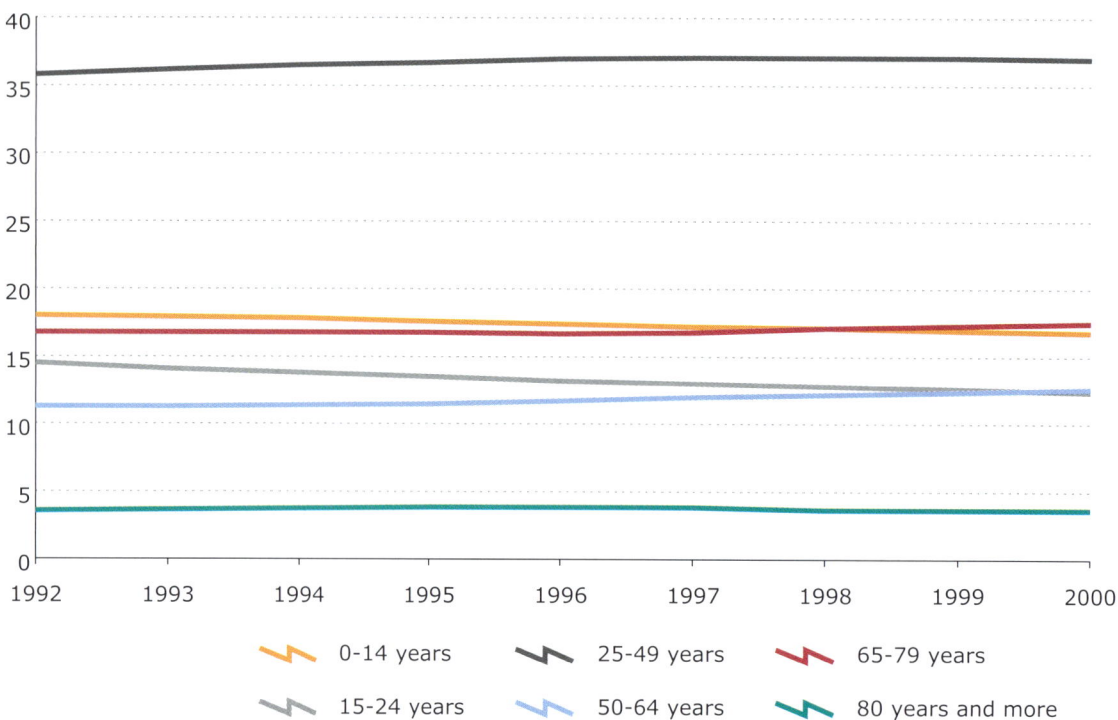

Legend	
0-14 years	25-49 years	65-79 years
15-24 years	50-64 years	80 years and more

The share of the young population is decreasing. In 2000, the population aged up to 14 years made up 16.8 % of the total population compared with 18.0 % in 1992. The population aged 15 to 24 years had a share of 12.4 % (2000) as against 14.5 % (1992).

The population aged 25 to 49 years represents more than one third of the total EU population (2000: 37.0 %). From 1992 to 2000, the share of the population aged over 50 years increased all over the EU. The share of the age group 65 to 79 years rose from 11.3 % of the total population in 1992 to 12.6 % in 2000. There are marked differences between countries regarding this age group.

Population density
In inhabitants per km²

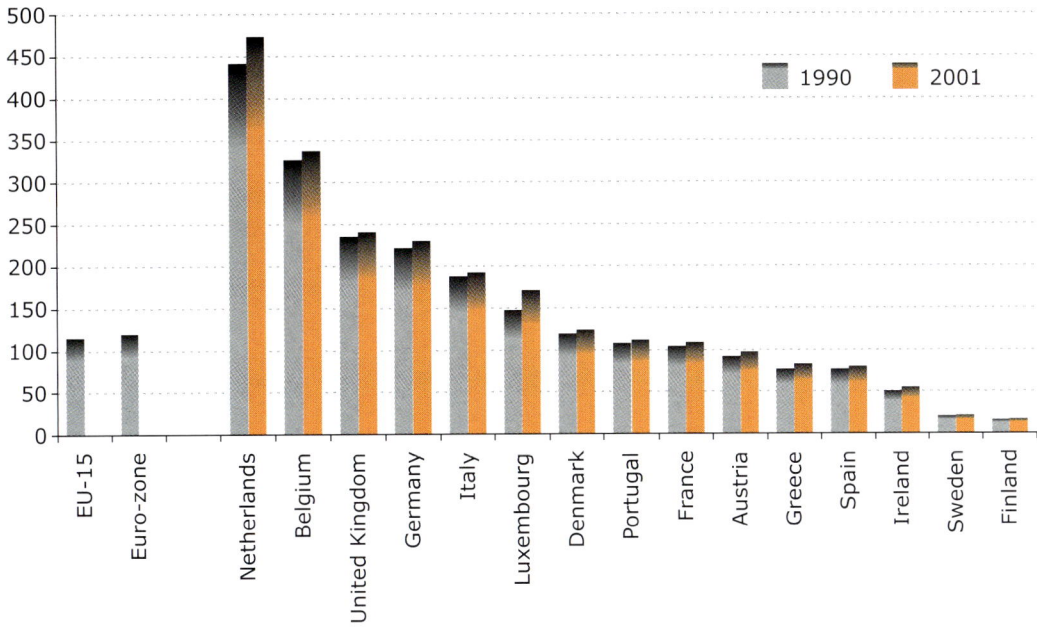

The ratio of the mid-year population of a territory on a given date to the size of the territory.

There are significant differences in population density: it is much higher in the Netherlands (474 inhabitants per km²) and in Belgium (337) than in some Nordic countries such as Finland (17) and Sweden (22).

Women per 100 men

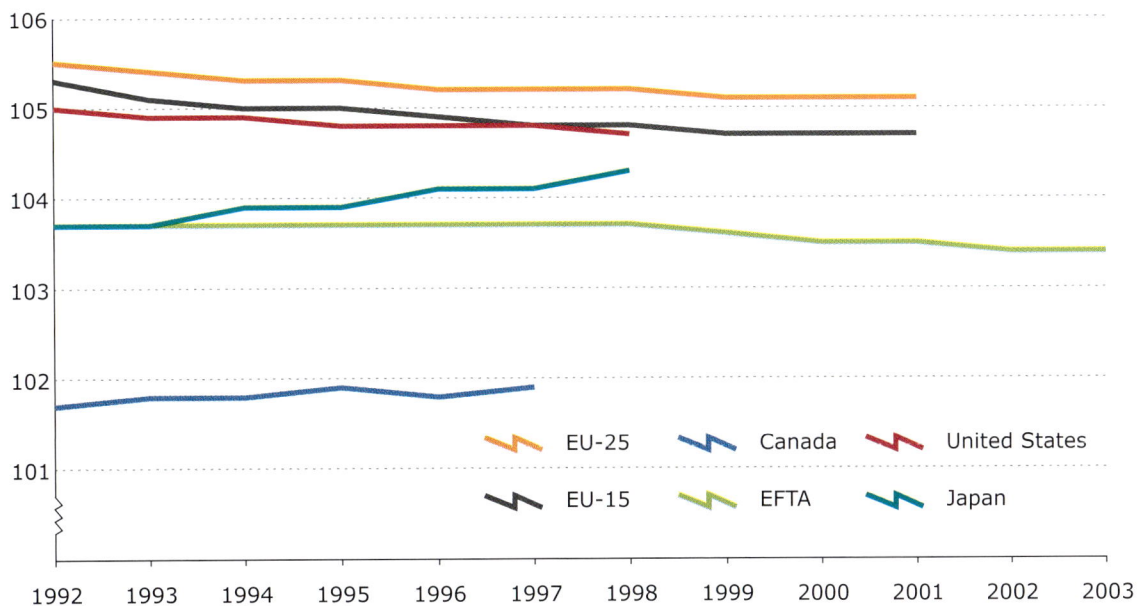

2

World population in 2002
In %

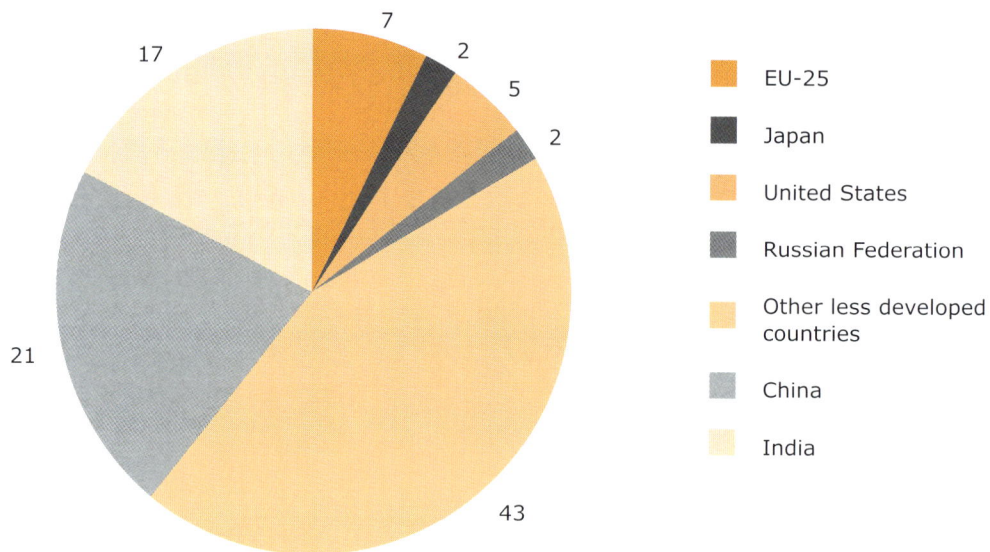

■	EU-25
■	Japan
■	United States
■	Russian Federation
■	Other less developed countries
■	China
■	India

Shares of the world population increase, 2002 as against 1990
In %

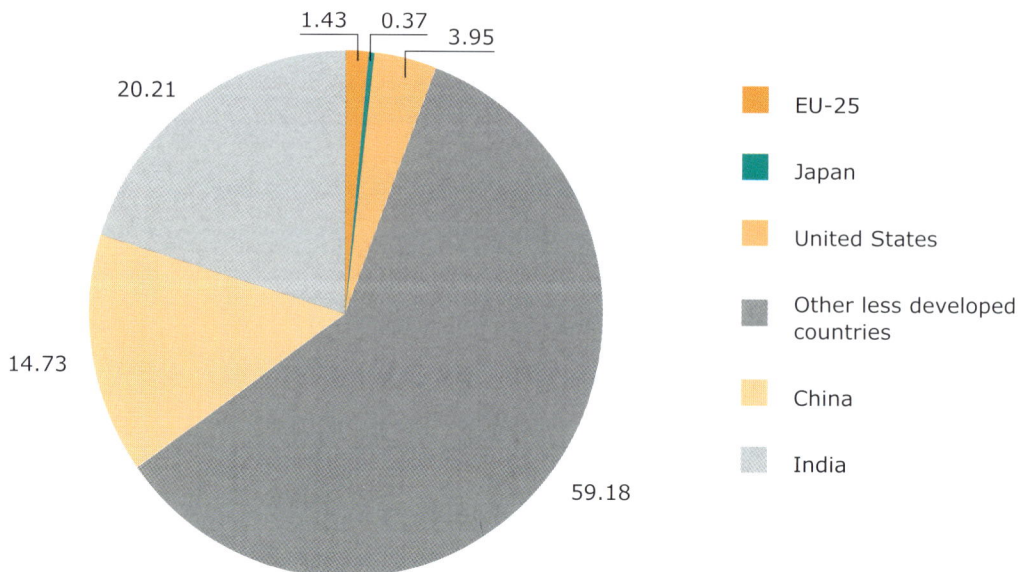

■	EU-25
■	Japan
■	United States
■	Other less developed countries
■	China
■	India

The Russian Federation contributed — 0.32 % to the development of the world population.

Families and births

Eurostat data

Eurostat provides a wide range of data on:

— First marriages by sex and age
— Marriages by previous marital status and sex
— Divorces by duration of marriage
— Marriage and divorce indicators
— Marriages and live births by month
— Live births by marital status and mother's age
— Live births by birth order
— Fertility rates by age
— Fertility indicators
— Abortions

2

Fewer and later marriages; more marital breakdowns

In 2002, there were only five marriages per 1 000 inhabitants in the EU compared with almost eight in 1970. The average age at which people first get married has increased: for men, from 26 years in 1980 to over 30 today, and for women from 23 to 28 years. The proportion of divorces is estimated at 15 % for marriages entered into in 1960, and at around 30 % for those entered into in 1985.

Fewer children, and later in life

The completed fertility of post-war generations has been steadily declining since the mid-1960s, but the total fertility rate remains relatively stable at almost 1.5. The completed fertility changes far less abruptly over time and is now around 1.7, still well below the reproduction level (2.1 children per woman).

A rise in births outside marriage

The proportion of births outside marriage continues to increase, basically reflecting the growing popularity of cohabitation: from 6 % of all births in 1970 to over 30 % in 2002. In Sweden, more than half (56 %) of the children born in 2002 had unmarried parents.

2

Marriages
Per 1 000 persons

	1991	1992	1993	1994	1995	1996	1997	1998	1999	2000	2001	2002
EU-25	5.77	5.63	5.38	5.24	5.17	5.08	5.09	:	5.15	5.14	:	:
EU-15	5.64	5.54	5.33	5.2	5.14	5.07	5.08	:	5.12	5.13	:	:
Euro-zone	5.59	5.45	5.25	5.12	5.08	5.03	5.06	:	5.13	5.11	4.85	:
Belgium	6.07	5.79	5.37	5.14	5.07	4.98	4.69	4.35	4.32	4.4	4.09	:
Czech Republic	6.96	7.18	6.39	5.66	5.32	5.22	5.61	5.35	5.2	5.39	5.12	:
Denmark	6.03	6.22	6.1	6.78	6.64	6.83	6.48	6.55	6.66	7.19	6.82	:
Germany	5.68	5.62	5.45	5.41	5.27	5.22	5.15	5.09	5.25	5.09	4.72	:
Estonia	6.59	5.79	5.18	5.04	4.88	3.9	3.99	3.92	4.06	4.01	4.14	:
Greece	6.39	4.69	5.94	5.38	6.02	4.24	5.62	5.12	5.62	4.48	5.2	:
Spain	5.6	5.57	5.14	5.09	5.1	4.92	4.97	5.22	5.22	5.39	5.08	:
France	4.92	4.74	4.44	4.4	4.4	4.83	4.88	4.65	4.88	5.18	5.13	:
Ireland	4.93	4.68	4.7	4.63	4.32	4.45	4.26	:	4.93	5.04	4.98	:
Italy	5.5	5.49	5.3	5.1	5.06	4.85	4.83	4.86	4.86	4.86	4.54	:
Cyprus	10.46	8.04	9.71	9.7	10.25	8.71	10.71	11.4	13.22	13.37	15.07	14.48
Latvia	8.43	7.23	5.69	4.59	4.46	3.92	3.98	4	3.93	3.88	3.93	:
Lithuania	9.24	8.14	6.44	6.38	6.1	5.67	5.26	5.21	5.07	4.83	4.53	:
Luxembourg	6.7	6.4	5.98	5.84	5.08	5.08	4.78	4.8	4.85	4.92	4.49	:
Hungary	5.9	5.5	5.22	5.23	5.18	4.75	4.56	4.37	4.44	4.71	4.28	:
Malta	7.1	6.58	6.79	6.75	6.26	6.36	6.43	6.51	6.28	6.52	5.58	:
Netherlands	6.3	6.17	5.77	5.39	5.27	5.48	5.45	5.54	5.66	5.53	4.97	:
Austria	5.69	5.83	5.69	5.45	5.4	5.31	5.2	4.91	4.94	4.9	4.26	:
Poland	6.1	5.66	5.4	5.39	5.37	5.27	5.3	5.42	5.68	5.46	5.05	:
Portugal	7.24	7.01	6.84	6.6	6.56	6.33	6.52	6.57	6.75	6.23	5.67	:
Slovenia	4.09	4.57	4.53	4.18	4.14	3.8	3.78	3.8	3.89	3.62	3.48	:
Slovakia	6.19	6.39	5.78	5.27	5.13	5.11	5.19	5.1	5.07	4.81	4.42	:
Finland	4.93	4.67	4.87	4.89	4.65	4.77	4.56	4.66	4.7	5.05	4.79	:
Sweden	4.27	4.29	3.9	3.9	3.81	3.79	3.65	3.57	4.03	4.5	4.02	:
United Kingdom	6.05	6.14	5.87	5.67	5.5	5.33	5.26	5.15	5.06	5.12	:	:
Iceland	4.79	4.75	4.62	4.92	4.63	5.02	5.46	5.58	5.62	6.32	5.21	:
Liechtenstein	6.27	14.19	7.48	12.98	13.18	14.16	12.56	:	:	:	:	:
Norway	4.66	4.49	4.51	4.75	4.97	5.29	5.41	5.27	5.26	5.65	5.09	:
United States	:	:	:	:	:	:	:	:	8.38	:	:	:

Source: Eurostat/US Bureau of the Census.

In the last decades, the rate of marriages per 1 000 inhabitants in EU-15 has decreased from almost eight at the beginning of the 1980s to around six at the end of this decade, approaching five in 2001. This might partly be the result of the growing popularity of cohabitation. Low rates are reported for Slovenia, Latvia, Sweden and Belgium (around four). In contrast, the rate for Cyprus stands at 15.

As well as the decrease in the rate of marriages, demographical changes are marked by the increase in the average age at which people get married for the first time. In 2002, men as well as women in EU-15 married about two years later in their lives than in 1991.

Mean age at first marriage in 2002
Years

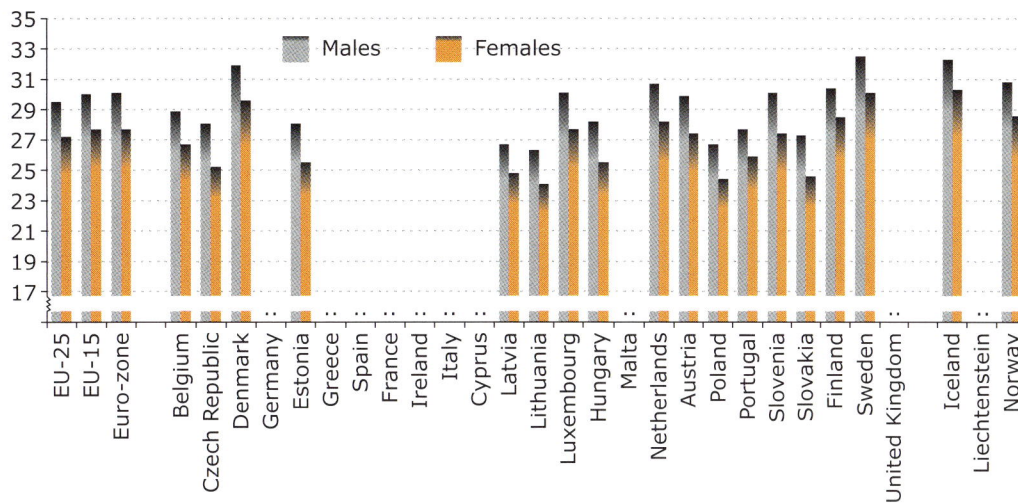

Divorces
Per 1 000 persons

	1991	1992	1993	1994	1995	1996	1997	1998	1999	2000	2001	2002
EU-25	:	:	:	:	:	:	:	:	:	:	:	:
EU-15	:	:	:	:	:	:	:	:	:	:	1.9	:
Euro-zone	:	:	:	:	:	:	:	:	:	:	1.7	:
Belgium	2.1	2.2	2.1	2.2	3.5	2.8	2.6	2.6	2.6	2.6	2.8	3
Czech Republic	2.8	2.8	2.9	3	3	3.2	3.2	3.1	2.3	2.9	3.1	3.1
Denmark	2.5	2.5	2.5	2.6	2.5	2.4	2.4	2.5	2.5	2.7	2.7	2.8
Germany	1.7	1.7	1.9	2	2.1	2.1	2.3	2.3	2.3	2.4	2.4	:
Estonia	3.7	4.3	3.9	3.8	5.2	4	3.8	3.2	3.3	3.1	3.2	3
Greece	0.6	0.6	0.7	0.7	1	1	1.1	0.7	0.9	1	1	1.1
Spain	0.7	0.7	0.7	0.8	0.8	0.8	0.9	:	:	1	0.9	:
France	1.9	1.9	1.9	2	2.1	2	2	2	2	:	1.9	:
Ireland	:	:	:	:	:	:	:	:	:	0.7	0.7	:
Italy	0.5	0.5	0.4	0.5	0.5	0.6	0.6	0.6	0.6	0.7	0.7	0.7
Cyprus	0.5	0.7	0.8	0.9	1.2	1.1	1.3	1.3	1.7	1.7	1.7	1.9
Latvia	4.2	5.6	4	3.3	3.1	2.5	2.5	2.6	2.5	2.6	2.4	2.5
Lithuania	4.1	3.8	3.8	3	2.8	3.1	3.2	3.3	3.2	3.1	3.2	3
Luxembourg	2	1.8	1.9	1.7	1.8	2	2.4	2.4	2.4	2.4	2.3	2.4
Hungary	2.4	2.1	2.2	2.3	2.4	2.2	2.4	2.5	2.5	2.3	2.4	2.5
Malta	:	:	:	:	:	:	:	:	:	:	:	:
Netherlands	1.9	2	2	2.4	2.2	2.2	2.2	2.1	2.1	2.2	2.3	2.1
Austria	2.1	2.1	2.1	2.1	2.3	2.3	2.3	2.2	2.3	2.4	2.6	2.4
Poland	0.9	0.8	0.7	0.8	1	1	1.1	1.2	1.1	1.1	1.2	1.2
Portugal	1.1	1.2	1.2	1.4	1.2	1.3	1.4	1.5	1.7	1.9	1.8	2.6
Slovenia	0.9	1	1	1	0.8	1	1	1	1	1.1	1.1	1.2
Slovakia	1.5	1.5	1.5	1.6	1.7	1.7	1.7	1.7	1.8	1.7	1.8	2
Finland	2.6	2.6	2.5	2.7	2.7	2.7	2.6	2.7	2.7	2.7	2.6	2.6
Sweden	2.3	2.5	2.5	2.5	2.6	2.4	2.4	2.3	2.4	2.4	2.4	2.4
United Kingdom	3	3	3.1	3	2.9	2.9	2.7	2.7	2.7	2.6	2.6	:
Iceland	2.1	2	2	1.8	1.8	2	1.9	1.8	1.7	1.9	1.9	1.8
Liechtenstein	1.2	1.1	1.3	1.3	1.2	1.4	2.1	:	:	:	2.8	3
Norway	2.4	2.4	2.5	2.5	2.4	2.3	2.3	2.1	2	2.2	2.3	:
Japan	:	:	:	:	1.6	1.6	:	:	:	:	:	:
United States	:	:	:	:	:	:	:	:	:	4.2	:	:

Completed fertility
By generation

	1961	1962	1963	1964	1965	1966	1967	1968	1969	1970	1971
EU-15	1.77	1.74	1.7	:	:	:	:	:	:	:	:
Euro-zone	1.73	1.7	1.66	:	:	:	:	:	:	:	:
Belgium	1.85	1.82	1.81	1.79	:	:	:	:	:	:	:
Czech Republic	2.01	1.99	1.96	1.94	1.93	1.91	1.88	1.86	1.82	1.78	1.73
Denmark	1.91	1.92	1.92	1.93	1.92	1.92	1.92	:	:	:	:
Germany	1.63	1.61	1.58	1.56	1.53	1.49	1.46	:	:	:	:
Estonia	1.98	1.94	1.91	1.9	1.87	1.84	1.83	1.8	1.76		:
Greece	1.89	1.83	1.8	1.76	1.72	1.7	:	:	:	:	:
Spain	1.71	1.66	1.66	1.64	1.59	:	:	:	:	:	:
France	2.1	2.08	2.06	2.04	2.02	2	:	:	:	:	:
Ireland	2.35	2.31	2.27	2.23	2.18	2.14	:	:	:	:	:
Italy	1.63	1.6	1.57	1.52	1.49	:	:	:	:	:	:
Latvia	1.92	1.88	1.83	1.79	1.77	1.77	1.76	1.73	1.69	1.62	:
Lithuania	1.83	1.78	1.74	1.72	1.72	1.71	1.71	1.72	1.72	1.69	1.64
Luxembourg	1.77	1.79	1.81	1.81	1.82	1.85	1.82	:	:	:	:
Hungary	2.03	2.02	2	1.98	1.97	1.96	1.93	1.89	1.84	1.8	:
Malta	2.08	2.07	2.06	2.03	2	1.95	1.89	1.81	:	:	:
Netherlands	1.84	1.82	1.81	1.79	1.77	1.76	1.75	:	:	:	:
Austria	1.68	1.67	1.66	1.65	1.64	1.62	1.6	1.57	:	:	:
Poland	2.14	2.11	2.07	2.03	2	1.98	1.96	1.91	1.85	1.79	:
Portugal	1.87	1.86	1.84	1.82	1.82	1.81	1.78	1.74	:	:	:
Slovenia	1.85	1.84	1.81	1.79	1.77	1.75	1.73	1.7	1.67	:	:
Slovakia	2.17	2.14	2.11	2.07	2.04	2.01	1.99	1.95	1.91	1.85	1.79
Finland	1.95	1.94	1.93	1.92	1.91	1.89	1.87	:	:	:	:
Sweden	2.03	2.02	2.01	2	1.98	1.96	1.94	:	:	:	:
United Kingdom	1.94	1.92	1.9	1.89	1.87	1.86	:	:	:	:	:
Iceland	2.43	2.4	2.38	2.4	2.36	2.34	2.32	:	:	:	:
Norway	2.1	2.09	2.08	2.07	2.06	2.05	2.04	2.02	:	:	:
Japan	:	:	:	:	:	:	:	:	:	:	:
United States	:	:	:	:	:	:	:	:	:	:	:

Source: Eurostat/US Bureau of the Census.

The mean number of children born to women of a given generation at the end of their childbearing years. This is calculated by adding the fertility rates by age of the mother observed for successive years, when the cohort has reached the age in question (in general, only ages between 15 and 49 years are considered). In practice, the fertility rates for older women can be estimated using the rates observed for previous generations, without waiting for the cohort to reach the end of the reproductive period.

In EU-15, the completed fertility rate for women born at the beginning of the 1960s stood at 1.8, well below the reproduction level. The total fertility rate, that allows comparison between the fertility of a population in different reporting years, decreased from 2.7 in 1965 to below the level of 1.5 in 1995 where it has remained since.

Total fertility rate in the EU-15

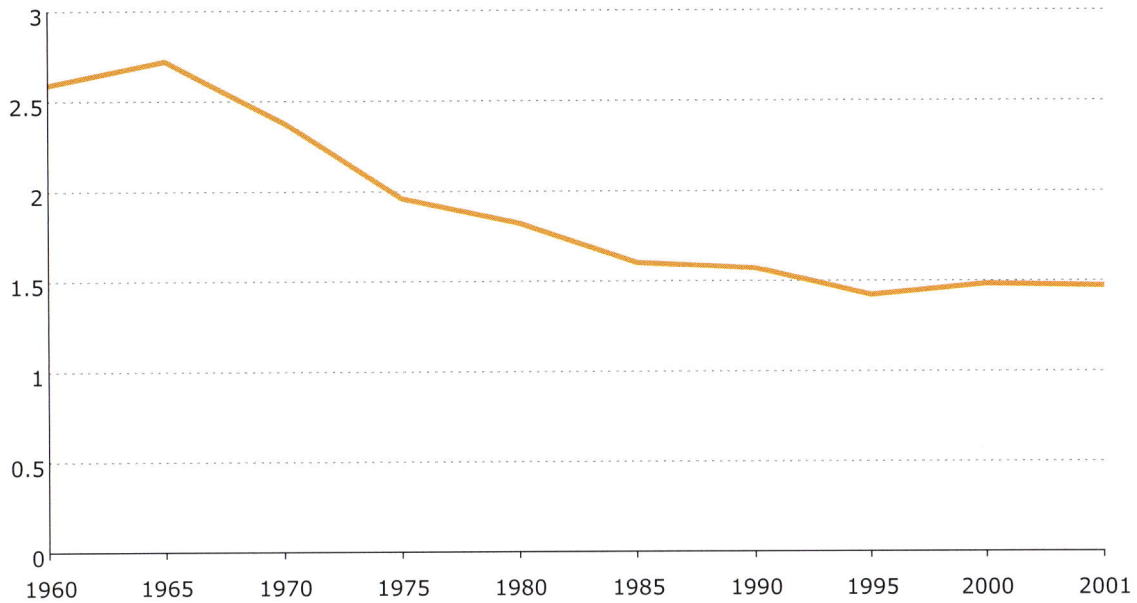

The total fertility rate is the mean number of children that would be born alive to a woman during her lifetime if she were to pass through her childbearing years conforming to the fertility rates by age of a given year. It is therefore the completed fertility of a hypothetical generation, computed by adding the fertility rates by age for women in a given year (the number of women at each age is assumed to be the same). The total fertility rate is also used to indicate the replacement level fertility; in more developed countries, a rate of 2.1 is considered to be replacement level.

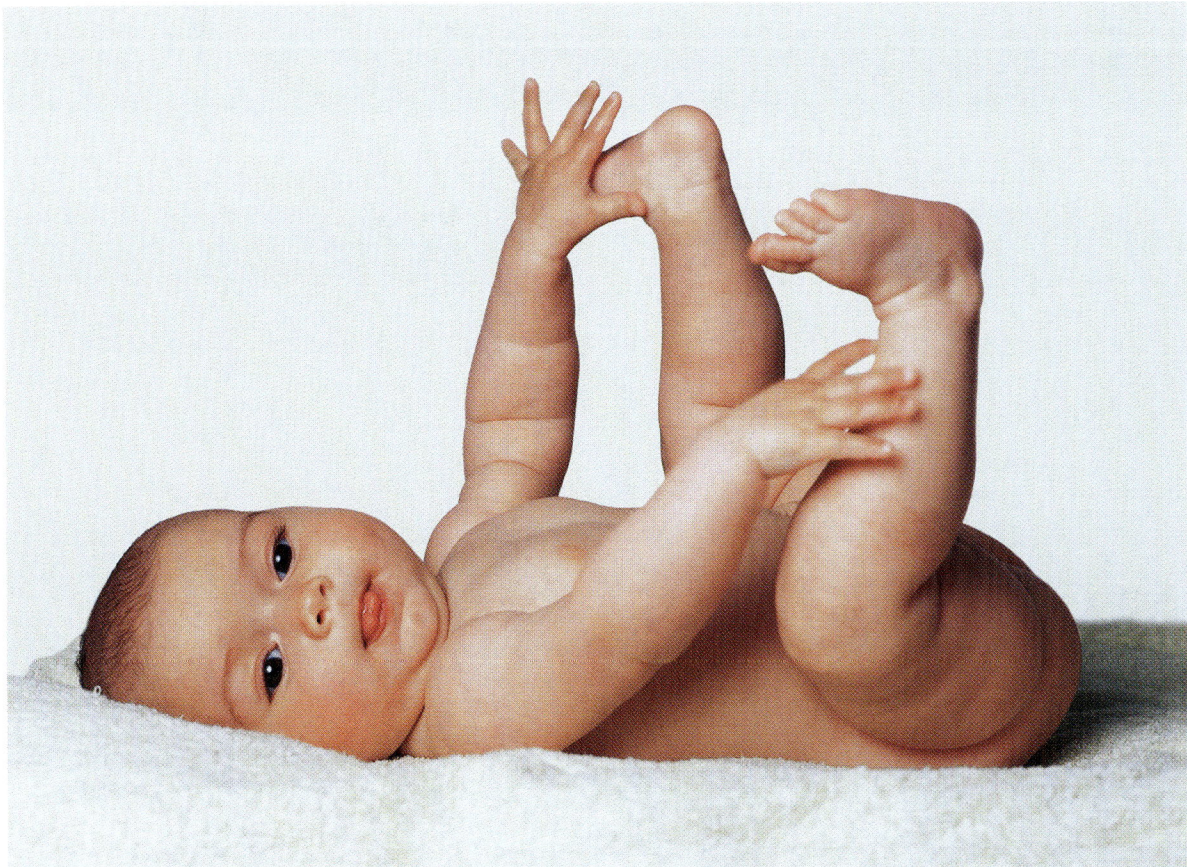

Mean age of women at childbearing
Years

	1991	1992	1993	1994	1995	1996	1997	1998	1999	2000	2001	2002
EU-25	:	:	:	:	:	:	:	:	:	29	29.1	29.2
EU-15	28.3	28.46	28.59	28.75	28.9	28.98	:	:	:	29.4	29.4	29.4
Euro-zone	28.46	28.63	28.76	28.92	29.09	29.16	:	:	:	29.5	29.5	29.6
Belgium	27.95	28.09	28.2	28.34	28.47(e)	28.50(e)	28.6	:	:	:	:	:
Czech Republic	24.72	24.82	25.05	25.4	25.77	26.1	26.38	26.64	26.9	27.2	27.6	27.8
Denmark	28.63	28.77	28.94	29.08	29.21	29.28	29.42p	29.52	29.62	29.7	29.7	29.9
Germany	27.79	27.93	28.07	28.19	28.31	28.37	28.52	28.58	28.7	28.7	28.8	:
Estonia	25.3	25.3	25.3	25.4	25.6	25.9	26.2	26.4	26.6	27	27.2	27.5
Greece	27.38	27.55	27.84	28.01	28.19	28.37	28.58	28.7	28.9	:	:	:
Spain	29.04	29.25	29.47	29.74	29.98	30.2	30.4	30.55	30.7	30.7	:	:
France	28.4	28.55	28.67	28.83	28.99	29.12	29.21	29.32	29.3	29.4	29.4	29.5
Ireland	29.88	30.01	30.05	30.12	30.24	30.20(p)	30.40(p)	30.3	30.3	30.4	30.5	30.6
Italy	29.01	29.21	29.29	29.48	29.72	30	:	:	30.3	30.3	30.3	:
Cyprus	27.3	27.5	27.8	28	28.2	28.2	28.4	28.4	28.6	28.7	28.9	29.1
Latvia	25.5	25.4	25.4	25.8	25.8	26	26.4	26.6	26.8	27.2	27.4	27.6
Lithuania	25.7	25.6	25.6	25.5	25.6	25.7	25.9	26.2	26.4	26.6	26.8	26.9
Luxembourg	28.43	28.58	28.6	28.73	28.93	29.16	29.18	29.25	29.36	29.3	29.3	29.5
Hungary	25.68	25.8	26	26.22	26.35	26.51	26.69	26.86	27.07	27.3	27.6	27.8
Malta	28.8	28.83	28.81	28.9	29.06	28.8	28.68	28.87	29	28.6	28.9	29.2
Netherlands	29.47	29.67	29.82	29.9	30.04	30.15	30.18	30.25	30.27	30.3	30.3	30.4
Austria	27.2	27.3	27.3	27.5	27.7	27.8	27.9	28	28.1	28.2	28.4	28.6
Poland	26.25	26.38	26.61	26.82	26.89	27.02	27.12	27.19	27.31	27.4	27.6	27.8
Portugal	27.5	27.6	27.7	27.8	28	28.1	28.3	28.4	28.5	28.6	28.7	28.8
Slovenia	26.12	26.18	26.55	26.78	27.04	27.27	27.53	27.81	27.97	28.2	28.5	28.8
Slovakia	24.99	25.13	25.26	25.45	25.63	25.82	:	:	26.39	26.6	26.8	27
Finland	28.87	28.95	29.02	29.13	29.3	29.35	29.45	29.55	29.58	29.6	29.7	29.7
Sweden	28.74	28.87	28.99	29.15	29.24	29.38	29.48	29.73	29.81	29.9	30	30.1
United Kingdom	27.72	27.84	27.94	28.11	28.16	28.17	28.26	28.32	28.4	28.5	28.6	28.7
Iceland	27.98	28.52	28.62	28.61	28.66	28.8	28.61	28.77	28.72	28.9	29.1	29.3
Liechtenstein	29.8	28.6	29.3	29.8	30	30	30	:	:	30.1	29.9	30
Norway	28.3	28.43	28.6	28.74	28.85	28.95	29.08	29.16	29.26	29.3	29.4	29.5
Canada	28.2	28.4	28.5	28.7	28.8	29	:	:	:	:	:	:
Japan	28.9	28.9	29	29	:	:	:	:	:	29.7	29.7	:
United States	27	:	:	:	:	:	:	:	:	27.4	:	:

The mean age of women when their children are born. For a given calendar year, the mean age of women at childbearing is calculated using the fertility rates by age as weights (in general, the reproductive period is between 15 and 49 years of age). When calculated in this way, the mean age is not influenced by a specific population structure (number of mothers in each age group) and is therefore better for geographical and temporal comparisons.

Migration and asylum

2

Migration: an important component of population change

Migration and asylum are topics of very high political importance. These statistics are used by the Commission in the development and monitoring of a common asylum policy and harmonised immigration policies for the EU.

The information is also of relevance to a number of other important areas of social and economic policy. In many Member States, migration is the principal component of population change. This is important when considering the effects of an ageing population on, for example, the future sustainability of health and social security systems. Similarly, these statistics are used as an input to work on assessing the socioeconomic inclusion of migrant populations and the success of measures to prevent discrimination.

Measuring migration

Eurostat produces statistics on a range of issues related to international migration and asylum. Data to produce these statistics are supplied on a monthly, quarterly and annual basis by national statistical institutes and by Ministries of Justice and the Interior. Many of these statistics are sent to Eurostat as part of a joint migration data collection organised by Eurostat in cooperation with the United Nations Statistical Division, the United Nations Economic Commission for Europe, the Council of Europe and the International Labour Office.

Countries differ in the way they produce migration statistics and who they consider to be a migrant. In some countries, migration statistics are based on administrative data taken, for example, from systems for issuing residence permits or from a population register. Some other countries use survey-based data. These variations in data sources and definitions result in problems when comparing the migrant counts for different countries.

The EU remains attractive to migrants

Migration is influenced by a combination of economic, political and social factors. These factors may act in a migrant's country of origin ('push' factors) or in the country of destination ('pull' factors). The relative economic prosperity and political stability of the EU exert a considerable pull effect. Various push factors in many parts of the world have also continued to have a strong effect on migrant flows.

Citizenship

Acquisition of citizenship is sometimes viewed as an indicator of the formal integration of migrants into their destination country, often requiring a period of legal residence together with other factors such as language proficiency.

Policy context

The Treaty of Amsterdam introduced a new Title IV ('Visas, asylum, immigration and other policies related to free movement of persons') into the EC Treaty. It covers the following fields: free movement of persons; controls on external borders; asylum, immigration and safeguarding of the rights of third-country nationals; judicial cooperation in civil and criminal matters, and administrative cooperation.

2

Net migration, including corrections
Per 1 000 inhabitants

	1991	1992	1993	1994	1995	1996	1997	1998	1999	2000	2001	2002
EU-25	2.5	2.9	2.2	1.7	1.8	1.7	1.2	1.5	2.1	2.6	3.0(p)	3.7(e)
EU-15	3.2	3.7	2.9	2.2	2.2	2.1	1.5	1.9	2.5	3.1	3.6(p)	4.4(e)
Euro-zone	3.6	4.4	3.1	2.2	2.3	2.2	1.5	1.6	2.5	3.2	3.8(p)	5.0(e)
Belgium	1.3	2.6	1.8	1.7	0.2	1.5	1	1.1	1.6	1.3	3.5	3.9
Czech Republic	-5.5	1.1	0.5	1	1	1	1.2	0.9	0.9	0.6	-0.8	1.2
Denmark	2.1	2.2	2.2	2	5.5	3.3	2.3	2.1	1.8	1.9	2.2	1.8
Germany	7.5	9.6	5.7	3.9	4.9	3.4	1.1	0.6	2.5	2	3.3	2.7(p)
Estonia	-8.1	-27.1	-19	-14.3	-10.8	-9.5	-4.9	-4.7	-0.8	0.2	0.1	0.1
Greece	11.7	9.1	8.3	7.4	7.3	6.6	5.7	5.1	4.1	2.7	3.1	2.9(e)
Spain	1.6	1.4	1.5	1.4	1.5	1.9	2.1	3.8	5.7	9.4	10.6(p)	15.8(e)
France	0.6	0.6	0.3	-0.1	-0.3	-0.3	-0.2	-0.1	0.8	0.8	1	1.1(e)
Ireland	1.4	0.5	-0.9	-0.8	1.6	3.6	5.6	5	5.4	6.9	11.8	8.3(p)
Italy	0.1	3.2	3.2	2.7	1.7	2.7	2.2	1.9	1.7	3.1	2.2	6.1(e)
Cyprus	19.1	17.7	13.9	11	10.3	9.1	8.2	6.2	6.1	5.7	6.6	9.7
Latvia	-5.7	-20.5	-12.6	-9.1	-5.5	-4.1	-3.9	-2.4	-1.7	-2.3	-2.2	-0.8
Lithuania	-2.9	-6.6	-6.5	-6.6	-6.5	-6.5	-6.3	-6.2	-5.9	-5.8	-0.7	-0.6
Luxembourg	10.2	10.3	10.1	9.4	10.6	8.3	8.6	9	10.4	7.9	7.5	5.9
Hungary	1.7	1.8	1.8	1.7	1.7	1.7	1.7	1.7	1.6	1.6	1	0.3
Malta	3.4	2.4	2.7	2.4	-0.5	1.6	1.6	1.1	23.7	3.4	5.9	4.7(p)
Netherlands	3.3	2.8	2.9	1.3	1	1.4	1.9	2.8	2.8	3.6	3.5	1.7
Austria	9.9	9.1	4.2	0.4	0.3	0.5	0.2	1.1	2.5	2.2	2.2	3.2
Poland	-0.4	-0.3	-0.4	-0.5	-0.5	-0.3	-0.3	-0.3	-0.4	-0.5	-0.4	-0.3
Portugal	7.2	-1	1	2	2.5	2.5	3	3.5	3.9	4.9	5.7	6.8
Slovenia	-1.6	-2.7	-2.2	0	0.4	-1.7	-0.7	-2.7	5.4	1.4	2.5	1.1
Slovakia	0	-0.6	0.3	0.9	0.5	0.4	0.3	0.2	0.3	0.3	0.2	0.2
Finland	2.9	1.8	1.8	0.7	0.8	0.8	0.9	0.9	0.7	0.5	1.2	1
Sweden	2.9	2.3	3.7	5.8	1.3	0.7	0.7	1.2	1.5	2.7	3.2	3.5
United Kingdom	1.3	0.8	1.5	1.4	2	1.8	1.5	3.6	2.8	2.8	3.1	2.1
Iceland	4.4	-0.9	-0.7	-3	-5.1	-2	0.7	3.6	4.1	6.7	3	-1.2
Liechtenstein	4.3	9.7	6.8	5.5	3.1	1.5	-0.9	15.9	6.5	7.3	14.4	4.7
Norway	1.9	2.4	2.9	1.7	1.5	1.3	2.2	3	4.3	2.2	1.8	3.8
Japan	:	:	:	:	-2.6	-9.3	9.4	:	0	-0.1	:	:
United States	:	:	:	:	:	:	:	:	3.5	3.5	:	:

Eurostat estimates that might be subject to change.

The difference between immigration into and emigration from the area during the year (net migration is therefore negative when the number of emigrants exceeds the number of immigrants). Since most countries either do not have accurate figures on immigration and emigration or have no figures at all, net migration is estimated on the basis of the difference between population change and natural increase between two dates. The statistics on net migration are therefore affected by all the statistical inaccuracies in the two components of this equation, especially population change.

The net inflow of foreign migrants into EU-15 increased to about 1 688 000 in 2002.

Spain, Italy, Germany and the United Kingdom together received 71 % of the net inflow of migrants into the EU Member States in 2003.

Net migration(¹), EU-15
In 1000

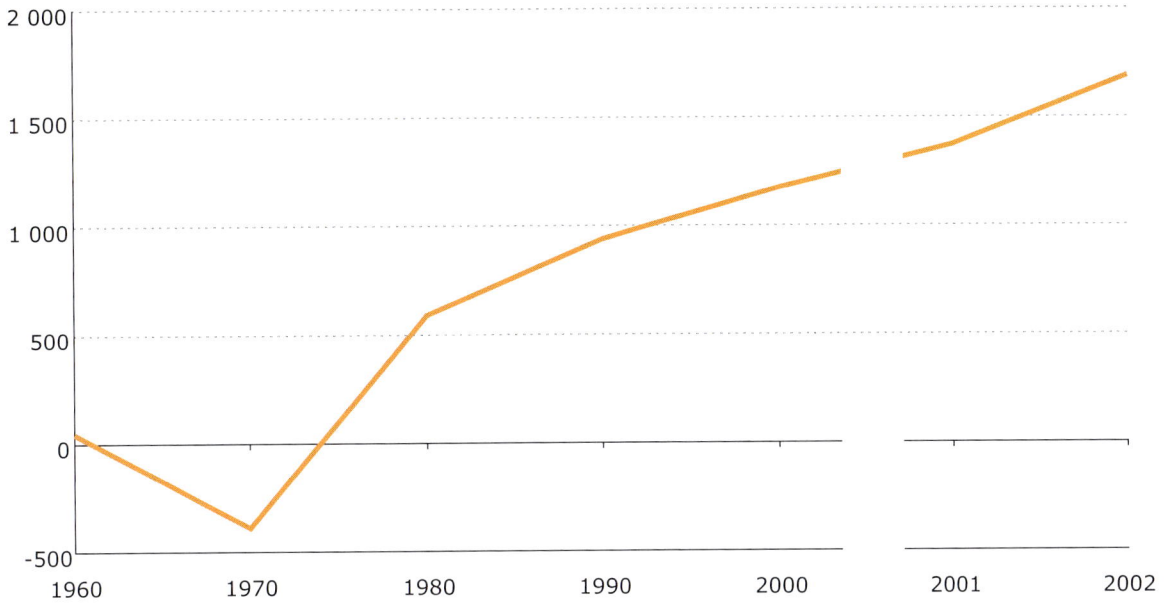

(¹) Including corrections due to population censuses, register counts, etc. which cannot be classified as births, deaths or migration.

Net migration by EU Member States in 2003
In %

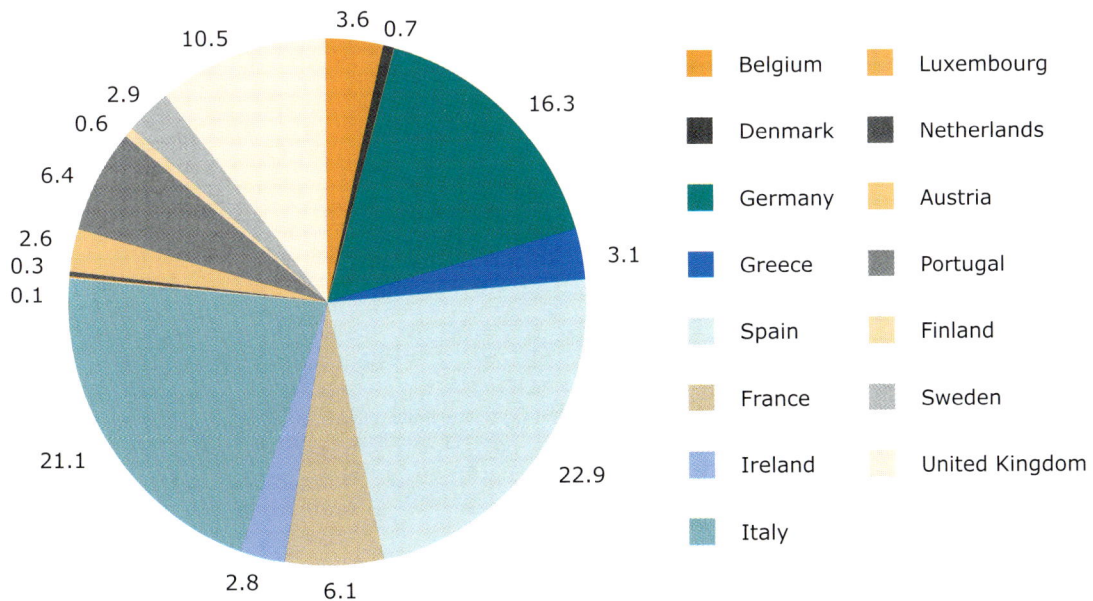

Belgium · Luxembourg · Denmark · Netherlands · Germany · Austria · Greece · Portugal · Spain · Finland · France · Sweden · Ireland · United Kingdom · Italy

Crude total population growth rate in 2003

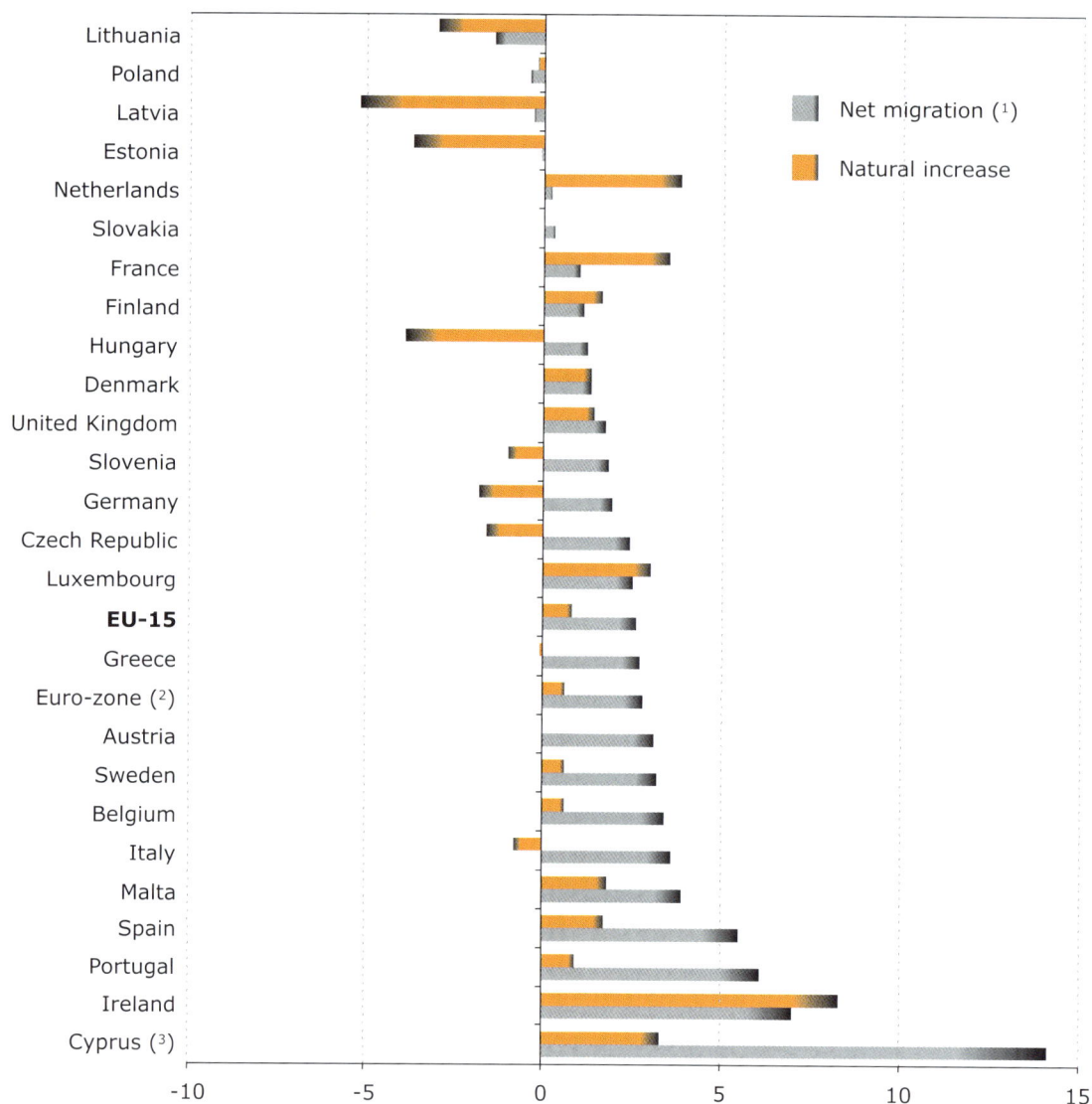

Legend:
- Net migration [1]
- Natural increase

Countries (top to bottom): Lithuania, Poland, Latvia, Estonia, Netherlands, Slovakia, France, Finland, Hungary, Denmark, United Kingdom, Slovenia, Germany, Czech Republic, Luxembourg, **EU-15**, Greece, Euro-zone [2], Austria, Sweden, Belgium, Italy, Malta, Spain, Portugal, Ireland, Cyprus [3]

X-axis: -10, -5, 0, 5, 10, 15

[1] Including corrections due to population censuses, register counts, etc. which cannot be classified as births, deaths or migrations.

[2] Total of the 12 EU countries that participate in the euro zone from 1 January 2001 (Belgium, Germany, Greece, Spain, France, Ireland, Italy, Luxembourg, the Netherlands, Austria, Portugal and Finland).

[3] Government-controlled area.

In 2003, the EU Member States had quite different rates of population growth. The population of Ireland continued to grow strongly, whereas population growth in Germany was lower. International migration is an important component of population change in many countries. Without immigration, Germany, Greece and Italy would have had a population loss.

Acquisition of citizenship

	1990	1991	1992	1993	1994	1995	1996	1997	1998	1999	2000	2001
EU-15	192 706	234 556	276 217	290 491	329 946	:	:	:	:	:	:	:
Euro-zone	114 547	141 881	198 277	195 199	244 729	252 999	:	:	:	:	:	:
Belgium	8 658	8 470	46 485	16 379	25808	26 149	:	:	:	24 196	:	62 160
Czech Republic	:	:	:	:	:	:	:	:	:	7 309	:	:
Denmark	3 028	5 484	5 104	5 037	5736	5 260	7 283	5482	10 262	12 416	18 811	11 902
Germany	20 078	27 162	37 000	45 016	61625	31 797	86 356	83 027	106 790	143 120	186 688	180 349
Estonia	:	:	:	:	:	:	:	:	9 969	4 534	3 425	3 090
Greece	1 090	886	1 204	1 803	383	1 258	716	930	807	:	:	:
Spain	7 033	3 752	5 226	8 348	7802	6 756	8 433	9 801	12 550	16 384	16 743	16 743
France	54 381	59 684	59 252	60 013	77515	92 410	63 055	83 676	81 449	94 002	:	:
Ireland	179	188	150	133	175	355	:	:	1 474	1 433	1 143	2 817
Italy	555	349	539	6 469	5993	7 442	:	:	:	:	:	:
Cyprus	:	:	:	:	:	:	:	:	:	97	296	:
Latvia	:	:	:	:	:	:	:	:	:	12 914	13 482	9 947
Lithuania	:	:	:	:	:	:	825	:	562	567	490	507
Luxembourg	893	748	739	800	293	270	305	761	631	549	684	496
Hungary	:	:	:	:	:	:	12 126	:	6 203	6 066	5 393	8 430
Netherlands	12 794	29 112	36 237	43 069	49448	71 445	82 690	59 831	59 173	62 090	49 968	46 667
Austria	8 980	11 137	11 656	14 131	15275	15 627	15 627	15 792	17 786	:	24 320	31 731
Poland	:	:	:	:	:	:	:	:	:	:	:	1 070
Portugal	97	43	117	2	144	80	1 154	1 364	519	584	1 143	1 419p
Slovenia	:	:	:	:	1451	1 973	981	:	3 321	2 337	2 102	1 346
Slovakia	:	:	:	:	:	:	:	:	:	:	:	2 886
Finland	899	1 236	876	839	651	668	981	1 439	4 017	4 730	2 977	2 720
Sweden	16 770	27 663	29 389	42 659	35065	:	25 549	28 875	46 520	37 777	43 474	36 399
United Kingdom	57 271	58 642	42 243	45 793	44033	40 516	43 069	37 010	53 934	54 902	82 210	89 785
Iceland	105	165	155	177	205	229	308	289	352	288	328	:
Liechtenstein	82	64	55	65	69	:	:	:	:	567	:	:
Norway	4 757	5 055	5 132	5 538	8 778	11 778	12 237	12 037	9 244	7 988	9474	10 838

These figures refer to grants of citizenship of the reporting country to persons who have previously been citizens of another country or who have been stateless.

2

Asylum applications in the EU-15 and EU-25
In 1 000

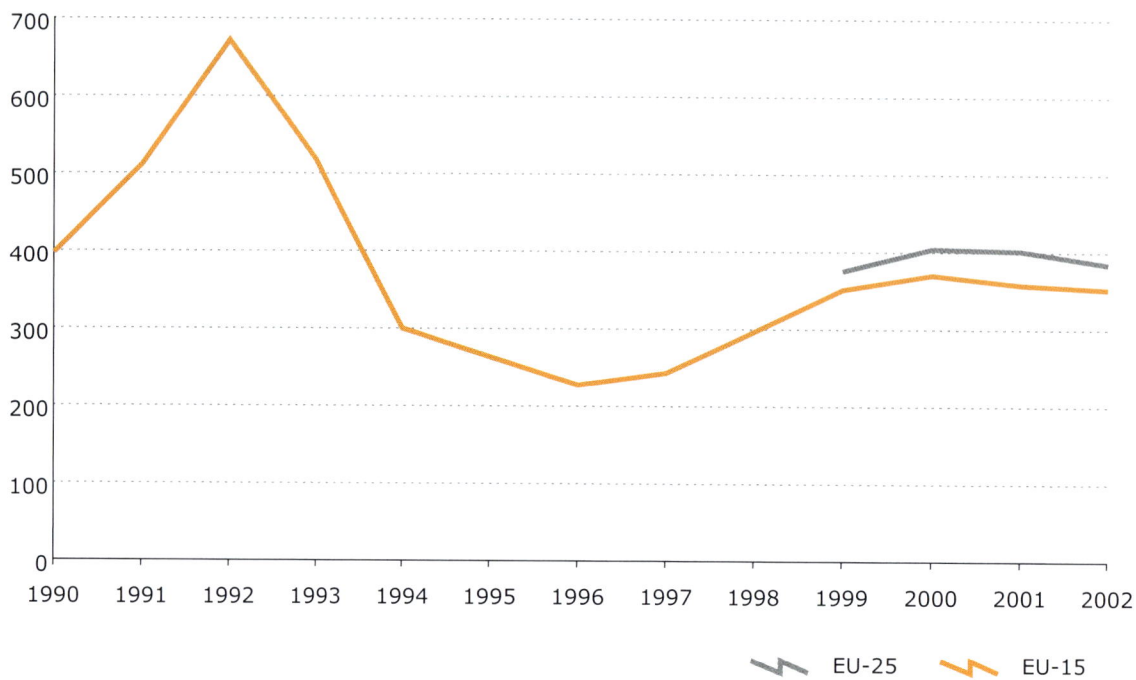

Life expectancy and mortality

Eurostat data

Eurostat provides a wide range of data on:

— Life expectancy by sex and age
— Deaths by sex and age
— Deaths by month
— Infant mortality (absolute numbers and rates)

2

Lower mortality and higher life expectancy

The EU population is characterised by a high life expectancy at birth which has increased by eight years for both sexes over the last 40 years. Although life expectancy is six years higher for women than men, due to a persistently higher male mortality throughout the entire life cycle, the gap is starting to narrow: life expectancy has increased more for men than women in the last decade in the majority of the Member States.

Life expectancies converge which is reflected in the adaptation of the mortality of men and women at all ages. This might be a consequence of more similar circumstances of life of men and women than in the past.

Increasing life expectancy, combined with changes in fertility, results in an EU population that is becoming increasingly older. This demographic ageing means that the number of older people is growing while the share of those of working age (15–64) is decreasing. These demographic trends will have economic and social consequences in a number of areas, including healthcare systems.

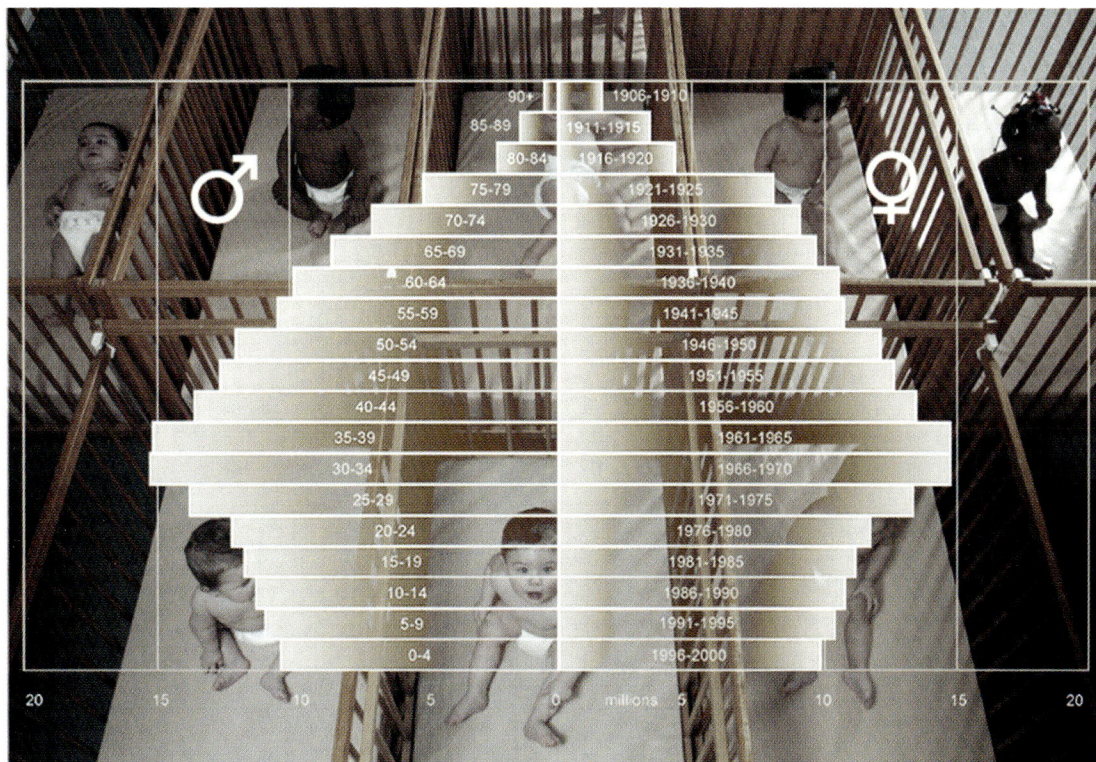

Life expectancy at birth in 2002
Years

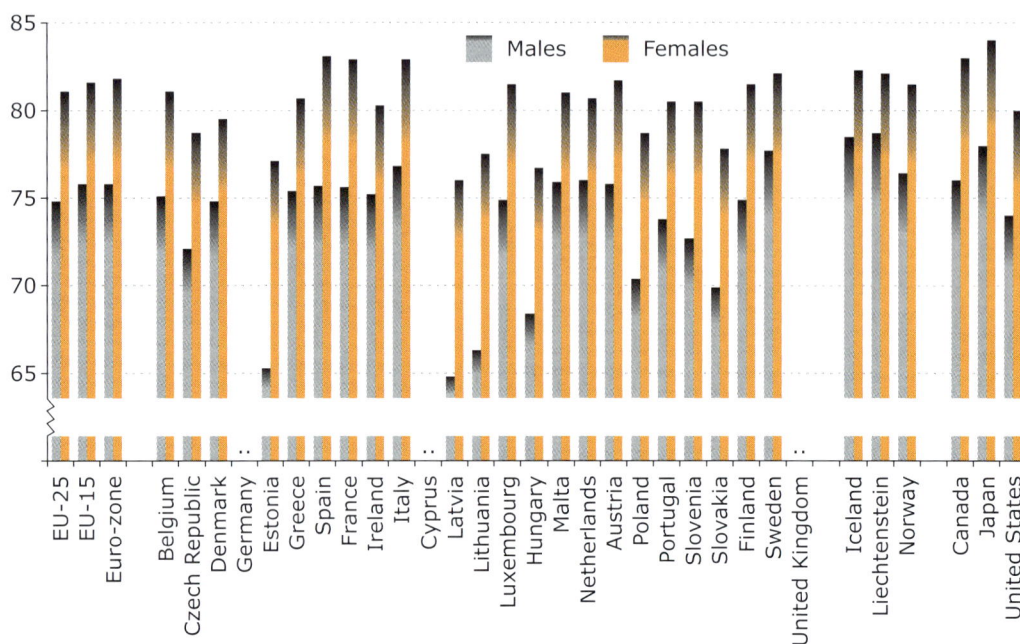

Source: Eurostat/US Bureau of the Census.

EU-25, EU-15, Eurozone, Spain, Italy: estimated values; Greece, France, Iceland: provisional data. Canada, Japan, United States: 2001.

The mean number of years that a newborn child can expect to live if subjected throughout his life to the current mortality conditions (age-specific probabilities of dying).

In the last decade, life expectancy at birth has increased by almost three years in the 25 countries of today's EU. In 2002, it was 75 years for men and 81 years for women. It was higher than in the United States (2001: 74 for men and 80 for women) but lower than in Japan (2001: 78 for men and 84 for women) and Canada (2001: 76 for men and 83 for women).

Life expectancy at birth in the EU-25
Years

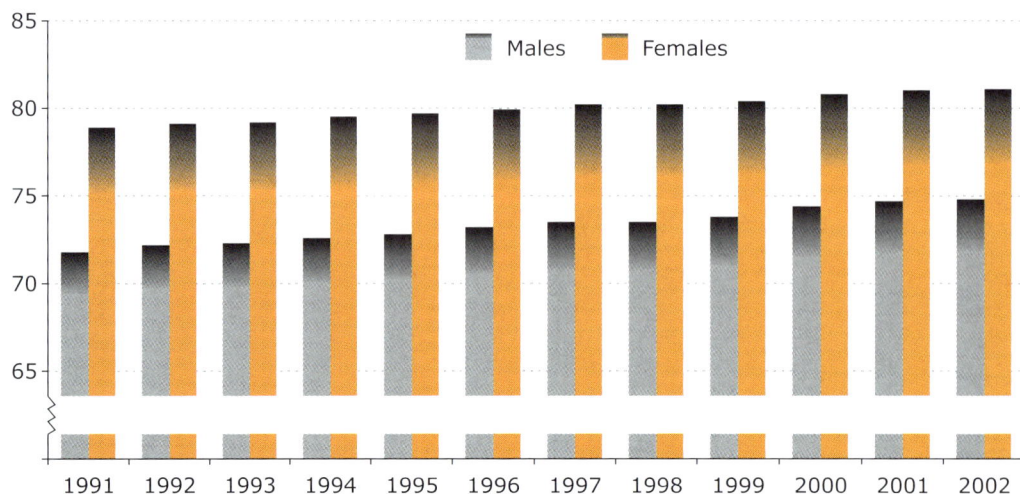

Estimated data.

Life expectancy at 60 in 2002
Years

Males   Females

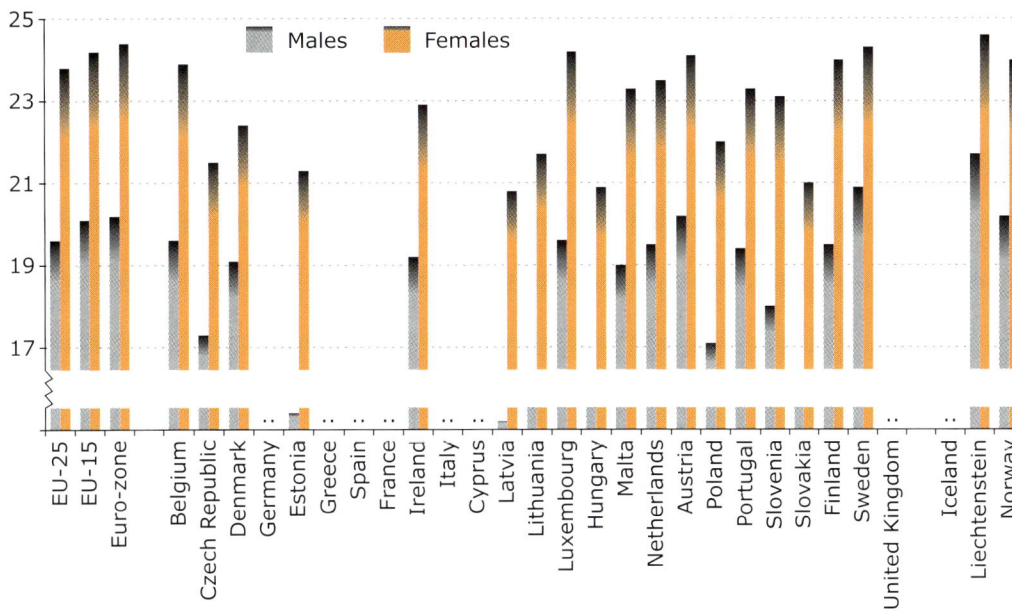

EU-25, EU-15, Eurozone: estimated data.

The mean number of years still to be lived by a person who has reached 60, if subjected throughout the rest of his life to the current mortality conditions (age-specific probabilities of dying).

In 2002, life expectancy at 60 was nearly two years more in the 25 countries of today's EU than in 1991, for both sexes. The difference in life expectancy between men and women aged 60 is less (four years more for women) when compared with the difference in the life expectancies of boys and girls at birth (six years more for girls).

Life expectancy at 60 in the EU-25
Years

Males   Females

1991 1992 1993 1994 1995 1996 1997 1998 1999 2000 2001 2002

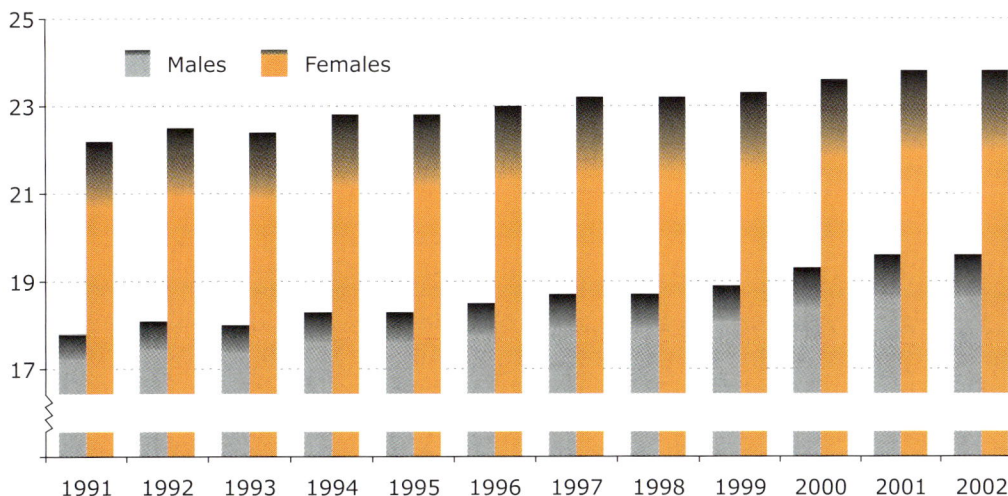

Estimated data.

Infant mortality rate in the EU-15
Per 1 000 live births

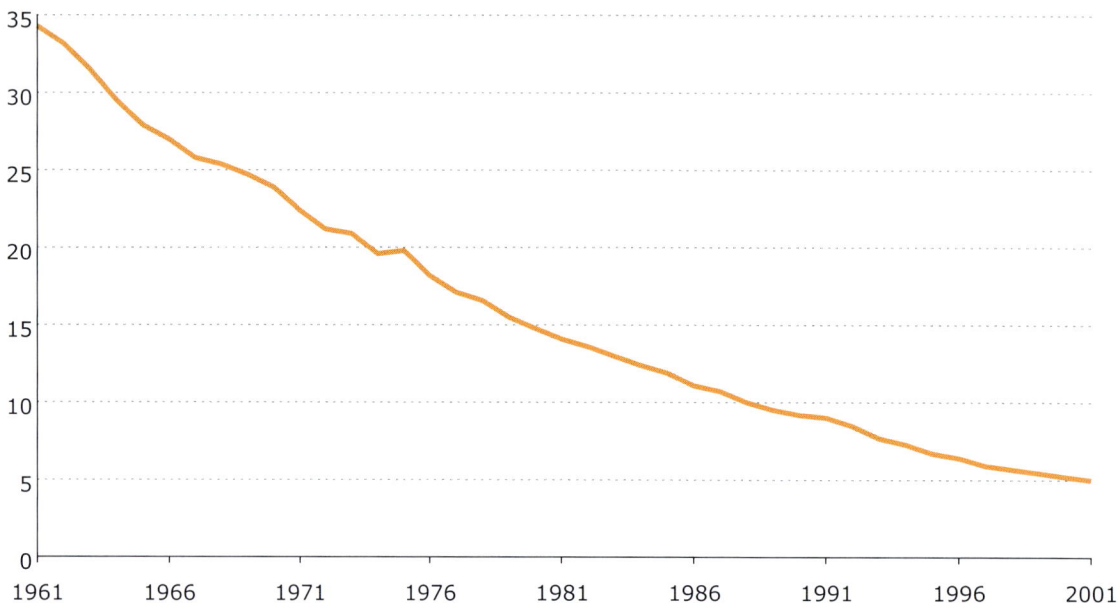

Deaths per 100 000 people in the EU-15 in 1998
By age

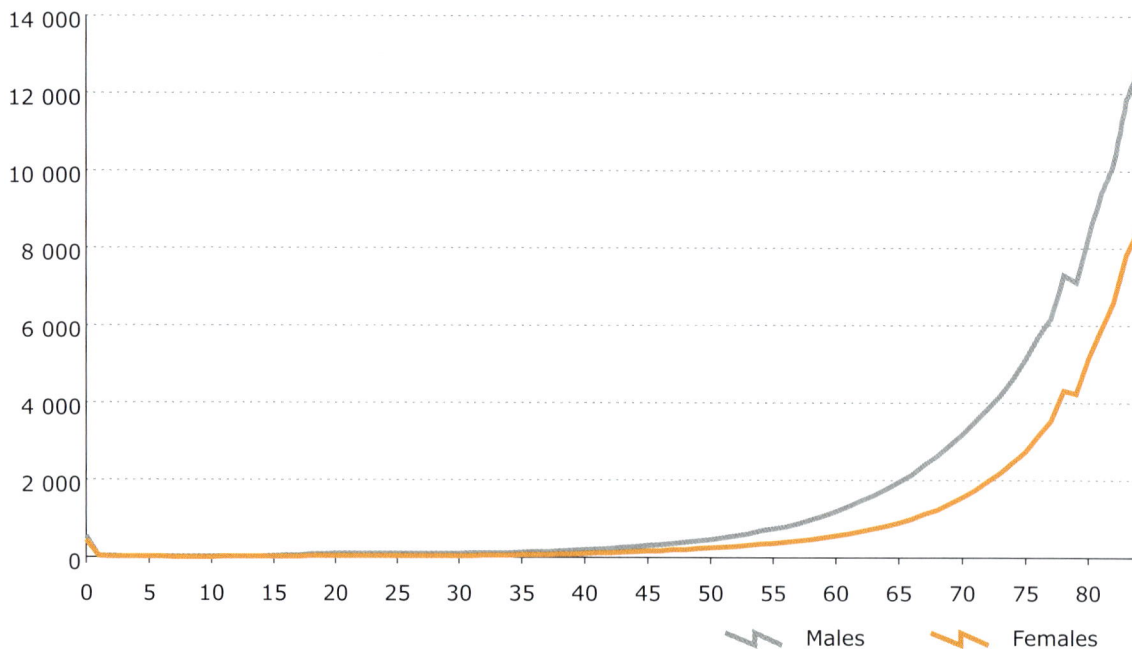

Males   Females

Probability of dying by age: The probability that a person of a given age will die during the period in question. In the case of annual probabilities, the denominator is the size of the generation of women (or men) who reach age n during the year in question, and the numerator is the number of women (or men) from this generation who die between age n and age n+1. Some of the deaths occur during the year in question, while other deaths occur the following year. The annual probability of dying by age therefore differs from the annual death rate by age because in the latter case the denominator is the average population of this age and the numerator is the number of persons of this age who die during the year (the age used can be either the age reached during the year or the age at last birthday).

Infant mortality rate
Per 1 000 live births

	1992	1993	1994	1995	1996	1997	1998	1999	2000	2001	2002
EU-25	8.5	7.7	7.3	6.7	6.4	5.9	5.7	:	5.2	5	:
EU-15	6.9	6.4	6	5.6	5.5	5.2	5.1	:	4.7	4.6	:
Euro-zone	7	6.5	6.1	5.6	5.4	5.1	5	:	4.5	4.5	:
Belgium	8.2	6.7	6.3	5.9	5	5.4	5.2	4.9	4.8	4.5	5
Czech Republic	9.9	8.5	7.9	7.7	6.1	5.9	5.2	4.6	4.1	4	4.1
Denmark	6.6	5.4	5.5	5.1	5.6	5.2	4.7	:	5.3	4.9	4.4
Germany	6.2	5.8	5.6	5.3	5	4.9	4.7	4.5	4.4	4.3	4.3
Estonia	15.7	15.6	14.4	14.9	10.5	10	9.3	9.6	8.4	8.8	5.7
Greece	8.4	8.5	7.9	8.1	7.2	6.4	6.7	6.2	5.9	5.1	5.9
Spain	7.1	6.7	6	5.5	5.5	5	4.9	4.5	3.9	3.5	:
France	6.8	6.5	5.9	4.9	4.8	4.7	4.6	4.3	4.4	4.5	:
Ireland	6.5	6.1	5.7	6.4	6	6.1	5.9	5.9	6.2	5.8	5.1
Italy	7.9	7.1	6.6	6.2	6.2	5.6	5.5	:	4.5	4.7	:
Cyprus	11.1	9.9	9.8	9.7	9.5	9	7	:	5.6	4.9	4.7
Latvia	17.6	16.2	15.7	18.8	15.9	15.4	15	11.3	10.4	11	9.9
Lithuania	16.5	15.7	14.2	12.5	10.1	10.3	9.3	8.7	8.6	7.9	7.9
Luxembourg	8.6	5.9	5.3	5.6	4.9	4.2	5	4.6	5.1	5.8	5.1
Hungary	14.1	12.5	11.5	10.7	10.9	9.9	9.7	8.4	9.2	8.1	7.2
Malta	10.7	8.2	9.2	8.9	10.8	6.5	5.2	7.2	6	4.4	6.1
Netherlands	6.3	6.3	5.6	5.5	5.7	5	5.2	5.2	5.1	5.4	5.1
Austria	7.5	6.5	6.3	5.4	5.1	4.7	4.9	4.4	4.8	4.8	4.1
Poland	17.5	15.4	15.1	13.6	12.2	10.2	9.5	8.9	8.1	7.7	7.5
Portugal	9.3	8.7	8.1	7.5	6.9	6.4	6	5.8	5.5	5	5
Slovenia	8.9	6.8	6.5	5.5	4.7	5.2	5.2	4.5	4.9	4.2	3.8
Slovakia	12.6	10.6	11.2	11	10.2	8.7	8.8	8.3	8.6	6.2	7.6
Finland	5.2	4.4	4.7	3.9	4	3.9	4.2	3.6	3.8	3.2	3
Sweden	5.4	4.8	4.4	4.1	4	3.6	3.6	3.4	3.4	3.7	3.3
United Kingdom	6.6	6.3	6.2	6.2	6.1	5.9	5.7	5.8	5.6	5.5	5.2
Iceland	4.8	4.8	3.4	6	3.7	5.5	2.6	2.4	3	2.7	2.3
Liechtenstein	10	0	5	0	7.5	20	7.5	:	:	0	2.5
Norway	5.8	5	5.2	4	4	4.1	4	3.9	3.8	3.9	3.5

Infant mortality rate: The ratio of the number of deaths of children under one year of age during the year to the number of live births in that year. The value is expressed per 1 000 live births.

The progress made in medical care services is reflected in a decreasing infant mortality rate. In the course of the last four decades, the infant mortality rate in EU-15 has fallen from over 34 per 1 000 live births (1961) to 5 (2002).

Proportion of population aged 65 and over
In % of total population

	1992	1993	1994	1995	1996	1997	1998	1999	2000	2001	2002	2003
EU-25	14.3	14.4	14.6	14.8	15	15.2	15.4	15.5	15.7	15.9	16.1	16.3
EU-15	14.9	15	15.2	15.4	15.6	15.8	15.9	16.1	16.3	16.4	16.6	16.8
Euro-zone	14.6	14.8	15	15.3	15.6	15.8	16	16.2	16.4	16.6	16.9	17.1
Belgium	15.2	15.4	15.6	15.8	16	16.3	16.5	16.6	16.8	16.9	16.9	17
Czech Republic	12.8	12.9	13	13.1	13.3	13.5	13.6	13.7	13.8	13.9	13.9	13.9
Denmark	15.6	15.5	15.4	15.3	15.1	15	14.9	14.9	14.8	14.8	14.8	14.8
Germany	15	15	15.2	15.4	15.6	15.7	15.8	15.9	16.2	16.6	17.1	17.5
Estonia	12	12.4	12.8	13.1	13.4	13.8	14.1	14.3	15	15.2	15.5	15.9
Greece	14.3	14.6	15	15.4	15.8	16.2	16.5	16.9	17.3	:	:	:
Spain	14.1	14.4	14.8	15.1	15.5	15.9	16.2	16.5	16.8	16.9	17.1	:
France	14.4	14.6	14.8	15	15.3	15.5	15.7	15.9	16	16.1	16.2	16.3
Ireland	11.4	11.4	11.4	11.4	11.4	11.4	11.4	11.3	11.2	11.2	11.1	11.1
Italy	15.5	15.7	16.1	16.4	16.8	17.2	17.4	17.7	18	18.2	:	:
Cyprus	:	11	11	11	11.1	11.1	11.2	11.2	11.2	11.3	11.7	11.8
Latvia	12.3	12.7	13.1	13.4	13.7	14	14.3	14.5	14.8	15.2	15.5	15.9
Lithuania	11	11.2	11.5	11.8	12.1	12.4	12.7	13.1	13.7	14.1	14.4	14.7
Luxembourg	13.5	13.6	13.8	13.9	14.4	14.2	14.3	14.3	14.3	13.9	13.9	14
Hungary	13.6	13.8	13.9	14.1	14.3	14.5	14.7	14.8	15	15.1	15.3	15.4
Malta	:	:	:	11	11.4	11.6	:	12	12.1	12.3	12.6	:
Netherlands	13	13	13.1	13.2	13.3	13.4	13.5	13.5	13.6	13.6	13.7	13.7
Austria	14.9	14.9	15	15.1	15.2	15.3	15.4	15.5	15.4	15.4	15.5	15.5
Poland	10.3	10.5	10.7	10.9	11.2	11.5	11.7	11.9	12.1	12.3	12.5	12.8
Portugal	13.8	14	14.2	14.5	14.9	15.2	15.5	15.8	16.1	16.4	16.5	16.7
Slovenia	11.1	11.4	11.7	12.1	12.5	12.9	13.2	13.6	13.9	14.1	14.5	14.8
Slovakia	10.4	10.5	10.7	10.8	10.9	11.1	11.3	11.3	11.4	11.4	11.4	11.6
Finland	13.6	13.8	13.9	14.1	14.3	14.5	14.6	14.7	14.8	15	15.2	15.3
Sweden	17.7	17.7	17.6	17.5	17.5	17.4	17.4	17.4	17.3	17.2	17.2	17.2
United Kingdom	15.7	15.8	15.7	15.7	15.7	15.7	15.7	15.7	15.6	15.6	:	:
Iceland	10.8	10.9	11	11.1	11.3	11.5	11.6	11.6	11.6	11.6	11.6	11.7
Liechtenstein	10.1	10.2	10.5	11.3	10.3	10.3	10.2	10.3	10.5	10.5	10.5	10.8
Norway	16.3	16.2	16.1	16	15.9	15.8	15.7	15.5	15.3	15.1	14.9	14.8

The ageing of the population is becoming gradually more important. Between 1993 and 2003, the share of those aged 65 and over in the total population rose by roughly 2 percentage points in the area of today's EU-25. The increase was even 3 percentage points in some southern, central and eastern countries where usually the values were lower before. In 2001, Italy, Sweden, Spain, Belgium and Germany had the highest shares of people aged 65 and over.

Health and safety

2

The European policy agenda on health

Health is a crosscutting issue in the European social agenda and an important item in the EU strategy for sustainable development, both of which constitute important elements in the Lisbon strategy.

In May 2000, the Commission proposed a new health strategy, which promotes an integrated approach to health-related initiatives at Community level. On this basis, a new programme of Community action in the field of public health for the period 2003–08 was adopted in 2002. The programme is focused on three main strands of action:

— improving health information and knowledge for the development of public health;
— enhancing the capability of responding rapidly and in a coordinated fashion to threats to health;
— promoting health and preventing disease through addressing health determinants across all policies and activities.

Health and safety at work

Health and safety at work are important dimensions in European social policy. Health at work is not only the absence of accidents or occupational illnesses, but involves physical, moral and social well-being, which are important for the quality of work and for the produc-tivity of the workforce. A new Community strategy on health and safety at work for the period 2002–06 has been developed, taking into account changes in society and the world of work. The strategy adopts a global approach to well-being at work, based on preventive measures and building partnerships between all players in the areas of employment, health and safety.

Data collection on health and safety

The health and safety statistical data collection of Eurostat responds to the specific requirements that result from the programme of Community action in the field of public health 2003–08 (Decision No 1786/2002/EC of the European Parliament and of the Council of 23 September 2002), covering health status, health determinants and health resources. For their part, the European statistics on accidents at work and on occupational diseases respond to the needs derived from the Community strategy on health and safety at work 2002–06 (Council Resolution 2002/C 161/01 of 3 June 2002). The general emphasis is on the infrastructure for the basic EU system on public health, safety at work and food safety statistics, on harmonisation of concepts, definitions and classifications for the whole area of health information and on improvement of the comparability of data.

The developments are carried out in coordination with competent international organisations (WHO, OECD, ILO).

2

Self-perception of a person's health in 2001
15 years and over; in %

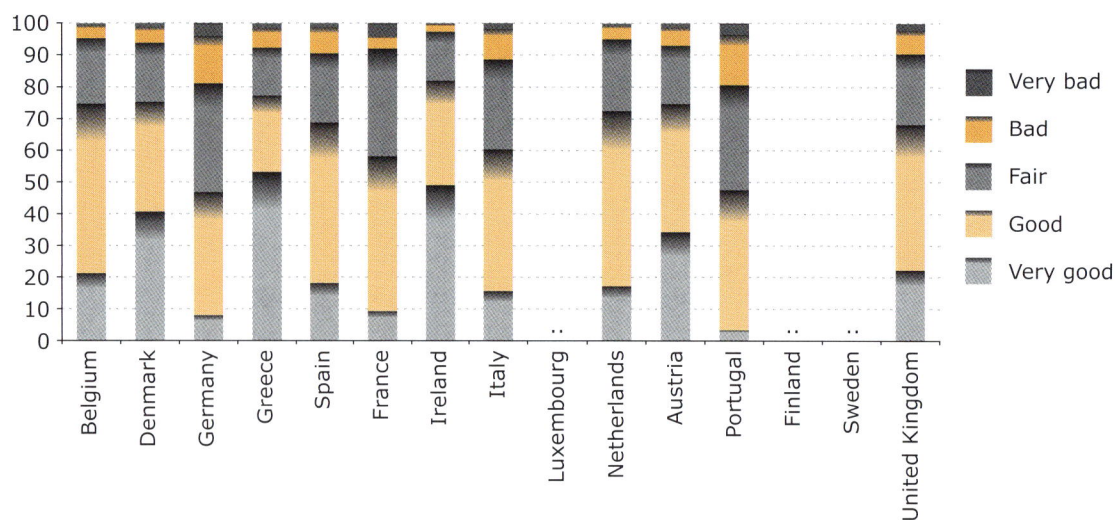

One of the ways used by governments to assess the positive aspects of health is through population survey measures of self-rated health status. Subjective, or self-reported, health status is not a substitute for more objective indicators but rather complements these measures: self reports of health introduce a consumer perspective into population health monitoring and reveal dimensions of health that may be inaccessible to the more traditional measures.

The results of the European Community household panel (ECHP) on the self-perception of the status of a person's health show that Ireland (82 %), Greece (77 %), Belgium, Denmark and Austria (75 % each) had the biggest percent- ages for a 'very good' and 'good' perception of health. In all, 4.1 % of those interviewed in Germany and France said they felt they had a 'very bad' health status.

Physicians
Per 100 000 inhabitants

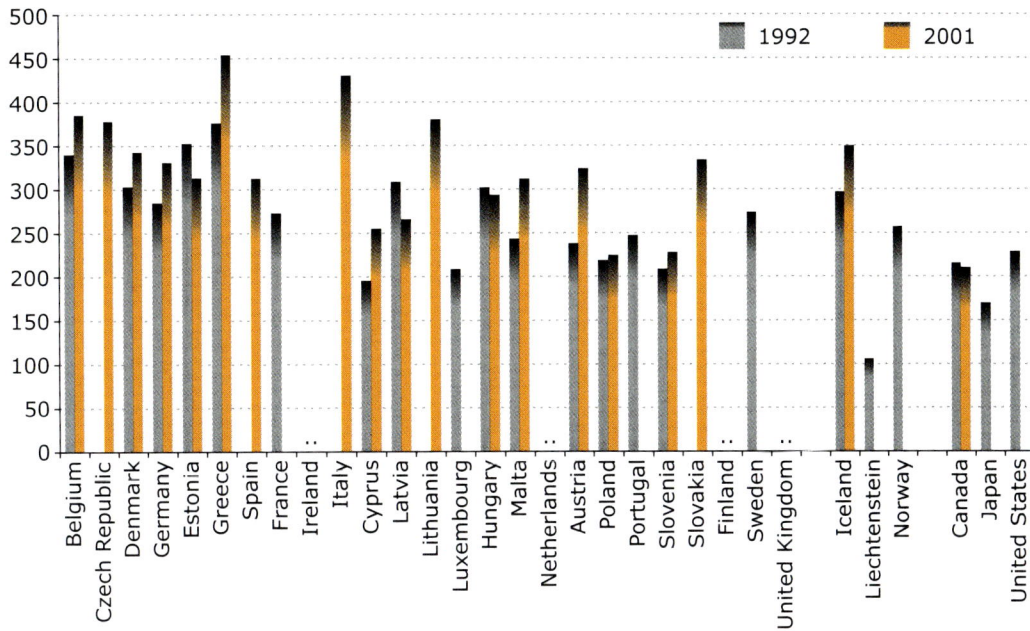

Physicians may be counted as 'licensed','economically active' or 'practising'. Data for two or more concepts are available in the majority of Member States. Practising physicians are those seeing patients either in a hospital, practice or elsewhere.

Hospital beds
Per 100 000 inhabitants

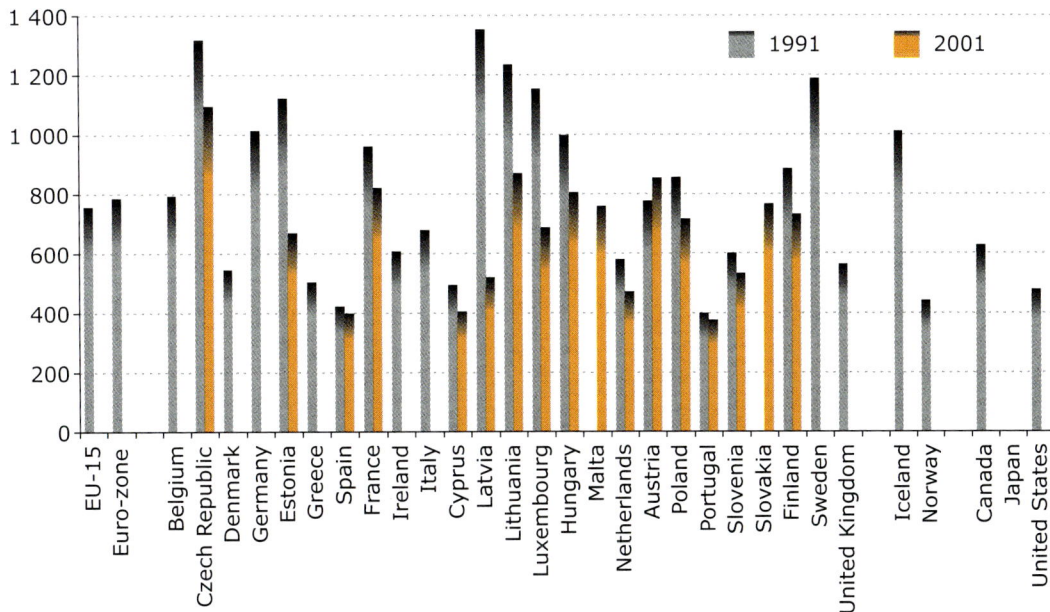

Beds accommodating patients who are formally admitted (or 'hospitalised') to an institution for treatment and/or care and who stay for a minimum of one night in the hospital or other institution providing in-patient care. In-patient care is delivered in hospitals, other nursing and residential care facilities or in establishments, which are classified according to their focus of care under the ambulatory care industry but perform in-patient care as a secondary activity.

Serious accidents at work 2001
1998 = 100

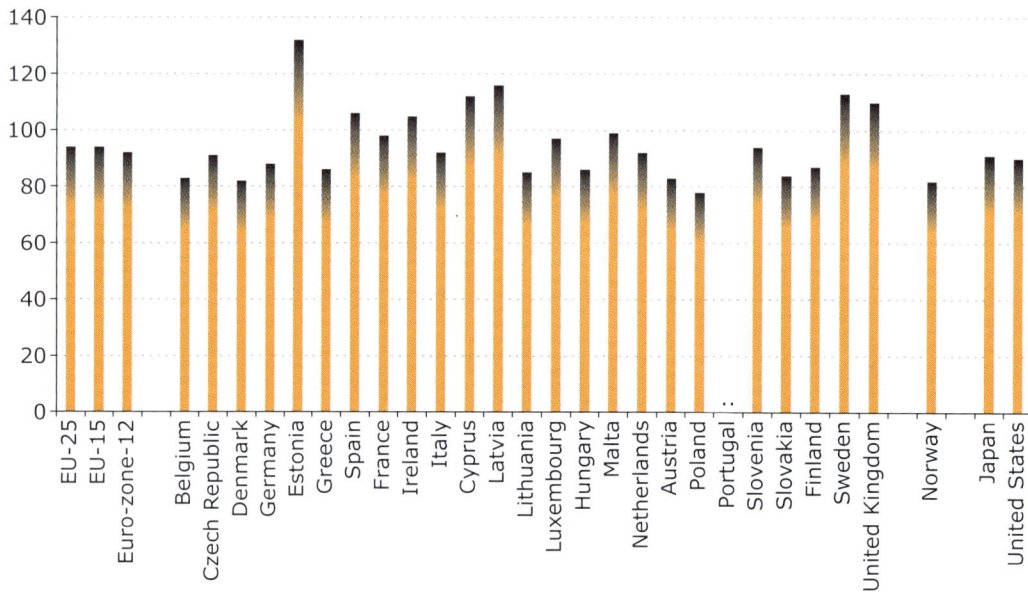

2001 EU-25, EU-15, Euro-zone-12: provisional data.

The index shows the evolution of the incidence rate of serious accidents at work in comparison to 1998 (= 100). The incidence rate = (number of accidents at work with more than 3 days' absence that occurred during the year/number of persons in employment in the reference population) x 100 000. An accident at work is a discrete occurrence in the course of work that leads to physical or mental harm. This includes accidents in the course of work outside the premises of his/her business, even if caused by a third party, and cases of acute poisoning. It excludes accidents on the way to or from work, occurrences having only a medical origin, and occupational diseases.

Fatal accidents at work: incidence rate
Per 100 000 persons employed

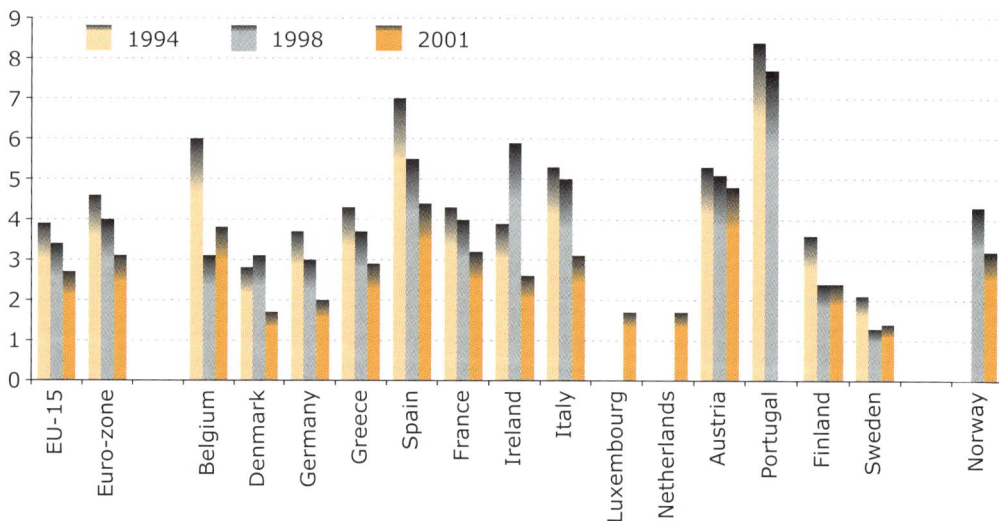

2001 EU-15, Eurozone: estimated value.

The incidence rate = (number of fatal accidents at work that occurred during the year/number of persons in employment in the reference population) x 100 000. A fatal accident at work is a discrete occurrence in the course of work with physical or mental harm, leading to death within one year of the accident. It excludes accidents on the way to or from work, occurrences having only a medical origin, and occupational diseases. To adjust for differences between the Member States in the distribution of workforce across the risk branches, a standardisation is made giving each branch the same weight at national level as in the European Union total.

Between 1998 and 2001, the incidence rate of serious accidents at work decreased by 6 % in EU-25, and the incidence rate of fatal accidents at work by 20 %. An accident at work is an occurrence in the course of work that leads to physical or mental harm; it excludes accidents on the way to or from work, occurrences having only a medical origin and occupational diseases.

Death in motor-vehicle traffic accidents in 1999
Per 100 000 persons

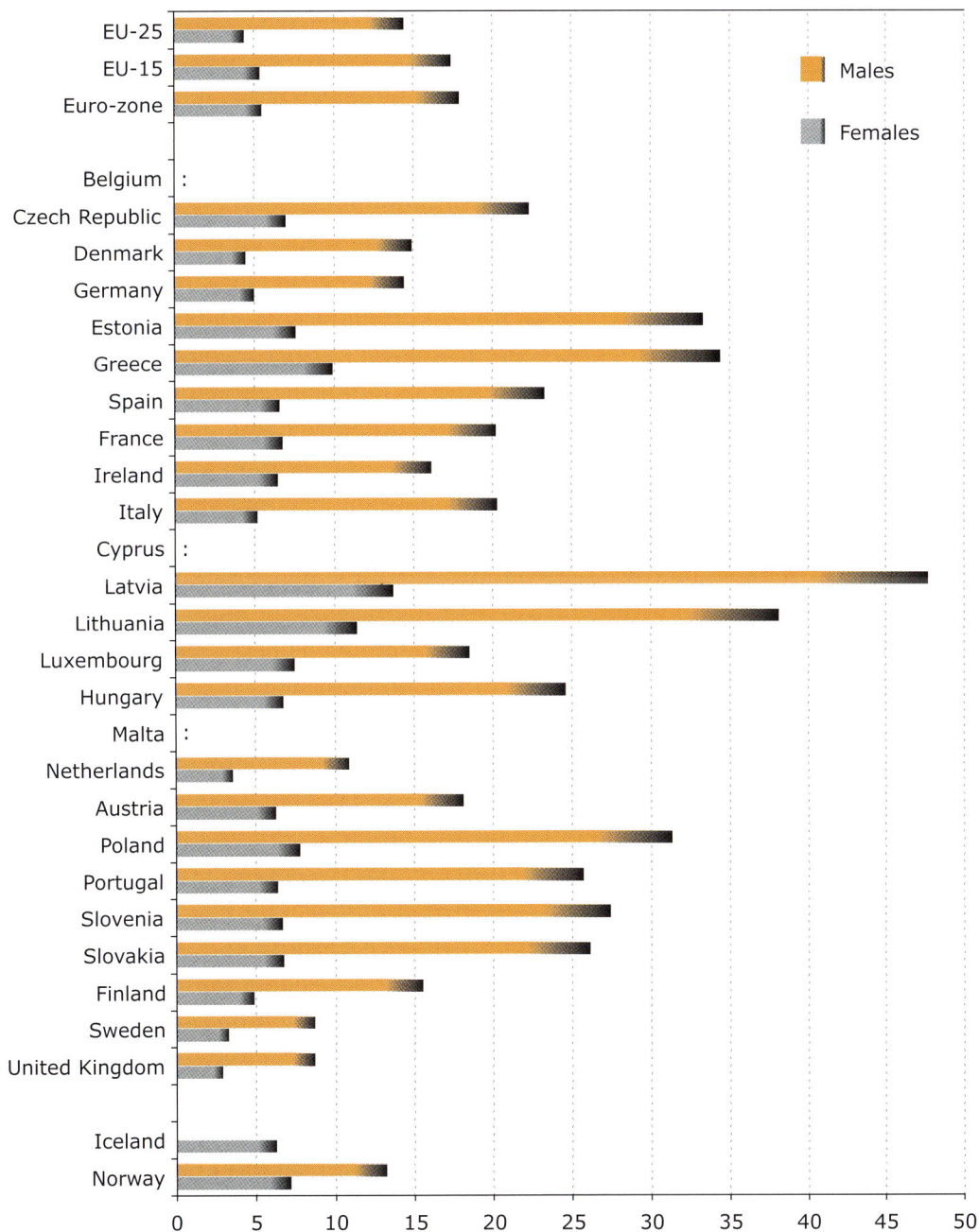

2

Death from ischaemic heart diseases in 1999
Per 100 000 persons

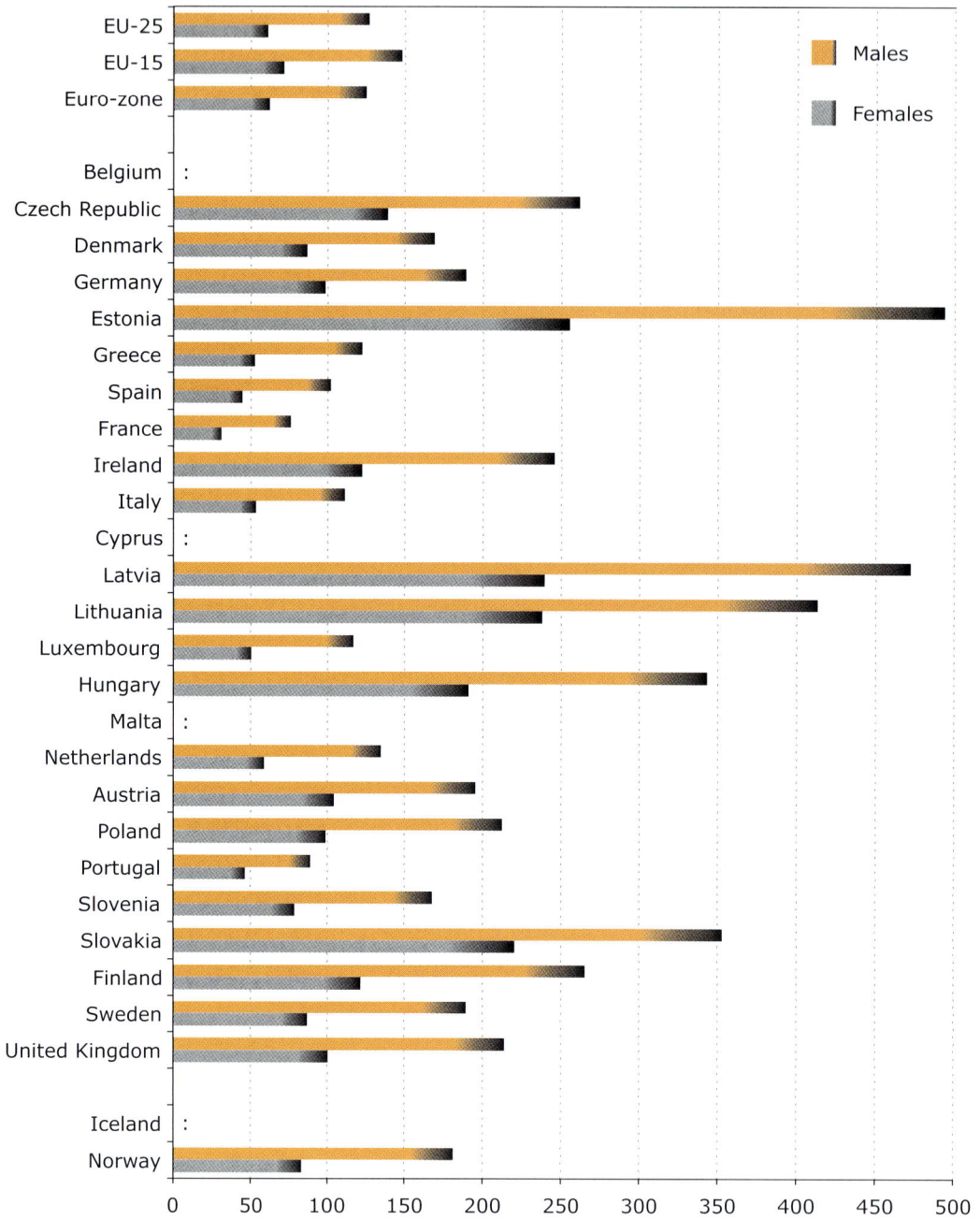

Legend: Males, Females

EU-25	
EU-15	
Euro-zone	
Belgium	:
Czech Republic	
Denmark	
Germany	
Estonia	
Greece	
Spain	
France	
Ireland	
Italy	
Cyprus	:
Latvia	
Lithuania	
Luxembourg	
Hungary	
Malta	:
Netherlands	
Austria	
Poland	
Portugal	
Slovenia	
Slovakia	
Finland	
Sweden	
United Kingdom	
Iceland	:
Norway	

Death from cancer in 1999
Per 100 000 persons

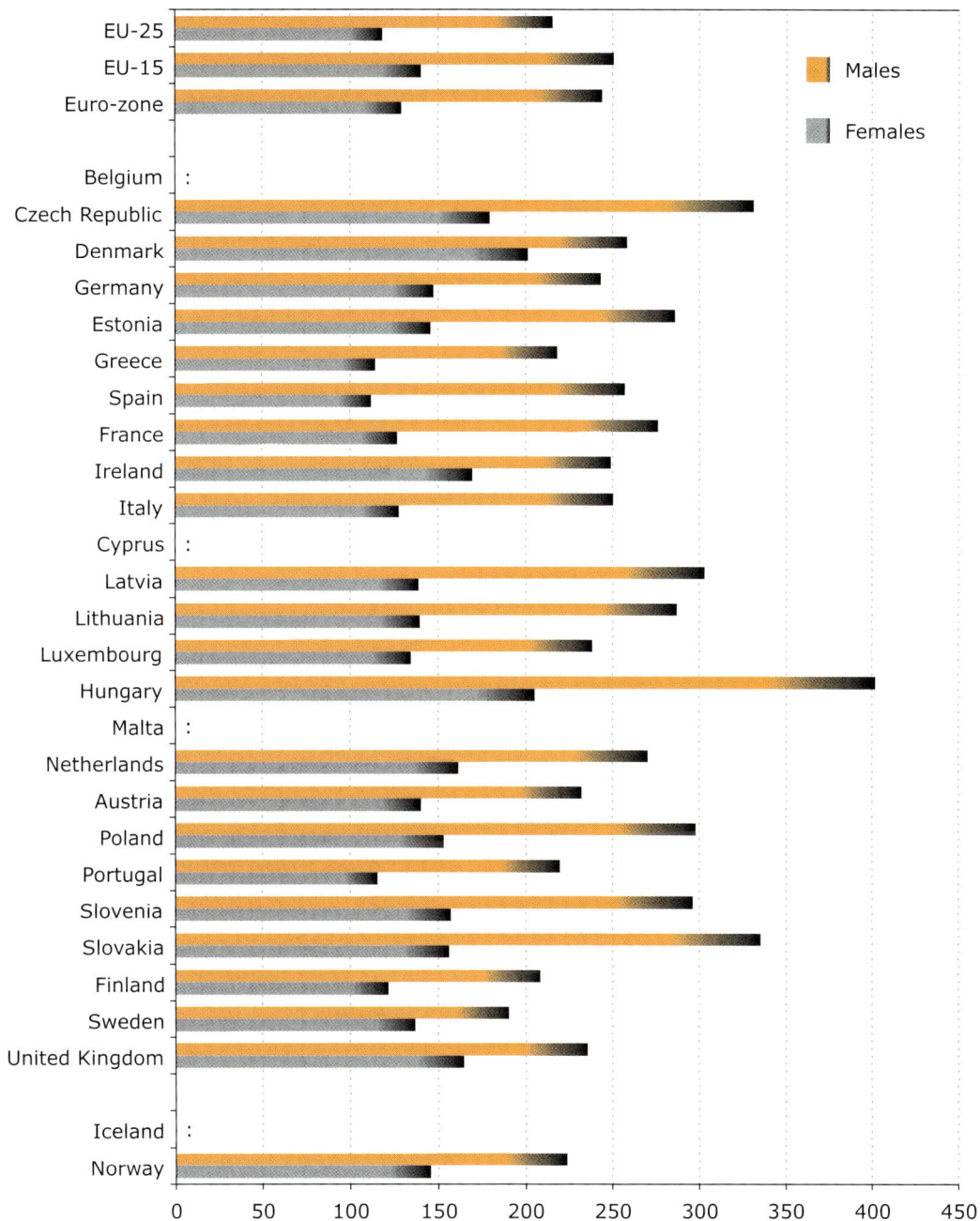

Legend:
- Males
- Females

EU-25	
EU-15	
Euro-zone	
Belgium	:
Czech Republic	
Denmark	
Germany	
Estonia	
Greece	
Spain	
France	
Ireland	
Italy	
Cyprus	:
Latvia	
Lithuania	
Luxembourg	
Hungary	
Malta	:
Netherlands	
Austria	
Poland	
Portugal	
Slovenia	
Slovakia	
Finland	
Sweden	
United Kingdom	
Iceland	:
Norway	

2

A comparison of the data for 1994 and 1999 shows a decrease in the death rates from cancer, ischaemic heart diseases, suicide and motor vehicle traffic accidents. There are large differences between the death rates for men and women. In the 25 countries that form the EU today, the death rate from cancer for men (1999: 216 per 100 000 persons) was higher than the rate for women (118). In 1999, the death rate from ischaemic heart diseases was more than twice as high for men (127) as for women (62). For the death rates from suicide and from motor vehicle traffic accidents, the values for men were more than three times as high as those for women (13.6 for men and 4.3 for women, and 14.4 for men and 4.4 for women, respectively).

Death by suicide in 1999
Per 100 000 persons

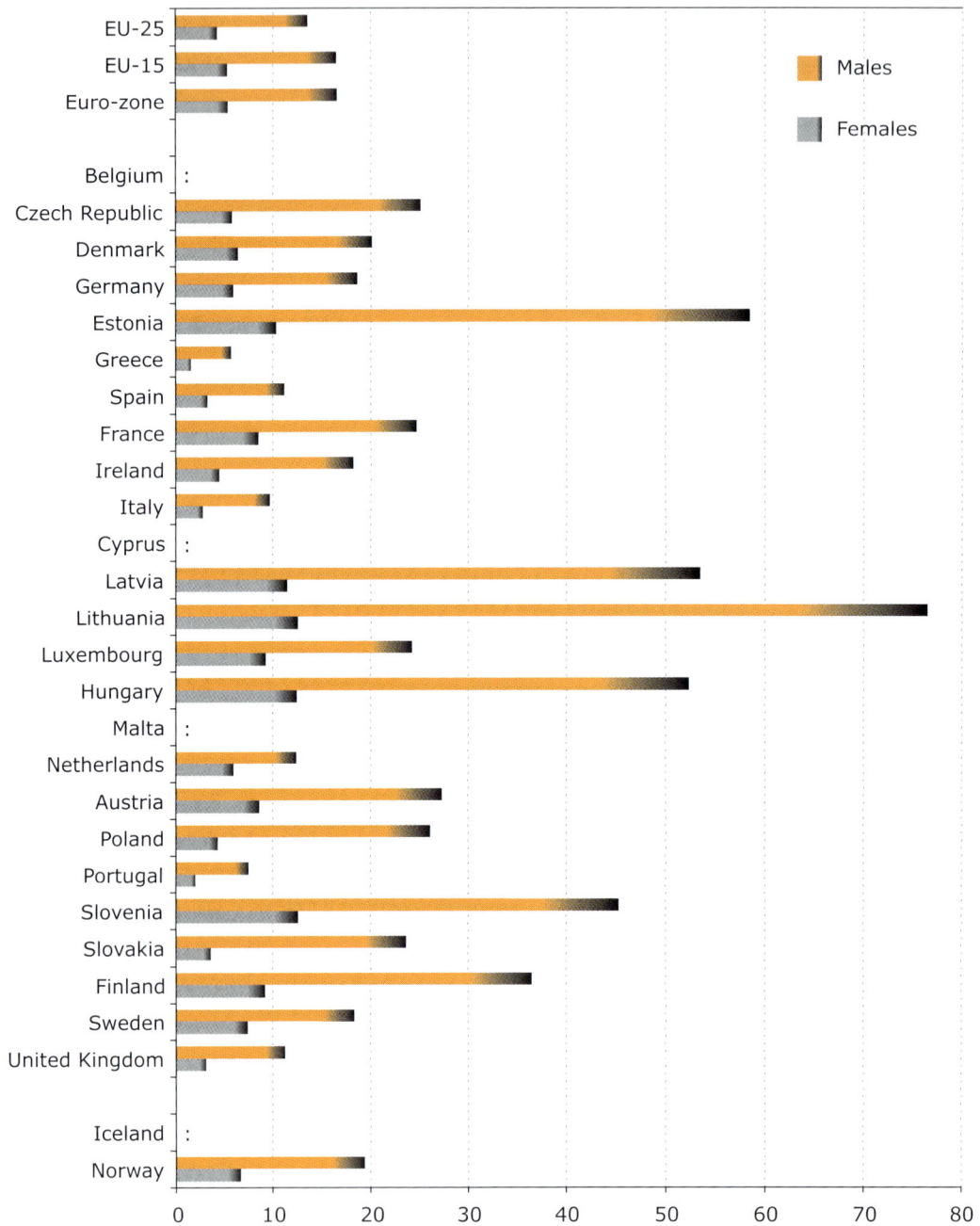

Legend:
- Males
- Females

Categories (top to bottom): EU-25, EU-15, Euro-zone, Belgium :, Czech Republic, Denmark, Germany, Estonia, Greece, Spain, France, Ireland, Italy, Cyprus :, Latvia, Lithuania, Luxembourg, Hungary, Malta :, Netherlands, Austria, Poland, Portugal, Slovenia, Slovakia, Finland, Sweden, United Kingdom, Iceland :, Norway

X-axis: 0, 10, 20, 30, 40, 50, 60, 70, 80

'Incidence' is a measure of the number of new cases arising in a population in a given period. It can be expressed as the number of new cases of a disease (or disorder) per 100 000 inhabitants in a given year. In 2001, the incidence of tuberculosis decreased strongly in most European countries compared with the situation in 1990. The Baltic countries had the highest rates within the 25 countries of today's European Union: Latvia (88.0 per 100 000 inhabitants), Lithuania (85.7) and Estonia (59.4). These values are more than double those of 1990. Among the former EU-15 countries, only Portugal recorded a high value in 2001 (42.9). The value was lowest in Malta (4.1).

Tuberculosis and salmonellosis are communicable diseases. Communicable or infectious diseases cause, or have the potential to cause, significant morbidity and/or mortality across the EU. Therefore, the exchange of information may provide early warning of threats to public health. Both tuberculosis and salmonellosis are covered by Commission Decision 2002/253/EC of 19 March 2002 which lays down case definitions for the reporting to the Community network. Data for tuberculosis are collected by the EuroTB network.

2

Incidence of tuberculosis
Per 100 000 persons

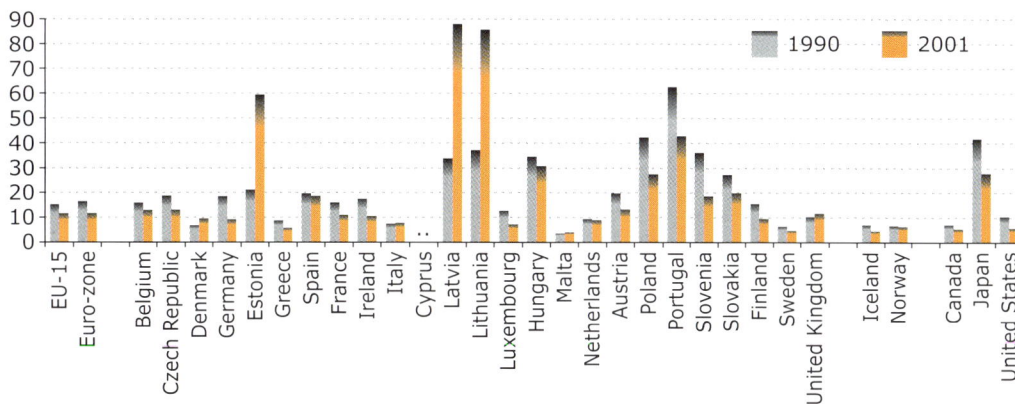

Source: EuroTB, mainly funded by the European Commission (Health and Consumer Protection DG) and managed jointly by the French Public Health Surveillance Institute (Institut de Veille Sanitaire, InVS) and by the Royal Netherlands Tuberculosis Association (KNCV).

Diseases such as as tuberculosis that cause, or have the potential to cause, significant morbidity and/or mortality across the EU and where the exchange of information may provide early warning of threats to public health are collected in the Member States in a compulsory legal basis. Data for tuberculosis are collected by EuroTB (network supported by the EC).

Incidence of salmonellosis in 2002
Per 100 000 persons

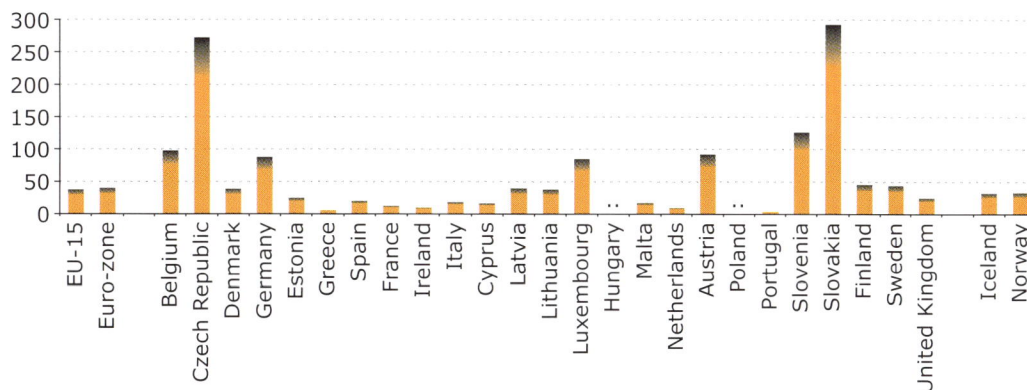

Source: Community Network on Communicable Disease.

Diseases (as salmonellosis) that cause, or have the potential to cause, significant morbidity and/or mortality across the EU and where the exchange of information may provide early warning of threats to public health are collected in the Member States in a compulsory legal basis.

Education

2

Education is crucial

Education, vocational training and lifelong learning play a vital role in the economic and social strategy of Europe. The Lisbon objectives can be attained only with efficient use of resources, quality improvements in the education and training systems and the implementation of a coherent lifelong learning strategy at the national level.

The European Council has adopted strategic goals and objectives for the education and training systems to be attained by 2010. The measurement of the progress towards the objectives requires a wide range of comparable statistics of good quality on educational attainment, enrolment in education and training, graduates, teachers, language learning, mobility and investments.

The European statistical system provides data on education and training which are the basis for indicators measuring the performance of the education and training systems in the Union and monitoring progress towards the knowledge-based economy and society within the broader policy for lifelong learning.

The younger generation is better qualified

By comparing those currently leaving the education system with older generations, it is possible to monitor the trends in educational attainment over a long time period of around 30 years.

Over the last 30 years or so, disparities in attainment levels between the sexes have been reduced throughout the Union. In the younger generation, women have even slightly overtaken men.

Higher qualifications tend to reduce the risk of unemployment ...

In general, higher education qualifications seem to reduce, albeit to differing degrees, the risk of unemployment in all Member States.

... and increase income

Data show also that a person's income is likely to be considerably higher if he/she is better qualified. On average, the equivalised income of a person with less than upper secondary education was 90 % of the national median compared with 147 % for those with tertiary education.

Policy context

'The Community shall contribute to the development of quality education by encouraging cooperation between Member States and, if necessary, by supporting and supplementing their action ...'. 'The Community shall implement a vocational training policy which shall support and supplement the action of the Member States ...'. (EC Treaty, Title XI, Chapter 3, Articles 149(1) and 150(1), respectively)

In its communication on the future of the European employment strategy (EES), the Commission outlines the need to reduce school failure and dropouts and raise the quality of education as a priority area for the new EES. Such policies should lay the ground for future access to lifelong learning, and remain important challenges for many current and future Member States.

Pupil/teacher ratio in primary education in 2001

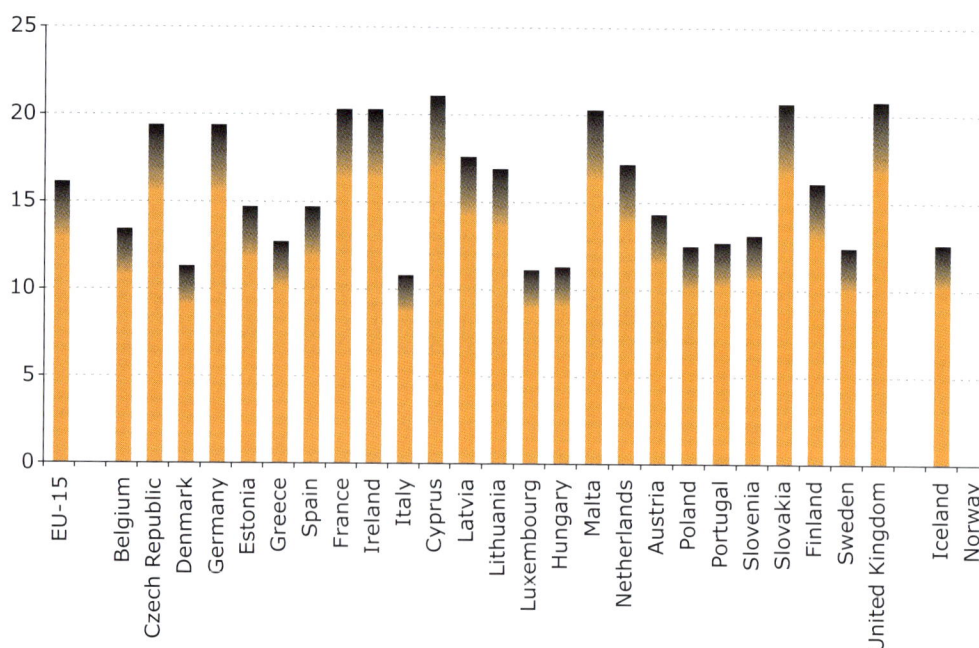

The pupil-teacher ratio is calculated by dividing the number of full-time equivalent pupils by the number of full-time equivalent teachers teaching at ISCED level 1. Only teachers in service (including special education teachers) are taken into account. The pupil-teacher ratio should not be confused with average class size as it does not take into account special cases, like the small size of groups of special needs pupils or specialised/minority subject areas, or the difference between the number of hours of teaching provided by teachers and the number of hours of instruction prescribed for pupils for example in the case a teacher is working in a shift system.

Pupils and students aged up to 29 years
Excluding pre-primary education; in 1 000

	1990	1991	1992	1993	1994	1995	1996	1997	1998	1999	2000	2001
EU-25	:	:	:	:	:	:	:	:	:	:	:	81 215.3
EU-15	67 516	70 242	70 917	72 345	73 014	73 027	73 380	73 296	64 198.8	66 285	66 204.2	65 913.1
Euro-zone	:	:	:	:	:	:	:	:	:	:	:	:
Belgium	2 072	2 056	2 033	2 087	2 113	2 153	2 160	2 168	:	1 978.3	1 988.1	2 009.8
Czech Republic	:	:	:	:	:	:	:	1 908.6	1 903.5	1 860	1 890.9	1 912.2
Denmark	960	948	933	938	942	943	942	955	909.6	919.5	935.7	959.3
Germany	10 484	13 218	13 338	13 629	13 858	14 035	14 210	14 441	14 082.2(i)	14 074.4(i)	14 058.2(i)	14 026.3(i)
Estonia	:	:	:	:	:	:	:	284.2	286.5	290.7	295.9	295.9
Greece	1 878	1 865	1 860	1 892	1 889	1 850	1 840	1 833	1904	1 858.8	1 881.3	1 901.1
Spain	8 860	8 830	8 773	8 813	8 778	8 637	8 509	8 239	7 748.4	7 555.1	7 467.8	7 328.4
France	11 711	11 800	11 911	11 998	12 145	12 148	12 137	12 131	11 923.5	11 862.9	11 784.3	11 699.6
Ireland	870	875	886	892	897	893	885	886	978.1	962.3	957.2	954.3
Italy	9 798	9 632	9 553	9 467	9 572	9 099	9 300	9 306	8 851.9	8 776.3	8 687.4(ip)	8 627.6
Cyprus	:	:	:	:	:	:	:	136	:(i)	138.0(i)	137.7(i)	139.3(i)
Latvia	:	:	:	:	:	:	:	453.8	464.4	472.2	478.3	484.4
Lithuania	:	:	:	:	:	:	:	685.1	708.4	732.3	757	774.4
Luxembourg	49	49	49	:	:	54	57	60	:(i)	64.6(i)	66.0(i)	67.4(i)
Hungary	:	:	:	:	:	:	:	1 809.2	1 803.8	1 832.6	1 847.5	1 854.1
Malta	:	:	:	:	:	:	:	:	:	76.9	76.6	76.7
Netherlands	3 529	3 550	3 534	3 539	3 241	3 201	3 179	3 116	2 997.7	3 027.4	3 046.8	3 078
Austria	1 321	1 323	1 352	1 372	1 387	1 402	1 412	1 416	1 363.7	1 372.5	1 371.5	1 376.5
Poland	:	:	:	:	:	:	:	8 679	8 649.6	8 747.2	8 778.1	8 780.7
Portugal	1 974	1 970	2 024	2 099	2 145	2 166	2 134	2 085	2 002.3	1 950.7	1 950.4	1 921.4
Slovenia	:	:	:	:	:	:	:	375.8	366.6(i)	368.5(i)	373.8(i)	383.2(i)
Slovakia	:	:	:	:	:	:	:	1 129.7	:	:	:	1 099.8
Finland	960	980	1 007	1 025	1 044	1 047	1 059	1 077	994.6	1 019.2	1 033.5	1 042.7
Sweden	1 361	1 359	1 377	1 623	1 656	1 698	1 753	1 814	1 677.3	1 736.9	1 753.8	1 764.1
United Kingdom	11 688	11 786	12 289	12 931	13 298	13 700	13 802	13 232	11 561.7	12 168.1	12 229.3	12 214
Iceland	:	61	62	:	:	67	67	68	67.3	67.3	68.8	69.5
Liechtenstein	:	:	:	:	:	:	:	:	:	:	4	:
Norway	:	843	850	:	895	858	856	884	902.6	915.6	921.7	920.6
Canada	6 422	6 563	6 681	7 434	7 519	6 666	6 717	6 670	6 530	8 511	:	:
Japan	23 833	:	:	:	22 842	22 408	22 346	:	:	:	:	15 928
United States	55 096	54 769	56 564	57 979	58 573	59 225	59 781	60 622	:	:	:	:

This table includes the total number of persons who are enrolled in the regular education system in each country. It covers all levels of education from primary education to postgraduate studies. It corresponds to the target population for education policy.

2

Total population having completed at least upper secondary education in 2002
Population aged 25 to 64; in %

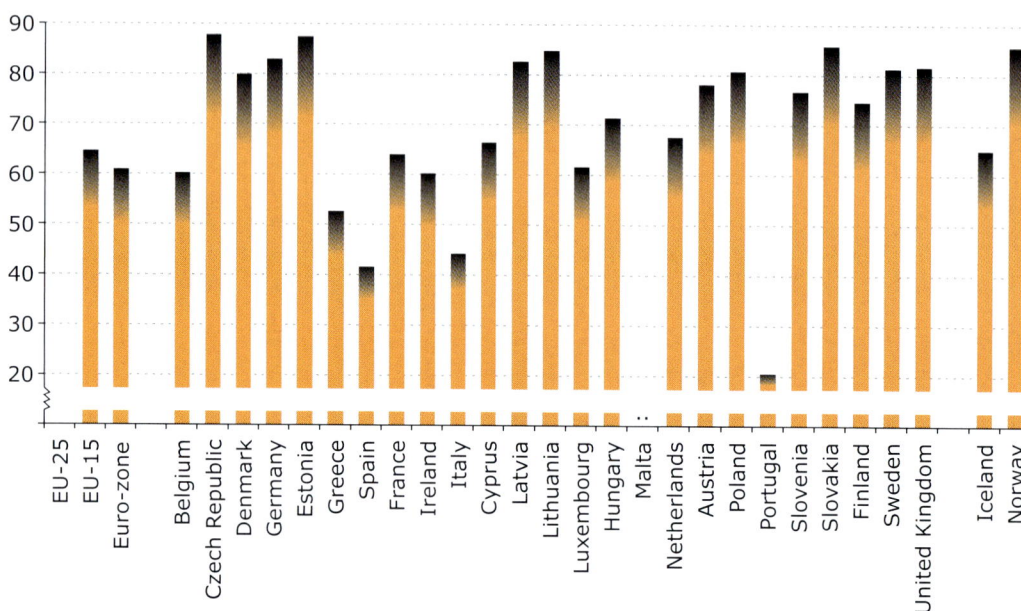

The indicator shows the percentage of the adult population (25–64 years old) that has completed upper secondary education. The indicator aims to measure the share of the population that is likely to have the minimum necessary qualifications to actively participate in social and economic life. It should be noted that completion of upper secondary education can be achieved in European countries after varying lengths of study, according to different national educational systems.

Unemployment rates in the EU-15 by level of education (*)
Population aged 25 to 59; in %

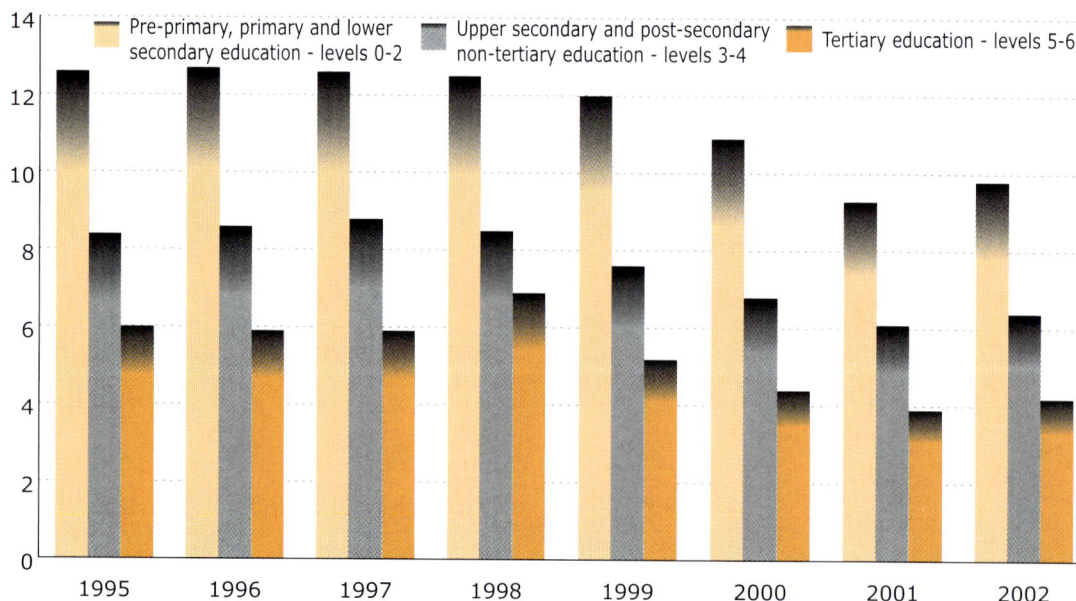

Pre-primary, primary and lower secondary education - levels 0-2
Upper secondary and post-secondary non-tertiary education - levels 3-4
Tertiary education - levels 5-6

(*) levels according ISCED 1997.

The indicators focus on the 25 to 59 years old. They show the 'probability' of being without a job for those who would like to have one, broken-down by level of education. The indicators provide a measure of difficulties that people with different levels of education have to face in the labour market and offer a first idea of the impact of education in reducing the chances of being unemployed.

Early school-leavers aged 18 to 24 in 2003
In % of the total population of the same age group

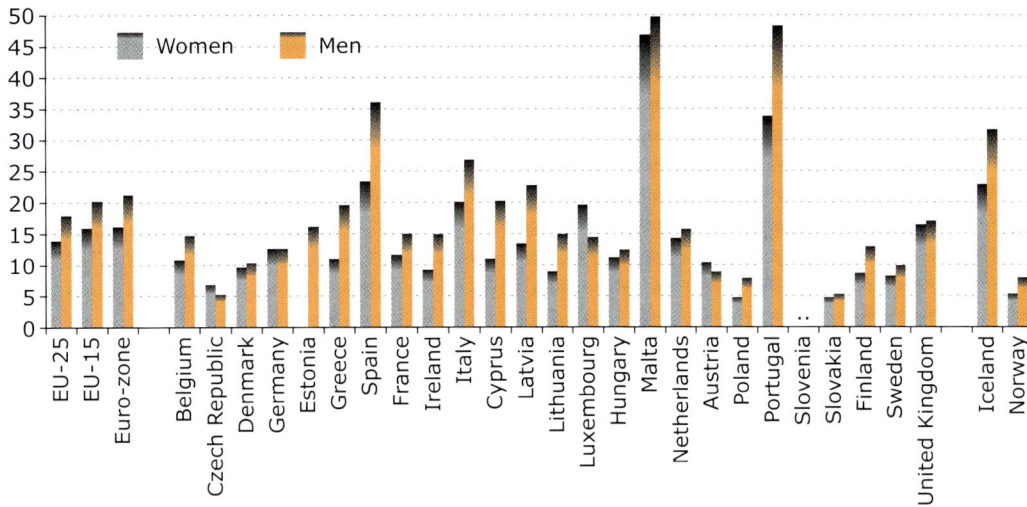

Germany, Luxembourg, Netherlands, Austria, United Kingdom, Iceland: provisional data.

The ages 17 to 19 are the typical ages for finishing upper secondary education in the EU countries. Eurostat reports the percentages of young people just above this last age who have no (completed) upper secondary education and who are currently not in any education or training either. In 2003, the lowest values were reached by Slovakia (4.9 %), the Czech Republic (6.0 %) and Poland (6.3 %). Malta (48.2 %), Portugal (41.1 %) and Spain

(29.8 %) are at the bottom of the list for this indicator. During the last decade, many countries have paid more and more attention to the younger people having a minimum level of education. In Luxembourg, the share of early school-leavers decreased from 42.2 % (1992) to 17.0 % (2003), and in the United Kingdom from 34.7 % (1992) to 16.7 % (2003), which is more than double in both cases.

Annual expenditure on public educational institutions per pupil/student in 2000
By level of education; in PPS, based on full-time equivalents

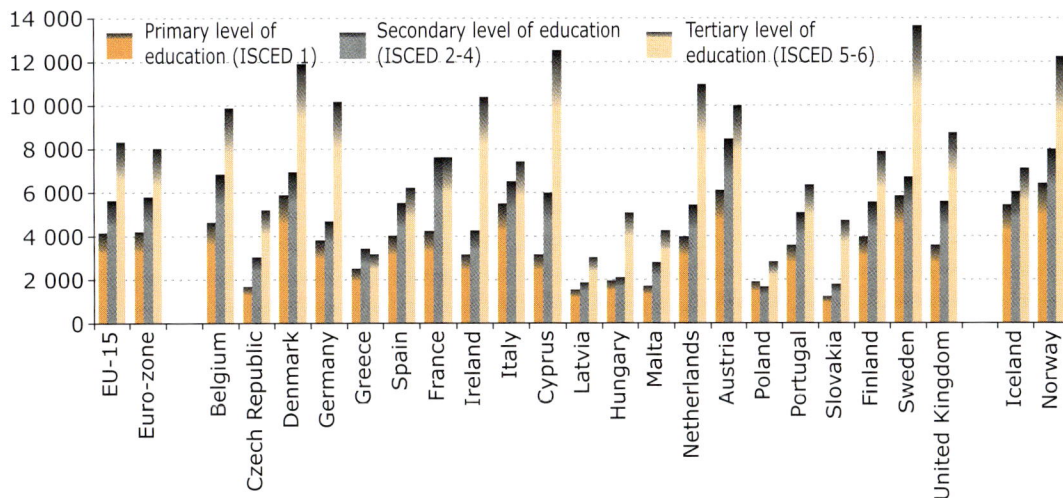

EU-15, Eurozone-12, Malta: estimated value.

Expenditure per pupil/student in public institutions measures how much central, regional and local levels of government, private households, religious institutions and firms spent per pupil/student. It includes expenditure for personnel, other current and capital expenditure.

2

Students
Tertiary education; in 1 000

	1990	1991	1992	1993	1994	1995	1996	1997	1998	1999	2000	2001
EU-15	8 816	9 614	10 114	10 854	11 528	11 790	11 934	12 266	12 329(e)	12 438	12 563.3	12 820.3
Euro-zone	:	:	:	:	:	:	:	:	:	:	:	:
Belgium	271	276	286	307	322	353	358	361	356.5(e)	352	355.7	359.3
Czech Republic	:	:	:	:	:	:	:	196(i)	215(i)	231(i)	253.7	260
Denmark	135	143	150	164	170	170	167	180	183	190	189.2(i)	190.8
Germany	1 720	2 049(i)	2 034(i)	2 113(i)	2 148(i)	2 156(i)	2 144(i)	2 132(i)	2 097.7(i)	2 087(i)	2 054.8(i)	2 083.9(i)
Estonia	:	:	:	:	:	:	:	39	43	49	53.6	57.8
Greece	194	195	200	299	314	296	329	363	374	388	422.3	478.2
Spain	1 166	1 222	1 302	1 371	1 469	1 527	1 592	1 684	1 746	1 787	1829	1 833.5
France	1 585	1 699	1 840	1 952	2 083	2 073	2 092	2 063	2 027	2 012	2 015.3	2 031.7
Ireland	85	90	101	108	118	122	128	135	143	151	160.6	166.6
Italy	1 373	1 452	1 533	1 615	1 770	1 792	1 775	1 893	1 869	1 797	1770	1 812.3
Cyprus	:	:	:	:	:	:	:	10(i)	11(i)	11(i)	10.4(i)	11.9(i)
Latvia	:	:	:	:	:	:	:	62	70	82	91.2	102.8
Lithuania	:	:	:	:	:	:	:	84	96	107	121.9	135.9
Luxembourg	1(i)	1(i)	1(i)	:	:	:	2(i)	2(i)	1.8(i)	2.7(i)	2.4(i)	2.5(i)
Hungary	:	:	:	:	:	:	:	203	255	279	307.1	330.5
Malta	:	:	:	:	:	:	:	:	:	6	6.3	7.4
Netherlands	437	479	494	507	532	503	492	469	461	470	487.6	504
Austria	200	206	217	221	227	234	239	241	248	253	261.2	264.7
Poland	:	:	:	:	:	:	:	:	1 191	1 399	1 579.6	1775
Portugal	131	186	191	248	276	301	320	351	352	357	373.7	387.7
Slovenia	:	:	:	:	:	:	:	53	68	79	83.8	91.5(i)
Slovakia	:	:	:	:	:	:	:	102	113	123	135.9	143.9
Finland	155	166	174	188	197	205	214	226	250	263	270.2	279.6
Sweden	185	193	207	223	234	246	261	275	281	335.1(i)	346.9(i)	358
United Kingdom	1 178	1 258	1 385	1 528	1 664	1 813	1 821	1 891	1 938	1 994	2 024.1(i)	2 067.3
Iceland	:	5	6	:	:	7	7	8	8	9	9.7(i)	10.2
Liechtenstein	:	:	:	:	:	:	:	:	:	:	0.5	:
Norway	:	142	154	:	177	173	180	185	183	188	190.9	189.9
Canada	1 822	1 898	1 943	2 633	2 662	1 784	1 763	1 717	1 179	1 193	:	:
Japan	2 683	:	:	:	3 841	3 918	3 945	:	3 964	3 941	:	3 972.5
United States	13 539	13 065	14 359	14 486	14 305	14 279	14 262	14 300	13 284	13 769	:	:

This table includes the total number of persons who are enrolled in tertiary education (including university and non-university studies) in the regular education system in each country. It corresponds to the target population for policy in higher education. It provides an indication of the number of persons who had access to tertiary education and are expected to complete their studies, contributing to an increase of the educational attainment level of the population in the country in case they continue to live and work in the country at the end of their studies.

Women among tertiary students in 2001
Total of science, mathematics, computing-engineering, manufacture and construction; in %

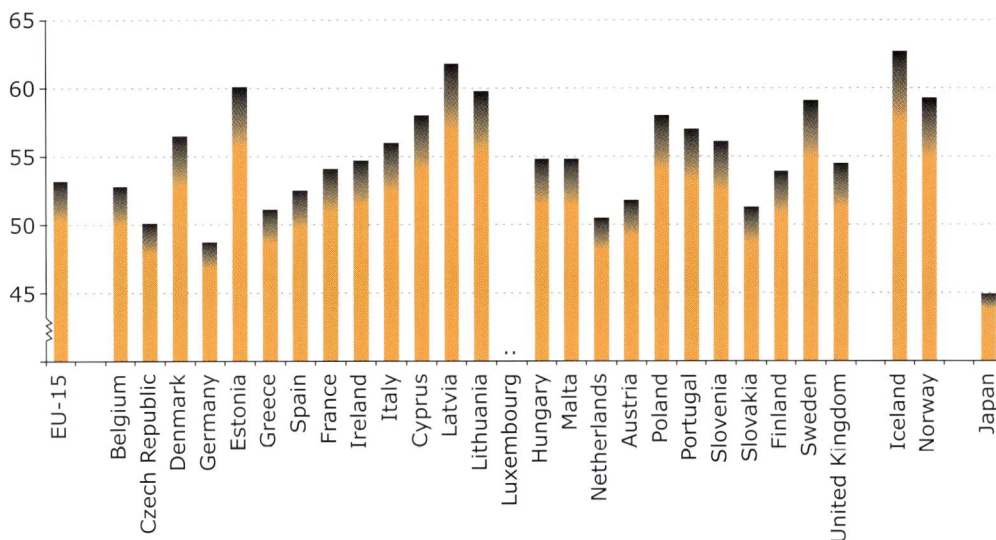

This indicator presents the percentage of women among all students in tertiary education irrespective of the field of education and among all students in the fields of mathematics, science and computing and in the fields of engineering, manufacturing and construction. The levels and fields of education and training used, follow the 1997 version of the International Standard Classification of Education (ISCED97) and the Eurostat Manual of fields of education and training (1999).

Throughout almost the entire European Union, there are more women than men among tertiary students. Exceptions are Germany, where male students are slightly more numerous than female students, and the Netherlands and Czech Republic with a balanced proportion. In Japan, the number of male tertiary students significantly exceeds that of female students.

Median age in tertiary education in 2001
Years

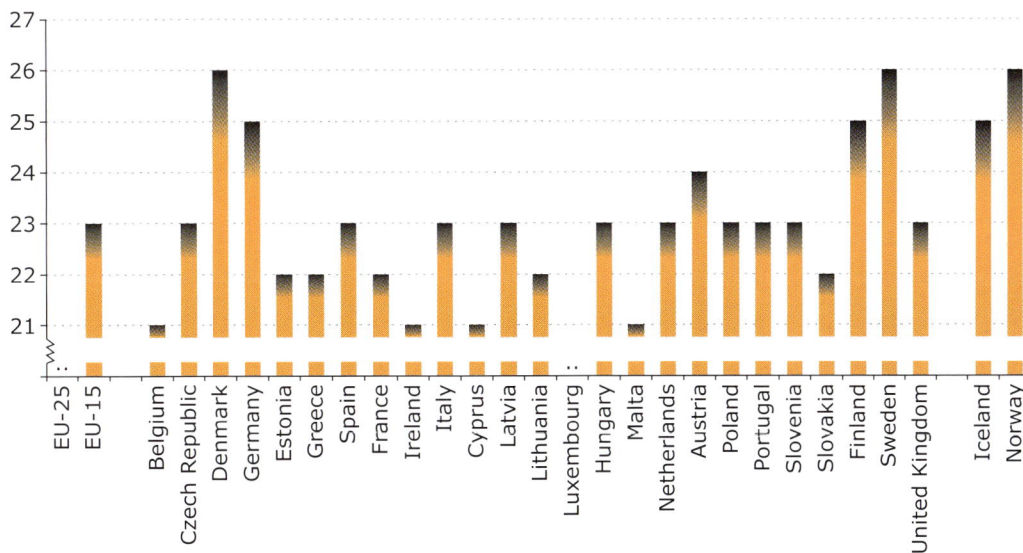

The median age of a given population is the age separating the group into two halves of equal size. In the case of this indicator it means that half of the student population, i.e. persons enrolled in tertiary education (ISCED levels 5 and 6), is younger than the median age and the other half is older.

Public expenditure on education in 2001
In % of GDP

Greece	Japan	Luxembourg	Slovakia	Czech Republic	Ireland	Spain	Germany	United Kingdom	Malta	Italy	Netherlands	Hungary	United States	Poland	Cyprus	France	Austria	Portugal	Lithuania	Belgium	Finland	Latvia	Estonia	Norway	Sweden	Denmark
3.51	3.59	3.84	4.03	4.28	4.36	4.42	4.53	4.54	4.73	4.98	4.99	5.15	5.16	5.42	5.69	5.77	5.82	5.89	6.03	6.12	6.25	6.39	6.83	7.07	7.32	8.38

Provisional data. Denmark, Germany, Ireland: 2000.

Generally the public sector funds the education either by bearing directly the current and capital expenses of educational institutions (direct expenditure for educational institutions) or by supporting students and their families with scholarships and public loans as well as by transferring public subsidies for educational activities to private firms or non-profit organisations (transfers to private households and firms). Both types of transaction together are reported as total public expenditure on education.

Total public expenditure on education in 2000
By level of education; in % of the GDP

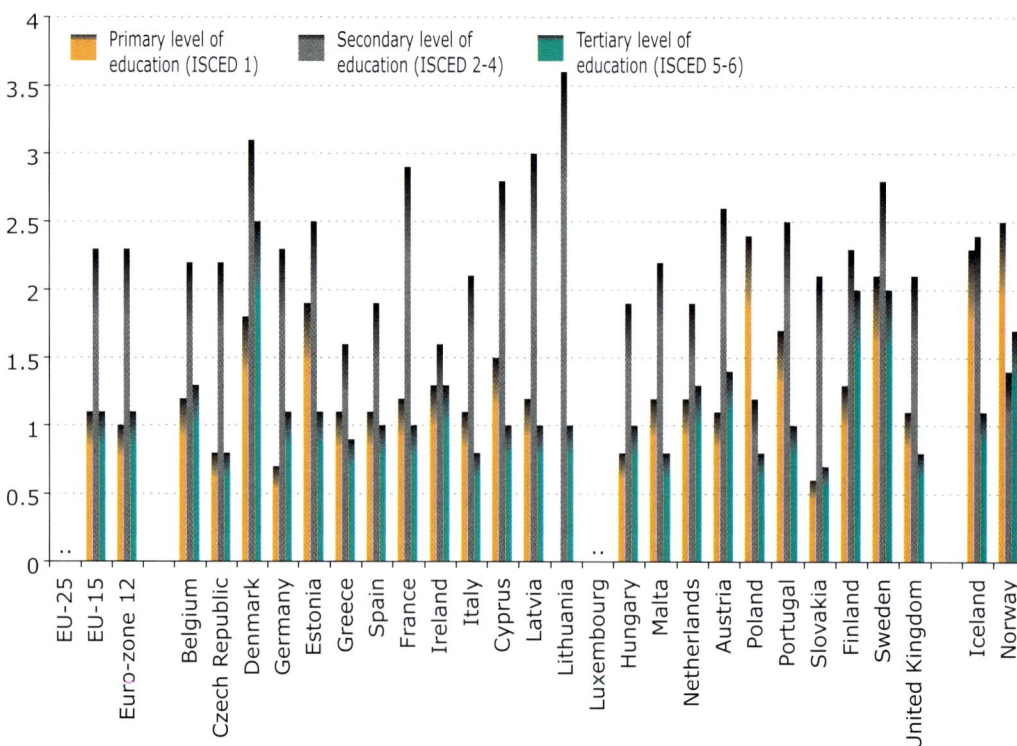

Source: Unesco/OECD/Eurostat data collection. EU-15, Eurozone-12: estimated value.

In general, the public sector funds education either by bearing directly the current and capital expenses of educational institutions (direct expenditure for educational institutions) or by supporting students and their families with scholarships and public loans as well as by transferring public subsidies for educational activities to private firms or non-profit organisations (transfers to private households and firms). Both types of transactions together are reported as total public expenditure on education.

Continuing vocational training

Eurostat data

Eurostat provides a wide range of data on:
— Training policy and management of training
— Training courses and 'other' forms of training
— Training and non-training enterprises
— Participation in courses
— Working time spent on courses
— Cost and funding of training courses
— Fields and providers of training courses
— Evaluation of training
— Introduction of new technologies and training

2

Developing human capital

Indicators of investment in human capital are becoming increasingly important, since they reflect the personal and economic impact of keeping the qualification of the workforce up to date. Developing abilities and skills through continuing vocational training at work is an essential part of lifelong learning and reflects the emphasis enterprises put on the qualification of their staff.

nomic performance and competitiveness extended to the whole life cycle. This perception reflects the long-term strategy of the Lisbon Summit to strengthen employment and social cohesion in a knowledge-based society and economy.

The Council resolution of 24 June 2003 on social and human capital underlines the importance of learning and training at work in building social and human capital in the

Policy context

'Community action shall aim to ... facilitate access to vocational training ...; stimulate cooperation on training between educational or training establishments and firms.' (EC Treaty, Title XI, Chapter 3, Article 150(2))

The Commission communication of November 2001 entitled 'Making a European area of lifelong learning a reality' underlines in paragraph 1.1 that the 'Lisbon European Council confirmed lifelong learning as a basic component of the European social model'. Learning is no longer given weight only in the area of education; it is also seen as a critical factor in the areas of employment and social security, eco-

2

knowledge-based society. Special reference is made to '… the importance of ensuring that all workers within their specific enterprises and organisations are fully involved and properly trained … which can help facilitate change, and are thus aware of the benefits in terms of improved competitiveness and quality of working life; …'. The resolution also highlights '… the problem of well-educated/trained people having more possibilities and, in reality, more access to learning opportunities than less well-educated/trained people, who should most benefit from training, such as women and older workers: …'.

The new European employment strategy (EES), agreed on 22 July 2003, has been revised to better account for the needs of an enlarged Eu-

ropean Union, to react better to the challenges facing a modern labour market, and to contribute better to the Lisbon strategy. Two key specific guidelines within the EES tackle the need to improve skill levels through lifelong learning. The guidelines call upon Member States to address labour shortages and skill bottlenecks. Member States are also encouraged to implement comprehensive lifelong learning strategies in order to equip all individuals with the skills required for a modern workforce, and to reduce skill mismatch and bottlenecks in the labour market. The guidelines state that policies will aim to achieve an increase in investment in human resources, in particular through a significant increase in investment by enterprises in the training of adults.

Lifelong learning in 2003
Percentage of the adult female/male population (25 to 64) participating in education and training

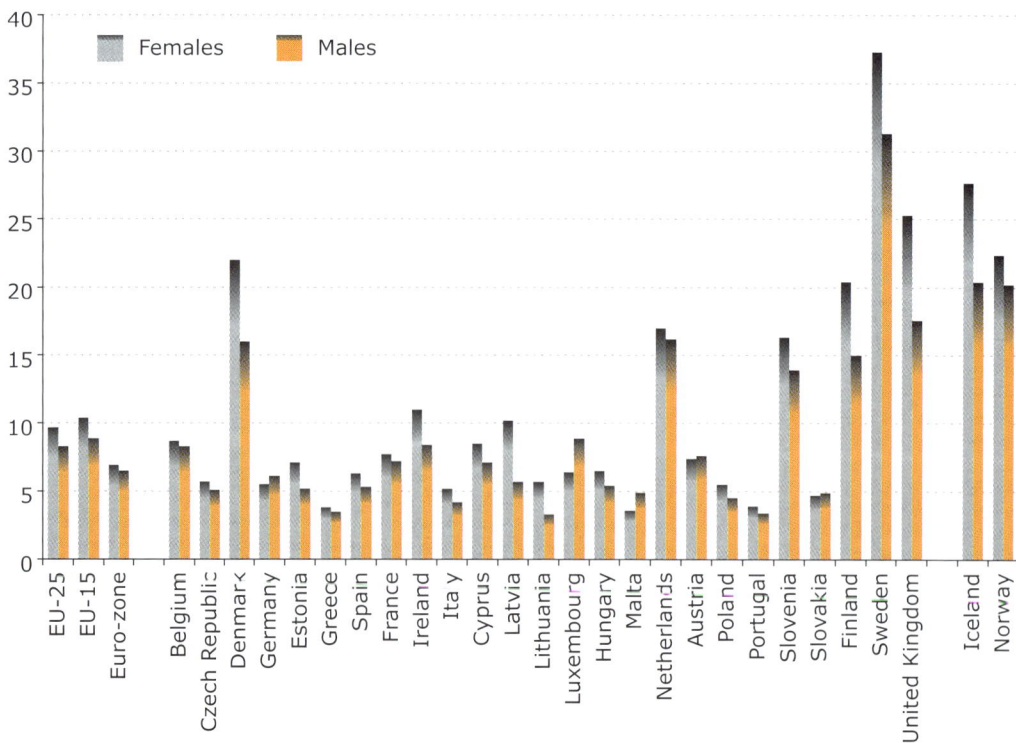

Germany, Luxembourg, Austria, Iceland: provisional data.

Lifelong learning
Percentage of the adult population (25 to 64) participating in education and training

	1992	1993	1994	1995	1996	1997	1998	1999	2000	2001	2002	2003
EU-25	:	:	:	:	:	:	:	:	:	7.9(e)	8	9.0(b)
EU-15	:	:	:	:	5.7(e)	5.8(e)	:	8.2(e)	8.5(e)	8.4(e)	8.5	9.7(b)
Euro-zone	:	:	:	:	:	:	:	5.7(e)	5.7(e)	5.5(e)	5.5	6.7(b)
Belgium	2.3	2.7	2.7	2.8	2.9	3	4.4	6.9(b)	6.8	7.3	6.5	8.5
Czech Republic	:	:	:	:	:	:	:	:	:	:	5.9	5.4
Denmark	16.2	15.6	15.1	16.8	18	18.9	19.8	19.8	20.8	17.8	18.4	18.9(b)
Germany	:	:	:	:	5.7	5.4	5.3	5.5	5.2	5.2	5.8	5.8(p)
Estonia	:	:	:	:	:	4.3	6.3	6.5	6	5.2	5.2	6.2
Greece	1.2	1.1	1	0.9	0.9	0.9	1	1.2	1.1	1.4	1.2	3.7(b)
Spain	3.4	3.5	3.9	4.3	4.4	4.5	4.3	5.1	5.1	4.9	5	5.8
France	2.9	3	2.9	2.9	2.7	2.9	2.7	2.6	2.8	2.7	2.7	7.4(b)
Ireland	3.4	3.5	3.9	4.3	4.8	5.2	:	:	:	:	7.7	9.7(b)
Italy	2.9	3.4(b)	3.7	4	4.4	4.9	4.8	5.5	5.5	5.1	4.6	4.7
Cyprus	:	:	:	:	:	:	:	2.6	3.1	3.4	3.7	7.9(b)
Latvia	:	:	:	:	:	:	:	:	:	:	8.2	8.1
Lithuania	:	:	:	:	:	:	:	4	2.8	3.6	3.3(b)	4.5
Luxembourg	2.9	2.6	3.3	2.9	2.9	2.8	5.1(b)	5.3	4.8	5.3	7.7	7.7(p)
Hungary	:	:	:	:	:	2.9	3.3	2.9	3.1	3	3.2	6.0(b)
Malta	:	:	:	:	:	:	:	:	:	:	4.4	4.2
Netherlands	15.1	14.3	13.6	13.1	12.5	12.6	12.9	13.6	15.6	16.3	16.4	16.5
Austria	:	:	:	7.7	7.9	7.8	:	9.1	8.3	8.2	7.5	7.5(p)
Poland	:	:	:	:	:	:	:	:	:	4.8	4.3	5
Portugal	3.6	3.2	3.5	3.3	3.4	3.5	3.0(b)	3.4	3.4	3.3	2.9	3.6
Slovenia	:	:	:	:	:	:	:	:	:	7.6	9.1	15.1(b)
Slovakia	:	:	:	:	:	:	:	:	:	:	9	4.8(b)
Finland	:	:	:	:	16.3	15.8	16.1	17.6	19.6(b)	19.3	18.9	17.6(b)
Sweden	:	:	:	:	26.5	25	:	25.8	21.6	17.5(b)	18.4	34.2(b)
United Kingdom	12.5	10.8	11.5	:	:	:	:	19.2	21.1	21.7	22.3	21.3
Iceland	:	:	:	14.1	15.7	16.5	19.3	20.2	23.5	23.5	24	24.0(p)
Norway	:	:	:	:	16.5	16.4	:	:	13.3	14.2	13.3	21.3(b)

Lifelong learning refers to persons aged 25 to 64 who stated that they received education or training in the four weeks preceding the survey (numerator). The denominator consists of the total population of the same age group, excluding those who did not answer to the question 'participation to education and training'. Both the numerator and the denominator come from the EU labour force survey. The information collected relates to all education or training whether or not relevant to the respondent's current or possible future job.

Age is not an impediment to having education or training. In 2003, the Nordic countries of Europe reached the highest levels of persons between 25 and 64 years that have had training: Sweden (34.2 %) had more than three times the EU-15 average, followed by the United Kingdom (21.3 %) and Denmark (18.9 %). A low share of people aged 25 to 64 years in training is observed in Portugal (3.6 %), Greece (3.7 %), Malta (4.2 %), Lithuania (4.5 %) and Italy (4.7 %).

People in the labour market

2

Labour market statistics are at the heart of EU policies

Employment is having an ever-important political profile for the European Union. Labour market statistics are now at the heart of many EU policies.

An employment chapter was introduced into the Amsterdam Treaty in 1997. The extraordinary European Council of Luxembourg in November 1997 endorsed an ambitious European employment strategy aiming at the reduction of unemployment and the sustainable increase of employment rates, as well as the reduction of gender gaps.

The Lisbon Summit (spring 2000) put full employment with more and better jobs on the European agenda. For the year 2010, it set targets for the total and female employment rate:

— 70 % for the total employment rate;
— 60 % for the female employment rate.

The Stockholm Council (spring 2001) subsequently added the employment target for persons aged between 55 and 64 years to reach 50 % by 2010. It also fixed the intermediate objectives (for 2005) of 67 % for the total employment rate and 57 % for the female employment rate.

The labour force survey: an indispensable tool for observing the labour market

In this context, the role of the Community labour force survey (LFS) has gained steadily in importance. It is now universally recognised as an indispensable tool for observing labour market de-

velopments and for taking the appropriate policy measures. The LFS is the only source of information in these areas to provide data that are truly comparable. The definitions and methods are harmonised for all Member States. The LFS is the main source of data for this section.

Comparable data on Europe's labour market

An objective of the LFS is to report on the EU's population of working age (15–64 years) which is composed of persons in employment, unemployed persons and economically inactive persons.

The LFS provides comprehensive information on these three categories. It describes the employment situation of employed persons by reporting, for example, on their education, the branches in which they work, and their occupation, as well as on part-time work, the duration of the work contract and the search for a new job. The data presented in the Eurostat yearbook refer to the situation in spring.

Numerous *Statistics in Focus* show the wide range of information that the LFS provides. The complete list of LFS variables (more than 100) can be consulted in the 2001 edition of *Labour force survey — Methods and definitions*.

Persons in employment
Annual average; in 1 000

	1992	1993	1994	1995	1996	1997	1998	1999	2000	2001	2002	2003
EU-25	:	:	:	:	:	:	:	:	:	:	:	:
EU-15	157 911	155 448	155 328	156 404	157 370	158 900	161 643	164 441	167 732	169 807	170 548	170 960
Euro-zone	120 243	118 257	117 915	118 647	119 231	120 322	122 462	124 686	127 481	133 198	133 888	134 093
Belgium	3 853	3 828	3 812	3 839	3 851	3 886	3 957	4 011	4 088	4 149	4 136	4 115
Czech Republic	:	:	:	4 959	4 968	4 933	4 863	4 761	4 728	4 724	4 760	4 731
Denmark	2 600	2 562	2 599	2 642	2 652	2 675	2 718	2 776	2 784	2 792	2 782	2 755
Germany	37 878	37 365	37 304	37 382	37 270	37 208	37 616	38 077	38 752	38 917	38 668	38 248
Estonia	:	:	:	634	619	619	608	581	572	577	584	593
Greece	3 807	3 838	3 834	3 820	3 805	3 784	3 940	3 941	3 935	3 921	3 914	3 966
Spain	13 772	13 381	13 318	13 572	13 745	14 147	14 698	15 209	15 744	16 107	16 343	16 646
France	22 742	22 449	22 483	22 682	22 767	22 867	23 215	23 680	24 308	24 720	24 888	24 934
Ireland	1 155	1 170	1 220	1 274	1 324	1 408	1 522	1 617	1 692	1 741	1 765	1 797
Italy	22 920	22 348	22 017	21 993	22 130	22 215	22 448	22 698	23 128	23 581	24 008	24 286
Cyprus	:	:	:	:	288	287	290	294	302	:	:	:
Latvia	1 294	1 205	1 083	1 046	1 018	1 037	1 043	1 038	1 038	:	:	:
Lithuania	:	:	:	:	:	:	:	:	1 585	1 522	1 411	1 442
Luxembourg	201	204	209	214	220	226	237	248	262	277	286	292
Hungary	:	:	:	3 623	3 605	3 611	3 675	3 792	3 829	3 845	3 856	3 969
Malta	:	:	:	:	:	:	132	131	134	138	137	:
Netherlands	6 986	6 986	7 036	7 143	7 308	7 544	7 742	7 946	8 124	8 274	8 349	8 316
Austria	3 959	3 934	3 929	3 928	3 904	3 924	3 965	4 020	4 050	4 076	4 066	4 079
Poland	:	:	:	14 791	14 969	15 177	15 354	14 757	14 526	14 207	13 782	13 617
Portugal	4 602	4 545	4 570	4 567	4 629	4 744	4 868	4 928	5 029	5 098	5 107	5 064
Slovenia	:	:	:	:	:	:	:	:	900	905	899	898
Slovakia	:	:	:	2 107	2 156	2 129	2 120	2 063	2 025	2 037	2 016	2 061
Finland	2 177	2 047	2 018	2 056	2 084	2 154	2 197	2 253	2 304	2 338	2 360	2 350
Sweden	:	4 077	4 041	4 103	4 069	4 015	4 078	4 163	4 264	4 345	4 352	4 341
United Kingdom	26 933	26 714	26 940	27 191	27 614	28 104	28 446	28 876	29 267	29 472	29 526	29 771

The indicator 'persons in employment (men and women)' refers to all persons who did any work for pay or profit, or were not working but had jobs from which they were temporarily absent. Family workers are included.

In 2002, there were, on average, over 170 million people employed in the 15 countries that at that time formed the European Union.

In 2003, the employment rate stood at 62.9 % in the 25 countries that today form the European Union, ranging from 51.2 % in Poland to 75.1 % in Denmark. The employment rate for women (55 %) stood lower than that for men (71 %).

Total employment rate
In %

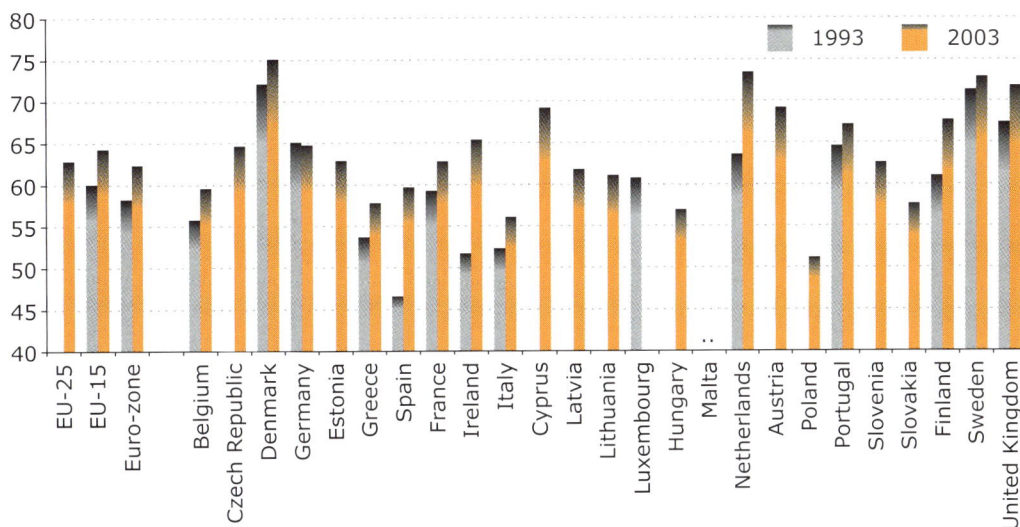

The employment rate is calculated by dividing the number of persons aged 15 to 64 in employment by the total population of the same age group. The indicator is based on the EU labour force survey. The survey covers the entire population living in private households and excludes those in collective households such as boarding houses, halls of residence and hospitals. Employed population consists of those persons who during the reference week did any work for pay or profit for at least one hour, or were not working but had jobs from which they were temporarily absent.

Employment rate of women
In %

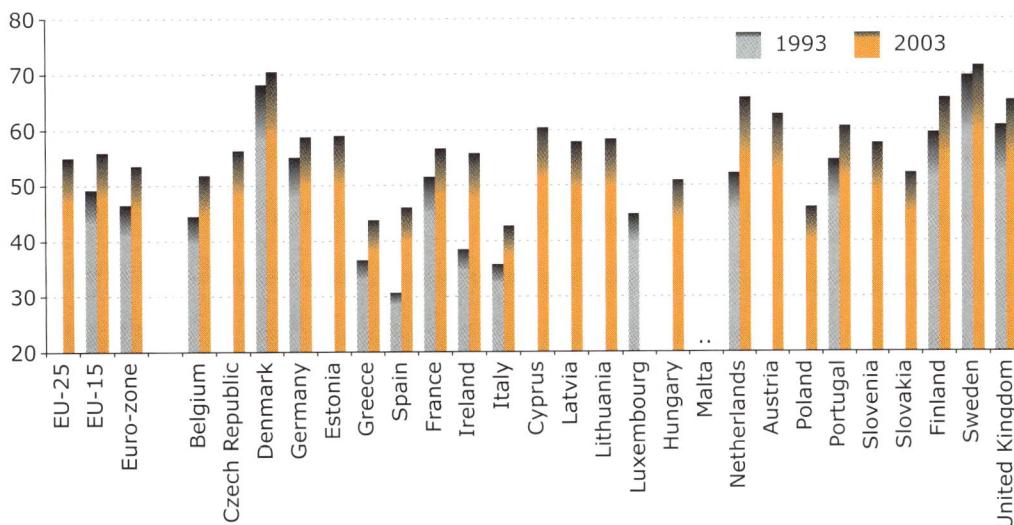

The female employment rate is calculated by dividing the number of women aged 15 to 64 in employment by the total female population of the same age group. The indicator is based on the EU labour force survey. The survey covers the entire population living in private households and excludes those in collective households such as boarding houses, halls of residence and hospitals. Employed population consists of those persons who during the reference week did any work for pay or profit for at least one hour, or were not working but had jobs from which they were temporarily absent.

Employment in the different sectors of the economy in 2003
Share in total employment in %

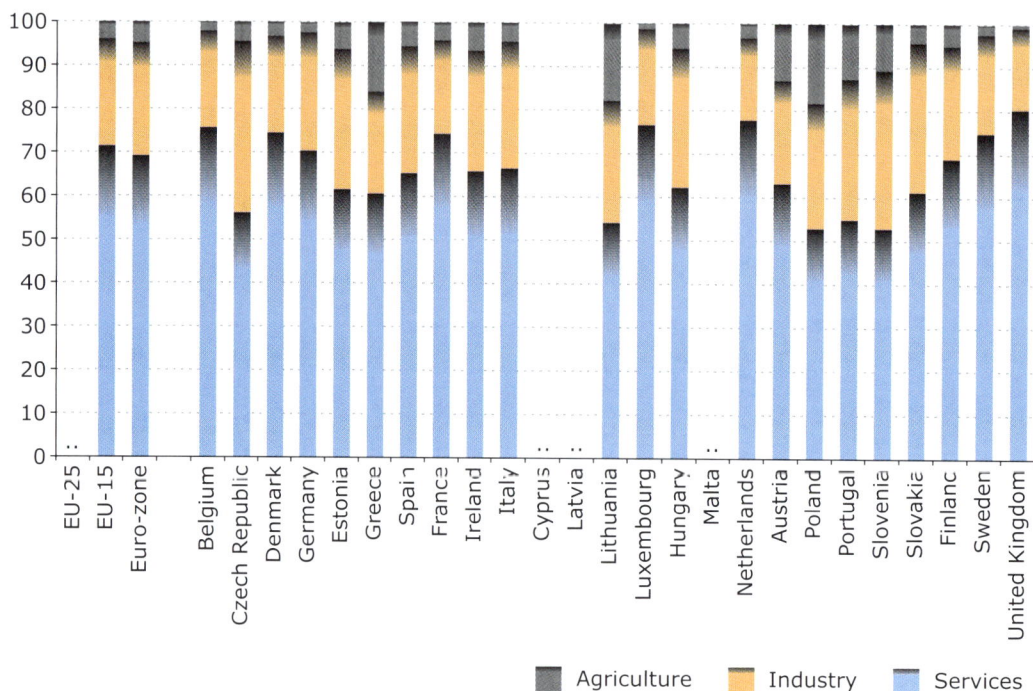

Legend: Agriculture | Industry | Services

All persons employed by sector as a share of all persons employed. Employed persons are those who did any work for pay or profit, or were not working but had jobs from which they were temporarily absent. Family workers are included.

There are marked differences in the structure of employment in the European Union: in 2003, employment in agriculture was above the 10 % threshold in Poland (18 %), Lithuania (18 %), Greece (16 %), Austria (13 %), Portugal (13 %) and Slovenia (11 %), while in many other countries it was about 5 % or lower. The United Kingdom (80 %), the Netherlands (78 %), Luxembourg (77 %) and Belgium (76 %) had the highest share of people working in the service sector.

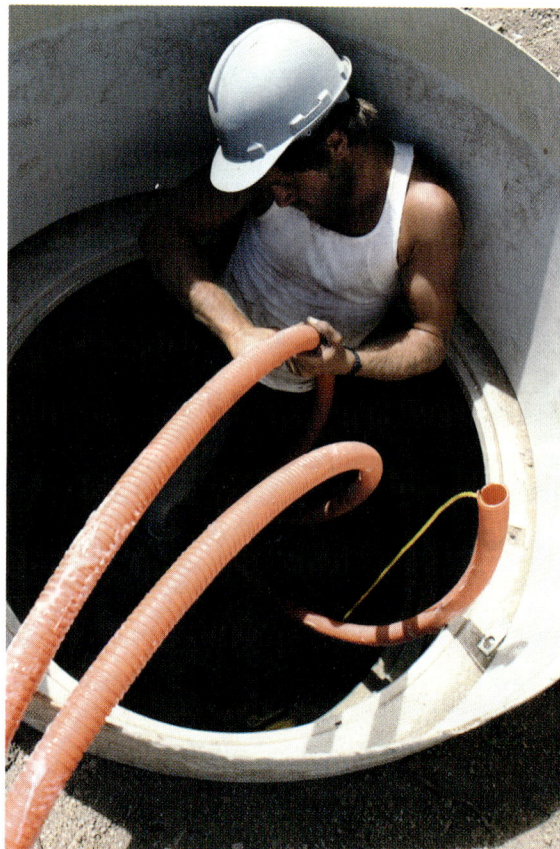

Unemployment rate for men and women in 2003
Unemployed persons as a percentage of the labour force

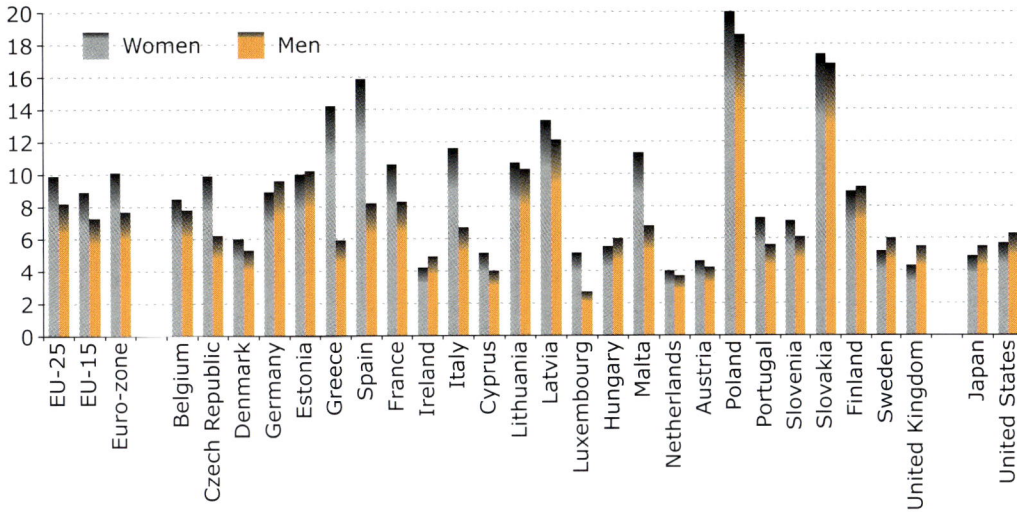

Unemployment rate represent unemployed persons as a percentage of the labour force = active population. The labour force is the total number of people employed and unemployed. Unemployed persons comprise persons aged 15–74 who were: without work during the reference week; currently available for work, i.e. were available for paid employment or self-employment before the end of the two weeks following the reference week; actively seeking work, i.e. had taken specific steps in the four weeks period ending with the reference week to seek paid employment or self-employment or who found a job to start later, i.e. within a period of at most three months.

Unemployment has remained a problem in the European Union: in 2002, the unemployment rate for the 25 countries that today form the European Union was 8.8 %; 3.9 % of the economically active population was 'long-term un-employed', i.e. they could not find a job for over one year. The unemployment rate for women (2003: 9.9 %) is higher than that for men (2003: 8.2 %).

Total and long-term unemployment in 2002
(Long-term) unemployed as a percentage of the total active population

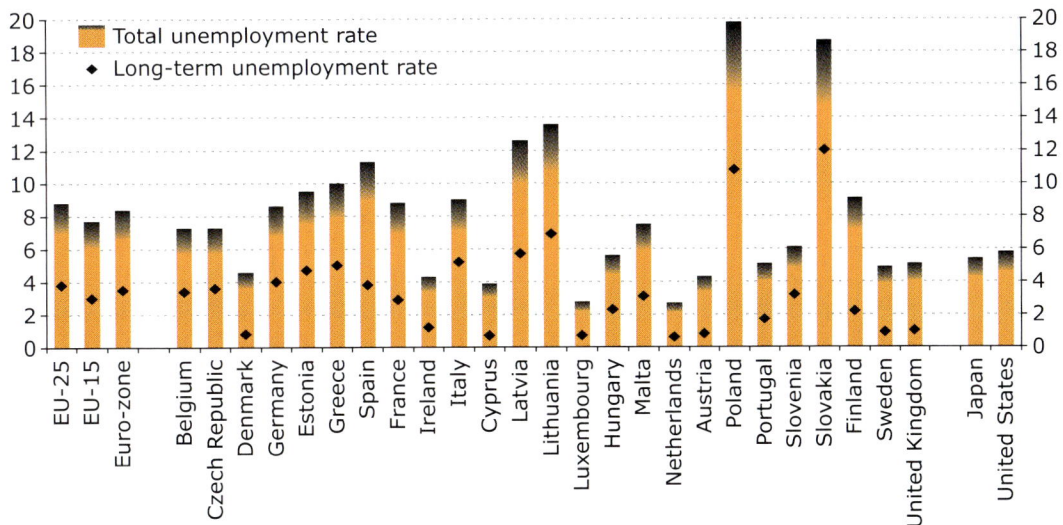

Long-term unemployed (12 months and more) persons are those aged at least 15 years not living in collective households who are without work within the next two weeks, are available to start work within the next two weeks and who are seeking work (have actively sought employment at some time during the previous four weeks or are not seeking a job because they have already found a job to start later). The total active population (labour force) is the total number of the employed and unemployed population. The duration of unemployment is defined as the duration of a search for a job or as the length of the period since the last job was held (if this period is shorter than the duration of search for a job).

Hours worked per week in 2003
Spring

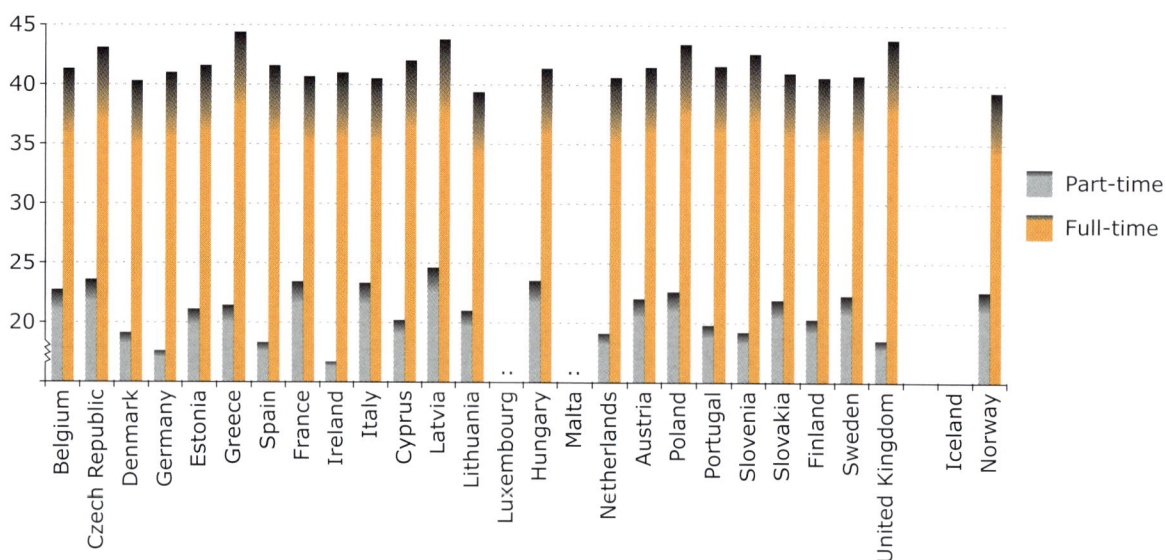

The average number of hours corresponds to the number of hours the person normally works. This covers all hours including extra hours, either paid or unpaid, which the person normally works. It excludes the travel time between the home and the place of work as well as the main meal breaks (normally taken at midday). The distinction between full-time and part-time work is made on the basis of a spontaneous answer given by the respondent.

Persons employed part-time in 2003
Share in total employment in %; Spring

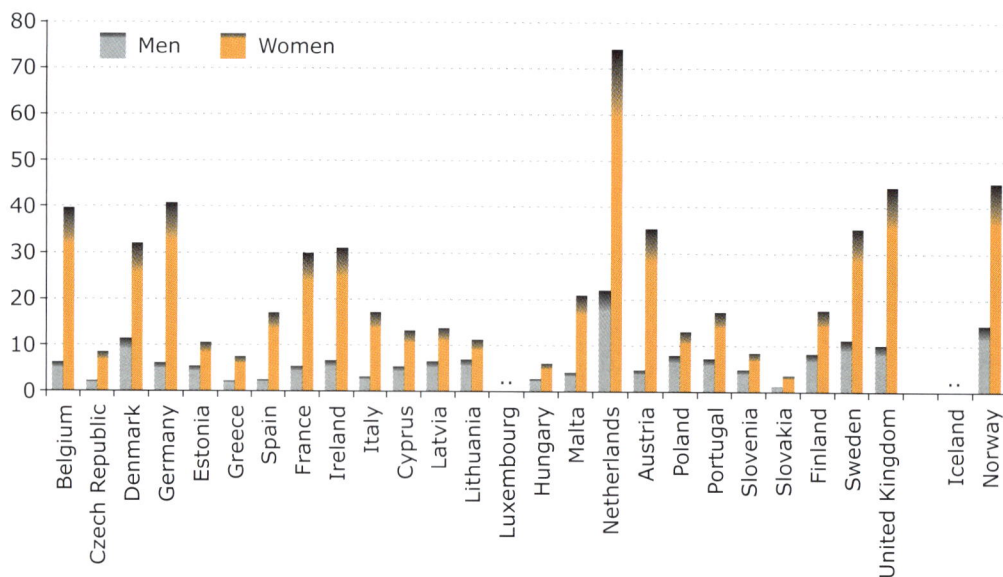

Persons in employment are those who, during the reference week, did any work for pay or profit for at least one hour, or were not working but had jobs from which they were temporarily absent. Family workers are included. The distinction between full-time and part-time work is made on the basis of a spontaneous answer given by the respondent. It is impossible to establish a more exact distinction between part-time and full-time work, due to variations in working hours between Member States and branches of industry.

Working part-time is still much more widespread amongst women than amongst men.

Labour market policy data

Eurostat data

Eurostat provides a wide range of data on:
— Labour market policy total expenditure
— Labour market policy expenditure by category
— Labour market policy expenditure by recipient of the transfers
— Detailed labour market expenditure by category and by country
— Total participants (stocks) in labour market policy measures by category
— Total participants (entrants) in labour market policy measures by category
— Detailed figures on participants in labour market measures by category and by country

2

Labour market policies

Labour market policies (LMPs) are, by definition, restricted in scope, covering only those political interventions targeted at the unemployed and other groups of people with particular difficulties in entering or retaining their position in the labour market. Primary target groups are the unemployed who are registered with the public employment services. However, public expenditure on LMPs should not be interpreted exclusively as demonstrating the strength of the political will to combat unemployment. Other factors such as the demographic situation and the GDP per capita of each country contribute to the differences. Expenditure on targeted programmes, including training, job rotation/job sharing, employment incentives, integration of the disabled, direct job-creation and start-up incentives, is usually considered as active expenditure, whereas expenditure on unemployment benefits and on early retirement is considered as passive expenditure. However, it should be taken into account that in the past few years the conditions for maintaining eligibility to receive unemployment benefits have been increasingly tied to individualised job-search activities and may also involve active intervention by the public employment service.

Public expenditure on labour market policy measures in the EU-15 in 2002
In % of GDP

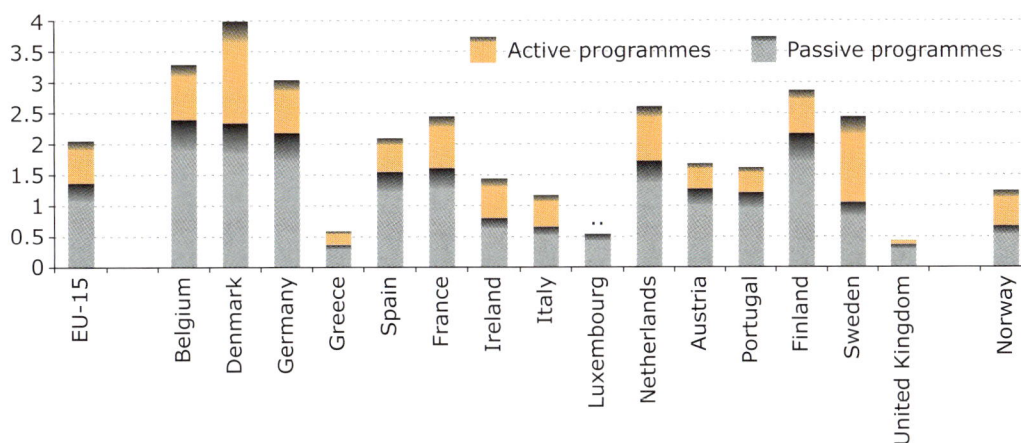

EU-15, active programmes: estimated data.

Public expenditure on labour market policy measures is explicitly devoted to unemployed, employed at risk, and inactive persons who would like to enter the labour market. Total expenditure includes two main groups of measures: total categories 2–7 — Expenditure on active programmes involving training, job rotation/job sharing, employment incentives, integration of the disabled, direct job creation and start-up incentives, and total categories 8–9 — Expenditure on passive programmes such as 'out-of-work income maintenance' (mostly unemployment benefits) and 'early retirement'.

2

Labour market policy expenditure in active measures in the EU-15 in 2002
In million EUR

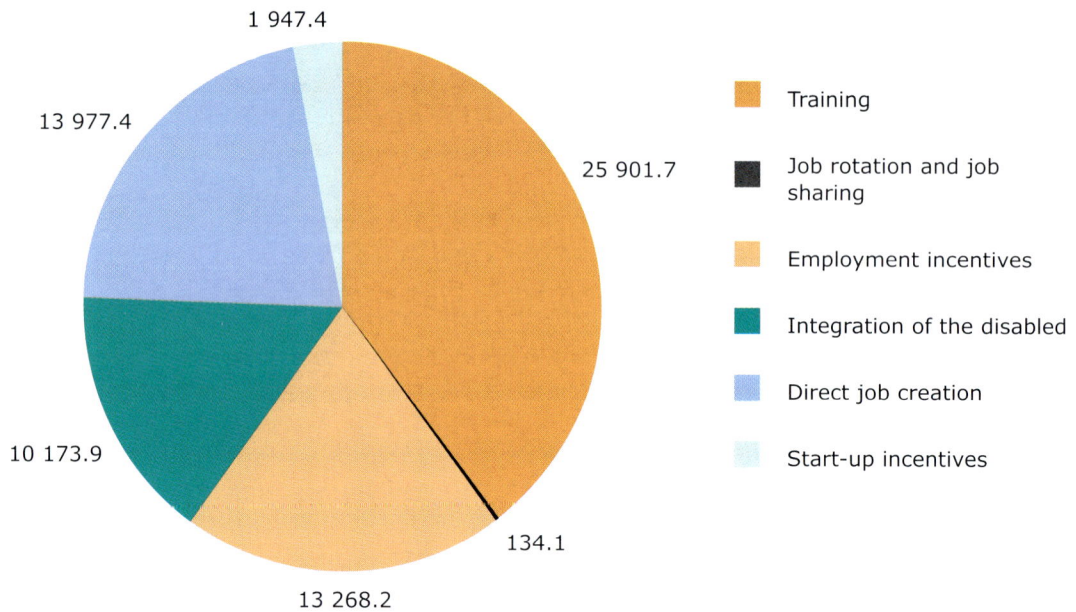

1 947.4

13 977.4

25 901.7

10 173.9

134.1

13 268.2

- Training
- Job rotation and job sharing
- Employment incentives
- Integration of the disabled
- Direct job creation
- Start-up incentives

Total labour market policy expenditure on active measures refers to public expenditure on programmes targeted at the unemployed, employed at risk and inactive persons who would like to enter the labour market. The coverage includes six categories of measures: training for the unemployed and groups at risk, job rotation/job sharing, employment incentives, integration of the disabled, direct job creation and start-up incentives.

Labour market policy expenditure in passive measures in the EU-15 in 2002
In million EUR

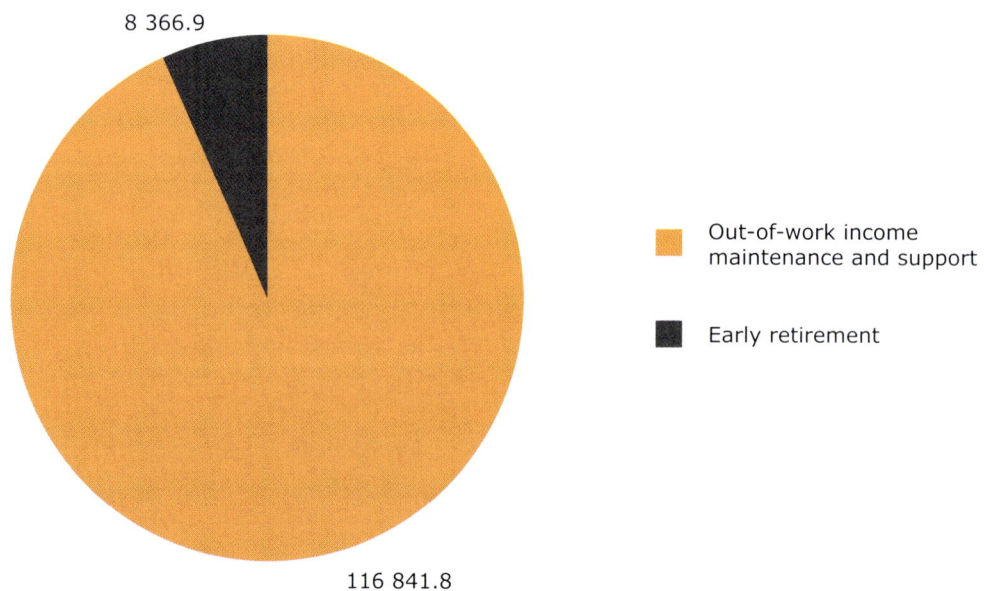

8 366.9

116 841.8

- Out-of-work income maintenance and support
- Early retirement

Total labour market expenditure on passive measures refers to public expenditure on out-of-work income maintenance (mostly unemployment benefits and other programmes which aim to compensate for loss of wage and salary) and on early retirement (programmes which facilitate the full or partial early retirement of older workers).

Household consumption expenditure

Eurostat data

Eurostat provides a wide range of data on household consumption expenditure, broken down by consumption purposes:

— Food, beverages and tobacco
— Clothes and footwear
— Housing (including rentals)
— Health
— Transport
— Communication
— Leisure and culture
— Education
— Restaurants and hotels
— Miscellaneous (personal care, social protection, insurance, etc.)

2

Making consumer markets transparent

For everyone who wants to know more about consumer markets in the EU, this is a fundamental question: How do the volumes and the proportions of the markets develop?

The Eurostat yearbook answers this question. It presents data on household consumption expenditure for so-called consumption purposes. The yearbook presents data broken down according to the 'classification of individual consumption by purpose' (Coicop). This nomenclature for consumption is accessible on the website http://europa.eu.int/ comm/eurostat/ramon/ (option 'Classifications'), line 17 'Coicop'.

Reliable source, harmonised definitions

Statistics on final consumption expenditure of households come from Eurostat's national accounts statistics.

Consumption refers to goods and services used for the direct satisfaction of individual needs.

It covers the purchases of goods and services, the consumption of own production (such as garden produce) and the imputed rent of owner-occupied dwellings.

The word 'expenditure' added in ESA 95 explicitly relates to direct spending by households; it excludes consumption financed by general government or by NPISHs (non-profit institutions serving households).

Household consumption expenditure in the EU-15 in 2001
In % of total household consumption expenditure

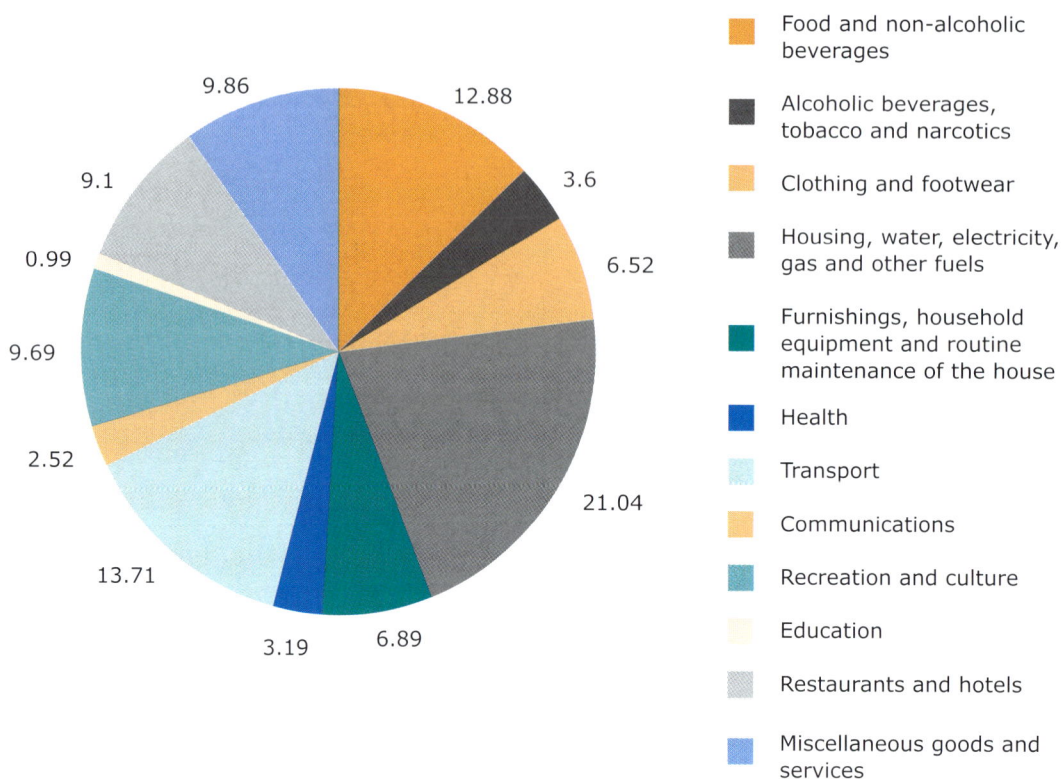

	Food and non-alcoholic beverages
	Alcoholic beverages, tobacco and narcotics
	Clothing and footwear
	Housing, water, electricity, gas and other fuels
	Furnishings, household equipment and routine maintenance of the house
	Health
	Transport
	Communications
	Recreation and culture
	Education
	Restaurants and hotels
	Miscellaneous goods and services

Pie chart values: 12.88, 3.6, 6.52, 21.04, 6.89, 3.19, 13.71, 2.52, 9.69, 0.99, 9.1, 9.86

Estimated values.

In 2001, the households in EU-15 spent one fifth of their expenditure on housing, water, and energy linked to housing (21 %). This is by far the biggest share when compared with other consumption purposes. It ranged from almost 29 % in Sweden to below 10 % in Cyprus and Malta.

About 14 % of total household consumption expenditure was spent on transport.

Household consumption expenditure in the EU-15 in 2001: housing, water, electricity, gas and other fuels
In % of total household consumption expenditure

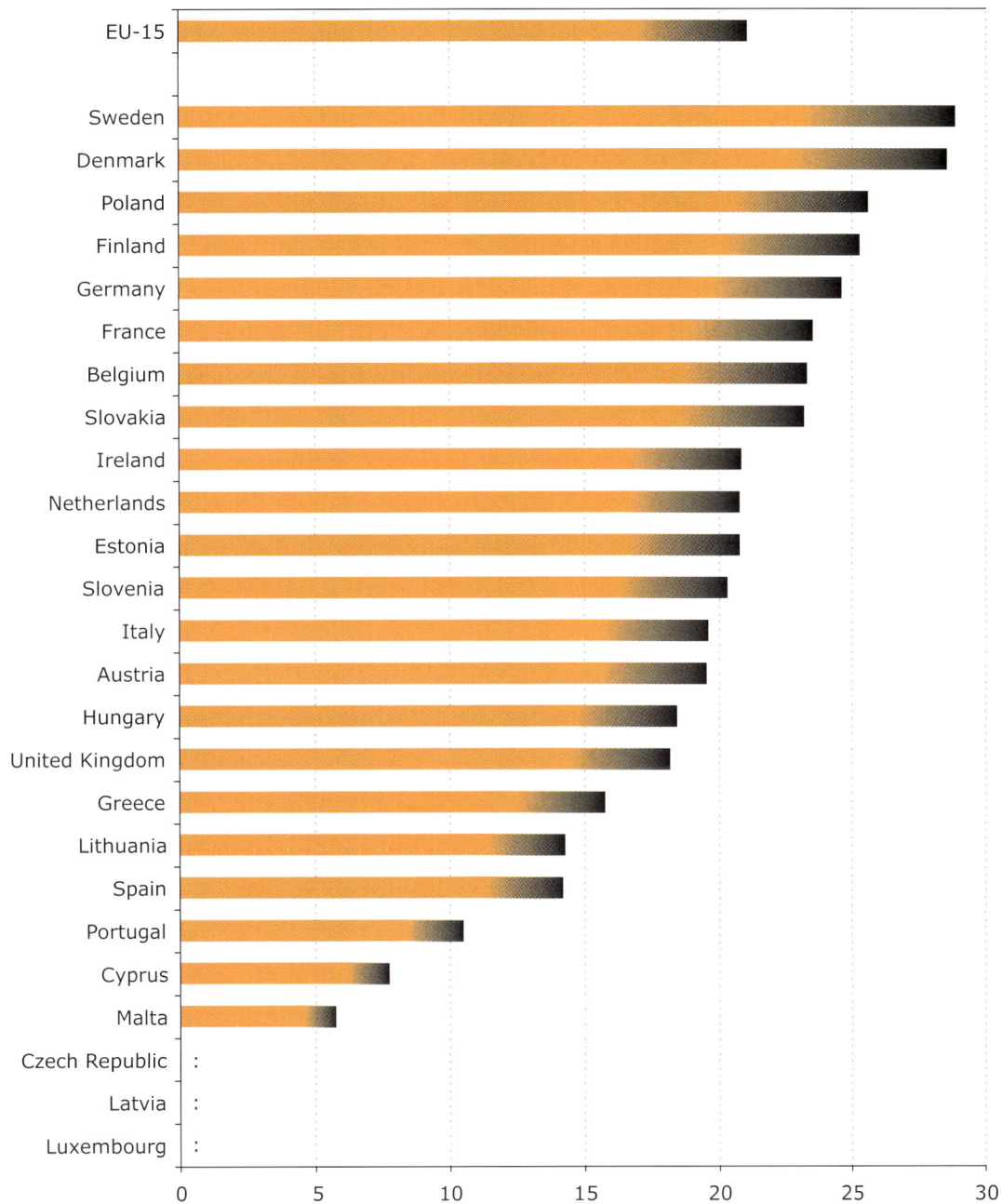

EU-15	21
Sweden	29
Denmark	28.5
Poland	25.5
Finland	25
Germany	24.5
France	23
Belgium	23
Slovakia	23
Ireland	20.5
Netherlands	20.5
Estonia	20.5
Slovenia	20
Italy	19.5
Austria	19.5
Hungary	18
United Kingdom	18
Greece	15.5
Lithuania	14
Spain	14
Portugal	10.5
Cyprus	7.5
Malta	5.5
Czech Republic	:
Latvia	:
Luxembourg	:

At current prices.

2

Household expenditure on food (1) versus GDP per head (2) in 2001

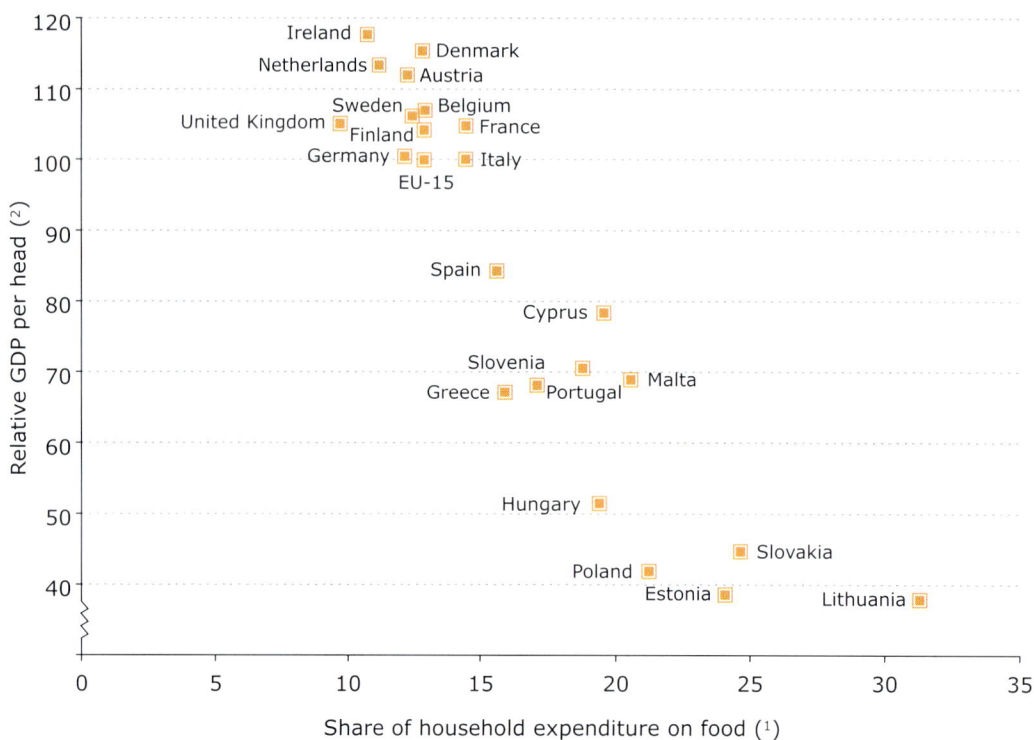

Y-axis: Relative GDP per head (²)

Country	Share	GDP
Ireland		~118
Denmark		~115
Netherlands		~113
Austria		~112
Sweden, Belgium		~107
United Kingdom, Finland, France		~105
Germany, Italy		~100
EU-15		100
Spain		~84
Cyprus		~78
Slovenia		~71
Portugal, Malta		~69
Greece		~67
Hungary		~51
Slovakia		~45
Poland		~42
Estonia		~39
Lithuania		~39

X-axis: Share of household expenditure on food (¹) — 0, 5, 10, 15, 20, 25, 30, 35

(¹) Share of household consumption expenditure on food and non-alcoholic beverages in total household consumption expenditure; in %; measured at current prices.

(²) Gross domestic product in PPS per inhabitant; EU-15 = 100.

About 13 % was spent on food and non-alcoholic beverages. This share varies with GDP per head: the lower GDP per head of a country, the higher the share of money spent on food.

Household consumption expenditure in the EU-15 in 2001: food and non-alcoholic beverages

In % of total household consumption expenditure

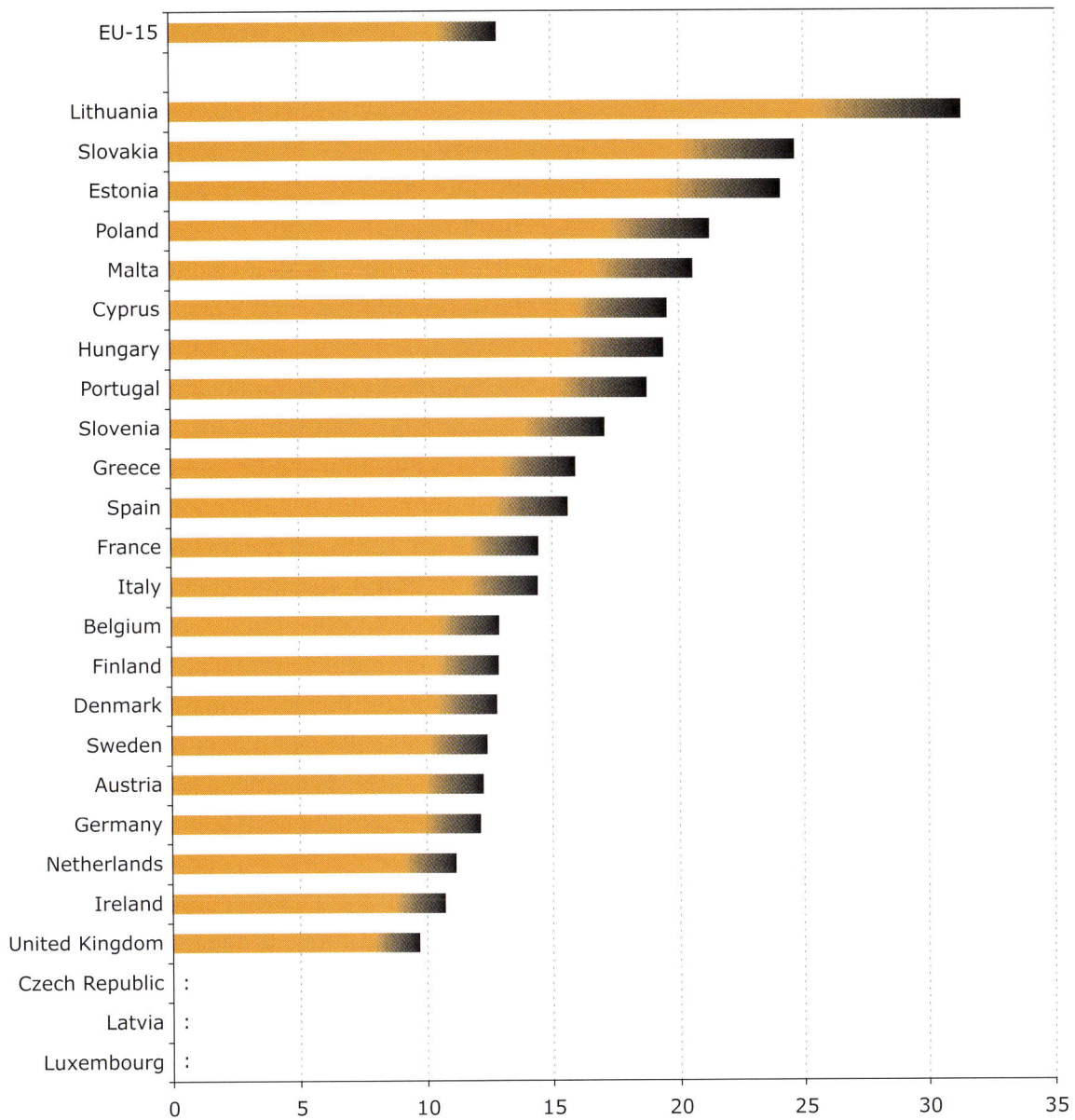

EU-15	
Lithuania	
Slovakia	
Estonia	
Poland	
Malta	
Cyprus	
Hungary	
Portugal	
Slovenia	
Greece	
Spain	
France	
Italy	
Belgium	
Finland	
Denmark	
Sweden	
Austria	
Germany	
Netherlands	
Ireland	
United Kingdom	
Czech Republic	:
Latvia	:
Luxembourg	:

At current prices.

Household consumption expenditure in the EU-15 in 2001: clothing and footwear

In % of total household consumption expenditure

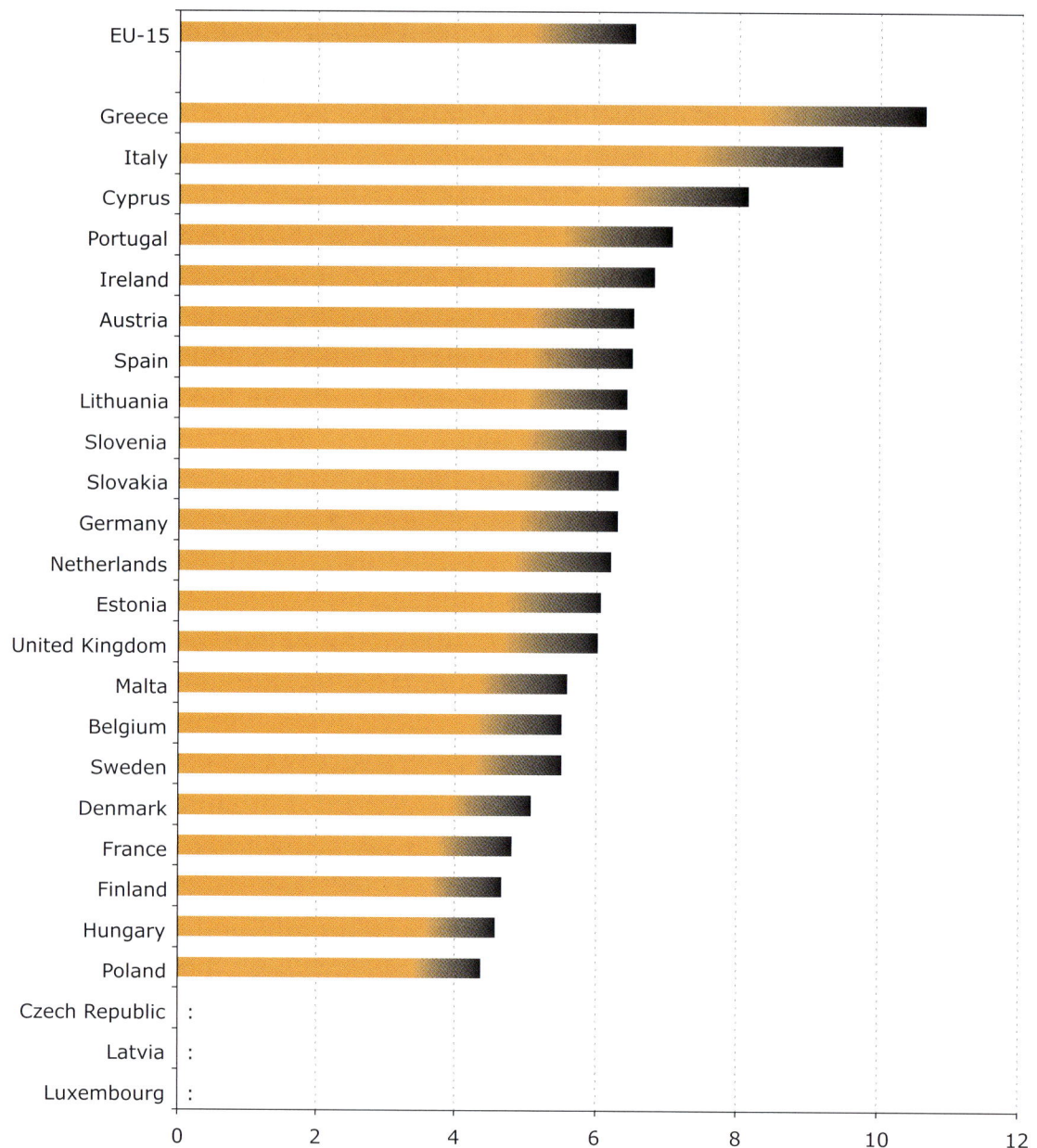

EU-15	6.6
Greece	10.7
Italy	9.5
Cyprus	8.2
Portugal	7.1
Ireland	6.9
Austria	6.6
Spain	6.6
Lithuania	6.5
Slovenia	6.5
Slovakia	6.4
Germany	6.3
Netherlands	6.2
Estonia	6.1
United Kingdom	6.1
Malta	5.6
Belgium	5.5
Sweden	5.5
Denmark	5.1
France	4.8
Finland	4.7
Hungary	4.6
Poland	4.4
Czech Republic	:
Latvia	:
Luxembourg	:

At current prices.

Income and living conditions

Eurostat data

Eurostat provides a wide range of data on:

— Situation of private households

— Inequality of income distribution

— At-risk-of-poverty rates

— Jobless households

2

full range of goods and services? Is the situation stable over time? Are there differences between countries?

The demand for such information has received a new impetus in recent years following the social chapter in the Amsterdam Treaty (1997) which became the driving force for EU social statistics generally. This impetus was reinforced by successive European Councils that keep the social dimension high on the political agenda. Effective monitoring is an essential element in making operational the strategies agreed under the open method of coordination.

The statistical indicators

Income, poverty and social exclusion are multidimensional problems. To monitor them effectively at European level, a subset of so-called 'social cohesion indicators' has been developed within the Structural indicators which are produced for the Commission's annual Spring report to the Council.

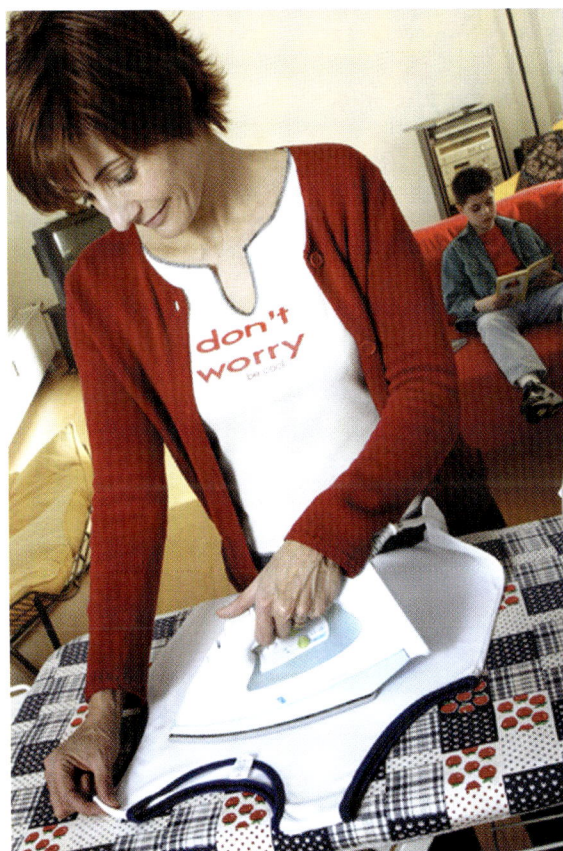

Income, poverty and social exclusion: statistics answer many questions

What is the average income level? Are some components more important than others? Is there a divide between the 'haves' and the 'have-nots', and, if so, how big is it? Are certain groups more at risk of poverty than others? Are they less involved in society? Do they have lower education attainment levels? Or worse health? Or larger families? Are their incomes less secure? Do they have access to a

Where do the data come from?

To calculate indicators for EU Member States in recent years, Eurostat has principally used micro-data from the European Community household panel (ECHP). However, after eight years of using this data source, it was replaced in 2003 by a new instrument, the EU statistics on income and living conditions (EU-SILC). One of the main reasons for this change was the need to adapt the content and timeliness of data production to reflect current political needs.

2

The ECHP is a 'longitudinal' survey that involves annual interviews with participant households (around 80 000 across the EU: samples are designed to be nationally representative). This makes it possible to follow up the same individuals over consecutive years and to provide information on social dynamics (for example, transition from education to working life; from working life to retirement) which are not possible from more typical cross-sectional surveys (separate sample each year).

EU-SILC aspires to become the EU reference source for comparative income distribution and social exclusion statistics, with the two main goals of high quality, especially regarding comparability and timeliness, and flexibility. It will comprise both a cross-sectional dimension — the first priority — and a longitudinal dimension. Greater reliance will be placed on existing national data sources in an attempt to harmonise outcomes rather than inputs and improve timeliness.

During the transition period, data is compiled by Eurostat from the best available national sources (typically household budget surveys), ex-post harmonised for maximum consistency. Nevertheless, due to the differences in underlying data sources, results cannot be considered to be perfectly comparable.

Brief methodological details

Household income is established by summing all monetary income received from any source by each member of the household (including income from work, investment and social benefits) net of taxes and social contributions paid. In order to reflect differences in household size and composition, this total is divided by the number of 'equivalent adults' using a standard scale (the so-called 'modified OECD' scale), and the resulting figure is attributed to each member of the household. EU-level estimates are calculated as population weighted averages of available national values.

At-risk-of-poverty rate in 2001
Before and after social transfers; in %

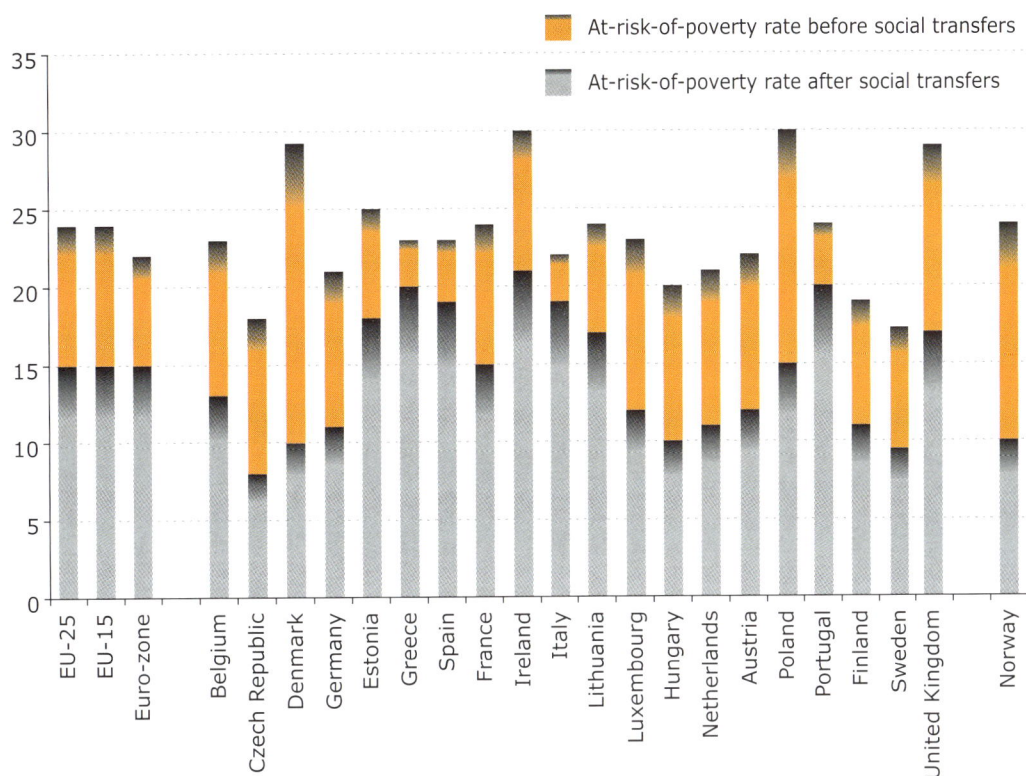

Legend:
- At-risk-of-poverty rate before social transfers
- At-risk-of-poverty rate after social transfers

Countries: EU-25, EU-15, Euro-zone, Belgium, Czech Republic, Denmark, Germany, Estonia, Greece, Spain, France, Ireland, Italy, Lithuania, Luxembourg, Hungary, Netherlands, Austria, Poland, Portugal, Finland, Sweden, United Kingdom, Norway

No data for Cyprus, Latvia, Malta, Slovenia and Slovakia.

Source: Eurostat; EU-15: ECHP.UDB wave 8 (1994-2001) version December 2003, except Denmark: Law Model Database and Sweden: HEK survey; NMS-10: 2nd round pilot project, transitional data collection 2003; Norway: national source.

The share of persons with an equivalised disposable income, before social transfers, below the risk-of-poverty threshold, which is set at 60 % of the national median equivalised disposable income (after social transfers). Retirement and survivor's pensions are counted as income before transfers and not as social transfers.

To measure the share of people that are at risk of poverty, a threshold is set at 60 % of the median income in a country. Below that threshold, a person is considered to be at risk of poverty. The respective shares are measured before and after social transfers. In 2001, 15 % of the population in the 25 countries that make up the European Union today were at risk of poverty.

This figure masks considerable variation between countries: the at-risk-of-poverty rate after social transfers was highest in Ireland (21%), the United Kingdom and Southern countries. It was lowest in Central European and Scandinavian countries, notably the Czech Republic (8%).

Without social transfers, the EU-25 rate would have been almost a quarter of the population (24%). The impact of social transfers is greatest (with a reduction of more than 40%) in Scandinavian and Central European countries, notably Denmark (65%). It is least apparent (with a reduction of less than 20%) in Southern countries. Note: this analysis only refers to the impact of social transfers other than pensions. Pensions play an important role in all countries.

2

Inequality of income distribution in 2001
Income quintile share ratio

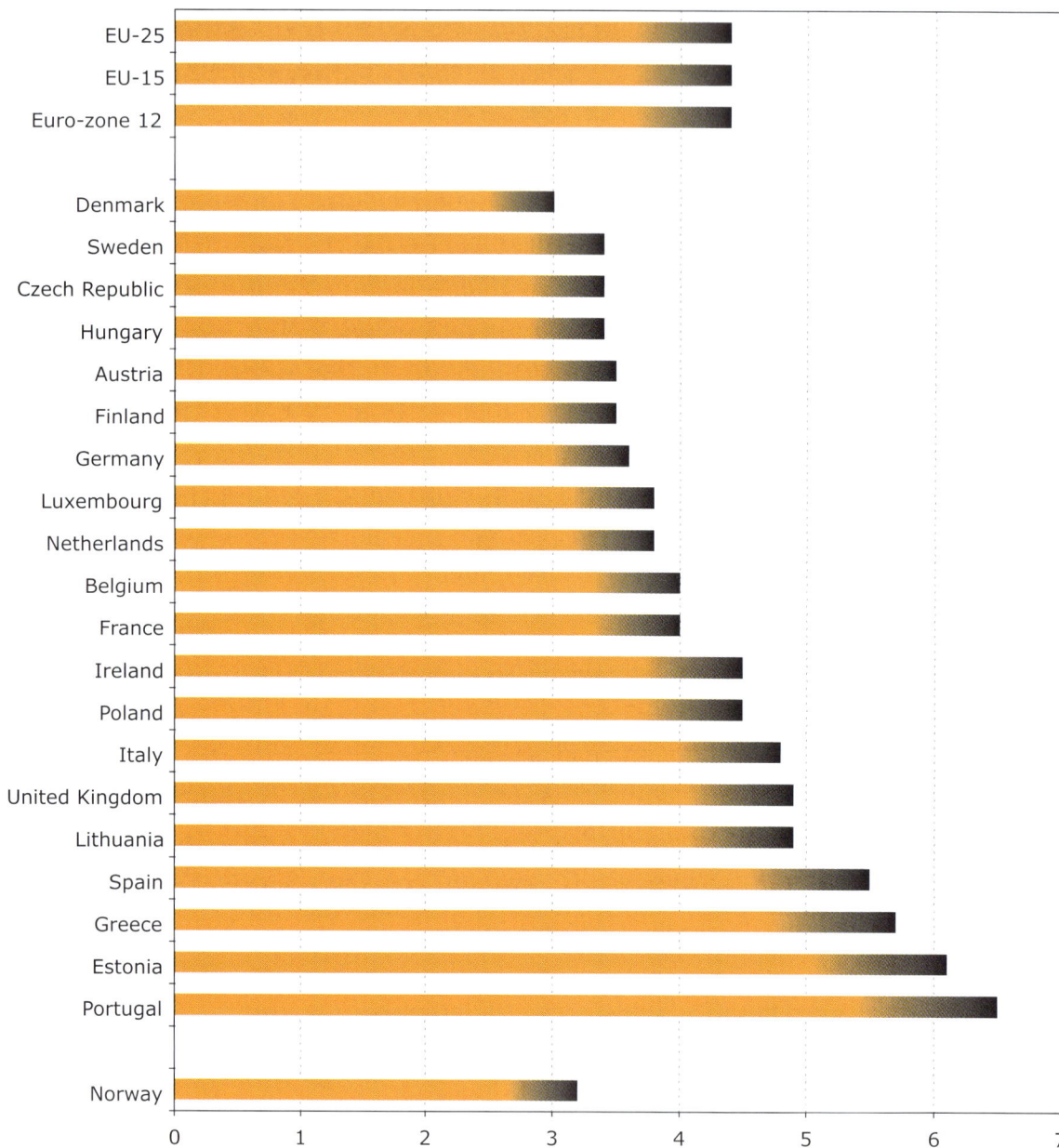

EU-25	4.4
EU-15	4.4
Euro-zone 12	4.4
Denmark	3.0
Sweden	3.4
Czech Republic	3.4
Hungary	3.4
Austria	3.5
Finland	3.5
Germany	3.6
Luxembourg	3.8
Netherlands	3.8
Belgium	4.0
France	4.0
Ireland	4.5
Poland	4.5
Italy	4.8
United Kingdom	4.9
Lithuania	4.9
Spain	5.5
Greece	5.7
Estonia	6.1
Portugal	6.5
Norway	3.2

The aggregates are Eurostat estimates. No data for Cyprus, Latvia, Malta, Slovenia and Slovakia.

Source: Eurostat; EU-15: ECHP.UDB wave 8 (1994-2001) version December 2003, except Denmark: Law Model Database and Sweden: HEK survey; NMS-10: 2nd round pilot project, transitional data collection 2003; Norway: national source.

The ratio of total income received by the 20 % of the population with the highest income (top quintile) to that received by the 20 % of the population with the lowest income (lowest quintile). Income must be understood as equivalised disposable income.

Income inequality is a sensitive issue, and it is difficult to measure. Eurostat calculates the following ratio to compare 'rich' and 'poor': total income received by the 20 % of the population with the highest income in relation to that received by the 20 % of the population with the lowest income. In EU-25 in 2001, the 20 % of the population with the highest income received more than four times as much income as the 20 % of the population with the lowest income. The indicator varies greatly between the countries, reaching from 3.0 in Denmark to 6.5 in Portugal.

Persons living in jobless households in 2003
Children aged up to 17 and adults aged 18 to 59

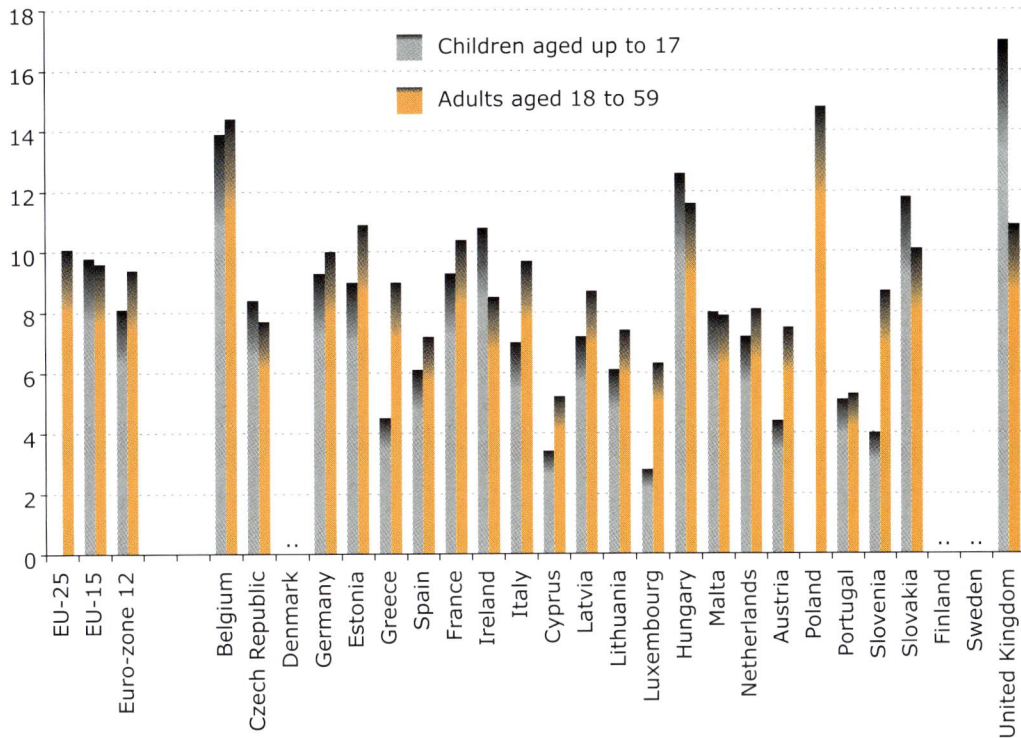

Children aged up to 17

Adults aged 18 to 59

The aggregates are estimated values.

The indicator 'persons living jobless households' is calculated as a share of persons of the respective age who are living in households where no one works. Students aged 18–24 who live in households composed solely of students of the same age class are not counted in either numerator nor denominator. Both the numerators and the denominators come from the EU labour force survey (LFS).

In 2003, about 10 % of the population aged between 18 and 59 years in EU-15 lived in jobless households. The share for children (up to 17 years) was equally high.

Average number of persons per private household in 2002

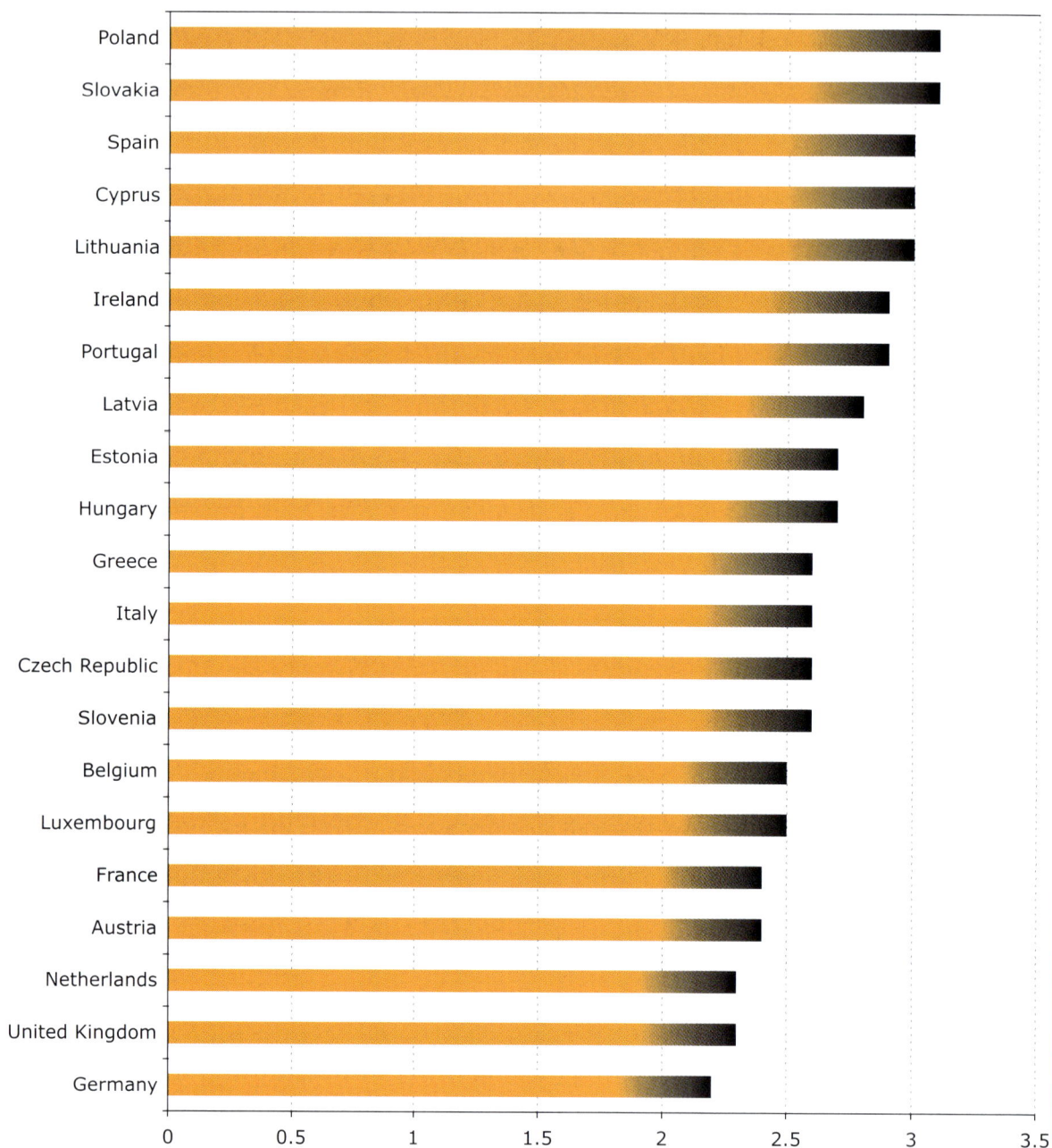

Poland	3.1
Slovakia	3.1
Spain	3.0
Cyprus	3.0
Lithuania	3.0
Ireland	2.9
Portugal	2.9
Latvia	2.8
Estonia	2.7
Hungary	2.7
Greece	2.6
Italy	2.6
Czech Republic	2.6
Slovenia	2.6
Belgium	2.5
Luxembourg	2.5
France	2.4
Austria	2.4
Netherlands	2.3
United Kingdom	2.3
Germany	2.2

No data for Denmark, Finland and Sweden.

Number of persons living in private households divided by the number of private households. Collective households such as boarding houses, halls of residence and hospitals and the persons living in them are excluded.

Housing

Eurostat data

Eurostat provides a wide range of data on:

— Type of housing of several groups of households

— Tenure status of households by socioeconomic status

— Lack of amenities by economic status of households

— Housing problems of several groups of households

— Households in overcrowded conditions (more than one person per room)

— Durables and affordability of households

— Dissatisfaction of households with their accommodation

— Financial burden of households due to the housing costs

2

Housing conditions

Is the type of accommodation or the tenure status an indicator for the welfare of households?

Two different trends concerning the type of housing of European households are revealed. In southern countries, low-income households (household income less than 60 % compared with median actual current income) seem to live predominantly in houses, compared with higher-income households (household income greater than 140 % compared with median actual current income) that live predominantly in flats. An opposite trend is observed for northern countries.

It is very difficult to pinpoint the reasons for such differences. The distribution of households in individual houses or flats is related to the degree of urbanisation in each country and to the quality of accommodation.

Within one's own four walls

Ownership of accommodation is higher in southern than in northern countries where the income level has a much stronger impact on whether the household lives in its own accommodation. However, considering the fact that ownership of accommodation is more important in southern countries, many owners there may have smaller accommodation.

2

Share of households living in a house, EU-15 in 2001
In %

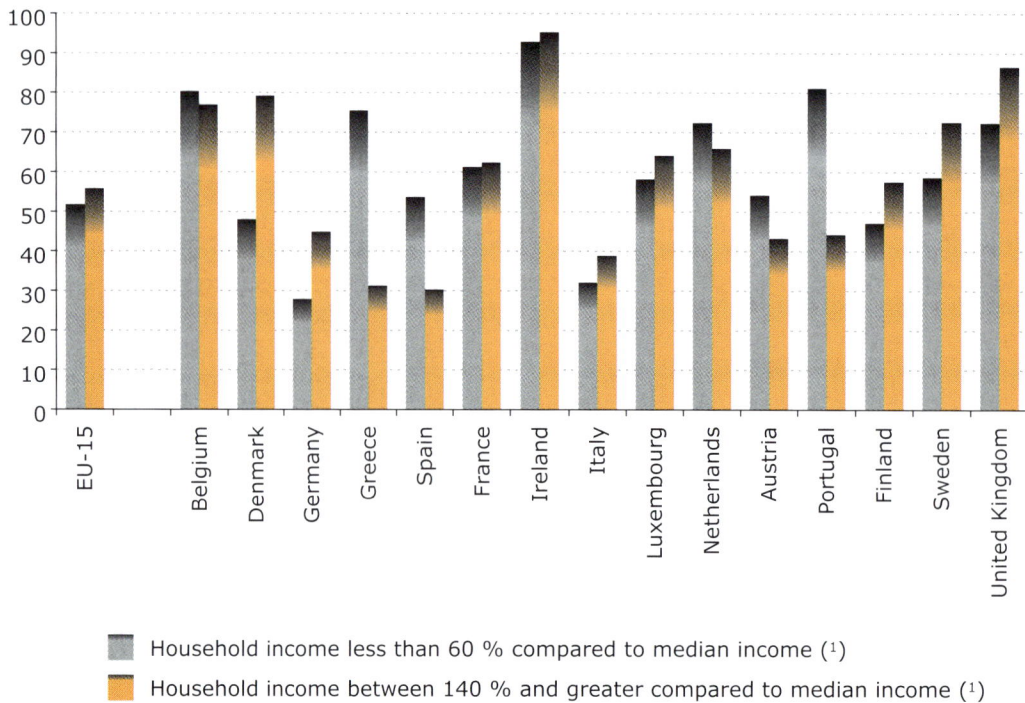

Household income less than 60 % compared to median income (¹)

Household income between 140 % and greater compared to median income (¹)

(¹) Median actual current income.

The indicator shows the share of all households that are situated in single, attached or detached house (versus flat or other accommodation). Four income groups: lower than 60 % of the median income of all households; 60 % to 100 %; 100 % to 140 %; greater than 140 %.

Share of households owning their accommodation, EU-15 in 2001
In %

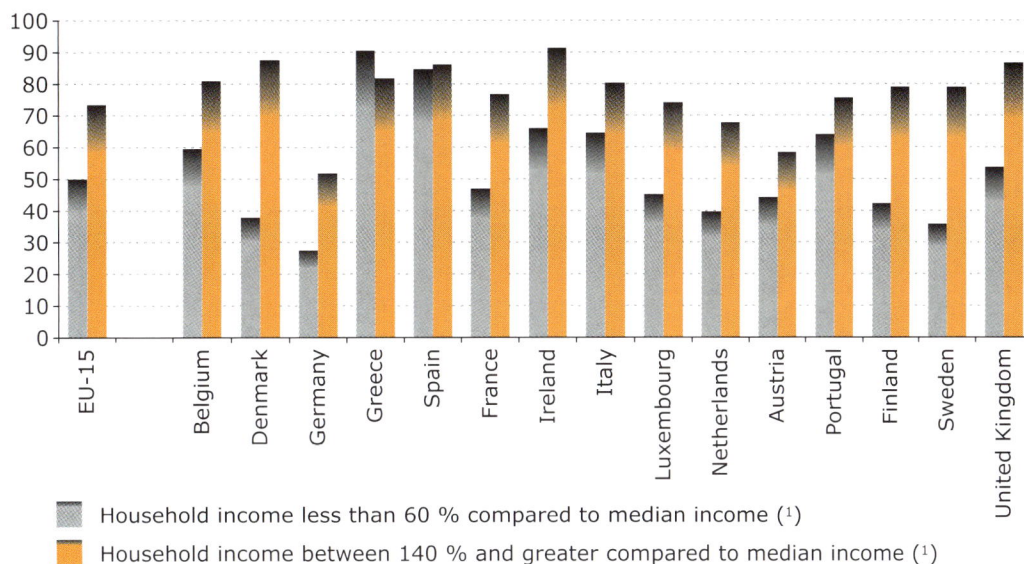

Household income less than 60 % compared to median income [1]

Household income between 140 % and greater compared to median income [1]

[1] Median actual current income.

The indicator shows the share of all households that are owner of their accommodation. Four income groups: lower than 60 % of the median income of all households; 60 % to 100 %; 100 % to 140 %; greater than 140 %.

Share of households with/without financial burden due to housing costs, EU-15 in 2001
In %

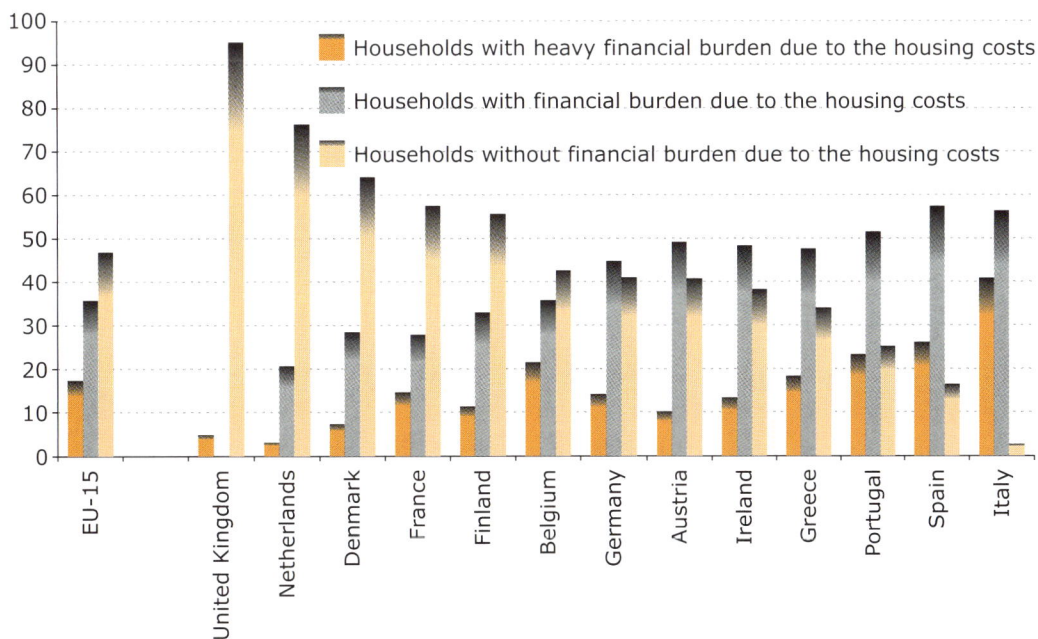

Households with heavy financial burden due to the housing costs

Households with financial burden due to the housing costs

Households without financial burden due to the housing costs

No data for Luxembourg and Sweden.

This indicator shows the share of households that have a financial burden, a very heavy financial burden or no financial burden due to the housing costs.

Share of households living in overcrowded houses, EU-15 in 2001
In %

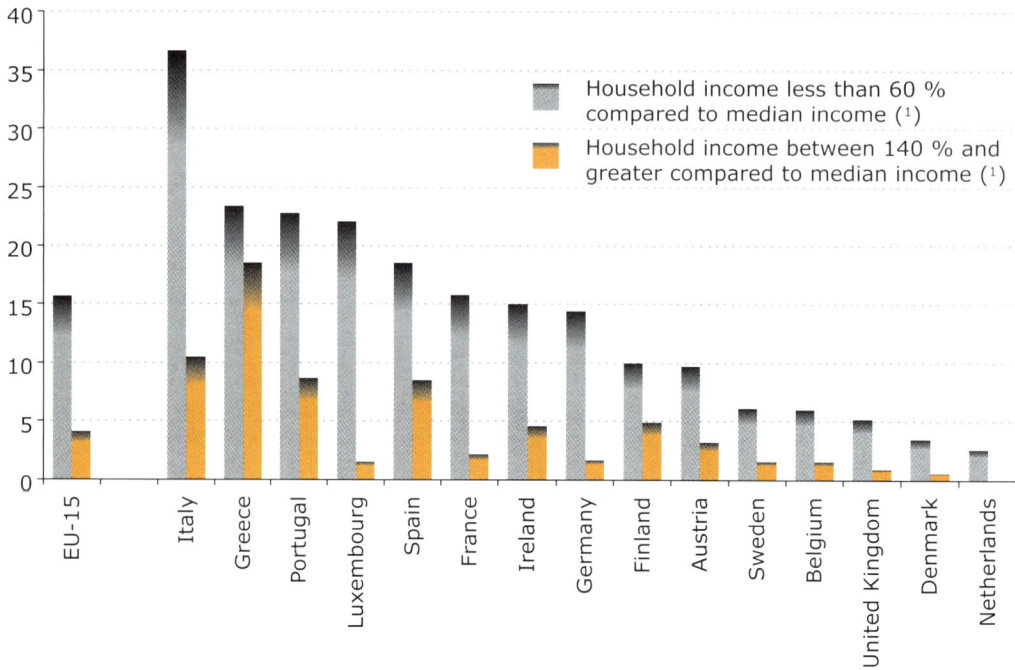

Legend:
- Household income less than 60 % compared to median income ([1])
- Household income between 140 % and greater compared to median income ([1])

([1]) Median actual current income.

The indicator shows the share of all persons that live in overcrowded conditions (more than one person per room). Four income groups: lower than 60 % of the median income of all households; 60 % to 100 %; 100 % to 140 %; greater than 140 %.

Rooms per person, EU-15 in 2001
By tenure status

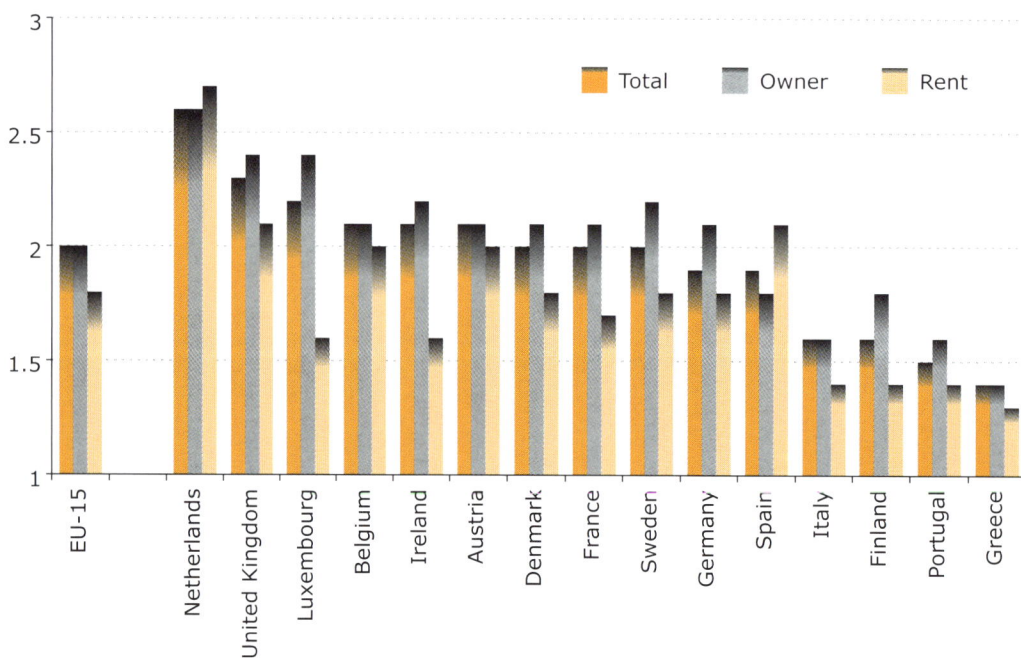

Legend: Total, Owner, Rent

This indicator shows the number of rooms that each person in a household has in his disposal by tenure status of the household.

Social protection

Social protection: relieving the burden

Social protection encompasses all action by public or private bodies to relieve households and individuals of the burden of a defined set of risks or needs associated with old age, sickness, childbearing and family, disability, unemployment, etc.

The eight 'functions' to classify social protection benefits

Social protection expenditure includes provision of social benefits, administration costs and other expenditure (for example, interest paid to banks). Benefits provision represents the core of social protection expenditure. Expenditure on education is excluded.

Social benefits are direct transfers in cash or kind by social protection schemes to households and individuals to relieve them of the burden of distinct risks or needs. Benefits via the fiscal system are excluded.

Benefits are classified according to eight social protection 'functions':

1. **Sickness/healthcare benefits** include mainly paid sick leave, medical care and provision of pharmaceutical products.

2. **Disability benefits** include mainly disability pensions and the provision of goods and services (other than medical care) to the disabled.

3. **Old-age benefits** include mainly old-age pensions and the provision of goods and

services (other than medical care) to the elderly.

4. **Survivors' benefits** include income maintenance and support in connection with the death of a family member, such as survivors' pensions.

5. **Family/children benefits** include support (except healthcare) in connection with the costs of pregnancy, childbirth, childbearing and caring for other family members.

6. **Unemployment benefits** also include vocational training financed by public agencies.

7. **Housing benefits** include interventions by public authorities to help households meet the cost of housing.

8. **Social exclusion benefits** include income support, rehabilitation of alcohol and drug abusers and other miscellaneous benefits (except healthcare).

2

Financing social protection

Units responsible for providing social protection are financed in different ways. Their receipts comprise social contributions paid by employers and by protected persons, contributions by general government and other receipts. Other receipts come from a variety of sources, for example interest, dividends, rent and claims against third parties.

Social contributions are paid by employers and by the protected persons.

Social contributions by employers are all costs incurred by employers to secure employees' entitlement to social benefits. These include all payments by employers to social protection institutions (actual contributions) and social benefits paid directly by employers to employees (imputed contributions). Social contributions by protected persons comprise contributions paid by employees, by the self-employed and by pensioners and other persons.

Social benefits are recorded without any deduction of taxes or other compulsory levies payable on them by beneficiaries. 'Tax benefits' (tax reductions granted to households for social protection purposes) are generally excluded.

Esspros: the statistical tool to compare social policy

The data on social protection expenditure and receipts are harmonised according to the European system of integrated social protection statistics (Esspros). Built on the concept of functions of social protection and according to a common methodology, Esspros is a unique tool to compare the social policy of the various European countries. The comparisons can relate, for example, to the way in which the social needs or risks are covered or to the effort provided by the countries for their satisfaction. Esspros also allows an analysis in terms of organisation of social protection because it is built on the basis of 'statistical units' charged to provide the households or the individuals with the various social benefits.

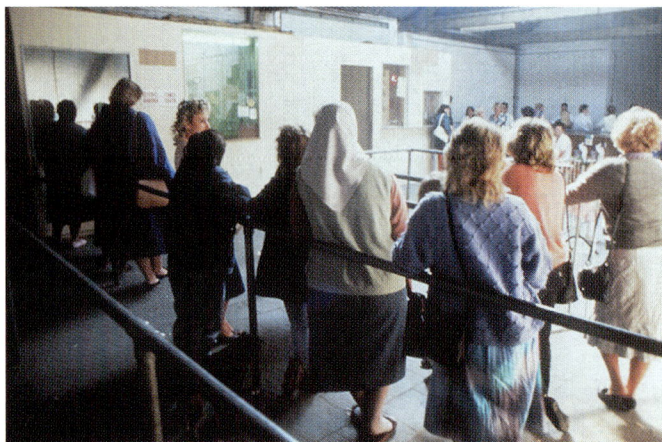

Total expenditure on social protection
At current prices; in % of GDP

	1990	1991	1992	1993	1994	1995	1996	1997	1998	1999	2000	2001
EU-25	:	:	:	:	:	:	:	:	:	:	:	:
EU-15	25.4	26.4	27.7	28.7	28.4	28.2	28.4	28	27.5	27.4(p)	27.3(e)	27.5(e)
Euro-zone	:	:	:	:	:	:	:	:	:	:	:	:
Belgium	26.4	27	27.7	29.3	28.7	28.1	28.6	27.9	27.6	27.3(p)	26.8(e)	27.5(e)
Czech Republic	:	:	:	:	:	:	:	:	:	:	:	:
Denmark	28.7	29.7	30.3	31.9	32.8	32.2	31.4	30.4	30.2	30	29.2	29.5
Germany	25.4	26.1	27.6	28.4	28.3	28.9	29.9	29.5	29.3	29.6	29.6	29.8(p)
Estonia	:	:	:	:	:	:	:	:	:	:	:	:
Greece	22.9	21.5	21.2	22	22.1	22.3	22.9	23.3	24.2	25.5	26.3	27.2
Spain	19.9	21.2	22.4	24	22.8	22.1	21.9	21.2	20.6	20.2(p)	20.2(p)	20.0(p)
France	27.9	28.4	29.3	30.7	30.5	30.7	31	30.8	30.5	30.2	29.8	30.0(p)
Ireland	18.4	19.6	20.3	20.2	19.7	18.9	17.8	16.6	15.4	14.7	14.1	14.6(p)
Italy	24.7	25.2	26.2	26.4	26	24.8	24.8	25.5	25	25.2	25.2(p)	25.6(p)
Cyprus	:	:	:	:	:	:	:	:	:	:	:	:
Latvia	:	:	:	:	:	:	:	:	:	:	:	:
Lithuania	:	:	:	:	:	:	:	:	:	:	:	:
Luxembourg	21.4	22	22.5	23.3	22.9	23.7	24.1	22.8	21.7	21.7	20.3	21.2(p)
Hungary	:	:	:	:	:	:	:	:	:	20.9(p)	20.3(p)	19.9(p)
Malta	:	:	:	:	:	:	:	:	18.8	18.4	17.9	18.3
Netherlands	31.1	31.2	31.9	32.3	31.7	30.9	30.1	29.4	28.4	28	27.4	27.6(p)
Austria	27	27.3	27.8	29.1	29.9	29.8	29.8	28.7	28.3	28.9	28.4	28.4
Poland												
Portugal	16.3	17.2	18.4	21	21.3	22.1	21.2	21.4	22.1	22.6	23	23.9(p)
Slovenia	:	:	:	:	:	:	24.7	25.2	25.3	25.2	25.4	25.6(p)
Slovakia	:	:	:	:	:	18.7	19.8	20	20.2	20.2	19.5	19.1(p)
Finland	25.1	29.8	33.6	34.5	33.8	31.7	31.6	29.2	27.2	26.8	25.5	25.8
Sweden	33.1	34.3	37.1	38.2	36.7	34.6	33.9	33	32.2	31.8	30.7	31.3(p)
United Kingdom	22.9	25.7	27.9	29	28.6	28.2	28	27.5	26.9	26.4	27.1	27.2(p)
Iceland	16.8	17.6	18.2	18.8	18.4	19	18.8	18.9	18.9	19.5	19.8	20.1
Norway	26.2	27	28.2	28.2	27.6	26.7	26	25.3	27.1	27.1	24.6	25.6

Expenditure on social protection contain: social benefits, which consist of transfers, in cash or in kind, to households and individuals to relieve them of the burden of a defined set of risks or needs; administration costs, which represent the costs charged to the scheme for its management and administration; other expenditure, which consists of miscellaneous expenditure by social protection schemes (payment of property income and other).

In 2001, 27.5 % of the GDP was spent on social protection in EU-15, 1.1 percentage point more than in 1991. The share was highest in Sweden with 31.3 %, and lowest in Ireland with 14.6 %.

Total expenditure on social protection per head of population
In PPS

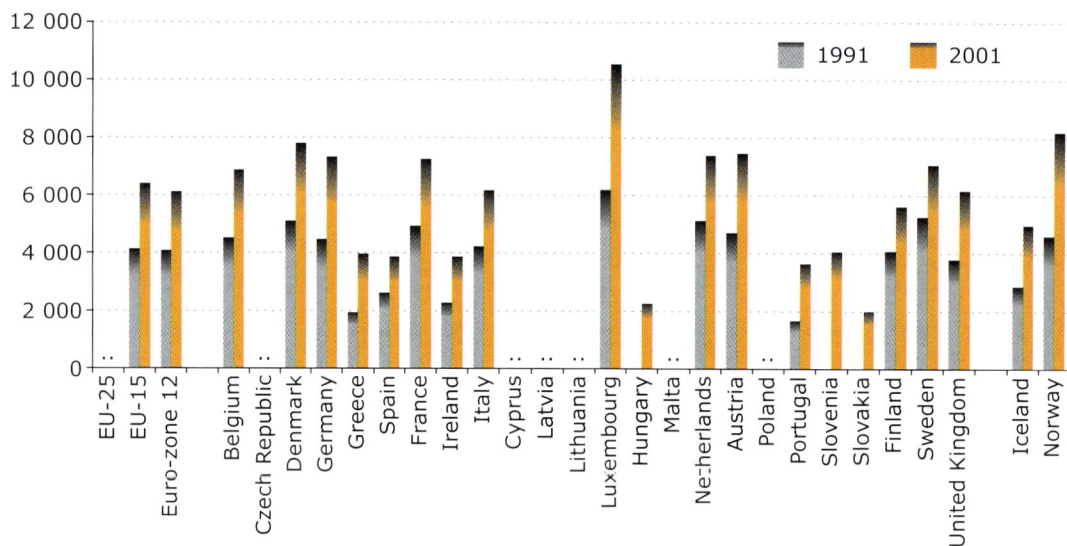

2001 EU-15, EU-25: estimated values.

Expenditure on social protection contain: social benefits, which consist of transfers, in cash or in kind, to households and individuals to relieve them of the burden of a defined set of risks or needs; administration costs, which represent the costs charged to the scheme for its management and administration; other expenditure, which consist of miscellaneous expenditure by social protection schemes (payment of property income and other).

The expenditure on social protection has also been calculated per head of the population. The unit is the purchasing power standard (PPS) that allows an unbiased comparison between countries. In 2001, the expenditure on social protection was about 6 405 PPS per head in EU-15, ranging from 10 559 PPS in Luxembourg to 3 644 PPS in Portugal. A decade earlier, the expenditure on social protection per head in EU-15 was about a third below the 2001 value.

Social benefits per head of population by function: EU-15 in 2001
In PPS

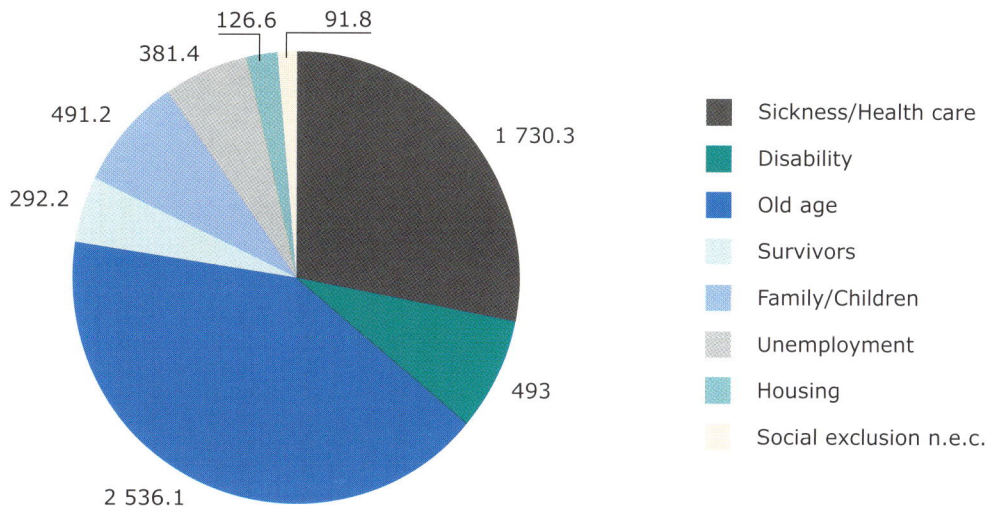

- Sickness/Health care
- Disability
- Old age
- Survivors
- Family/Children
- Unemployment
- Housing
- Social exclusion n.e.c.

1 730.3
493
2 536.1
292.2
491.2
381.4
126.6
91.8

Estimated values.

Social benefits consist of transfers, in cash or in kind, by social protection schemes to households and individuals to relieve them of the burden of a defined set of risks or needs.

The social benefits per head are presented by the abovementioned functions. The highest amount is spent on the elderly (2 536 PPS in EU-15 in 2001), followed by benefits for sickness and healthcare (1 730 PPS in EU-15 in 2001). About 38.8 % of the social protection receipts were financed by the employers, 36.0 % by the government and 21.7 % by the protected persons themselves.

Social protection receipts by type: EU-15 in 2001
In % of total receipts

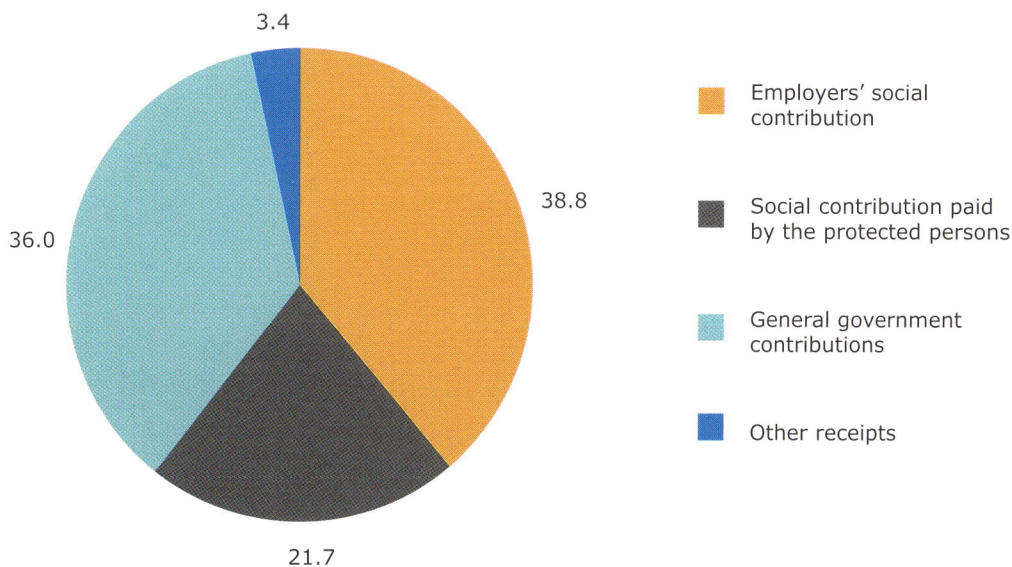

- Employers' social contribution
- Social contribution paid by the protected persons
- General government contributions
- Other receipts

3.4
38.8
36.0
21.7

Estimated values.

Receipts of social protection schemes comprise social contributions, general government contributions and other receipts. Employers' social contributions are the costs incurred by employers to secure entitlement to social benefits for their employees, former employees and their dependants. Employers' social contributions may be actual or imputed; they can be paid by resident or non-resident employers.

The biggest share of the expenditure on social protection is actually spent on social benefits (95.9 % of the total in EU-15 in 2001).

Total expenditure on social protection by type in 2001
In % of total expenditure on social protection

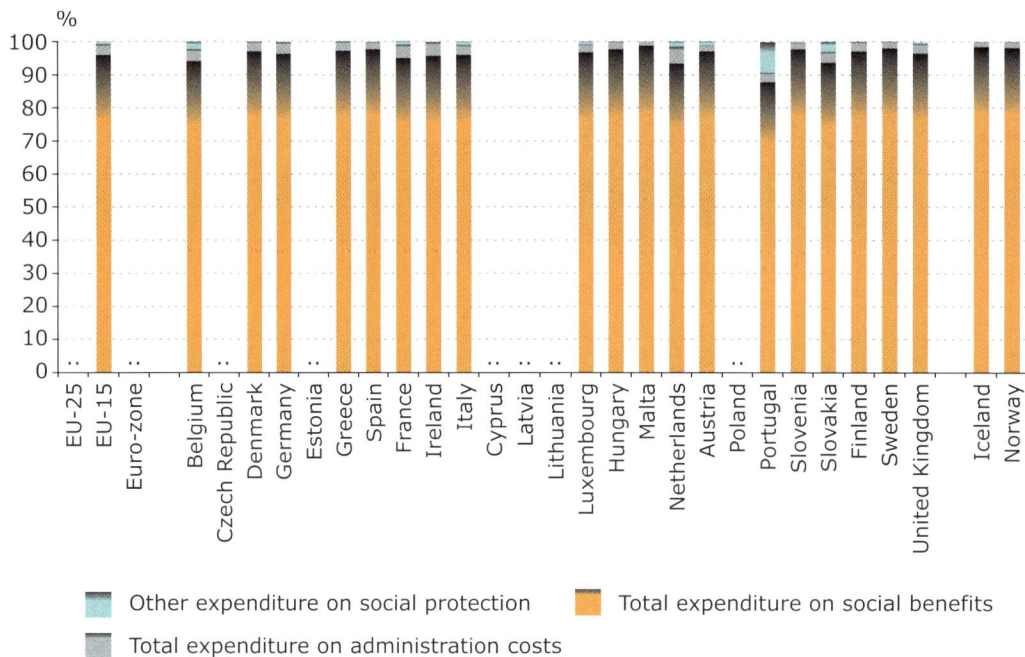

Legend:
- Other expenditure on social protection
- Total expenditure on social benefits
- Total expenditure on administration costs

EU-15, Belgium: estimated values.

Social benefits consists of transfers, in cash or in kind, to households and individuals to relieve them of the burden of a defined set of risks or needs. Expenditure on social protection contain: social benefits, administration costs, which represent the costs charged to the scheme for its management and administration, other expenditure, which consists of miscellaneous expenditure (payment of property income and other).

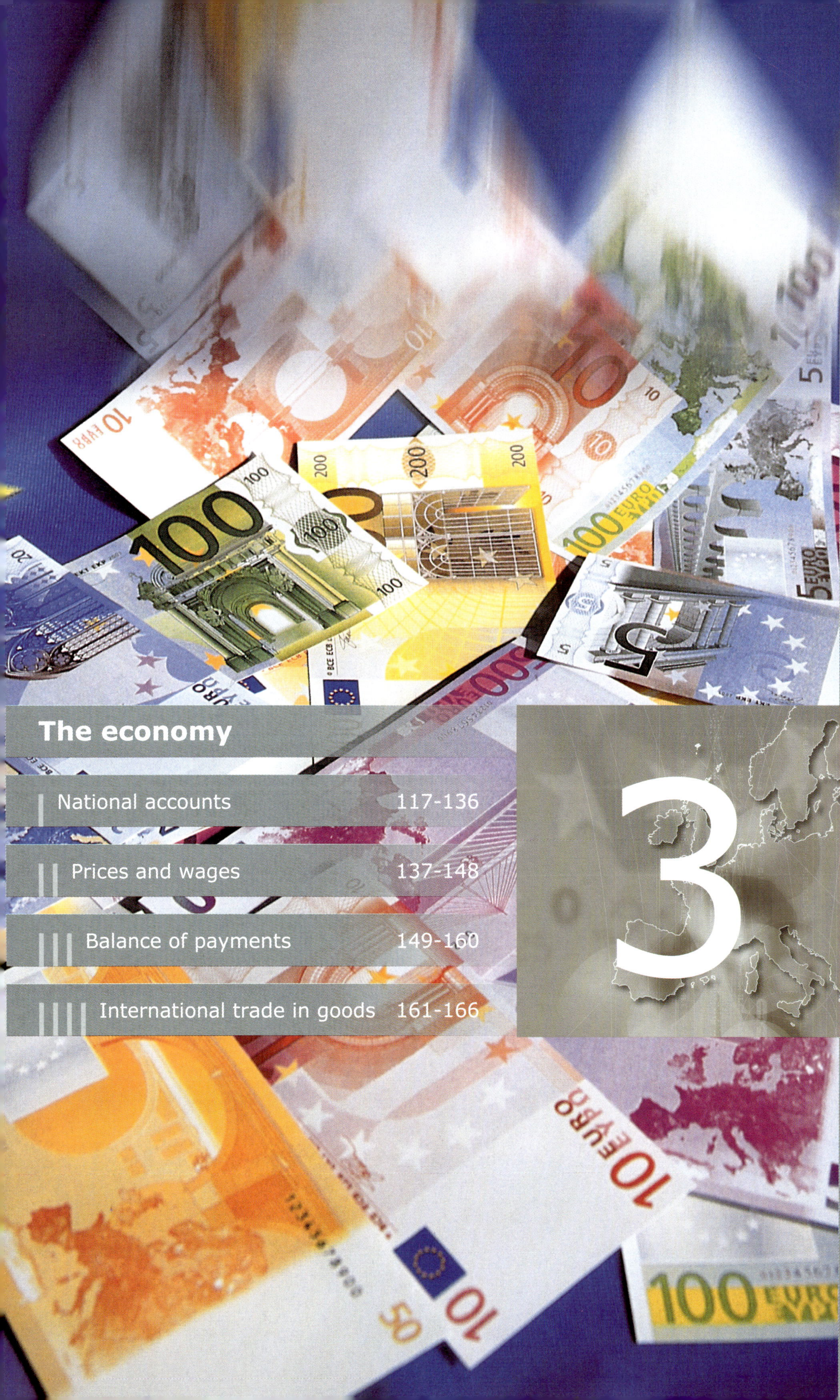

The economy

3

National accounts

National accounts – monitoring the state of the economy

The national accounts provide a comprehensive and consistent framework to measure the level and structure of economic activity. This framework of accounts provides many key macroeconomic statistics including Gross Domestic Product (GDP), production, income, consumption, exports and imports.

National accounts shed light on both the supply and the demand side of an economy. They are compiled for regions, Member States and the European Union. The accounts show which sectors of the economy are particularly important for GDP and economic growth; how much of the income generated in the economic process is retained by enterprises and what amount is received by households and government; how much of the income is spent on consumption goods and investment, and how high savings are.

These features make national accounts particularly relevant for economic analysis, decision-taking and policy-making.

ESA95 – a common standard for national accounts in Europe

In Europe, national accounts are compiled according to fully harmonised standards which are laid down in the European System of National and Regional Accounts (ESA 95). ESA 95 is the subject of council regulation 2223/96 which entered into force in 1996 and is thus legally binding for all European Union Member States. This common methodology ensures the full comparability of national accounts data across economic areas, and all national accounts data in this publication are according to this standard. The ESA95 is the European version of the world-wide guidelines, the System of National Accounts (SNA93). SNA93 was prepared and published jointly by the Commission of the European Communities, the International Monetary Fund, the Organisation for Economic Co-operation and Development, the Statistics Division of the former Department for Economic and Social Information and Policy Analysis and the regional commissions of the United Nations Secretariat, and the World Bank.

3

Gross domestic product per inhabitant in PPS
At current market prices

	1994	1995	1996	1997	1998	1999	2000	2001	2002	2003	2004	2005
EU-25	:	:	:	:	18 470	19 400	20 630	21 300	21 990	22 280 (f)	23 160 (f)	24 120 (f)
EU-15	17 060	17 680	18 530	19 460	20 330	21 340	22 660	23 340	24 040	24 360	25 690 (f)	27 160 (f)
Euro-zone	17 220	17 840	18 640	19 480	20 380	21 370	22 650	23 010	23 630	23 800 (f)	24 660 (f)	25 580 (f)
Belgium	18 510	19 190	19 870	20 750	21 430	22 470	24 110	24 970	25 620	25 900 (f)	26 830 (f)	27 860 (f)
Czech Republic	:	:	:	:	:	:	13 530	14 100	14 820 (f)	15 410 (f)	16 230 (f)	17 190 (f)
Denmark	19 210	19 940	21 100	22 260	23 050	24 710	26 180	26 930	27 000 (f)	27 310 (f)	28 400 (f)	29 440 (f)
Germany	18 520	19 060	19 850	20 450	21 130	21 990	23 120	23 460	23 950 (f)	24 080 (f)	24 900 (f)	25 770 (f)
Estonia	5 260	5 510	5 980	6 810	7 280	7 510	8 490	9 020	9 650 (f)	10 560 (f)	11 480 (f)	12 840 (f)
Greece	11 340	11 520	12 000	12 750	13 260	13 930	14 950	15 680 (f)	16 990 (f)	17 760 (f)	18 880 (f)	19 870 (f)
Spain	13 420	13 970	14 730	15 510	16 460	17 820	18 900	19 670	20 710 (f)	21 250 (f)	22 190 (f)	23 260 (f)
France	17 890	18 400	19 150	20 240	21 160	22 180	23 530	24 460	25 240 (f)	25 280 (f)	26 150 (f)	27 180 (f)
Ireland	14 350	15 870	17 360	19 910	21 600	23 720	26 080	27 480	30 160 (f)	29 360 (f)	30 370 (f)	31 950 (f)
Italy	17 670	18 420	19 270	19 940	20 990	21 750	22 960	23 370 (f)	23 680 (f)	23 900 (f)	24 600 (f)	25 560 (f)
Cyprus	13 130	13 320	13 740	14 230	14 960	15 900	17 280	18 290	18 380	18 840 (f)	19 550 (f)	20 500 (f)
Latvia	4 530	4 640	5 010	5 630	6 050	6 430	7 140	7 790	8 370 (f)	8 940 (f)	9 680 (f)	10 490 (f)
Lithuania	4 740	5 040	6 070	6 710	7 340	7 440	8 109	8 850	9 570 (f)	10 630 (f)	11 610 (f)	12 620 (f)
Luxembourg	28 120	28 540	29 810	32 610	35 620	40 370	45 080	45 330	45 630 (f)	46 370 (f)	47 920 (f)	50 100 (f)
Hungary	7 900	7 930	8 280	8 910	9 510	10 200	11 050	12 020	12 830 (f)	13 370 (f)	14 130 (f)	14 940 (f)
Malta	:	:	:	:	:	15 050	16 110	16 110	16 530 (f)	16 690 (f)	17 170 (f)	17 780 (f)
Netherlands	18 460	19 200	20 190	21 370	22 380	23 410	25 100	26 460	26 800 (f)	26 630 (f)	27 270 (f)	27 970 (f)
Austria	19 660	20 240	21 280	22 050	22 960	24 260	25 920	26 140	26 680 (f)	26 990 (f)	27 910 (f)	28 990 (f)
Poland	:	6 810	7 250	7 350	8 210	8 920	9 460	9 770	10 010 (f)	10 340 (f)	10 940 (f)	11 600 (f)
Portugal	11 070	11 670	12 260	13 070	13 920	14 980	15 950	16 480	17 050 (f)	16 740 (f)	17 110 (f)	17 680 (f)
Slovenia	10 670	10 950	11 670	12 580	13 250	14 340	15 160	15 920	16 710 (f)	17 200 (f)	18 070 (f)	19 090 (f)
Slovakia	7 740	7 120	7 730	8 370	8 820	9 160	9 920	10 430	11 340 (f)	11 740 (f)	12 240 (f)	12 860 (f)
Finland	16 149	16 890	17 750	19 570	20 980	21 660	23 590	24 320	24 490 (f)	24 580 (f)	25 500 (f)	26 420 (f)
Sweden	17 980	18 890	19 740	20 540	21 240	22 980	24 720	24 790	25 190 (f)	25 410 (f)	26 260 (f)	27 220 (f)
United Kingdom	16 960	17 660	18 740	20 160	21 010	21 980	23 560	24 540	25 840 (f)	26 490 (f)	27 820 (f)	29 010 (f)
Iceland	19 870	19 960	21 470	22 370	23 730	24 830	26 000	26 750	26 250 (f)	26 140 (f)	27 510 (f)	29 420 (f)
Norway	20 090	21 170	23 490	25 070	24 670	27 460	33 320	33 700	32 810 (f)	32 970 (f)	34 080 (f)	35 000 (f)
Canada	19 630	20 440	21 960	23 230	23 900	24 870	27 510 (f)	27 910 (f)	28 270 (f)	29 230 (f)	30 290 (f)	31 490 (f)
Japan	20 370	20 930	22 550	23 430	23 470	22 680	24 050	24 350 (f)	24 220 (f)	24 820 (f)	26 060 (f)	27 090 (f)
United States	25 080	25 710	26 730	28 340	29 640	30 480	32 280	32 560	33 010 (f)	33 740 (f)	35 320 (f)	36 660 (f)

(f): forecasts

GDP (gross domestic product) is an indicator for a nation's economic situation. It reflects the total value of all goods and services produced less the value of goods and services used for intermediate consumption in their production. Expressing GDP in PPS (purchasing power standards) eliminates differences in price levels between countries, and calculation on a per head basis allows the comparison of economies significantly different in absolute size.

Gross domestic product (GDP) is an indicator for a nation's economic situation. It is equal to the value of all goods and services either consumed, invested, put in inventories or exported, minus the value of goods and services imported. To compare economies of different sizes and with different price levels, Eurostat has calculated the indicator 'GDP per inhabitant in purchasing power standards'.

Economic output

Eurostat data

Eurostat provides a wide range of data on economic output, broken down by the branches of the economy that have generated it:

— Agriculture, hunting and forestry
— Fishing
— Mining and quarrying
— Manufacturing
— Energy (electricity, gas, etc.) and water supply
— Construction
— Services (wholesale and repair, hotels and restaurants, transport, storage, communication, finance, real estate, renting, business, public administration and defence, compulsory social security, education, health and social work, etc.)
— Miscellaneous (community, social and personal services, etc.)

GDP: the result of all production activity

Gross domestic product (GDP) at market prices is the final result of the production activity of resident producer units. It can be defined in three ways:

— GDP is the sum of gross value added of the various institutional sectors or the various industries, plus taxes and less subsidies on products (which are not allocated to sectors and industries).
— GDP is the sum of final uses of goods and services by resident institutional units (final consumption and gross capital formation), plus exports and minus imports of goods and services (expenditure approach).
— GDP is the sum of compensation of employees, taxes on production and imports less subsidies and gross operating surplus, and mixed income of the total economy (income approach) (ESA 95, 8.89).

In these tables, GDP corresponds to the economy's output of goods and services less intermediate consumption, plus taxes less subsidies on products. Valuation at constant prices means valuing the flows and stocks in an accounting period at the prices of the reference period (ESA 95, 1.56).

GDP per person

GDP, and in particular GDP per capita, is one of the main indicators for economic analysis as well as spatial and/or temporal international comparisons.

In order to facilitate these international comparisons, the GDP in national currency of each Member State is converted into a common currency (ecu until 1998, euro from the beginning of 1999) by means of its official exchange rate. However, the exchange rate does not necessarily reflect the actual purchasing power of each national currency on its economic territory.

In order to remove price-level differences, purchasing power parities (PPPs) are calculated and used as a factor of conversion (exchange

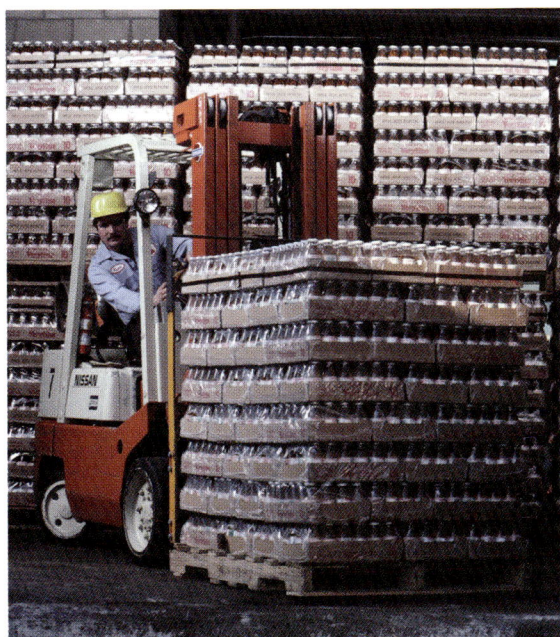

rate from national currency to PPS). These parities are obtained as a weighted average of relative price ratios regarding a homogeneous basket of goods and services, comparable and representative for each Member State.

The 'comparable volume' values of GDP obtained in this way are hence expressed in terms of purchasing power standards (PPS), a unit that is independent of any national currency.

Gross value added

Gross value added is recorded at basic prices. It is the net result of output valued at basic prices less intermediate consumption valued at purchasers' prices (ESA 95, 9.23). The basic price is the price receivable by the producers from the purchaser for a unit of a good or service produced as output minus any tax payable on that unit as a consequence of its production or sale (i.e. taxes on products), plus any subsidy receivable on that unit as a consequence of its production or sale (i.e. subsidies on products). It excludes any transport charges invoiced separately by the producer. It includes any transport margins charged by the producer on the same invoice, even when they are included as a separate item on the invoice (ESA 95, 3.48).

Gross domestic product at current market prices
In million ECU/EUR

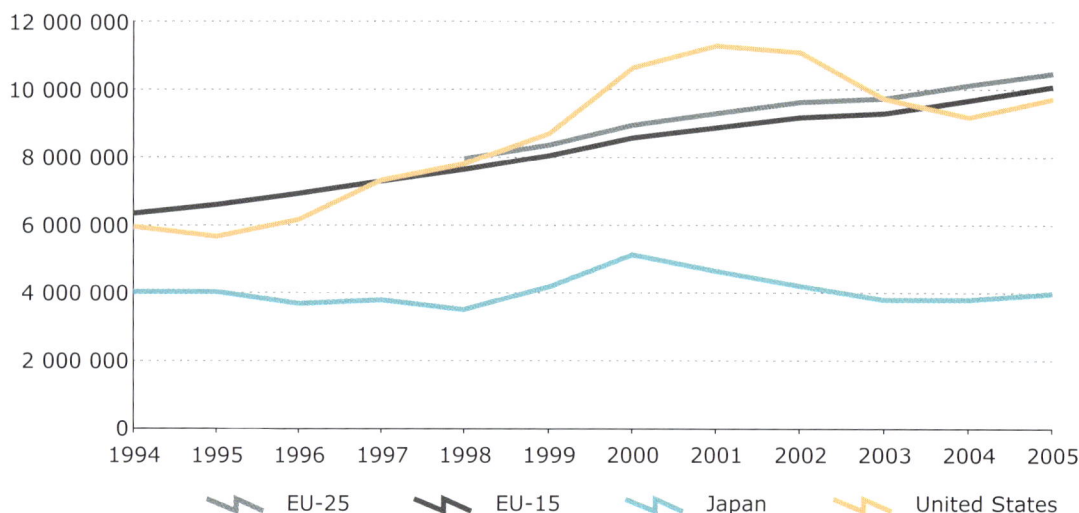

2004 and 2005: forecast; 2003 EU-15 and Japan: forecast.

GDP (gross domestic product) is an indicator for a nation´s economic situation. It reflects the total value of all goods and services produced less the value of goods and services used for intermediate consumption in their production. Expressing GDP in PPS (purchasing power standards) eliminates differences in price levels between countries, and calculations on a per head basis allows the comparison of economies significantly different in absolute size.

GDP per inhabitant in PPS in 1995 and 2005
EU-15 =100

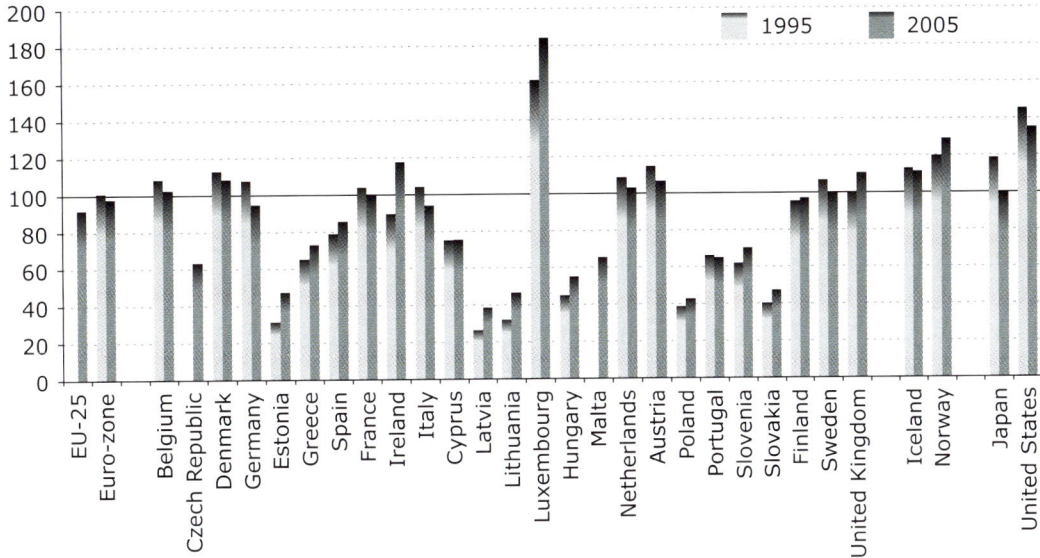

Legend: 1995, 2005

Countries (x-axis): EU-25, Euro-zone, Belgium, Czech Republic, Denmark, Germany, Estonia, Greece, Spain, France, Ireland, Italy, Cyprus, Latvia, Lithuania, Luxembourg, Hungary, Malta, Netherlands, Austria, Poland, Portugal, Slovenia, Slovakia, Finland, Sweden, United Kingdom, Iceland, Norway, Japan, United States

2005: forecast.

Gross domestic product (GDP) is a measure for the economic activity. It is defined as the value of all goods and services produced less the value of any goods or services used in their creation. The volume index of GDP per capita in purchasing power standards (PPS) is expressed in relation to the European Union (EU-15) average set to equal 100. If the index of a country is higher than 100, this country's level of GDP per head is higher than the EU average and vice versa. Basic figures are expressed in PPS, i.e. a common currency that eliminates the differences in price levels between countries allowing meaningful volume comparisons of GDP between countries. Please note that the index, calculated from PPS figures and expressed with respect to EU-15 = 100, is intended for cross-country comparisons rather than for temporal comparisons.

Real GDP growth rate
Growth rate of GDP at constant prices (1995) — percentage change on previous year

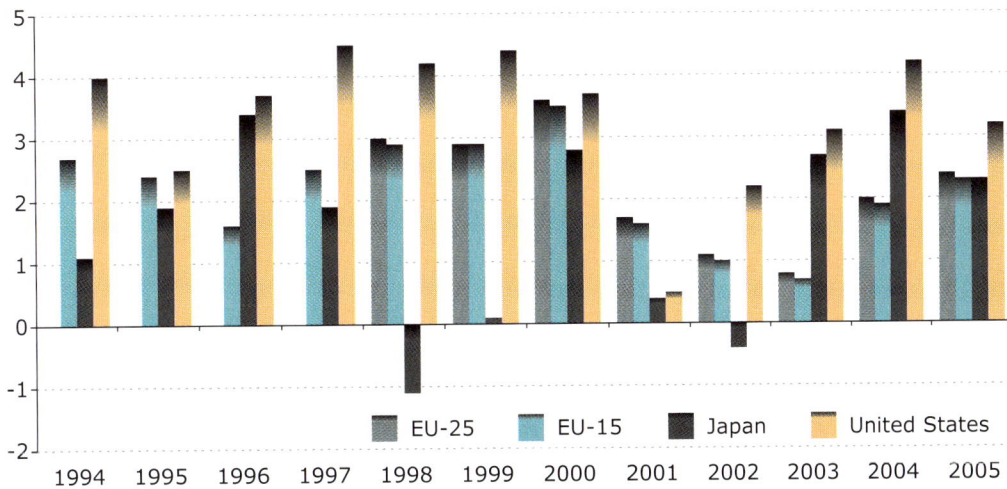

Legend: EU-25, EU-15, Japan, United States

Years (x-axis): 1994, 1995, 1996, 1997, 1998, 1999, 2000, 2001, 2002, 2003, 2004, 2005

2004 and 2005: forecast; 2003 EU-25 and Japan: forecast.

Gross domestic product (GDP) is a measure for the economic activity. It is defined as the value of all goods and services produced less the value of any goods or services used in their creation. The calculation of the annual growth rate of GDP at constant prices is intended to allow comparisons of the dynamics of economic development both over time and between economies of different sizes. The growth rate is calculated from figures at constant prices since these give volume movements only, i.e. price movements will not inflate the growth rate.

Labour productivity in 1993 and 2003

GDP in purchasing power standards (PPS) per hour worked, relative to the EU-15 (= 100)

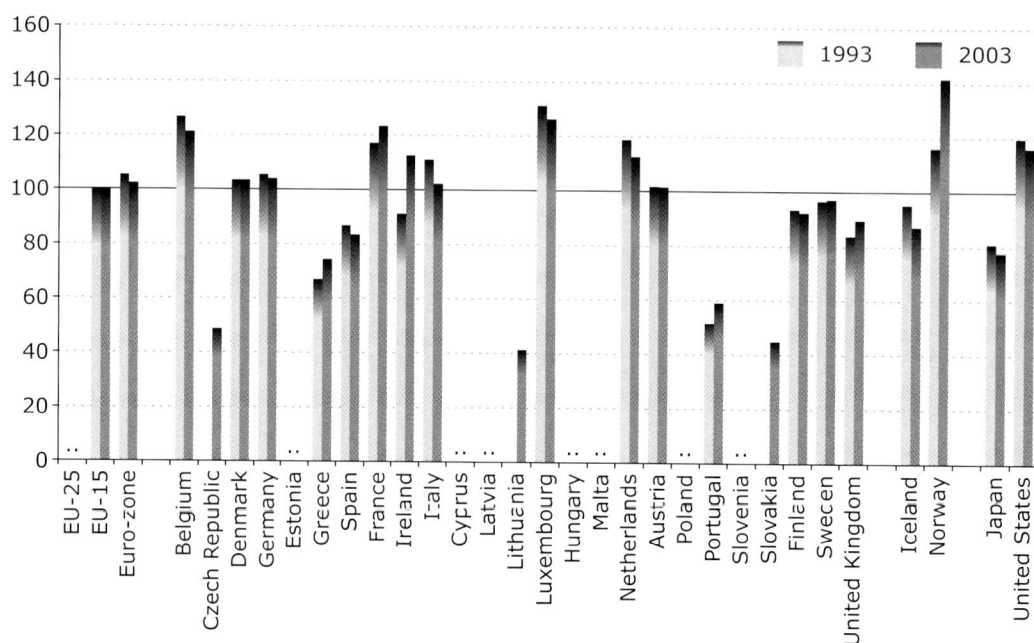

1993: estimated values; 2003: forecasts.

Gross domestic product (GDP) is a measure for the economic activity in an economy. It is defined as the value of all goods and services produced less the value of any goods or services used in their creation. GDP per hour worked gives a picture of the productivity of national economies expressed in relation to the European Union (EU-15) average. If the index of a country is higher than 100, this country's level of GDP per hour worked is higher than the EU average and vice versa. Basic figures are expressed in PPS, i.e. a common currency that eliminates the differences in price levels between countries allowing meaningful volume comparisons of GDP between countries. Expressing productivity per hour worked will eliminate differences in the full-time/part-time composition of the workforce.

Consumption and spending

Central to both structural and business-cycle analysis of the economy

National accounts aggregates on consumption and spending are used by the European Central Bank and Commission services, in particular the Directorate-General for Economic and Financial Affairs, as important tools for structural economic analysis and policy decisions. The respective quarterly series are central to business-cycle analysis and subsequent policy decisions. These series are also widely employed for supporting business decisions in the private sector, in particular on financial markets.

Final consumption: 'spending' the GDP

Following the expenditure approach, the tables in this section show by broad category what GDP has been used for. The main domestic expenditure categories are consumption on one hand and investment on the other; domestically produced goods and services may also be exported. The counterpart to exports are imports, which can be consumed or invested without being the result of domestic production activity. Exports minus imports, i.e. the external balance, is the net contribution of external trade to GDP.

— **Private final consumption expenditure** includes households' and NPISHs' final consumption expenditure, i.e. their expenditure on goods or services that are used for the direct satisfaction of individual needs. NPISHs consist of non-profit institutions which are separate legal entities, which serve households and which are private non-market producers. Their principal resources, apart from those derived from occasional sales, are derived from voluntary contributions in cash or in kind from households in their capacity as consumers, from payments made by general governments and from property income.

— **Government final consumption expenditure** (ESA 95, 3.79) includes two categories of expenditure: the value of goods and services produced by general government itself other than own-account capital formation and sales, and purchases by general government of goods and services produced by market producers that are supplied to households — without any transformation — as social transfers in kind.

— **Gross fixed capital formation** (ESA 95, 3.102) consists of resident producers' acquisitions, less disposals, of fixed assets during a given period plus certain additions to the value of non-produced assets realised by productive activity. Fixed assets are tangible or intangible assets produced as outputs from processes of production that are themselves used repeatedly, or continuously, in processes of production for more than one year.

— **Changes in inventories** (ESA 95, 3.117) are measured by the value of the entries into inventories less the value of withdrawals and the value of any recurrent losses of goods held in inventories.

— **External balance** (ESA 95, 8.68): imports of goods and services are recorded on the resources side of the account and exports of goods and services on the uses side. The difference between resources and uses is the balancing item in the account, called 'external balance of goods and services'.

Expenditure components of the EU-25's GDP in 2003
In % of total GDP

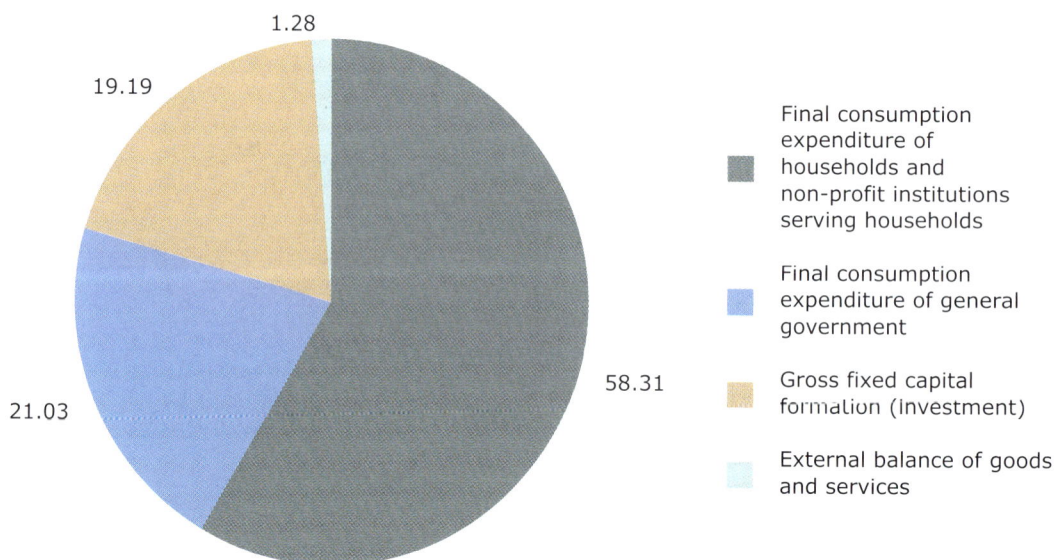

1.28
19.19
21.03
58.31

Final consumption expenditure of households and non-profit institutions serving households

Final consumption expenditure of general government

Gross fixed capital formation (investment)

External balance of goods and services

In 2003, there has been a negative change in inventories of about 0.2 % of GDP in the EU-25. Estimated values.

Final consumption expenditure of households and non-profit institutions serving households
Share in the GDP in %

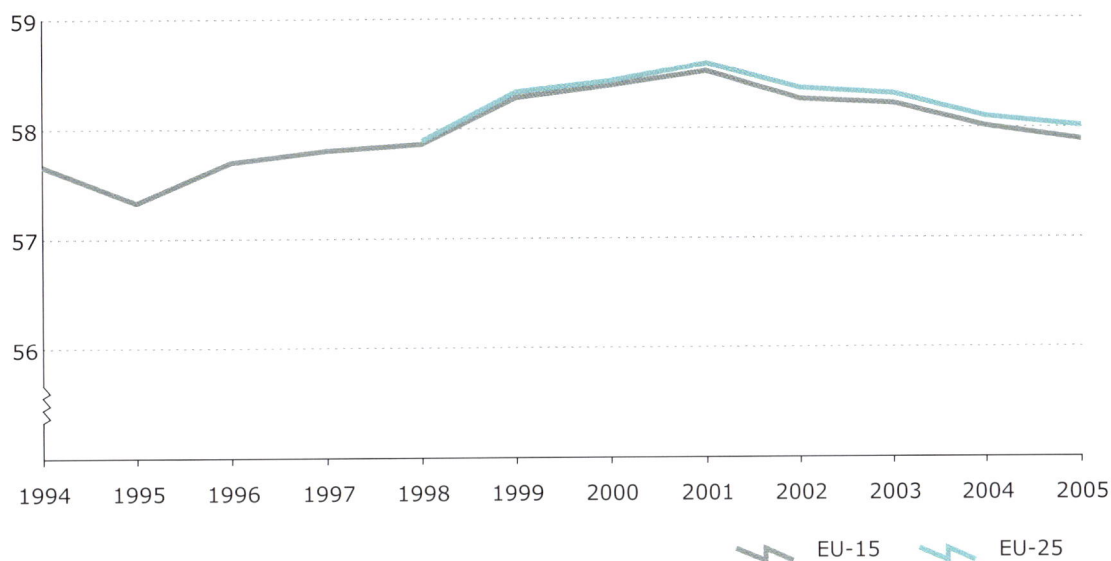

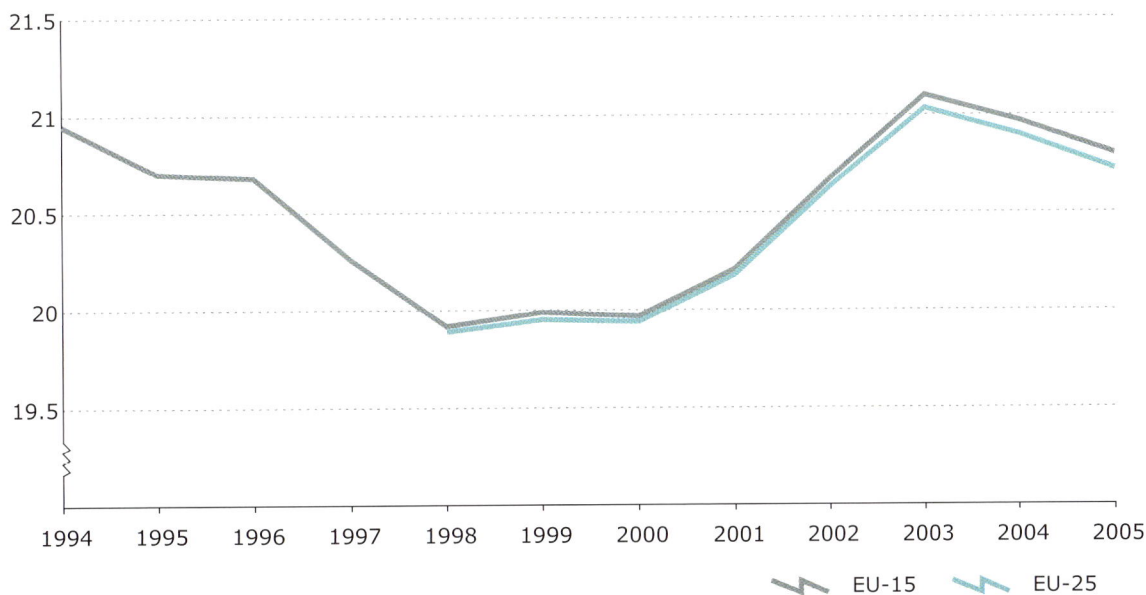

2004 and 2005: forecast; EU-25 2003: forecast.

In 2003, 58.3 % of the GDP of today's EU-25 was spent by households on consumption. Two years before, this share touched 58.6 % of GDP; it is forecast to fall to about 58 % by 2005.

Final consumption expenditure of general government
Share in the GDP in %

2004 and 2005: forecast; EU-25 2003: forecast.

Gross fixed capital formation (Investment) in 2003
Share in the GDP in %

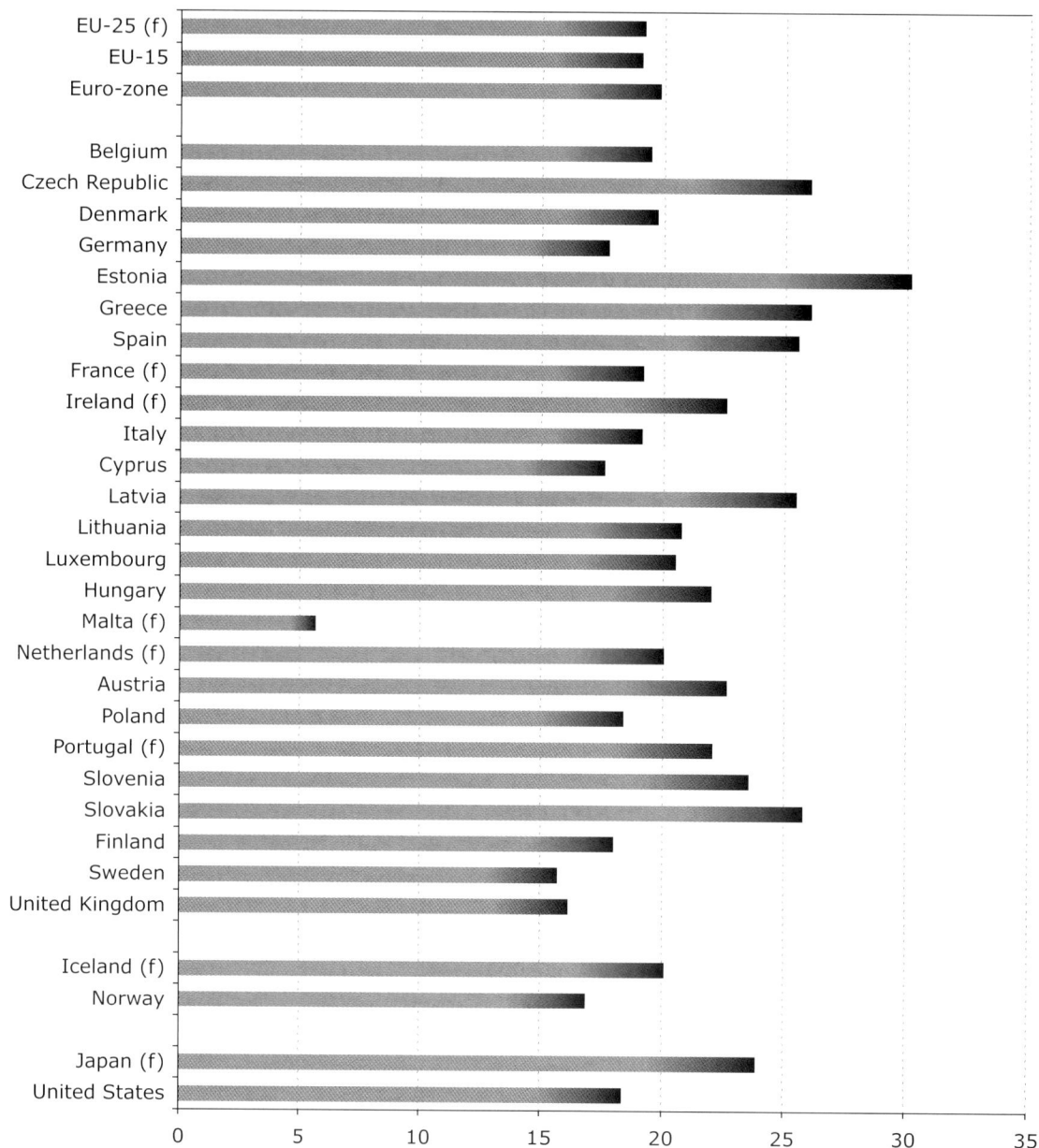

EU-25 (f)	
EU-15	
Euro-zone	
Belgium	
Czech Republic	
Denmark	
Germany	
Estonia	
Greece	
Spain	
France (f)	
Ireland (f)	
Italy	
Cyprus	
Latvia	
Lithuania	
Luxembourg	
Hungary	
Malta (f)	
Netherlands (f)	
Austria	
Poland	
Portugal (f)	
Slovenia	
Slovakia	
Finland	
Sweden	
United Kingdom	
Iceland (f)	
Norway	
Japan (f)	
United States	

(axis: 0 5 10 15 20 25 30 35)

(f): forecast.

Gross fixed capital formation consists of resident producers' acquisitions, less disposals, of fixed tangible or intangible assets. This covers in particular machinery and equipment, vehicles, dwellings and other buildings.

In 2003, about 21.0 % of EU-25's GDP was consumption expenditure of general government, while about 19.2 % of the GDP was invested. In 2000, when the share of investment in GDP peaked at 20.8 %, it exceeded consumption expenditure of general government which, at that time, stood at about 19.9 %. The European Commission forecasts that the current trend of an increased share of government expenditure and a falling one of investment will be reversed: by 2005, investment is forecast to go up to stand again at about 19 % of GDP, while government expenditure will be kept limited at well below the share of 2003.

External balance of goods and services
Share in the GDP in %

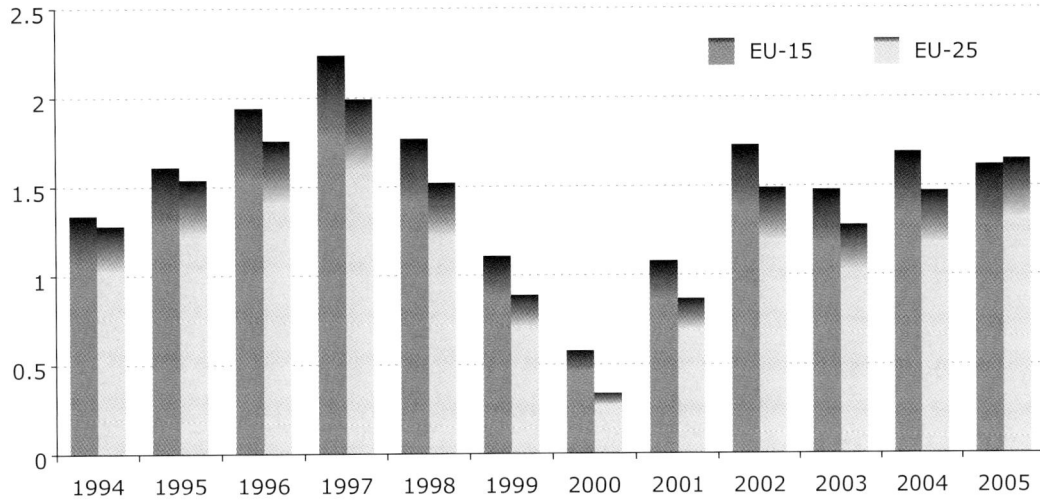

2004 and 2005: forecast; EU-25 2003: forecast.

The external balance of EU-25 is positive and amounted to nearly 1.3 % of GDP in 2003, and is forecast to rise to over 1.6 % by 2005.

Income of the input factors

Eurostat data

Eurostat provides a wide range of data on:

— Compensation of employees, including a breakdown by branch of activity
— Wages and salaries, including a breakdown by branch of activity
— Gross operating surplus and mixed income
— Taxes on production and imports
— Gross national income
— Consumption of fixed capital
— Disposable income
— Net saving of the economy
— Net lending/net borrowing of the economy

Crucial to economic analysis

Eurostat data on the income of the input factors are crucial to economic analysis in a number of contexts inside and outside the European Commission. Typical examples are studies of competitiveness, of income distribution inequalities and of long-term economic developments. Users outside the Commission include, in particular, academia and financial institutions.

Factor income: 'earning' the GDP

Producing the GDP requires 'input factors' such as the work of employees and capital. These income factors have to be paid for. The income side approach shows GDP as it is distributed among different participants in the production process. It is therefore represented as the sum of:

— **the compensation of employees:** this is defined as the total remuneration, in cash or in kind, payable by an employer to an employee in return for work done by the latter during the accounting period (ESA 95, 4.02). The compensation of employees is broken down into: (i) wages and salaries (in cash and in kind); (ii) employers' social contributions (employers' actual social con-

tributions, employers' imputed social contributions);

— **the gross operating surplus of the total economy:** this is the surplus (or deficit) on production activities before account has been taken of the interest, rents or charges paid or received for the use of assets.

— **the mixed income of the total economy:** this is the remuneration for the work carried out by the owner (or by members of his/her family) of an unincorporated enterprise. This is referred to as 'mixed income' since it cannot be distinguished from the entrepreneurial profit of the owner.

— **taxes on production and imports less subsidies:** this consists of compulsory, unrequited payments to general government or institutions of the European Union, in respect of the production or import of goods and services, the employment of labour, and the ownership or use of land, buildings or other assets used in production.

3

Income of the input factors in the EU-15
In million ECU/EUR; at current prices

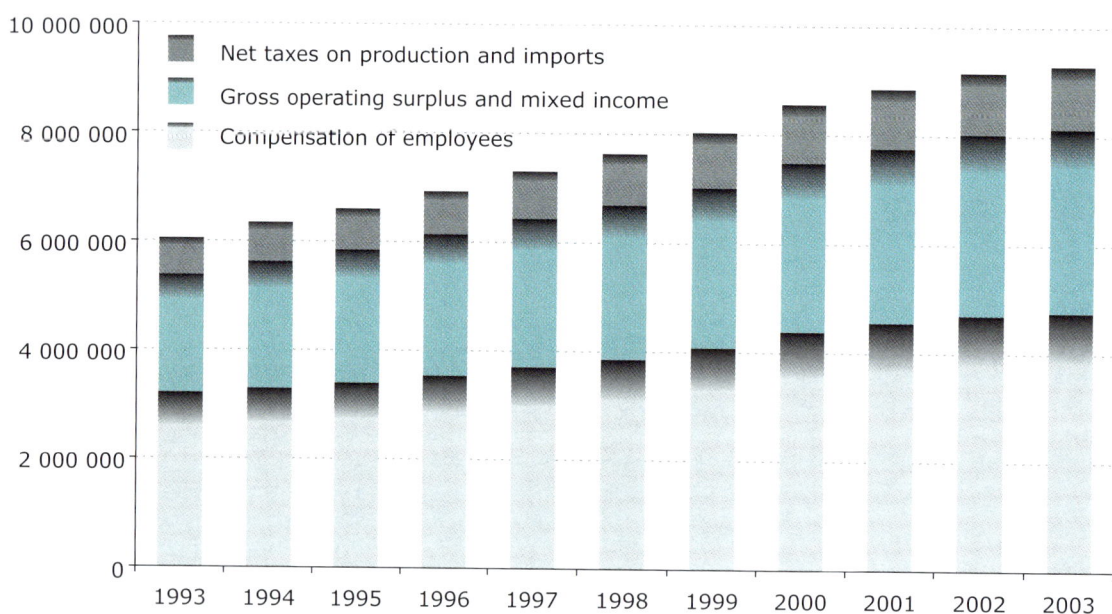

The higher the output of an economy, the more income can be distributed to the factors that have provided an input to its creation. Between 1993 and 2003, the GDP of EU-15 (measured at current prices) grew by more than a half (+ 54 %). Both the overall income of the employees and that of the capital owners have grown at about the same rate. However, the growth of the 'gross operating surplus and mixed income' was higher (+ 56 %) than that of 'compensation of employees' (+ 48 %).

Compensation of employees versus gross operating surplus and mixed income
Share in the EU-15's GDP in %

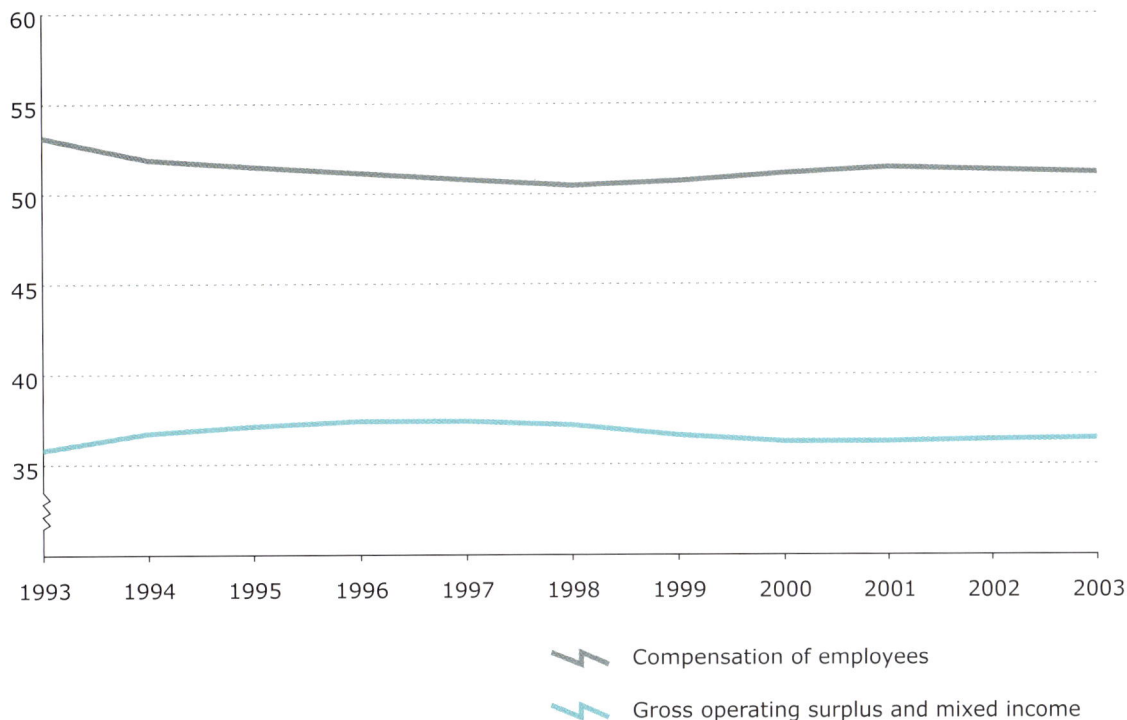

Compensation of employees

Gross operating surplus and mixed income

Current series.

Compensation of employees is defined as the total remuneration, in cash or in kind, payable by an employer to an employee in return for work done by the latter. In particular, it also includes social contributions paid by the employer.

Operating surplus is the surplus (or deficit) on production activities before account has been taken of the interest, rents or charges paid or received for the use of assets. Mixed income is the remuneration for the work carried out by the owner (or by members of his family) of an unincorporated enterprise. This is referred to as 'mixed income' since it cannot be distinguished from the entrepreneurial profit of the owner.

Closer analysis shows that the share of 'compensation of employees' fell from 1993 to 1998 from about 53 % to 50 %, and increased afterwards to stand at about 51 % in 2003. In contrast, the share of the 'gross operating surplus and mixed income' grew strongly from 1993 (36 %) to 1997 (37 $\frac{1}{2}$ %), but fell afterwards to settle at below 36 $\frac{1}{2}$ % in 2003.

Government finances

Eurostat data

Eurostat provides a wide range of data on:

— Government surplus and deficit
— Total general government revenue
— Taxes on production and imports
— Current taxes on income and wealth
— Social contributions
— Total general government expenditure
— Subsidies
— Social benefits (other than social transfers in kind)
— Final consumption expenditure
— Gross fixed capital formation

3

stantially and continuously). The rules on budgetary discipline were clarified and tightened under the Stability and Growth Pact (Amsterdam, 1997).

The EU Member States notify their government deficit and debt statistics to the European Commission on 1 March and 1 September of each year under the 'excessive deficit procedure'.

Eurostat collects the data and ensures that data from all Member States are in accordance with the relevant regulations.

Measuring government finances in the EU and the euro-zone ...

The EU Member States that participate in the euro zone acknowledge the need for solid and sustainable government finances. Member States are to avoid situations of 'excessive government deficits': their ratio of planned or actual government deficit to gross domestic product (GDP) should be no more than 3 %, and their ratio of government debt to GDP should be no more than 60 % (unless the excess over the reference value is only exceptional or temporary, or unless the ratios have declined substantially and continuously). The rules on budgetary discipline were clarified and tightened under the Stability and Growth Pact (Amsterdam, 1997).

... more than just about the surplus or deficit

Government finance statistics offer much more information on the general government sector. Some examples are given in the box 'Eurostat data' at the beginning of this section.

The main aggregates of general government are provided by the Member States to Eurostat twice a year in March and August, according to the ESA 95 transmission programme.

For a detailed description of the terms, please refer to the glossary.

Public balance
Net borrowing/lending of the general government sector as a percentage of GDP

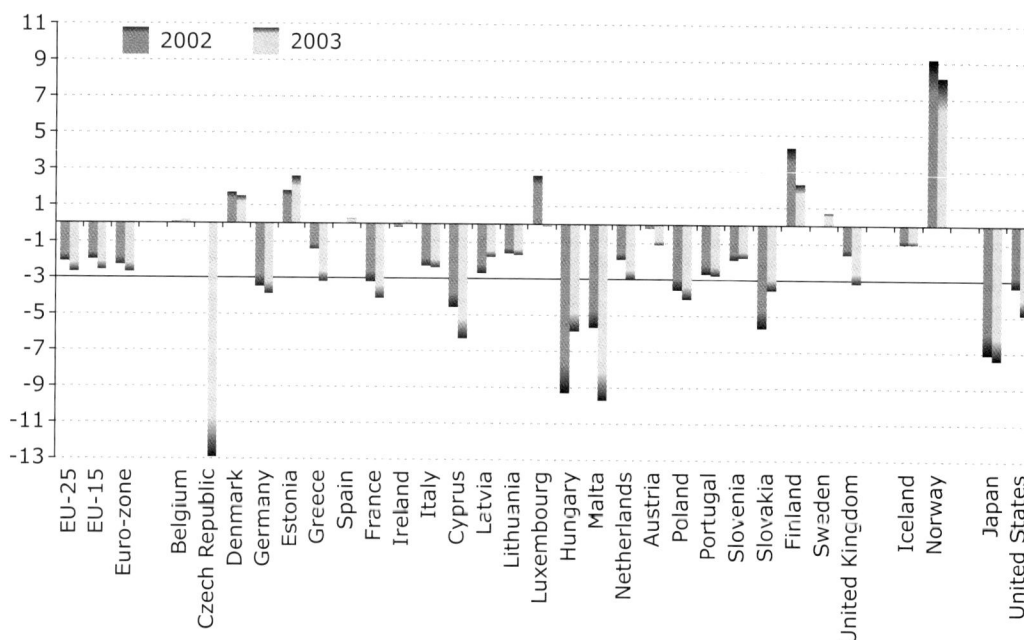

Source: Eurostat / OECD.

The net borrowing (+)/net lending (–) of general government is the difference between the revenue and the expenditure of the general government sector. The general government sector comprises the following subsectors: central government, State government, local government, and social security funds. GDP used as a denominator is the gross domestic product at current market prices.

General government debt
General government consolidated gross debt as a percentage of GDP

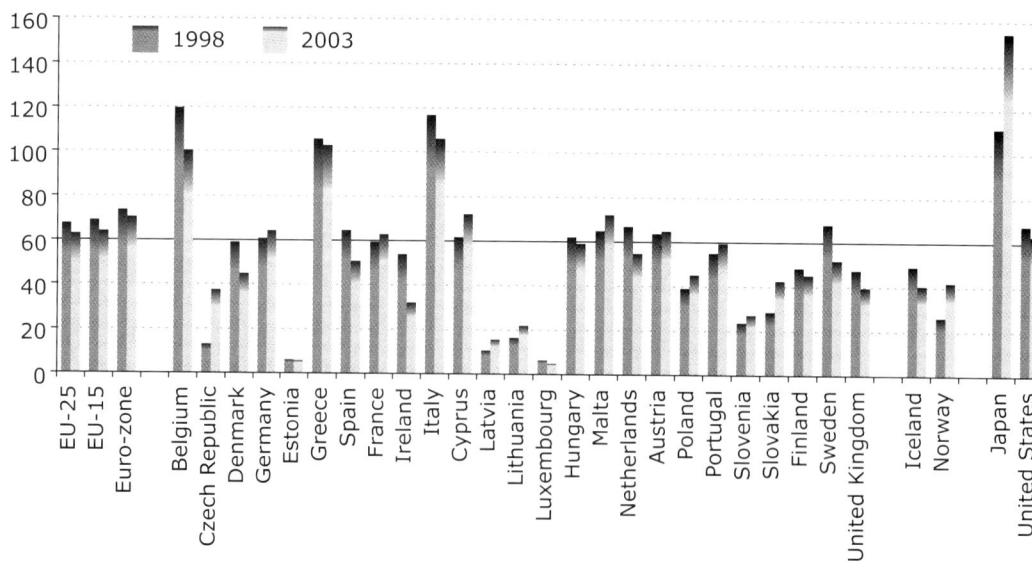

Source: Eurostat, OECD (Japan, US).

The general government sector comprises the subsectors of central government, State government, local government and social security funds. GDP used as a denominator is the gross domestic product at current market prices. Debt is valued at nominal (face) value, and foreign currency debt is converted into national currency using end-year market exchange rates (though special rules apply to contracts). The national data for the general government sector are consolidated between the subsectors. Basic data are expressed in national currency, converted into euro using end-year exchange rates for the euro provided by the European Central Bank. Data are compiled on an accrual basis.

The public deficit of EU-25, measured in terms of GDP, increased between 2002 and 2003 from 2.1 % to 2.7 %. Within the euro zone, notably France and Germany already had deficits of above 3 % in 2002 that continued to grow in 2003 to 4.1 % in France and 3.9 % in Germany, respectively. The public deficit of Greece stood at 3.2 % of GDP in 2003.

The trend in general government consolidated gross debt as a percentage of GDP has developed differently among the Member States. Some 'old' Member States that had a particu-

larly high level of government debt in 1998 managed to reduce it, even if the 2003 value is still well above the 60 % mark. This is true for Belgium (1998: 119.6 %; 2003: 100.5 %), Italy (1998: 116.7 %; 2003: 106.2 %) and Greece (1998: 105.8 %; 2003: 103.0 %). On the contrary, the general government debt increased in Germany (1998: 60.9 %; 2003: 64.2 %), France (1998: 59.5 %; 2003: 63.0 %), and Portugal (1998: 55.0 %; 2003: 59.4 %).

Current taxes on income, wealth, etc. and taxes on production and imports
Taxes of general government in 2003; in % of GDP

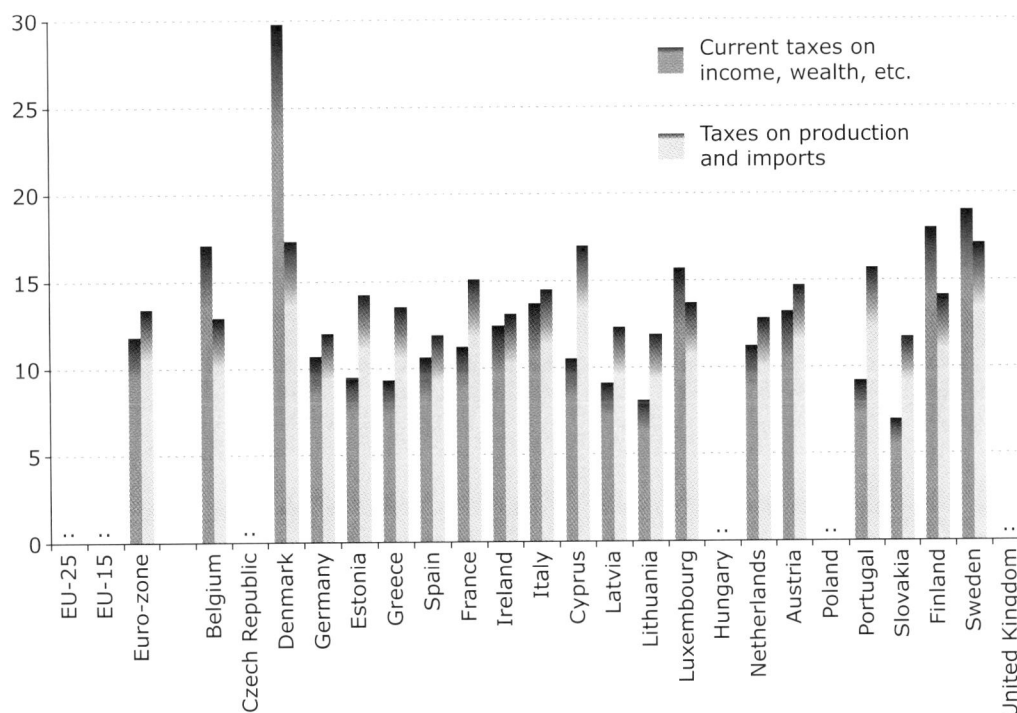

Current taxes on income, wealth, etc. (ESA 95 code D.5) cover all compulsory, unrequited payment, in cash or in kind, levied periodically by general government and by the rest of the world on the income and wealth of institutional units, and some periodic taxes which are assessed neither on the income nor the wealth. In ESA 95, current taxes on income, wealth, etc. are divided into taxes on income and other current taxes.

Taxes on production and imports (ESA 95 code D.2) consist of compulsory, unrequited payments, in cash or in kind which are levied by general government, or by EU institutions, in respect of the production and importation of goods and services, the employment of labour, the ownership or use of land, buildings or other assets used in production. In ESA 95, taxes on production and imports comprise: taxes on products and other taxes on production.

The share in GDP of taxes on income and wealth as well as on production and imports varies significantly between Member States. In 2003, five EU countries reported higher rev-

enues from taxes on income and wealth than from taxes on production and imports (Belgium, Denmark, Luxembourg, Finland and Sweden).

Total general government expenditure in 2003
In % of GDP

EU-15	:
Euro-zone	~49
Belgium	~51
Czech Republic	:
Denmark	~56
Germany	~49
Estonia	~43
Greece	~47
Spain	~40
France	~55
Ireland	~35
Italy	~49
Cyprus	~47
Latvia	~38
Lithuania	~34
Luxembourg	~46
Hungary	:
Malta	:
Netherlands	~49
Austria	~51
Poland	:
Portugal	~48
Slovenia	:
Slovakia	:
Finland	~51
Sweden	~58
United Kingdom	:

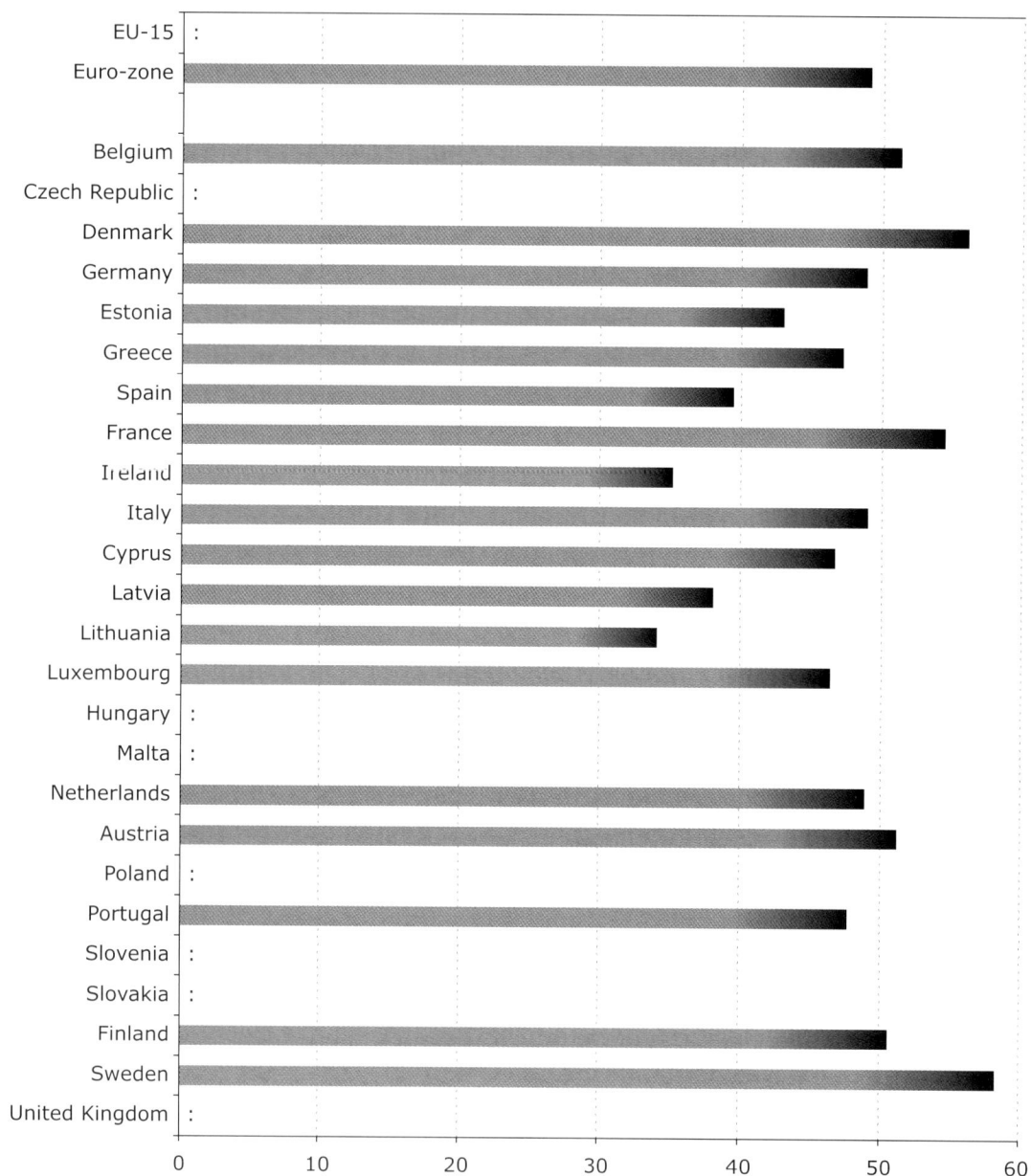

General government expenditure is defined in a new paragraph 8.99 (a) of ESA 95 as follows: intermediate consumption, gross capital formation, compensation of employees, other taxes on production, subsidies, payable, property income, current taxes on income, wealth, etc., social benefits other than social transfers in kind, social transfers in kind related to expenditure on products supplied to households via market producers, other current transfers, adjustment for the change in net equity of households in pension fund reserves, capital transfers, payable, and acquisitions less disposals of non-financial non-produced assets.

In 2003, the indicator for total government expenditure in GDP varied significantly between the Member States of today's European Union, from 34.1 % in Lithuania and 35.2 % in Ireland to 56.1 % in Denmark and 58.3 % in Sweden.

Consumer prices

Eurostat data

Eurostat provides a wide range of data on:

— Harmonised indices of consumer prices (HICPs)
— Price stability
— Price convergence
— European index of consumer prices (EICP) — EU
— Monetary union index of consumer prices (MUICP) — euro zone
— Convergence criteria of the Maastricht Treaty

HICPs: a comparable measure of inflation in the EU

The harmonised indices of consumer prices (HICPs) provide the best statistical basis for comparisons of consumer price inflation within the EU. The methodology ensures comparability between Member States. Eurostat publishes the HICPs monthly, about 18 days after the end of the reporting month. The HICP series starts with the index for January 1995. For ease of comparison, they are presented with a common base year, 1996 = 100.

Information on the HICPs of the new Member States has been introduced with the enlargement of the European Union in May 2004 so that comparable price indices are available for the entire EU.

Methodological notes can be accessed via the Eurostat Internet site (http://europa.eu.int/comm/eurostat or http://forum.europa.eu.int/Public/irc/dsis/hiocp/library).

HICP coverage

HICPs cover virtually all forms of household expenditure on goods and services (household final monetary consumption expenditure — HFMCE). HICP coverage follows the international classification Coicop (classification of individual consumption by purpose), adapted to the needs of HICPs.

HICP aggregate indices

There are three aggregate indices of the HICPs: the monetary union index of consumer prices (MUICP) for the euro zone; the European index of consumer prices (EICP) covering all Member States; the European Economic Area index of consumer prices (EEAICP), which additionally covers Iceland and Norway.

The HICP methodology allows country weights to change each year: for the MUICP, a Member

State's weight is its share of HFMCE in the EMU total; for the EICP and the EEAICP, a Member State's weight is its share of HFMCE expressed in euro in the EU and EEA totals. For the latter two indices, expenditure in national currencies is converted using purchasing power parities. The HICP is computed as an annual chain index. Starting in 1999, the MUICP is treated as a single entity within the EICP.

Price stability in the euro zone

With the launch of the euro in January 1999, the MUICP is used for the monitoring of inflation in the EMU and for assessment of inflation convergence. As price stability is the primary objective of the European System of Central Banks, the MUICP is used by the European Central Bank (ECB) as a prime indicator for monetary policy management for the euro zone. The ECB has defined price stability as a year-on-year increase in the HICP for the euro zone of close to but below 2 %, in the medium term.

Consumer price indices in the EU-15

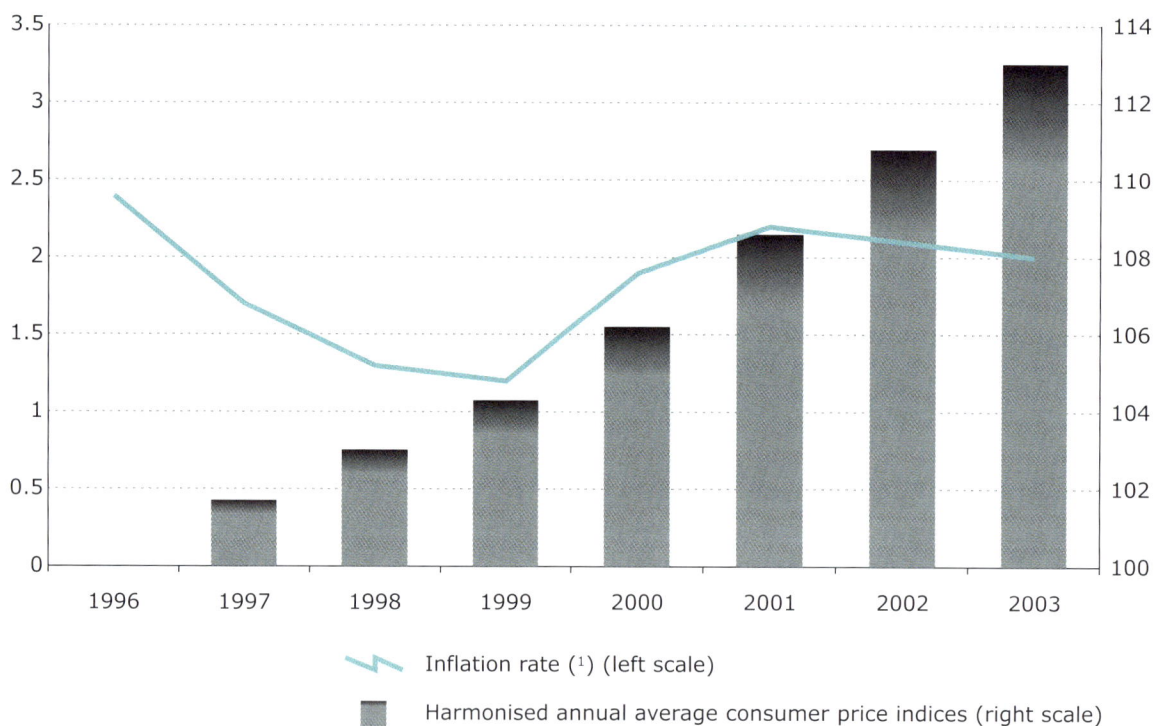

Inflation rate (^{1}) (left scale)

Harmonised annual average consumer price indices (right scale)

(1) Annual average rate of change in harmonised index of consumer prices (HICPs).

Harmonised index of consumer prices (HICPs) are designed for international comparisons of consumer price inflation. HICP is used by e.g. the European Central Bank for monitoring of inflation in the economic and monetary Union and for the assessment of inflation convergence as required under Article 121 of the Treaty of Amsterdam.

The EU Member States have made a successful effort to keep their inflation under control. Inflation, as measured by the annual average rate of change of the harmonised index of consumer prices for the EU Member States, decreased during the 1990s reaching 1.2 % in 1999. Inflation increased again in 2000 before settling at close to 2 % in 2003 and early 2004.

Purchasing power parities

Purchasing power parities (PPPs) estimate price-level differences between countries. They make it possible to produce meaningful volume or price-level indicators required for country comparisons. PPPs are aggregated price ratios calculated from detailed price comparisons of a large number of products.

PPPs are employed either:

— as currency converters to generate volume measures with which to compare levels of economic performance, economic welfare, consumption, investment, overall productivity and selected government expenditures, or

— as price measures with which to compare price levels, price convergence and competitiveness.

Eurostat produces three sets of data using PPPs:

— **Levels and indices of real final expenditure:** these are measures of volume. They indicate the relative magnitudes of the product groups or aggregates being compared. At the level of GDP, they are used to compare the economic size of countries.

— **Levels and indices of real final expenditure per head:** these are standardised measures of volume. They indicate the relative levels of the product groups or aggregates being compared after adjusting for differences in the size of populations between countries. At the level of GDP, they are often used to compare the economic well-being of populations.

— **Comparative price levels:** these are the ratios of PPPs to exchange rates. By expressing the PPPs in a common currency unit, they provide a measure of the differences in price levels between countries by indicating for a given product group the number of units of the common currency needed to buy the same volume of the product group in each country. At the level of GDP, they provide a measure of the differences in the general price levels of countries. Furthermore, comparative price levels provide a means of observing the movement of price levels over time. The coefficient of variation of comparative price levels is applied as the indicator of convergence among EU Member States.

3

Comparative price levels in 2002
Comparative price levels of final consumption by
private households, including indirect taxes (EU-15 = 100)

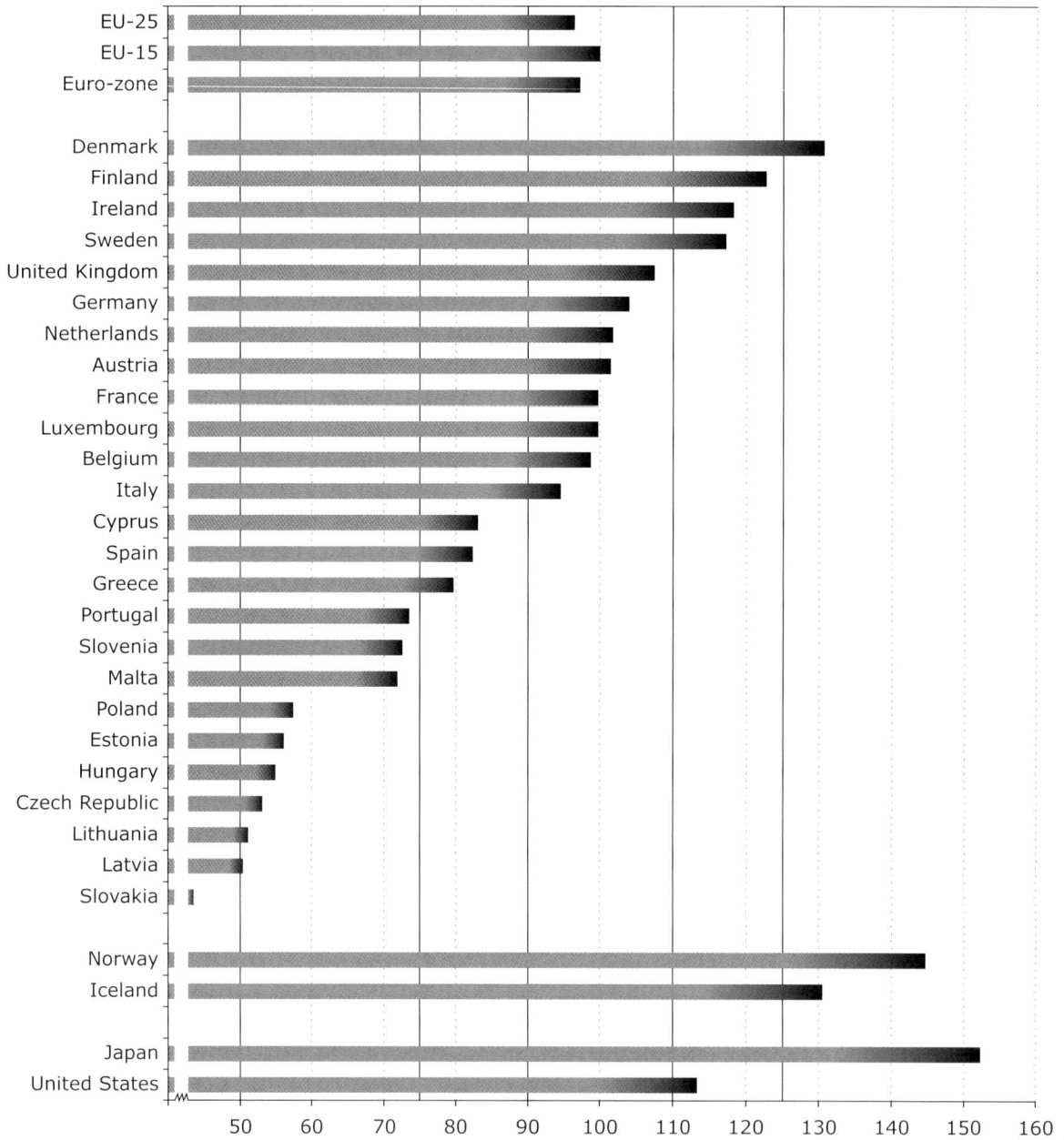

3

EU-25	
EU-15	
Euro-zone	
Denmark	
Finland	
Ireland	
Sweden	
United Kingdom	
Germany	
Netherlands	
Austria	
France	
Luxembourg	
Belgium	
Italy	
Cyprus	
Spain	
Greece	
Portugal	
Slovenia	
Malta	
Poland	
Estonia	
Hungary	
Czech Republic	
Lithuania	
Latvia	
Slovakia	
Norway	
Iceland	
Japan	
United States	

(x-axis: 50 60 70 80 90 100 110 120 130 140 150 160)

Provisional values.

Comparative price levels are the ratio between purchasing power parities (PPPs) and market exchange rate for each country. PPPs are currency conversion rates that convert economic indicators expressed in national currencies to a common currency, called purchasing power standard (PPS), which equalises the purchasing power of different national currencies and thus allows meaningful comparison. The ratio is shown in relation to the EU average (EU-15 = 100). If the index of the comparative price levels shown for a country is higher (lower) than 100, the country concerned is relatively expensive (cheap) as compared with the EU average.

The price levels that private households have to take into account for their consumption vary significantly between the Member States of the European Union. The average for EU-15 being defined as 100, the comparative price levels range, within the 25 countries that today form the European Union, from 131 in Denmark to 44 in Slovakia. The comparative value for Japan is 152, and for the United States 113.

Convergence of price levels between EU Member States
Coefficient of variation of comparative price levels of final
consumption by private households, including indirect taxes

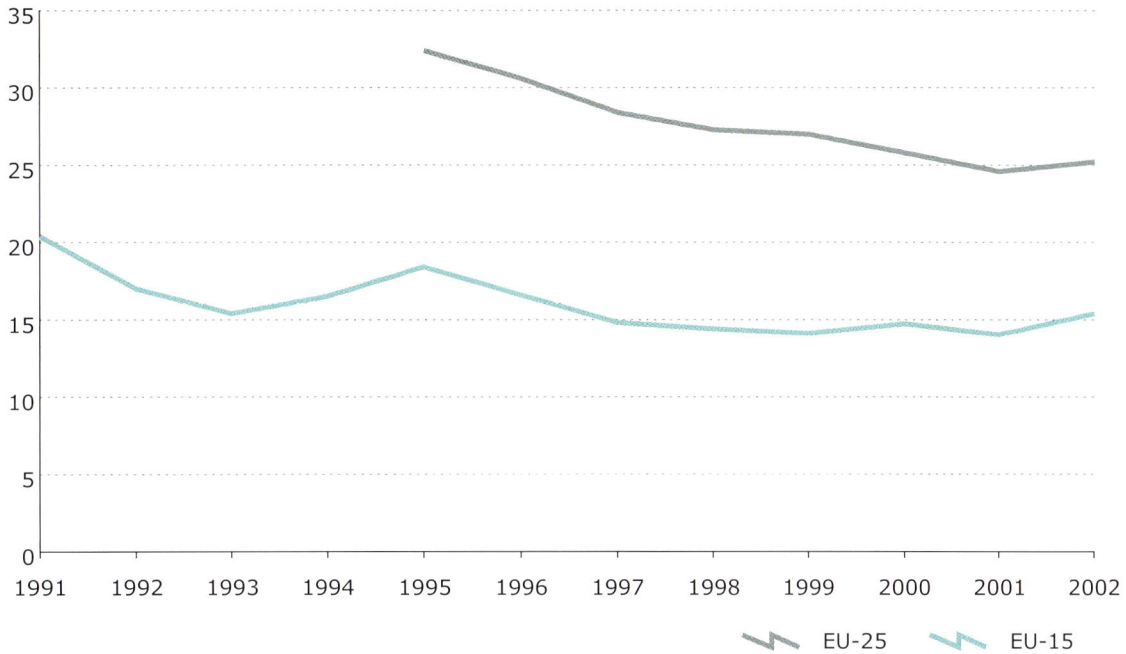

2002: provisional values; EU-25 1996 to 1999: estimated values.

Comparative price levels are the ratio between purchasing power parities (PPPs) and market exchange rate for each country. PPPs are currency conversion rates that convert economic indicators expressed in national currencies to a common currency, called purchasing power standard (PPS), which equalises the purchasing power of different national currencies and thus allows meaningful comparison. If the coefficient of variation of the comparative price levels for the EU decreases (increases) over time, the national price levels in the Member States are converging (diverging).

Given these differences, it must, however, also be pointed out that the price levels converged in EU-15 during the 1990s. The convergence of price levels within the 15 'old' Member States is currently much more advanced (15.4 in 2002) than within the whole EU-25 that includes the 'old' and the 'new' Member States (25.2 in 2003) (note that the lower the value, the more advanced the convergence of price levels).

Wages and labour costs

Eurostat provides a wide range of data on:

— Annual average gross earnings
— Annual net earnings in manufacturing
— Structure of earnings
— Labour costs
— Tax rates in manufacturing
— Minimum wages
— Labour cost index

Labour costs

Information on labour costs is of major importance for employers' associations, trade unions, political parties, economists and other users who are interested in the level and structure of labour costs.

The term 'labour costs' refers to the expenditure necessarily incurred by employers in order to employ personnel.

Eurostat provides detailed labour costs data from four-yearly surveys (the latest reference year available is 2000) as well as annual data on key figures: hourly and monthly labour costs, and components of labour costs. These data permit the comparison of total labour costs between different countries and between different industries within a country. The data on labour costs do not take into account the differences in labour productivity between the countries.

Gross annual earnings account for the largest share of total labour costs

Gross annual earnings are wages and salaries in cash paid directly to employees before any deductions for income tax and social security contributions. Eurostat provides information on the earnings of full-time employees broken down by industry and by gender, as well as the earnings of women as a percentage of men's.

Net earnings

Net earnings represent the part of remuneration that employees can actually spend. Compared with gross earnings, net earnings do not include social security contributions and taxes, but include family allowances.

National minimum wages in eighteen Member States

In 18 EU Member States and three candidate countries, collective bargaining is subject to a legal national minimum wage. The minimum wage usually applies to all employees in the economy and all occupations. The proportion of full-time employees with earnings at the minimum-wage level varies considerably between the countries, for both men and women. However, the percentage of women receiving a minimum wage is, broadly speaking, twice that of men.

Low-wage earners: tax wedge and unemployment trap

In connection with low pay, one of the Commission's Structural indicators is the 'tax rate on low-wage earners' that comprises two sub-indicators.

— The 'tax wedge on labour cost' measures the relative tax burden for an employed person with low earnings.

— The 'unemployment trap' measures what percentage of the gross earnings (after moving into employment) is 'taxed away' by the combined effects of the withdrawal of benefits and higher tax and social security contributions.

Average gross annual earnings in industry and services
Of full-time employees in enterprises with 10 or more employees; in ECU/EUR

	1995	1996	1997	1998	1999	2000	2001	2002
EU-15	:	:	:	22 142	23 080	25 527	26 288	:
Euro-zone	:	:	20 421	20 970	21 499	22 413	23 081	:
Belgium	28 945	29 131	28 901	29 616	30 701	31 644	33 109	34 330
Czech Republic	:	:	:	:	:	:	:	:
Denmark	:	36 376	36 235	37 209	39 515	40 962	41 661	43 577
Germany	34 584	35 254	35 093	36 033	36 862	37 253	38 204	39 440
Estonia	:	:	:	:	:	:	:	:
Greece	11 291	11 917	12 605	13 209	13 926	14 721	15 431	16 278
Spain	:	16 043	16 192	16 528	17 038	17 432	17 874	18 462
France	23 952	24 292	24 798	25 519	25 947	26 521	27 319	:
Ireland	:	:	:	:	:	:	:	:
Italy	:	:	:	:	:	:	:	:
Cyprus	:	12 980	14 021	14 709	15 161	16 335	16 948	17 740
Latvia	:	:	:	:	:	:	:	:
Lithuania	1 385	1 597	2 286	2 799	3 017	:	:	:
Luxembourg	:	:	32 746	33 462	34 534	35 910	37 801	38 551
Hungary	3 062	3 158	3 543	3 686	3 770	4 172	4 898	5 871
Malta	8 747	9 287	10 114	10 713	11 581	12 553	13 320	13 460
Netherlands	27 966	28 140	28 061	29 189	30 426	31 901	33 900	35 200
Austria	:	:	:	:	:	:	:	:
Poland	:	3 076	:	4 156	5 310	:	7 509	7 172
Portugal	:	:	:	:	:	12 620	13 338	:
Slovenia	:	:	:	:	:	:	:	:
Slovakia	:	:	3 179	3 292	3 125	3 583	3 837	4 582
Finland	23 584	23 883	24 005	24 944	25 739	27 398	28 555	:
Sweden	:	:	:	:	:	31 621	30 467	31 164
United Kingdom	:	:	:	29 370	32 269	37 677	39 233	40 553
Iceland	:	:	:	:	32 311	37 638	34 101	36 764
Norway	:	:	:	:	:	:	38 604	43 736

Gross earnings are remuneration (wages and salaries) in cash paid directly to the employee, before any deductions for income tax and social security contributions paid by the employee. Data is presented for full-time employees in 'industry and services'.

There are marked differences in earnings (average gross annual earnings in industry and services in euro) between the different countries of the EU.

Gender pay gap in 2001
In unadjusted form; in %

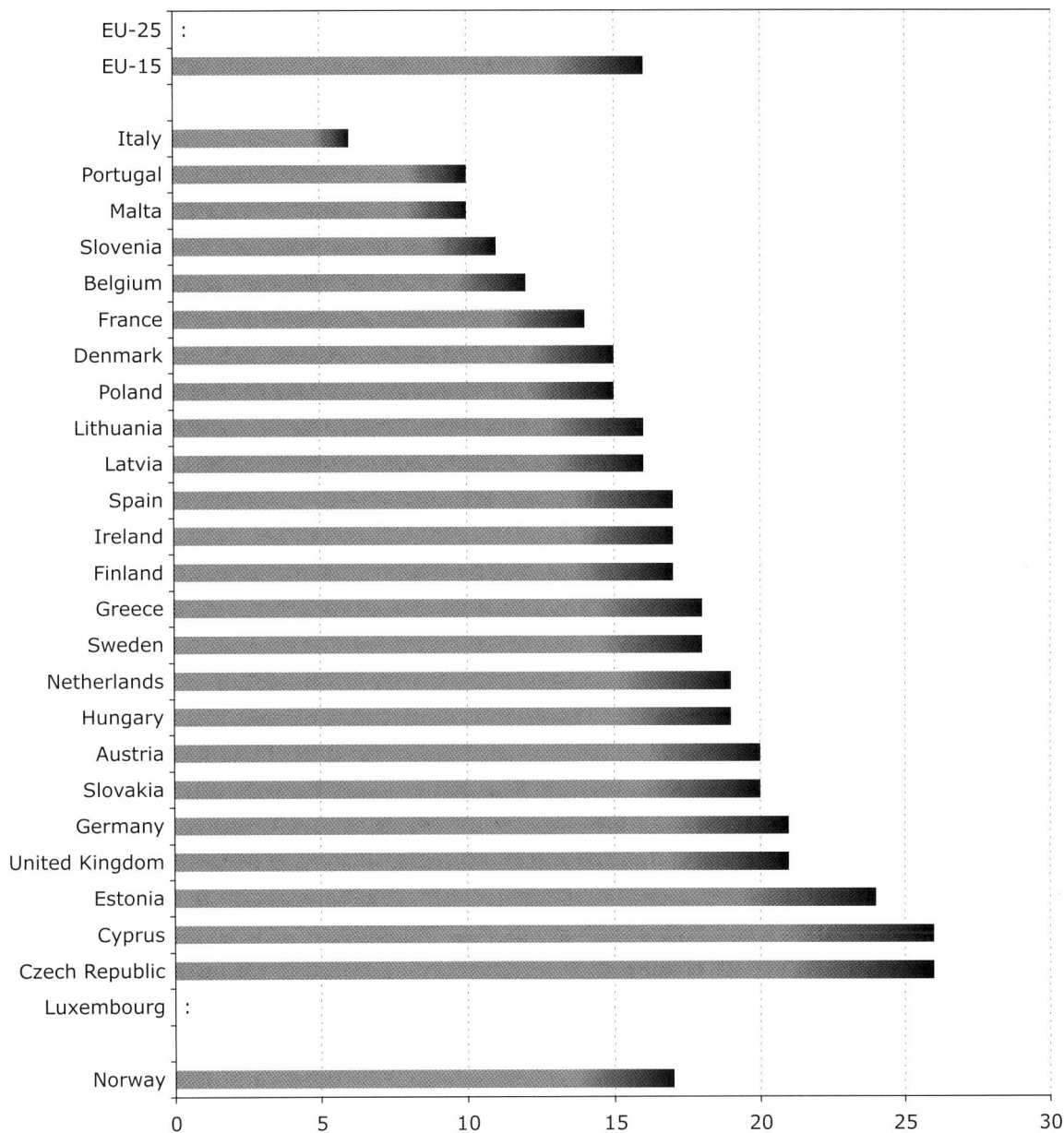

EU-25	:
EU-15	16
Italy	6
Portugal	10
Malta	10
Slovenia	11
Belgium	12
France	14
Denmark	15
Poland	15
Lithuania	16
Latvia	16
Spain	17
Ireland	17
Finland	17
Greece	18
Sweden	18
Netherlands	19
Hungary	19
Austria	20
Slovakia	20
Germany	21
United Kingdom	21
Estonia	24
Cyprus	26
Czech Republic	26
Luxembourg	:
Norway	17

Gender pay gap is given as the difference between average gross hourly earnings of male paid employees and of female paid employees as a percentage of average gross hourly earnings of male paid employees. The population consists of all paid employees aged 16–64 that are at work 15 + hours per week. The data for the remaining countries stem from the European Community household panel (ECHP), which is a survey based on a standardised questionnaire that involves annual interviewing of a representative panel of households and individuals, covering a wide range of topics. Data for CZ, EE, FR, CY, LV, LT, HU, MT, NL, PL, SI, SK, SE and NO originate from national data sources.

The gender pay gap sets the difference between hourly gross earnings of male and female employees in relation to the earnings of male employees. In 2001, it stood at about 16 % in EU-15. Within the 25 countries that make up today's European Union, it ranged from 6 % in Italy to 26 % in the Czech Republic.

Tax rate on low-wage earners: unemployment trap in 2002
In %

EU-25	:
EU-15	~79
Euro-zone	~81
Italy	~60
Czech Republic	~66
United Kingdom	~70
Hungary	~71
Austria	~72
Ireland	~73
Slovakia	~75
Poland	~75
Greece	~81
Spain	~82
Finland	~84
France	~84
Netherlands	~85
Luxembourg	~87
Portugal	~87
Sweden	~87
Germany	~88
Denmark	~91
Belgium	~91
Iceland	~69
Norway	~74
United States	~72
Japan	~74

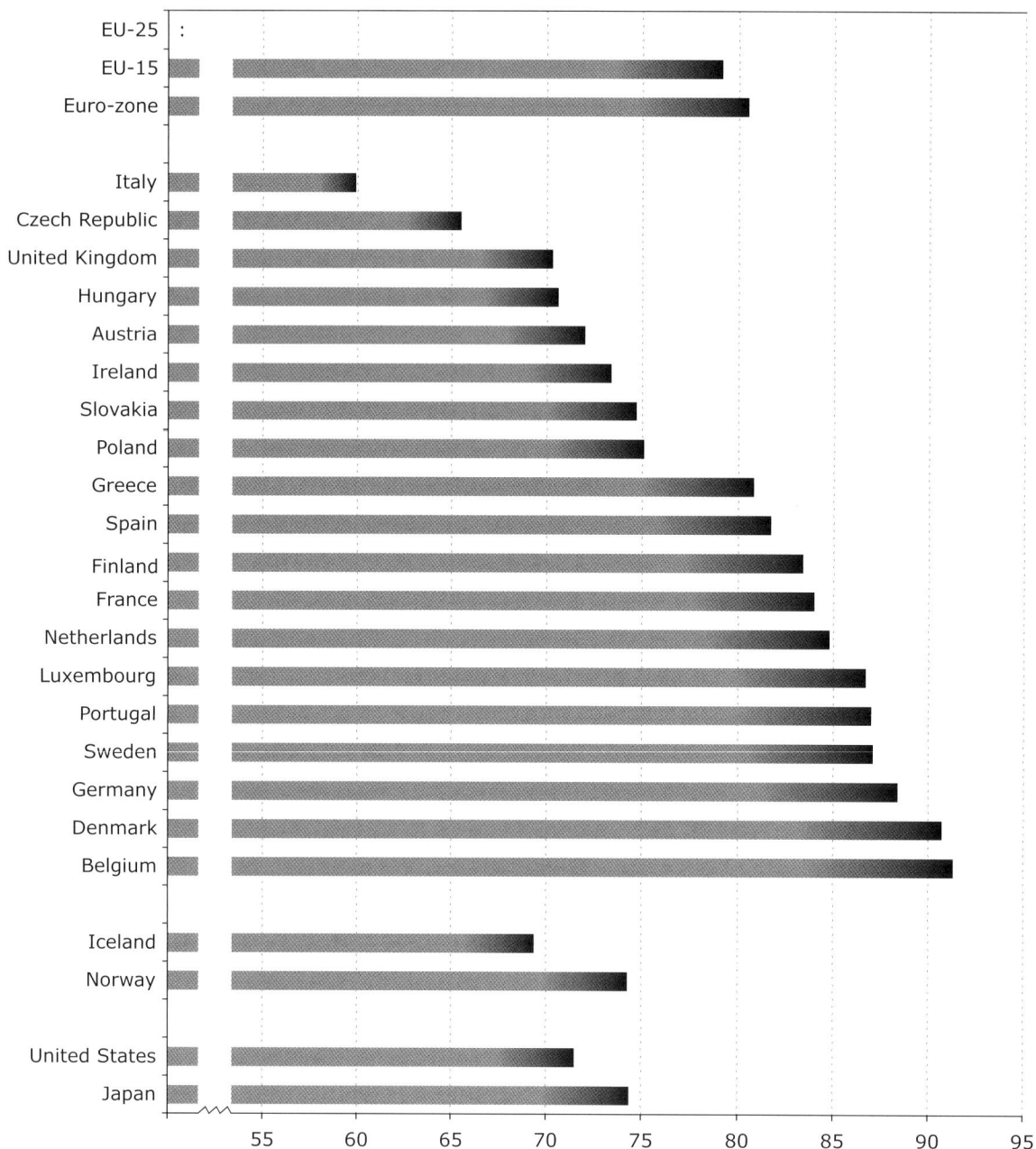

The unemployment trap measures what percentage of the gross earnings (from moving into employment) is 'taxed away' by the combined effects of the withdrawal of benefits and higher tax and social security contributions.

If a person moves from unemployment into employment, what part of the newly received gross earnings is 'taxed away' by the combined effects of the withdrawal of benefits and higher tax and social security contributions? The 'un- employment trap' answers this question: in 2002, it stood at about 79 % in EU-15. In oth- er words, the financial gain of moving from un- employment into employment was about 21 % of the gross earnings of the new employee.

Tax rate on low-wage earners: tax wedge on the labour cost in 2003
Relative tax burden for an employed person with low earnings; in %

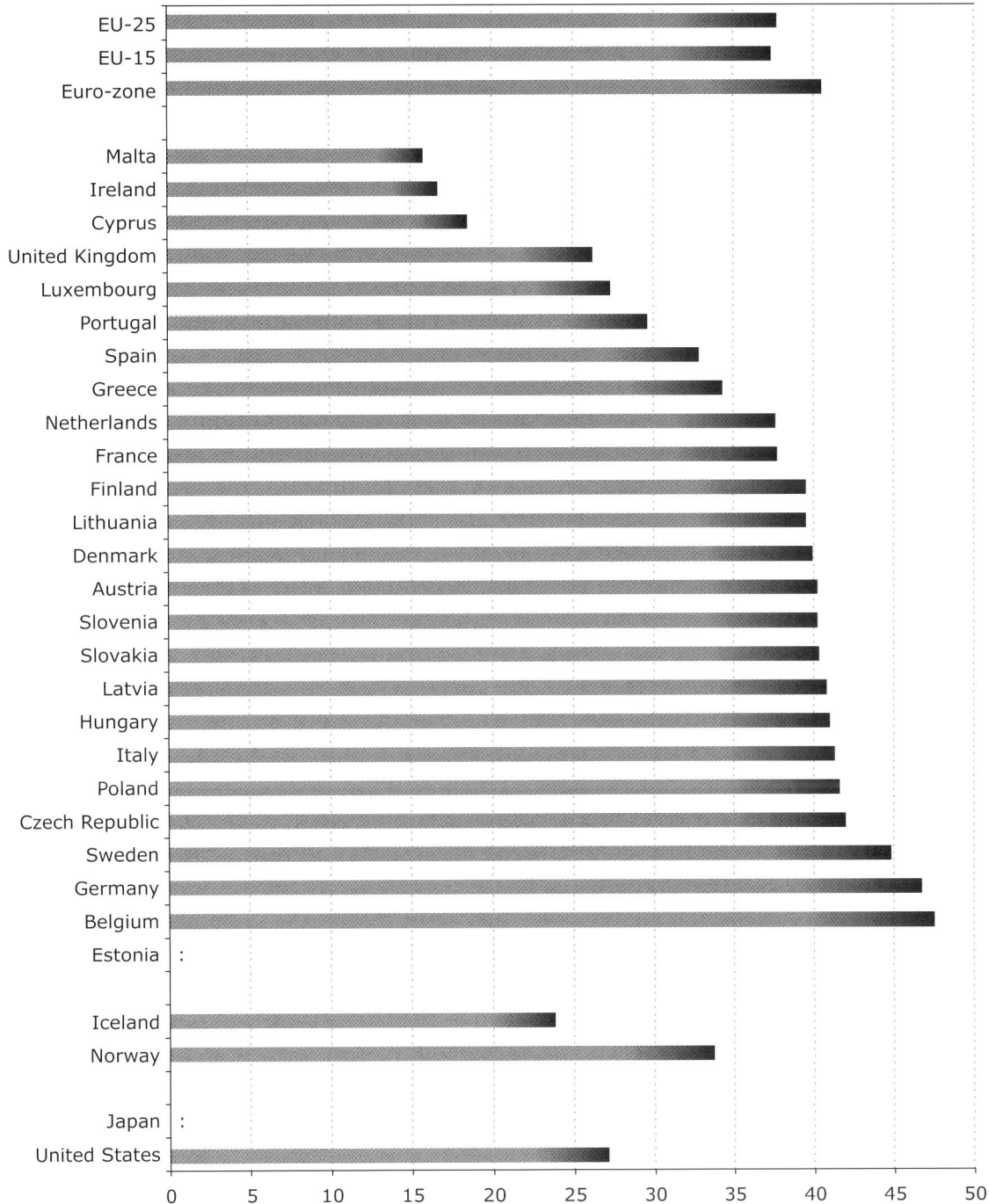

EU-25	
EU-15	
Euro-zone	
Malta	
Ireland	
Cyprus	
United Kingdom	
Luxembourg	
Portugal	
Spain	
Greece	
Netherlands	
France	
Finland	
Lithuania	
Denmark	
Austria	
Slovenia	
Slovakia	
Latvia	
Hungary	
Italy	
Poland	
Czech Republic	
Sweden	
Germany	
Belgium	
Estonia	:
Iceland	
Norway	
Japan	:
United States	

In 11 of the EU-25 countries, the tax wedge
(i.e. the relative tax burden for an employee
with low earnings) was above 40 % in 2003,
while in 3 countries, it was below 20 %.

Unit labour cost growth in the EU-15

Growth rate (in %) of the ratio: compensation per employee in current prices divided by GDP in current prices per total employment

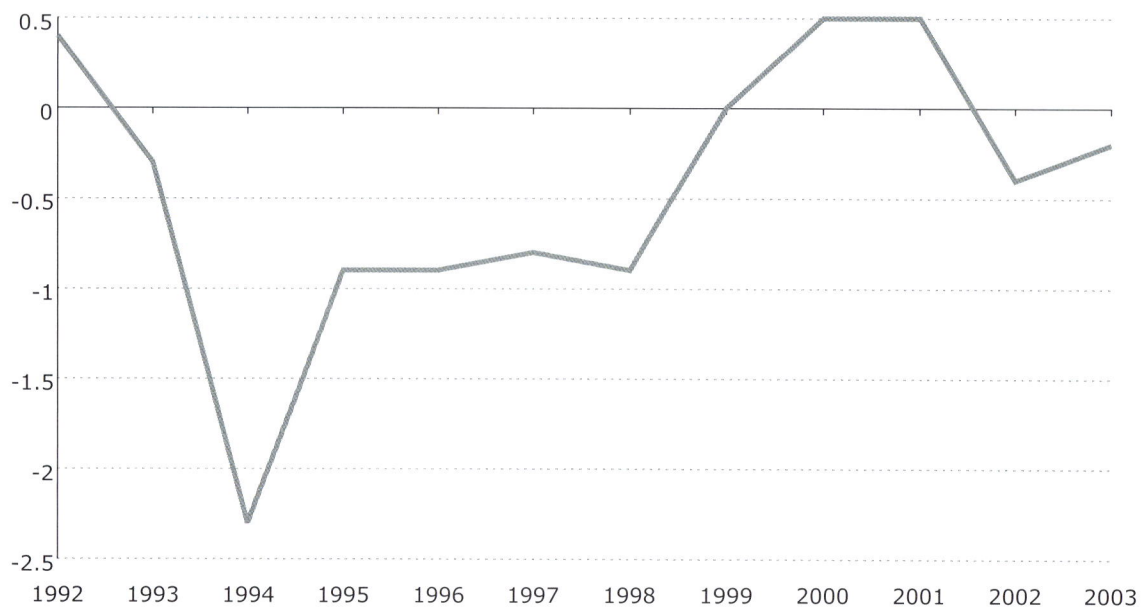

This derived indicator compares remuneration (compensation per employee) and productivity (gross domestic product (GDP) per employment) to show how the remuneration of employees is related to the productivity of their labour. Please note that the variables used in the numerator refer to employees only, while those in the denominator refer to all labour, including self-employed.

Current account

Gauging a country's economic position in the world

The current account covers all transactions (other than those recorded in the financial account) occurring between resident and non-resident entities. Within the current account, four main types of transactions are separately identified:

— The goods account covers general merchandise, goods for processing, repairs on goods, goods procured in ports by carriers and non-monetary gold. Exports and imports of goods are recorded on a fob/fob basis, i.e. at market value at the customs frontiers of exporting economies, including charges for insurance and transport services up to the frontier of the exporting country.

— The services account consists of the following items: transportation services performed by EU residents for non-EU residents, or vice versa, involving the carriage of passengers, the movement of goods, rentals of carriers with crew and related supporting and auxiliary services, travel, which includes primarily the goods and services EU travellers acquire from non-EU residents, or vice versa, and other services, which comprise those service transactions such as communication services, insurance, financial services, etc.

— The income account covers two types of transactions: compensation of employees paid to non-resident workers or received from non-resident employers, and investment income accrued on external financial assets and liabilities.

— The current transfers account includes general government current transfers, for example transfers related to international cooperation between governments, payments of current taxes on income and wealth, etc., and other current transfers, for example workers' remittances, insurance premiums — less service charges — and claims on non-life insurance companies.

Balance of the current account in 2002
In % of the GDP

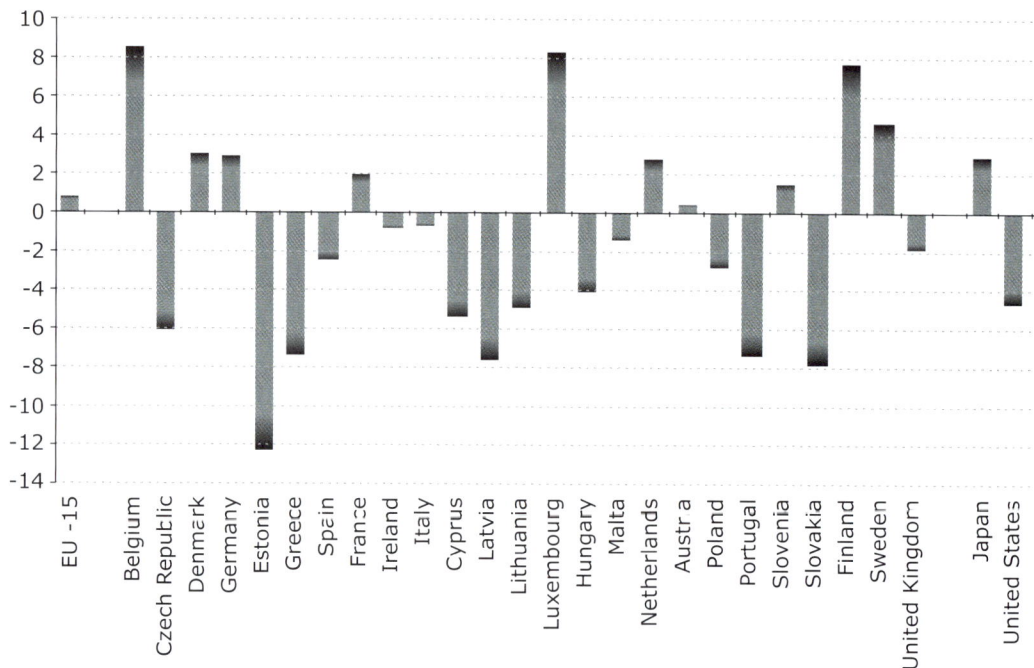

The balance of payments is composed of the current account and the capital and financial account. The current account is itself subdivided into goods, services, income and current transfers; it registers the value of exports (credits) and imports (debits). The difference between these two values is the 'balance' of each Member State's current transactions with all the other countries, and of the EU transactions with the extra EU countries.

Trade integration of the EU-15 of goods and services
Average value of imports and exports divided by GDP, multiplied by 100

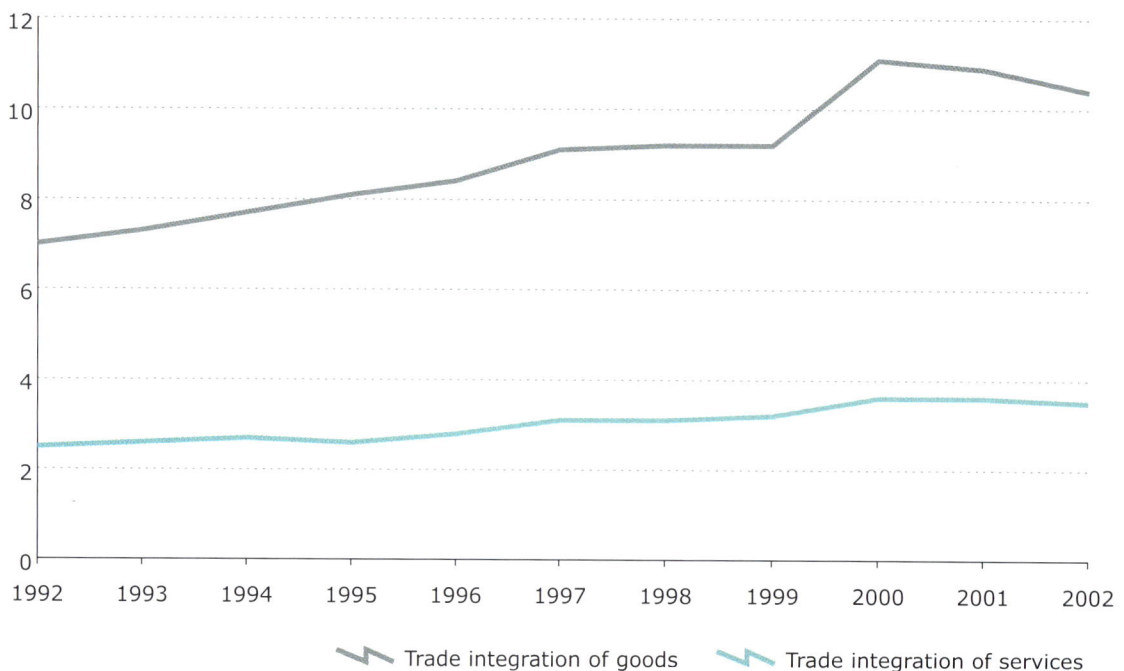

Trade integration of goods   Trade integration of services

An increasing index indicates that the EU becomes more integrated within the international economy.

Current account transactions of goods in the EU-15
In 1 000 million ECU/EUR

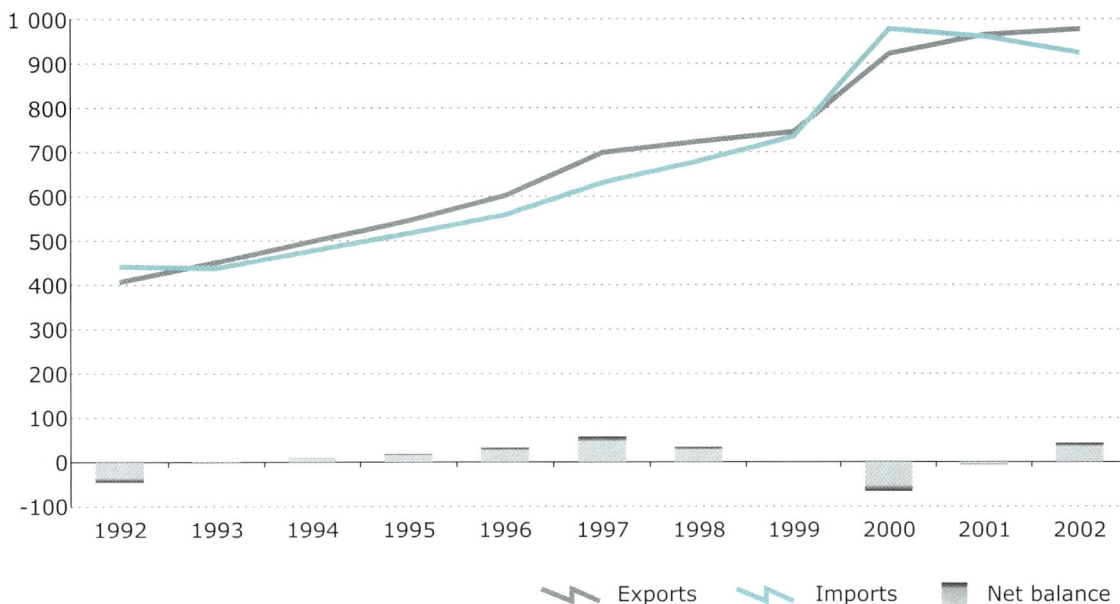

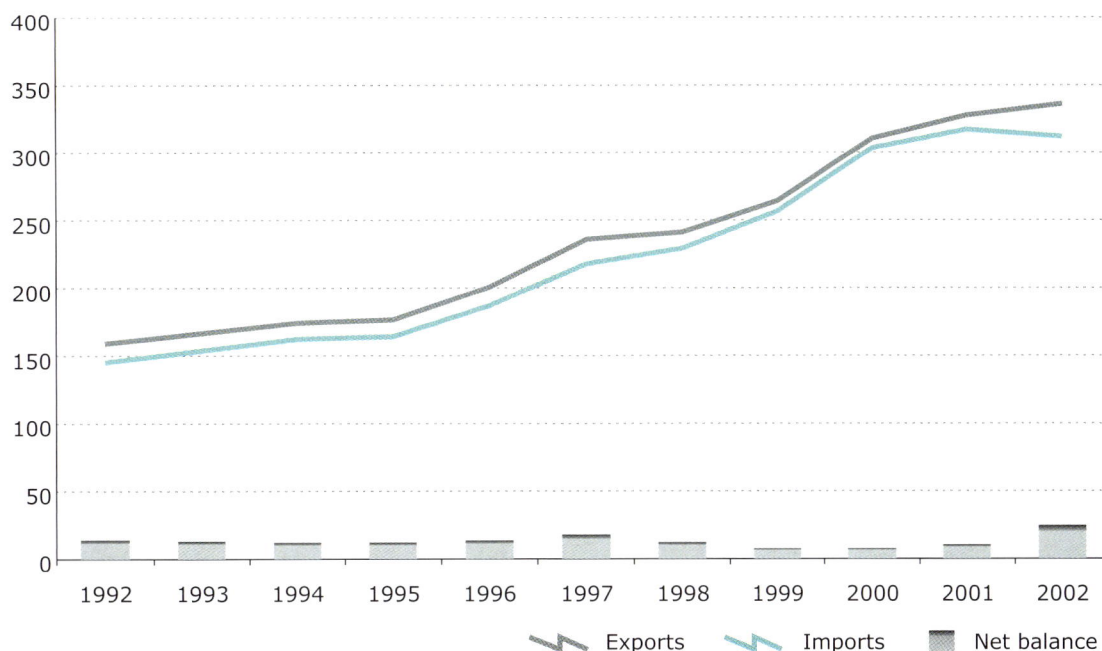

The balance of payments is a record of a country's international transactions with the rest of the world. The balance of payments is composed of two broad sub-balances: the current account and the capital and financial account. The current account is itself subdivided into four basic components: goods, services, income and current transfers. For each of these items, the current account registers the value of exports (credits) and imports (debits).

Current account transactions of services in the EU-15
In 1 000 million ECU/EUR

The balance of payments is a record of a country's international transactions with the rest of the world. It is composed of the current account and the capital and financial account. The current account is itself subdivided into goods, services, income and current transfers; it registers the value of exports (credits) and imports (debits). The difference between these two values is the 'balance'.

Trading partners

Eurostat data

Eurostat provides a wide range of data on:

— International transactions with individual countries

— International transactions with geographical zones

— International transactions with economic zones

Europe's trading partners in the world

Eurostat provides detailed information on the geographical breakdown of the current account of the European Union. The geographical breakdown distinguishes between:

— intra-EU transactions, corresponding to the sum of the transactions declared by EU Member States with other EU Member States; and

— extra-EU transactions, corresponding to the transactions declared by EU Member States with countries outside the European Union. Extra-EU transactions are further broken down into detailed partner zones: individual countries (e.g. Hungary, the United States, Japan), economic zones (e.g. OECD countries, ACP countries), and geographical zones (e.g. America, Asia).

World transactions are equal to the sum of intra-EU transactions and extra-EU transactions, plus a remainder that cannot be allocated.

Finding the residence

In the balance-of-payments statistics, the EU current account is geographically allocated according to the residence of the trading partner. However, precise information on residence is not always available. In this case, the currency in which transactions are recorded might be used to determine the origin or destination of the flows. The concept of residence thus corresponds to the concept of 'country of origin' (for imports) and 'country of destination' (for exports).

However, from 1997 onwards, the geographical allocation of imports of goods has changed. All goods imported by an EU Member State from outside the EU that transit through another EU Member State should be geographically allocated to the transit country and not the origin country.

3

EU-15 current account credits in 2002

Share of EU total credits in %

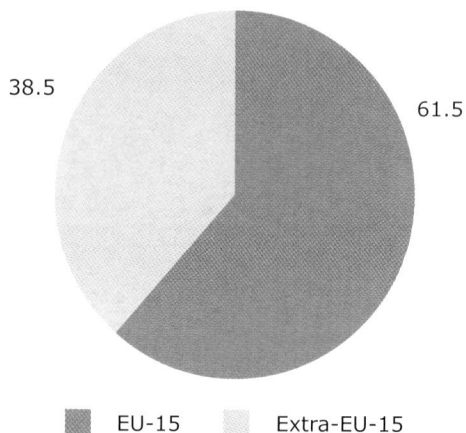

38.5

61.5

■ EU-15   ▨ Extra-EU-15

The balance of payments is a record of a country's international transactions with the rest of the world. It is composed of the current account and the capital and financial account. The current account is itself subdivided into goods, services, income and current transfers; it registers the value of exports (credits) and imports (debits).

EU-15 current account debits in 2002

Share of EU total debits in %

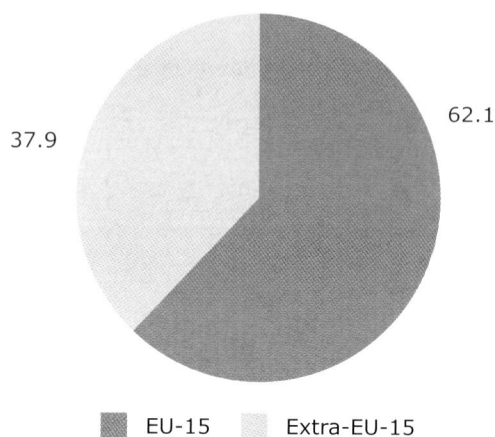

37.9

62.1

■ EU-15   ▨ Extra-EU-15

The balance of payments is a record of a country's international transactions with the rest of the world. It is composed of the current account and the capital and financial account. The current account is itself subdivided into goods, services, income and current transfers; it registers the value of exports (credits) and imports (debits).

EU-15 current account in 2002, by selected partner zones

Share of EU-15 total credits/debits in %

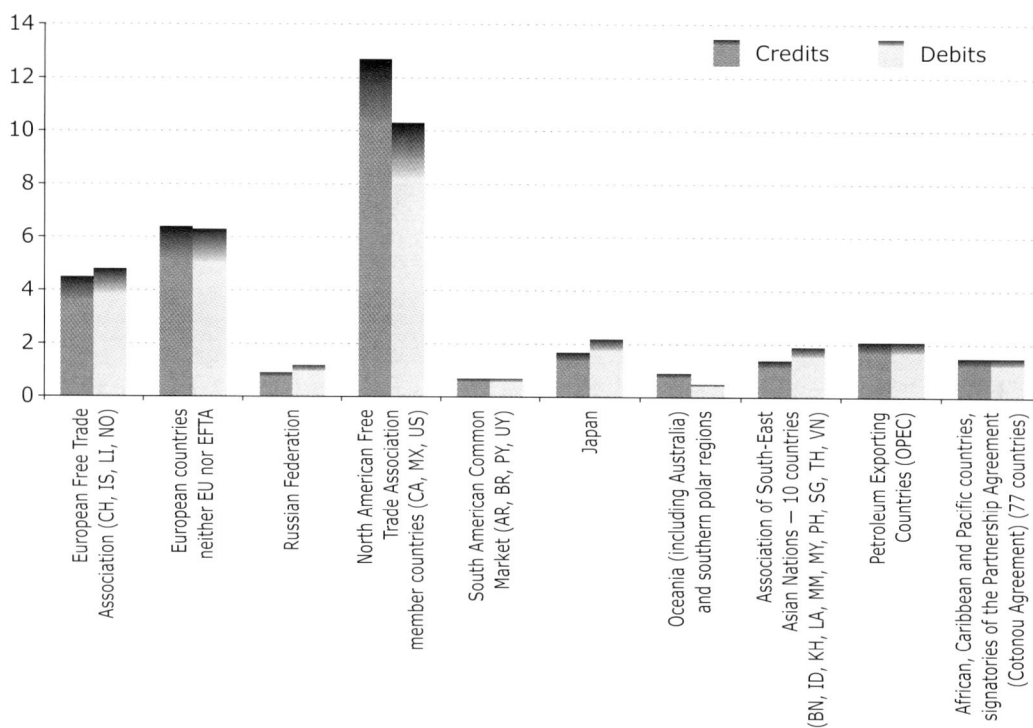

■ Credits   ▨ Debits

(Bar chart, x-axis categories:) European Free Trade Association (CH, IS, LI, NO); European countries neither EU nor EFTA; Russian Federation; North American Free Trade Association member countries (CA, MX, US); South American Common Market (AR, BR, PY, UY); Japan; Oceania (including Australia) and southern polar regions; Association of South-East Asian Nations – 10 countries (BN, ID, KH, LA, MM, MY, PH, SG, TH, VN); Petroleum Exporting Countries (OPEC); African, Caribbean and Pacific countries, signatories of the Partnership Agreement (Cotonou Agreement) (77 countries)

The balance of payments is a record of a country's international transactions with the rest of the world. It is composed of the current account and the capital and financial account. The current account is itself subdivided into goods, services, income and current transfers; it registers the value of exports (credits) and imports (debits).

EU-15 export in 2002, by selected partner zones
Share of EU-15 total exports in %

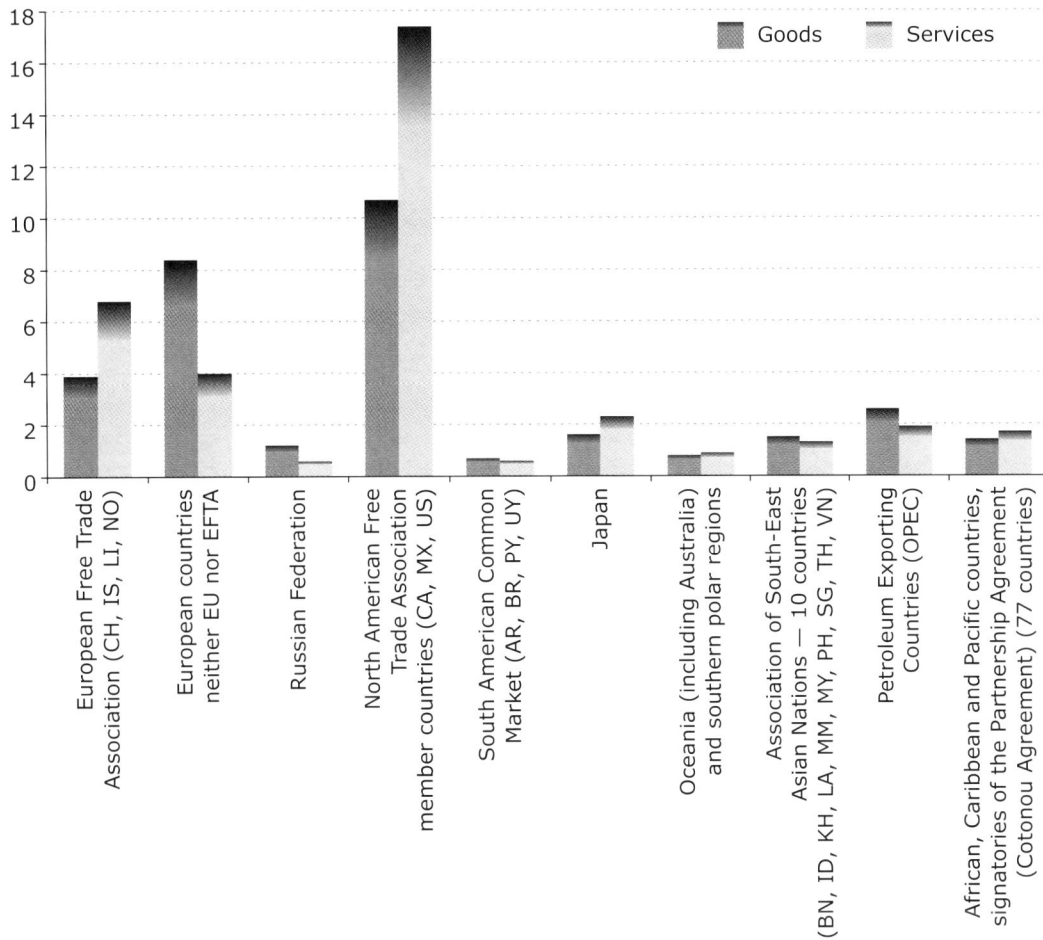

The balance of payments is a record of a country's international transactions with the rest of the world. It is composed of the current account and the capital and financial account. The current account is itself subdivided into goods, services, income and current transfers; it registers the value of exports (credits) and imports (debits).

EU-15 import in 2002, by selected partner zones
Share of EU-15 total imports in %

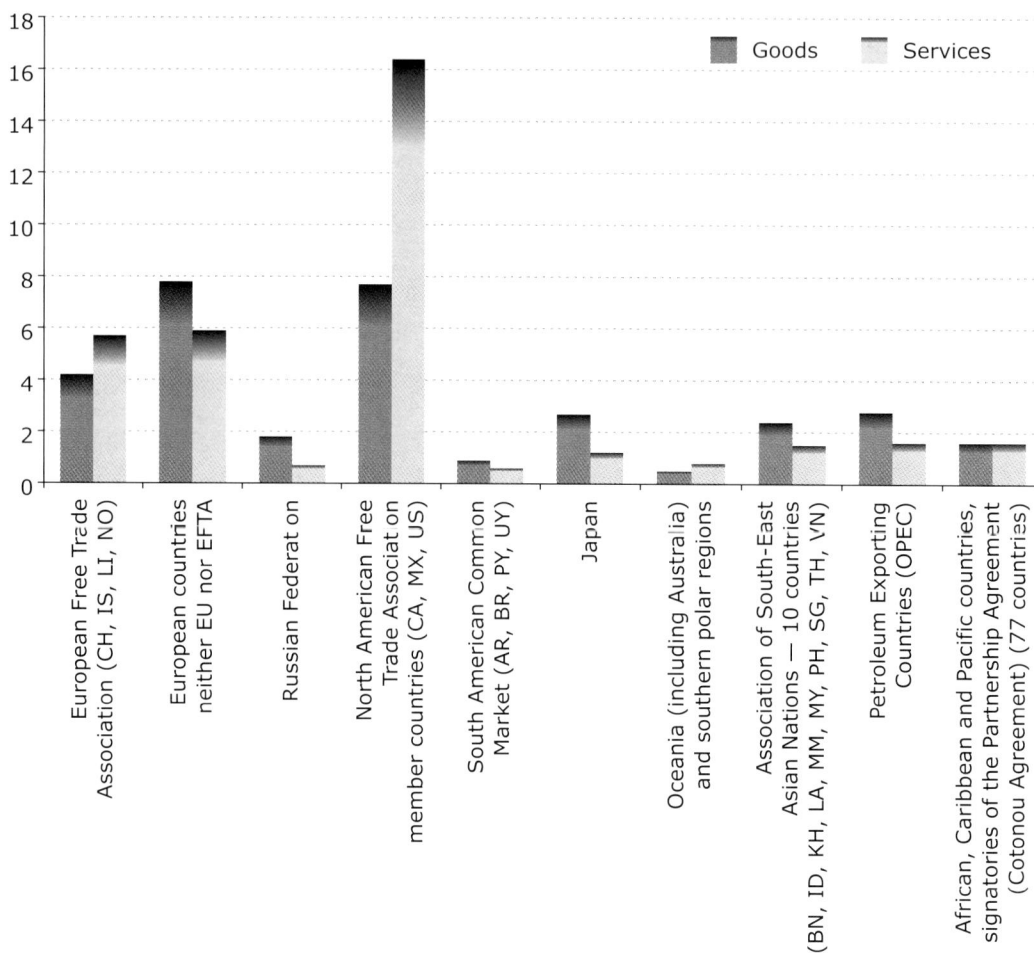

3

The balance of payments is a record of a country's international transactions with the rest of the world. It is composed of the current account and the capital and financial account. The current account is itself subdivided into goods, services, income and current transfers; it registers the value of exports (credits) and imports (debits).

Foreign direct investment

Eurostat data

Eurostat provides a wide range of data on:

— Direct investment flows (inflows and outflows)
— Direct investment stocks
— Investing countries (countries of origin)
— Receiving countries (countries of destination)

The financial account: dealing with money

The financial account records financial transactions. It includes foreign direct investment, portfolio investment, and other investment and reserve asset flows.

The annual European Union foreign direct investment statistics give a detailed presentation of foreign direct investment (FDI) flows and stocks, showing which Member State invests in which countries and in which sectors.

A firm wishing to sell overseas can choose between a variety of methods: exporting, licensing and using agents are some examples, with straightforward exporting up to now being the most common. FDI (producing and selling directly in the chosen country) is increasingly being adopted.

There are two kinds of FDI:

— the creation of productive assets by foreigners (greenfield investment);

— the purchase of existing assets by foreigners (acquisitions, mergers, takeovers, etc.).

FDI differs from portfolio investments because it is made with the purpose of having control or an effective voice in management and a lasting interest in the enterprise. Direct investment does not only include the initial acquisition of equity capital, but also subsequent capital transactions between the foreign investor and domestic and affiliated enterprises.

Eurostat collects FDI statistics for quarterly and annual flows as well as for stocks at the end of the year. The FDI stocks (assets and liabilities) are a part of the international investment position of an economy at the end of the year.

In the Eurostat yearbook, the sign convention adopted for the different sets of data (flows and stocks) is as follows: an investment is always recorded with a positive sign and a disinvestment with a negative sign.

3

Foreign direct investment intensity in 2002

Average value of inward and outward foreign direct investment flows divided by GDP, multiplied by 100

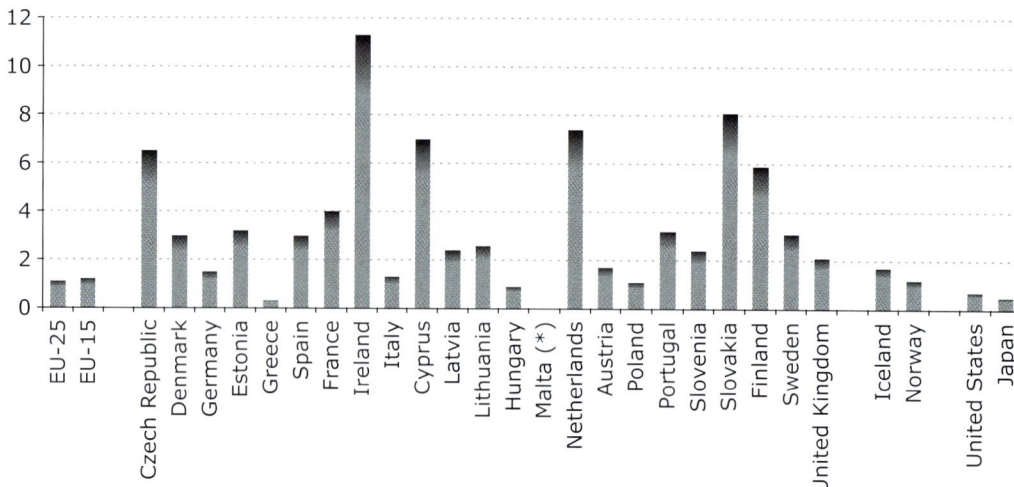

(*) In 2002, Malta had a disinvestment, i.e. a negative inward flow of FDI from the rest of the world. This has lead to a value of - 5.2. for the indicator on the FDI intensity.

For the aggregate of Belgium and Luxembourg (BLEU) the index stood at 51.4 in 2002 which is mainly due to a particularly high value for Luxembourg.

Foreign direct investment intensity is the sum of average inward and outward foreign direct investment (FDI) flows, divided by gross domestic product (GDP). The index measures the intensity of investment integration within the international economy.

For individual countries the partner is the 'rest of the world', for the EU-15 the 'extra-EU-15' and for the EU-25 the 'extra-EU-25'.

Direct investment flows

In million EUR/ECU

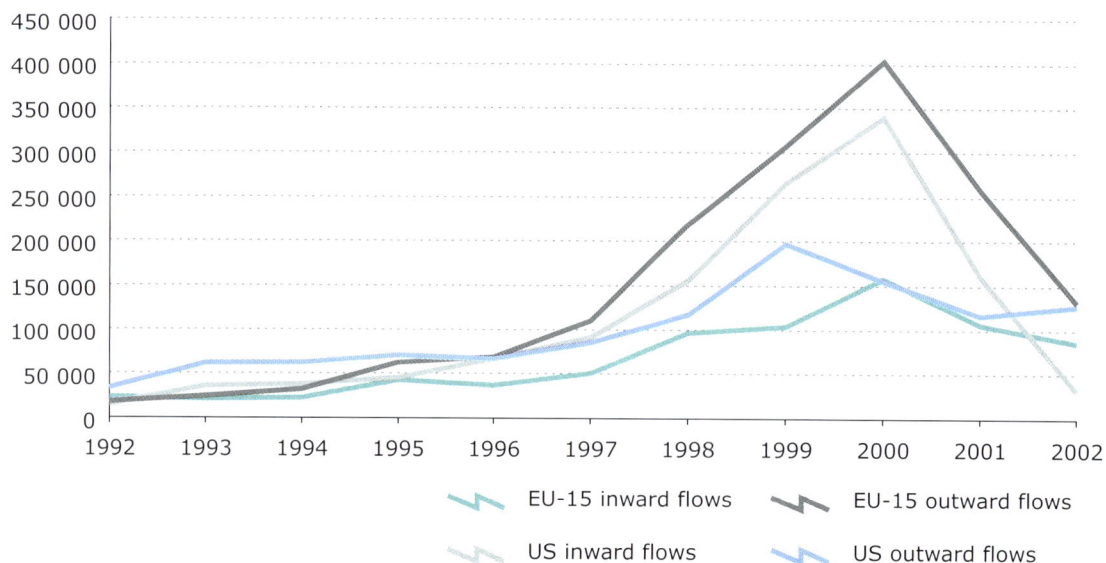

For the EU-15 the partner is the 'extra-EU-15', for the US the 'rest of the world'.

Foreign direct investment is an investment made by a resident entity (direct investor) to acquire a lasting interest in an entity operating in an economy other than that of the investor (direct investment enterprise).

Direct investment flows of the EU-15
In % of GDP

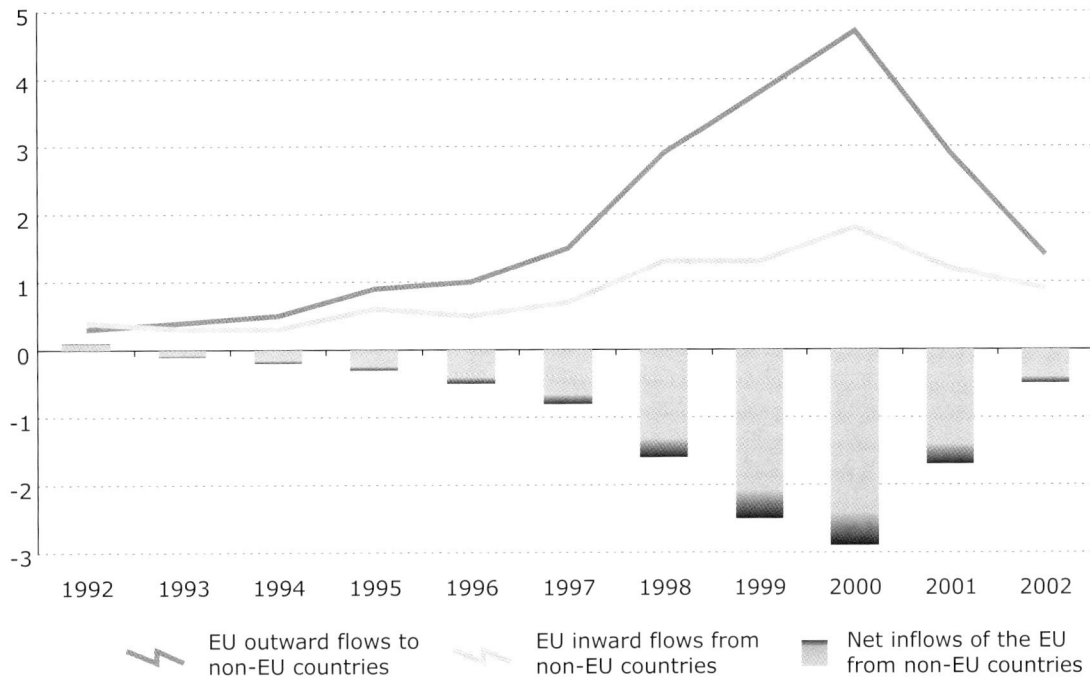

EU outward flows to non-EU countries

EU inward flows from non-EU countries

Net inflows of the EU from non-EU countries

Foreign direct investment is an investment made by a resident entity (direct investor) to acquire a lasting interest in an entity operating in an economy other than that of the investor (direct investment enterprise).

Direct investment flows of the United States
In % of GDP

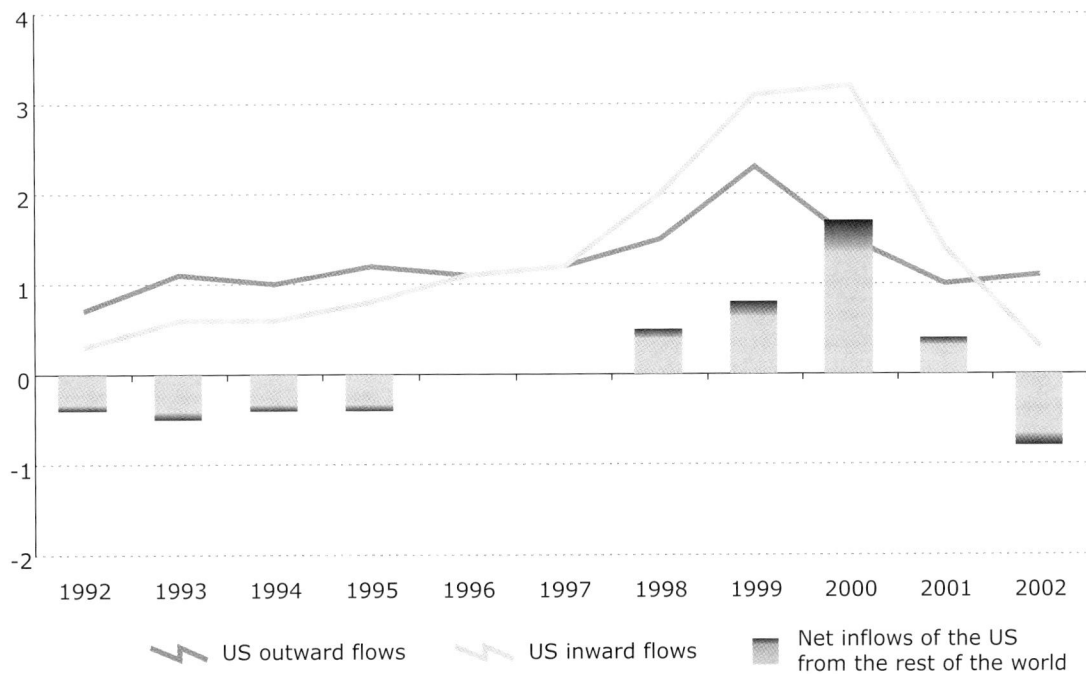

US outward flows

US inward flows

Net inflows of the US from the rest of the world

Foreign direct investment is an investment made by a resident entity (direct investor) to acquire a lasting interest in an entity operating in an economy other than that of the investor (direct investment enterprise).

3

Direct investment stocks of the EU-15
In % of GDP

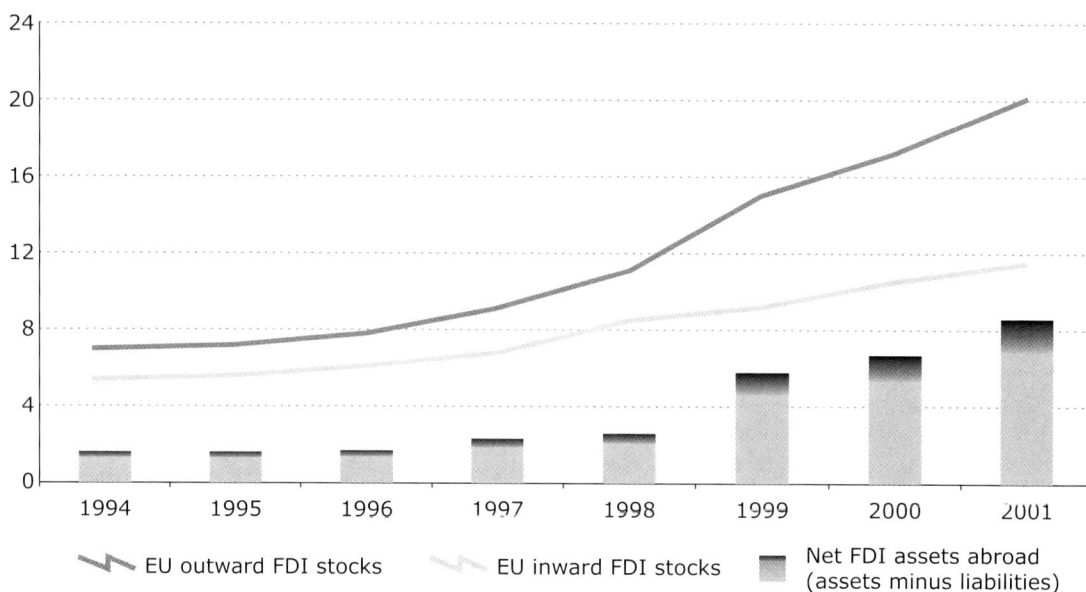

EU outward FDI stocks   EU inward FDI stocks   Net FDI assets abroad
(assets minus liabilities)

Foreign direct investment (FDI) is international investment made by a resident entity (direct investor) to acquire a lasting interest in an entity operating in an economy other than that of the investor (direct investment enterprise). FDI stocks are the value of FDI assets (for outward FDI stocks) and of FDI liabilities (for inward FDI stocks) at the end of the reference period.

Direct investment stocks of the US
In % of GDP

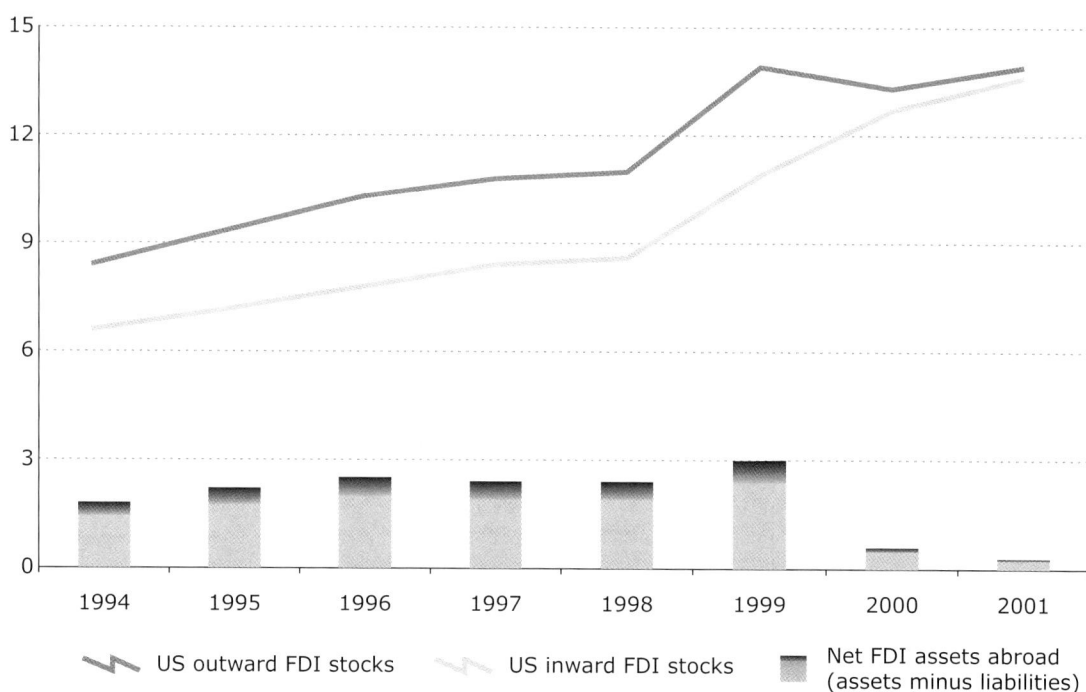

US outward FDI stocks   US inward FDI stocks   Net FDI assets abroad
(assets minus liabilities)

Foreign direct investment (FDI) is international investment made by a resident entity (direct investor) to acquire a lasting interest in an entity operating in an economy other than that of the investor (direct investment enterprise). FDI stocks are the value of FDI assets (for outward FDI stocks) and of FDI liabilities (for inward FDI stocks) at the end of the reference period.

International trade in goods

Essential information in a more and more open world economy

International trade in goods forms an increasing part of the world economy and, as such, must be measured reliably and the relevant data must be widely available and understood.

International trade statistics are an important primary source for most public and private sector decision-makers. For example, they help European companies carry out market research and define their commercial strategy. They enable Community authorities to prepare for multilateral and bilateral negotiations within the framework of the common commercial policy and to evaluate the progress of the single market or the integration of the European economies. Moreover, they constitute an essential source for balance-of-payments statistics, national accounts and studies of economic cycles.

Harmonised statistics on international trade in goods ...

The compilation of trade figures rests on a legal basis which is set out in a series of Council and Commission regulations. The concrete work is based on a cooperative effort between Eurostat and the appropriate bodies in the Member States which are responsible for collecting and processing the basic information.

Eurostat is responsible for harmonising Community legislation in the field of statistics on the trading of goods and ensuring that the legislation is applied correctly. The statistics provided to Eurostat are therefore based on precise legal texts directly applicable in the Member States and on definitions and procedures which have to a large extent been harmonised.

... which cover all physical movements of goods through the frontiers

In broad terms, the aim of international trade statistics is to record all goods that add to or subtract from the stock of material resources of a country by entering or leaving its territory. By their nature, international trade statistics are concerned with transportable goods.

The most important component of international trade statistics is related to transactions involving actual or intended transfer of ownership against compensation. Nevertheless, international trade statistics also cover movements of goods without a transfer of ownership such as operations following, or with a view to, processing under contract or repair.

Some methodological notes

Exports and imports valuation

In external trade statistics, exports are recorded at their fob value (fob — free on board) and imports at their cif value (cif — cost, insurance and freight). Therefore, and contrary to the balance-of-payments statistics, import value includes charges, such as transport and insurance, relating to that part of the journey which takes place outside the statistical territory of the importing country. Export value corresponds to the value of goods at the place and time where they leave the statistical territory of the exporting country.

Trade of country groups

EU-15, EU-25, the euro-zone and EEA (European Economic Area) are calculated as total trade less, respectively, intra-EU-15, intra-EU-25, intra-euro-zone and intra-EEA trade.

Trade in products

Agrifood products are food products obtained from agriculture. They are determined according to Sections 0 and 1 of the standard international trade classification (SITC), Rev. 3.

Trade in raw materials refers to Sections 2 and 4 of the SITC.

Trade in fuel products refers to products determined according to Section 3 of the SITC.

Trade in chemicals refers to products determined according to Section 5 of the SITC.

Machinery and transport equipment refers to products determined according to Section 7 of the SITC.

More concepts and definitions

Please refer to the publications *Statistics on the trading of goods — User guide or Geonomenclature* which can be downloaded from the Eurostat website.

International trade in goods in 2002: the EU and other main actors
In billion EUR

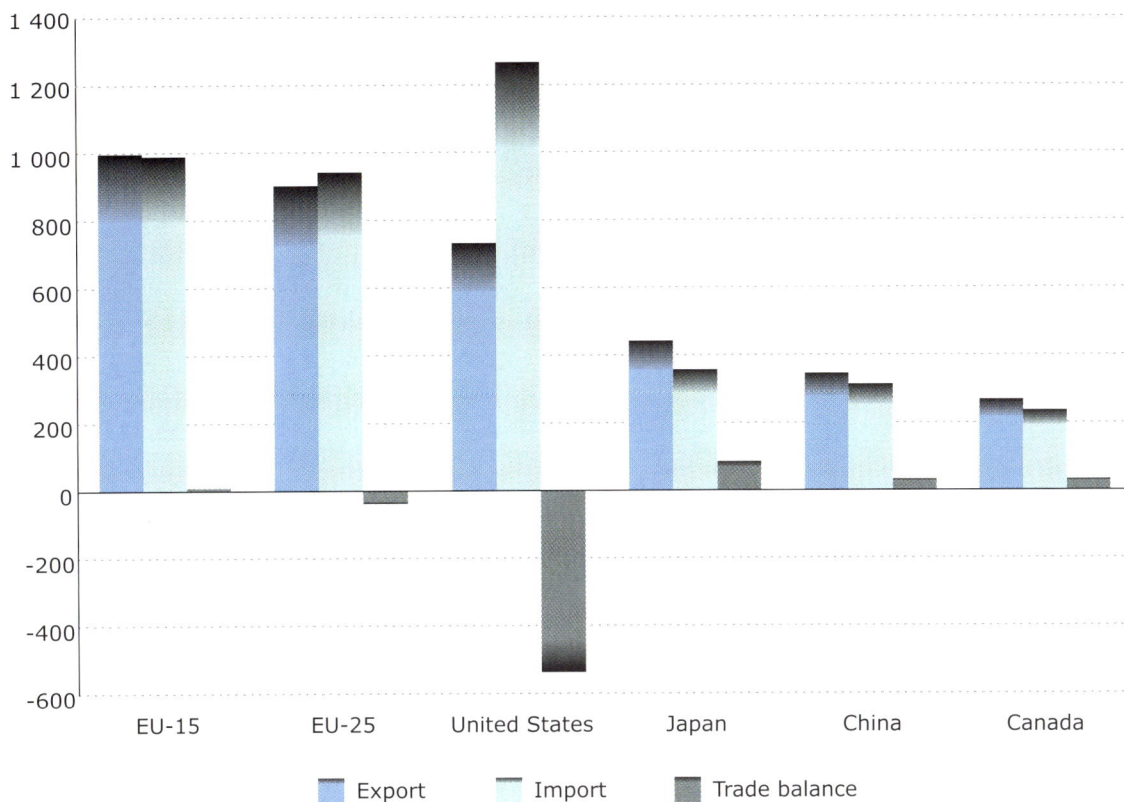

Legend: Export | Import | Trade balance

X-axis: EU-15, EU-25, United States, Japan, China, Canada

The EU-15's share in world trade(*) in 2002
In %

- United States — 20
- EU — 20
- Japan — 8
- China — 6
- Canada — 5
- Others — 42

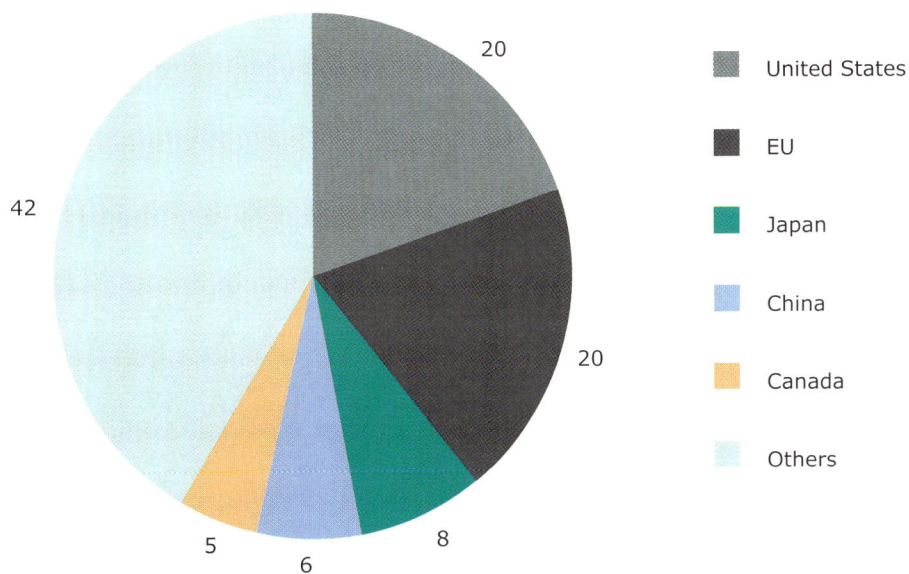

(*) imports + exports.

3

Evolution of the EU-15's trade from 1990 to 2003
In billion ECU/EUR

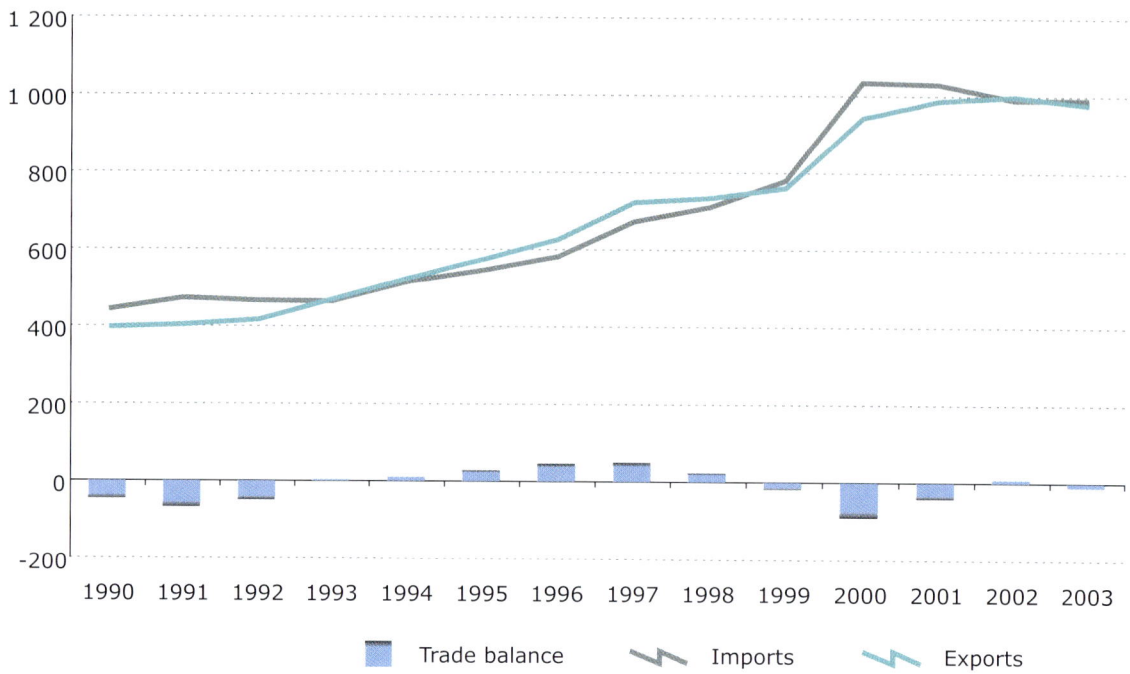

Trade balance   Imports   Exports

Shares of intra- and extra-EU-15 trade in total trade in 2003
In %

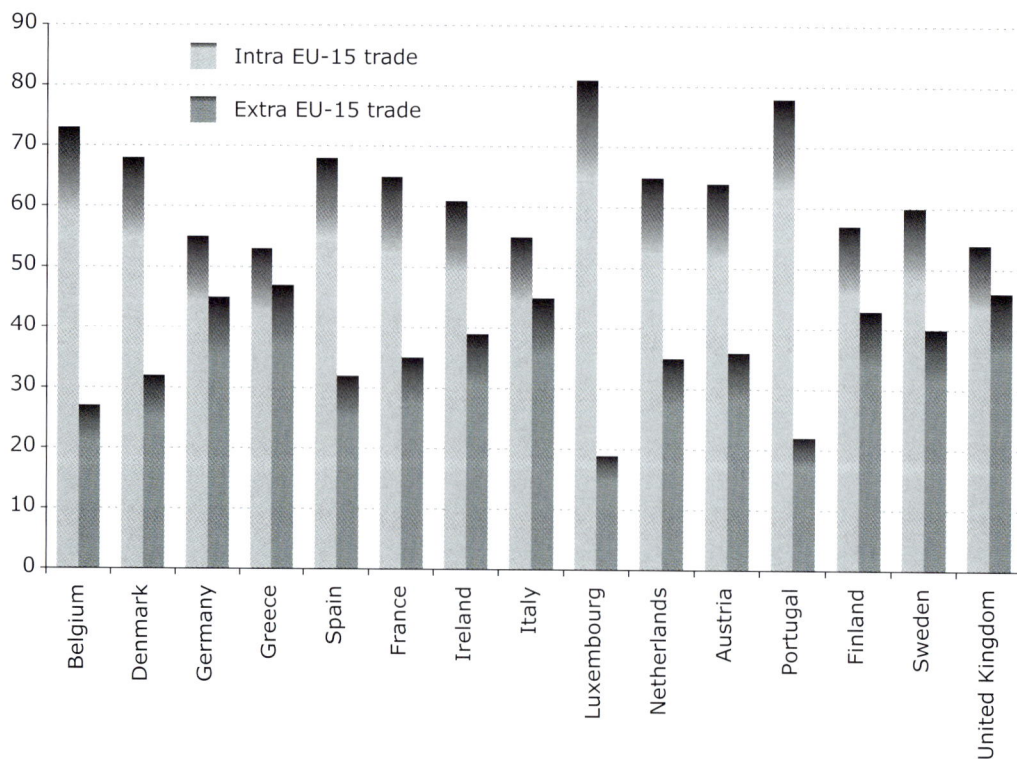

Intra EU-15 trade

Extra EU-15 trade

Belgium, Denmark, Germany, Greece, Spain, France, Ireland, Italy, Luxembourg, Netherlands, Austria, Portugal, Finland, Sweden, United Kingdom

Share of the main products in the EU-15's total imports
In %

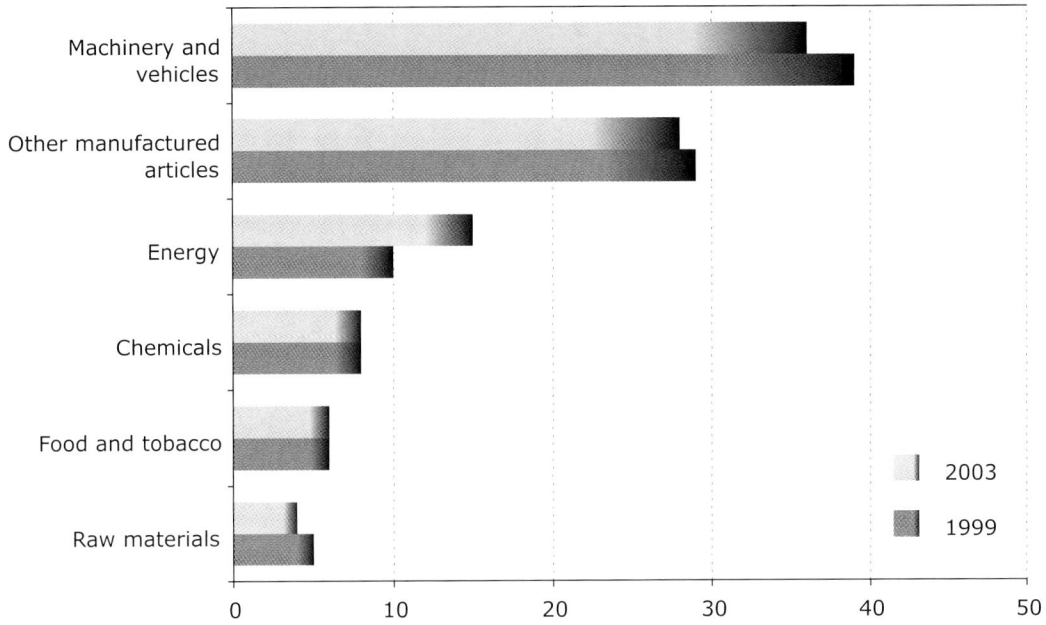

2003
1999

Share of the main products in the EU-15's total exports
In %

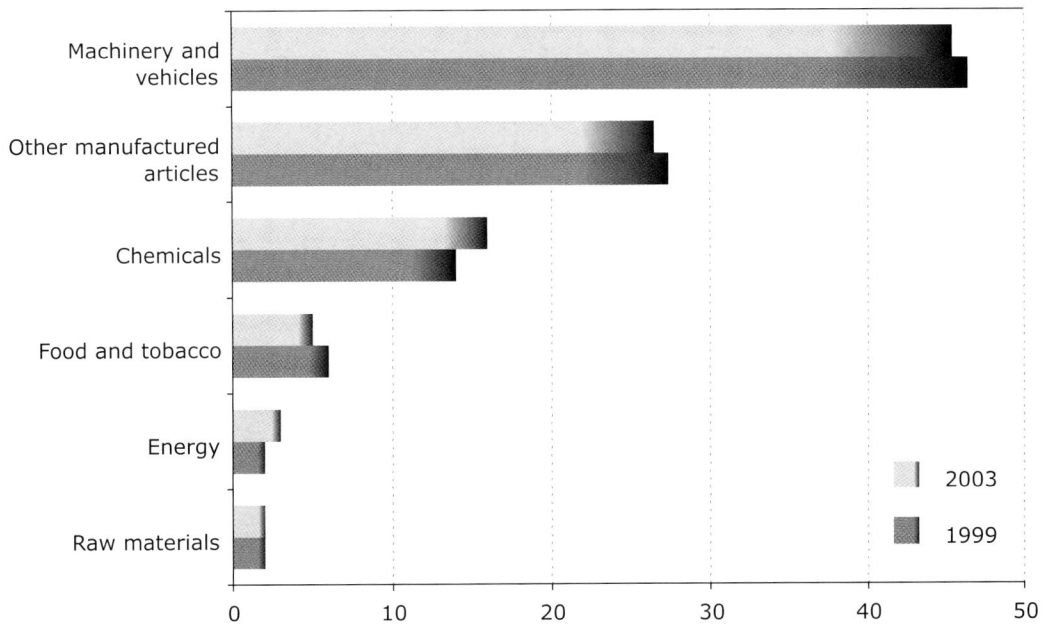

2003
1999

Total trade of the EU-15, EU-25 and the Member States in 2003
In billion EUR

	Export			Import			Trade balance	
	2003	2002	Change in %	2003	2002	Change in %	2003	2002
EU-15	976.7	997.2	-2	988.9	989.2	0	-12.2	8.0
EU-25	880.4	903.3	-3	936.3	942.0	-1	-55.9	-38.7
Belgium	225.7	228.6	-1	208.1	210.3	-1	17.6	18.3
Czech Republic	43.0	40.7	6	45.2	43.0	5	-2.2	-2.3
Denmark	59.6	60.8	-2	51.1	53.2	-4	8.5	7.6
Germany	661.6	651.3	2	531.9	518.5	3	129.6	132.8
Estonia	4.0	3.6	10	5.7	5.1	13	-1.7	-1.4
Greece	11.7	10.9	7	39.2	33.1	19	-27.5	-22.1
Spain	134.1	132.9	1	177.7	174.6	2	-43.6	-41.7
France	341.9	350.8	-3	345.2	348.2	-1	-3.4	2.6
Ireland	82.0	93.3	-12	47.2	55.4	-15	34.8	37.9
Italy	258.2	269.1	-4	257.1	261.2	-2	1.1	7.8
Cyprus	0.4	0.4	-6	3.6	3.9	-8	-3.2	-3.5
Latvia	6.1	5.5	11	8.4	8.0	6	-2.3	-2.4
Lithuania	2.6	2.4	6	4.6	4.3	8	-2.1	-1.9
Luxembourg	11.8	10.8	9	14.4	13.8	4	-2.6	-3.0
Hungary	37.7	36.5	3	42.1	39.9	6	-4.5	-3.4
Malta	2.0	2.1	-5	2.9	2.8	2	-0.8	-0.7
Netherlands	260.0	258.1	1	232.3	231.9	0	27.6	26.2
Austria	84.7	83.2	2	86.7	82.8	5	-1.9	0.4
Poland	47.5	43.5	9	60.4	58.5	3	-12.8	-15.0
Portugal	27.7	28.1	-1	39.9	42.4	-6	-12.1	-14.3
Slovenia	11.3	11.0	3	12.2	11.6	6	-1.0	-0.6
Slovak Republic	19.3	15.2	27	19.9	17.5	14	-0.6	-2.3
Finland	46.8	47.7	-2	37.1	36.2	3	9.7	11.6
Sweden	89.5	86.2	4	73.1	70.8	3	16.4	15.4
United Kingdom	269.3	296.3	-9	345.5	366.2	-6	-76.2	-69.9

Member States' contribution to the EU-25's total trade in 2003

	Export		Import		Trade balance
	Billion EUR	Share in %	Billion EUR	Share in %	Billion EUR
Extra EU-25	880.4	100	936.3	100	-55.9
Belgium	51.5	6	55.1	6	-3.6
Czech Republic	5.8	1	12.9	1	-7.1
Denmark	17.7	2	13.6	1	4.1
Germany	237.8	27	182.9	20	55.0
Estonia	0.7	0	2.0	0	-1.3
Greece	5.3	1	17.2	2	-11.9
Spain	34.5	4	56.8	6	-22.3
France	117.3	13	106.4	11	10.9
Ireland	30.9	4	17.7	2	13.2
Italy	104.4	12	101.5	11	2.9
Cyprus	0.2	0	1.4	0	-1.3
Latvia	0.5	0	1.1	0	-0.6
Lithuania	2.3	0	3.6	0	-1.3
Luxembourg	1.3	0	3.3	0	-2.0
Hungary	7.1	1	15.5	2	-8.4
Malta	1.1	0	0.9	0	0.1
Netherlands	51.9	6	105.8	11	-53.9
Austria	22.2	3	16.8	2	5.5
Poland	9.0	1	18.5	2	-9.5
Portugal	5.4	1	8.6	1	-3.2
Slovenia	3.7	0	3.0	0	0.8
Slovak Republic	3.0	0	5.1	1	-2.1
Finland	18.7	2	11.9	1	6.8
Sweden	37.0	4	20.5	2	16.4
United Kingdom	111.1	13	154.1	16	-43.0

The environment   167-178

4

Water

The pollution of rivers, lakes and groundwater remains a concern all over the world.

A directive to protect water

Because the quality of the water available is deteriorating and its quantity is limited, there is a need to reconsider the use of different sources of water as well as the demand on water. This has been set out in the Water Framework Directive 2000/60/EC. It states that sustainable water resource management has to be based on the principle of integrated river basin management. The directive also promotes a 'combined approach' of emission limit values and quality standards, getting the prices right and getting citizens more closely involved in water problems.

Water: essential and under strain

Water is a natural resource that both in terms of quality and availability is a major concern in many regions. Water resources are limited and water quality is affected by human activities such as industrial production, household discharges, animal husbandry, arable farming, etc.

At the same time, water is essential for human life and activities. Economic development and growing populations put increasing pressure on water quantity and quality. In many places on earth, freshwater resources are being consumed faster than nature can replenish them.

Keeping a close eye on water

Water statistics are collected from all European countries through the 'Inland waters' section of the joint OECD/Eurostat questionnaire which is continuously adapted to the EU policy framework. It reports on the following:

— **Freshwater resources in groundwater and surface waters:** these can be replenished by precipitation and by external inflows.

— **Water abstraction by source:** abstraction is a major pressure on resources, although a large part of the water abstracted (for domestic, industrial including energy production, or agricultural use) is returned to the environment and its water bodies, but often as wastewater with impaired quality.

— **Water use by supply category and by industrial activities.**

— **Treatment capacities of wastewater treatment plants and the share of the population connected to them:** this gives an overview of the development status of the infrastructure, in terms of quantity and qual-

ity, that is available for the protection of the environment from pollution by wastewater.

— **Sewage sludge production and disposal:** sewage sludge is an inevitable product of wastewater treatment processes; its impact on the environment depends on the methods chosen for its processing and disposal.

— **Generation and discharge of wastewater:** pollutants present in wastewater have different source profiles, and similarly the efficiency of treatment of any pollutant varies according to the method applied.

Total fresh water resources: long-term annual average
In million m^3

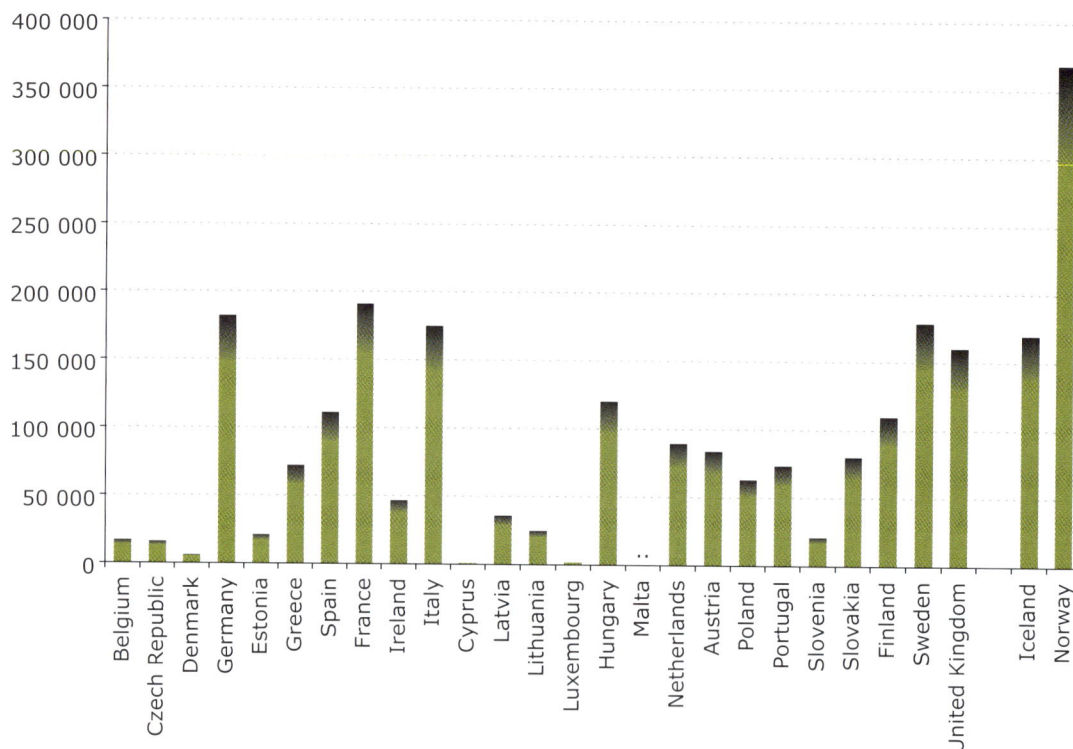

Ireland, Luxembourg, Norway: estimated value.

The minimum period taken into account for the calculation of long term annual averages is 20 years. Actual evapotranspiration is the volume of water transported from the ground (including inland water surfaces) into the atmosphere by evaporation and by transpiration of plants. Internal flow is the total volume of river run-off and groundwater renewal generated, in natural conditions, exclusively by precipitation into a territory. The internal flow is equal to precipitation less actual evapotranspiration. Actual external inflow is the total volume of actual inflow of rivers and groundwater coming from neighbouring territories. Total fresh water resources are the total volume of water that is additionally available due to internal flow and external inflow. Total actual outflow is the total actual outflow of rivers and groundwater into the sea and into neighbouring territories.

Waste

Eurostat data

Eurostat provides a wide range of data on:

— Waste generated

— Waste treatment

— Recycling

— Hazardous waste

Decoupling waste generation from economic growth

The generation of waste represents, on the one hand, a loss of materials and energy. On the other hand, its deposition contributes to major environmental problems such as climate change and an impaired quality of surface and groundwater bodies as well as landscapes. Waste generation might also lead to the deterioration of human health (through the release into the environment of hazardous substances that some types of waste contain).

The sixth environment action programme states the objective of decoupling economic growth from the generation of waste. A significant overall reduction in the volumes of waste generated will be achieved through improved waste-prevention initiatives, better resource efficiency and a shift to more sustainable consumption patterns.

Who generates waste ...

Municipal waste constitutes approximately 15 % of total waste produced and is the most reliable indicator for making comparisons among countries.

The economic activities that are large contributors to the waste mountain are construction, agriculture, mining and the manufacturing industry. Waste streams such as construction and demolition waste, and sewage sludge (a residual product of the treatment of municipal and industrial wastewater) pose various types

of management problems and environmental impacts.

... and what to do with it?

Landfilling, waste incineration (with or without energy recovery) and recycling are the most important treatment methods applied to municipal waste. Recycling is considered to be one of the most beneficial for the environment and is supported by several directives and policy measures in the EU.

Continuous improvement of statistics on waste

Waste statistics are collected from all European countries through the 'Waste' section of the joint Eurostat/OECD questionnaire.

It is generally recognised that differences in methods of data production among countries

4

plus the variances in interpretation of definitions and/or waste categories make comparison of data among countries rather difficult. It is expected that the recently adopted waste statistics regulation will, when fully implemented, significantly improve data availability and comparability on waste generation and treatment.

Municipal waste collected in 2001
In kg per inhabitant per year

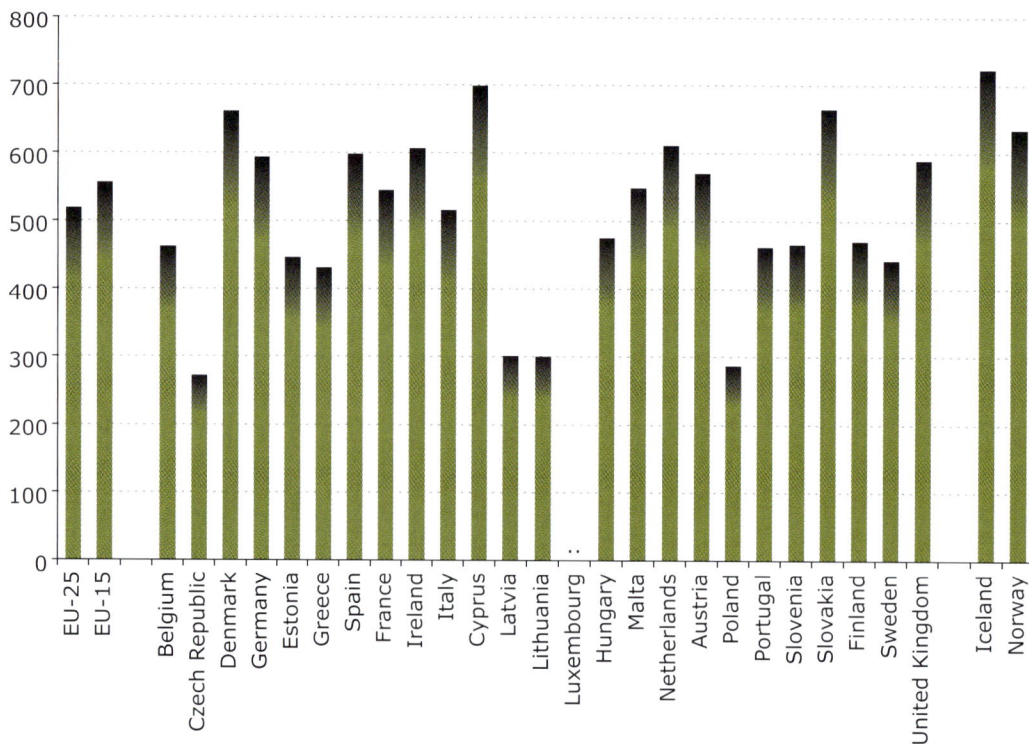

EU-25, EU-15, Belgium, Austria, Norway: estimated value

This indicator presents the amount of waste collected by or on behalf of municipal authorities and disposed of through the waste management system. The bulk of this waste stream is from households, though 'similar' wastes from sources such as commerce, offices and public institutions are included. The quantity collected is expressed in kg per capita per year.

Air pollution and climate change

Eurostat data

Eurostat provides a wide range of data on:

— Greenhouse gas emissions
— Air pollution by ozone
— Air pollution by particulate matter

Climate change

The earth's average surface temperature rose by around 0.6 °C during the 20th century and there is broad consensus among the scientific community that most of the warming over the last 50 years has been due to increased concentrations of greenhouse gases in the atmosphere, as a result of human activities, such as burning of fossil fuels and deforestation. The resulting increased energy in the weather system is predicted to lead to increased storms and rainfall in some areas, while others may suffer drought.

Under the 1997 Kyoto Protocol, the EU agreed to reduce its greenhouse gas emissions to 8 % below 1990 levels by 2008–12. In order to meet the 8 % target, individual targets for each of the EU Member States were set for the period 2008–12. This so-called 'burden-sharing' agreement allows several EU countries to increase emissions, provided these are offset by reductions in the rest of the EU. The EU climate change programme has been developed to identify common and coordinated policies and measures at Community level to ensure that the EU achieves its target.

For a more detailed analysis, see *Analysis of greenhouse gas emission trends and projections in Europe,* EEA, 2003.

Air pollution

The air we breathe contains gases and airborne particles released into the atmosphere by fuel combustion, industrial processes and other activities. Some of these are harmful to human health, and can result in various environmental problems such as acidification of soil and water, damage to buildings, eutrophication of water bodies, and the formation of tropospheric ozone.

Tropospheric ozone

Tropospheric ozone is formed by the reaction of some atmospheric pollutants such as nitrogen oxides and volatile organic compounds (VOCs) under the influence of sunlight; it is harmful to human health, causing damage to the respiratory tract. Although there are natural sources of nitrogen oxides, these are minor compared with emissions resulting from human activities, such as burning of fossil fuels and biomass. Areas with heavy traffic are particularly susceptible to the formation of tropospheric ozone.

Urban areas

Because many of these emissions are linked to human activities and heavy traffic, people living in urban areas are at most risk. Tropospheric ozone has already been mentioned, but human health is also at risk from high concentrations of particles, particularly those smaller than 10 μm, which penetrate deeply into the lungs, increasing the death rate in members of the population suffering from heart and lung diseases. The particles smaller than 2.5 μm are mostly soot, especially wood smoke and diesel engine exhaust. These can persist in the air for long periods and can be transported over long distances. Coarser particles (soil and mineral ash) originate mainly from mechanical processes such as mining, quarrying, and other industrial processes, as well as wear and tear of tyres and brakes in road traffic.

Data on emissions and on air quality

The European Environment Agency (EEA) and its European Topic Centre on Air and Climate Change compile data on greenhouse gas emissions, emissions of air pollutants and on air quality for the EU and candidate countries. These countries send to the EEA the same data they submit officially under various international conventions, such as the United Nations Framework Convention on Climate Change (UNFCCC) and the Convention on Long-range Transboundary Air Pollution (CLRTAP), and under various EU directives and regulations. Based on this data, the EEA produces reports and assessments, published regularly on its website (http://www.eea.eu.int).

Greenhouse gas emissions in 2001
Base year = 100

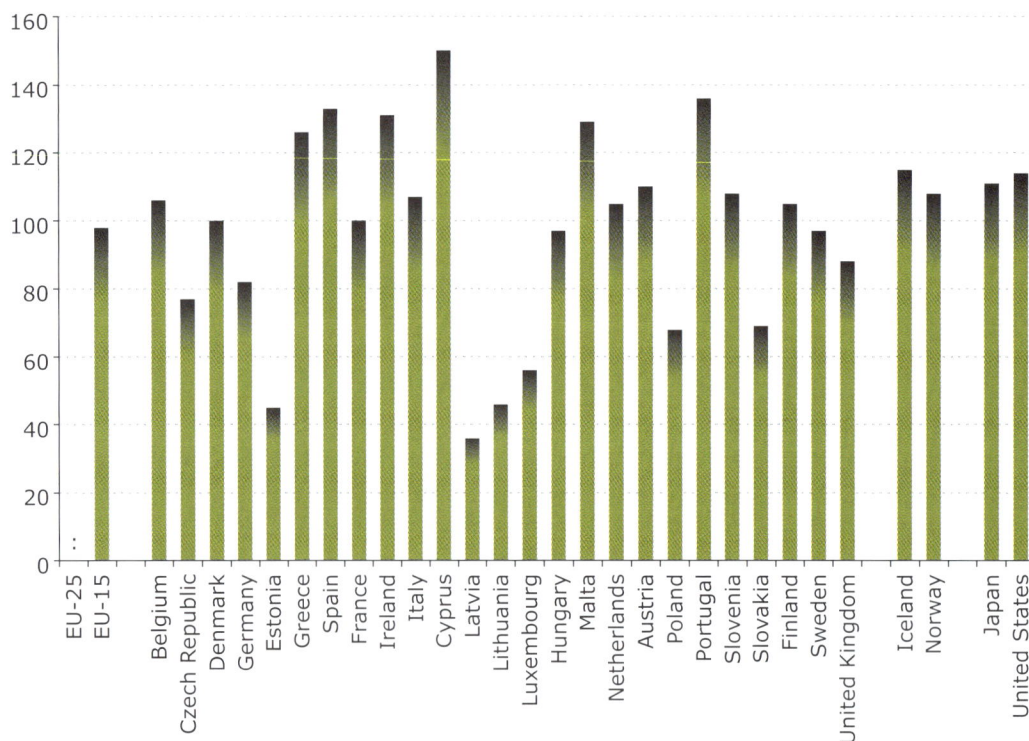

Source: European Environment Agency, European Topic Centre on Air and Climate Change

Under the Kyoto Protocol, the EU has agreed to an 8 % reduction in its greenhouse gas emissions by 2008–12, compared to the base year 1990. The reductions for each of the EU-15 countries have been agreed under the so-called EU burden-sharing agreement, which allows some countries to increase emissions, provided these are offset by reductions in other Member States. The ACCs have chosen other reduction targets and other base years, as allowed under the protocol. These and the 'burden sharing' targets for 2008–12 are shown in the table as figures for 2010. Emissions of the six greenhouse gases covered by the protocol are weighted by their global warming potentials (GWPs) and aggregated to give total emissions in CO_2 equivalents. The total emissions are presented as indices, with the base year = 100.

Environmental protection expenditure

Eurostat data

Eurostat provides a wide range of data on:

— Environmental expenditure

— Environmental investment

— Environmental tax revenues

About encouragement, regulations and 'the polluter shall pay'

The public has become increasingly aware of the need to protect the environment against pollution. Environmental protection is now being integrated into all policy fields with the general aim of ensuring sustainable development.

To encourage firms and private households to protect the environment, governments can use regulatory measures or levy taxes directly linked to pollution. The 'polluter pays' principle is another weapon in the fight against pollution. The data on environmental protection expenditure are an indicator of the response of society to reduce pollution.

Protecting the environment benefits the economy

Environmental protection measures cost money but can also generate revenues. Measures to protect the environment are increasingly being taken on a voluntary basis, for example, to meet the expectations of consumers or stakeholders, to increase market shares, or to improve company image. By the same token, environmental protection creates new markets for environmental goods and services, with benefits for exports and employment.

Spending on environmental protection occurs in all sectors of the economy. The public sector and industry are the sectors for which data are available for most Member States.

Statistical data on environmental protection expenditure

The legal framework for the statistical data on environmental protection expenditure by industry is Council Regulation (EC, Euratom) No 58/97 of 20 December 1996 concerning structural business statistics. The regulation provides a tool for the development in the coming years of regular data collection on the variables and economic activities of the highest policy interest.

Total expenditure is the sum of investments and current expenditure. Effective interpretations need to take into account that:

— high levels of spending in one country could, for example, be the result of new stricter policies or of long periods of no spending;

— the proportion of public sector expenditure versus industry expenditure could vary between countries depending on the degree of privatisation of the basic environmental protection activities, i.e. waste collection, waste treatment and sewage treatment.

Environmental protection expenditure statistics are collected through the joint Eurostat/OECD questionnaire.

Environmental protection expenditure by the public sector in the EU-15

Latest available year

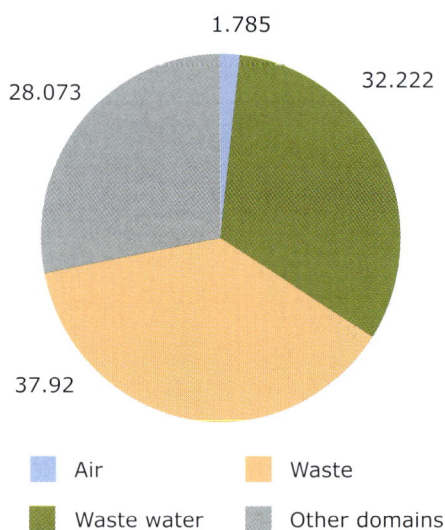

- Air
- Waste
- Waste water
- Other domains

Estimated values.

Environmental protection investment by the public sector in the EU-15

Latest available year

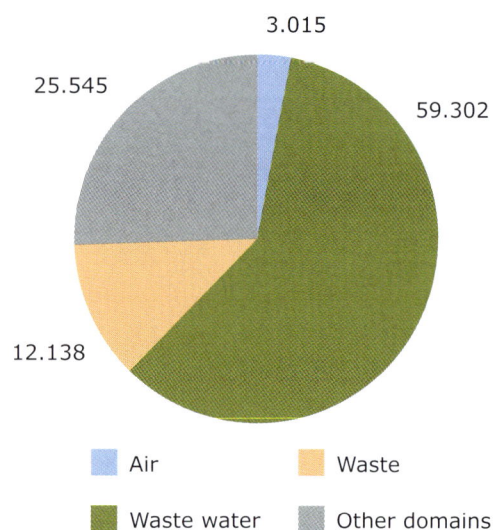

- Air
- Waste
- Waste water
- Other domains

Estimated values.

Agriculture and the environment

Eurostat data

Eurostat provides a wide range of data on:

— Sales and use of pesticides

— Consumption of commercial fertilisers

— Organic farming

Agriculture and the environment: a multifaceted relationship

The links between the richness of the natural environment and farming practices are complex. Farming has contributed over the centuries to creating and maintaining a variety of valuable semi-natural habitats. While many of these are maintained by extensive farming and a wide range of wild species rely on this for their survival, agricultural practices can also have an adverse impact on natural resources. Pollution of soil, water and air, fragmentation of habitats and loss of wildlife can be the result of inappropriate agricultural practices and land use. EU policies, and notably the common agricultural policy, are therefore increasingly aimed at reducing the risks of environmental degradation, while encouraging farmers to continue to play a positive role in the maintenance of the countryside and the environment.

Organic farming

Organic farming is one example of a sustainable farming system. Its importance has grown worldwide due to increased consumer awareness of organically grown products and government support for conversion. Since the start of the implementation of the EU regulation on organic farming (Council Regulation (EEC) No 2092/91), many agricultural holdings across the EU have converted to certified organic production methods. This regulation has established procedures for the Member States to report data on organic farming to the European Commission.

Use of fertilisers

The intensive use of fertilisers can have a negative impact on the environment. Maintaining a proper balance between nutrients added to the soil and removed from the soil by crops is essential to ensure the optimal use of resources and to limit pollution problems, such as environmental damage to surface water and groundwater particularly associated with nitrogen and phosphorus surpluses.

The Food and Agriculture Organisation (FAO) of the United Nations compiles information on commercial fertilisers. Country-level data are collected through: annual tailored questionnaires; electronic files and access to country websites; national/international publications; country visits made by FAO statisticians; and reports of FAO representatives in member nations.

Use of pesticides

The intensive use of pesticides, i.e. plant protection products, can have a negative impact on biodiversity and increases the risk of them finding their way into drinking water and the food chain.

Eurostat collects plant protection product sales data from Member States and the European Crop Protection Association produces data on the estimated use of plant protection products for Eurostat.

Total sales of pesticides in 1999
In tonnes of active ingredient

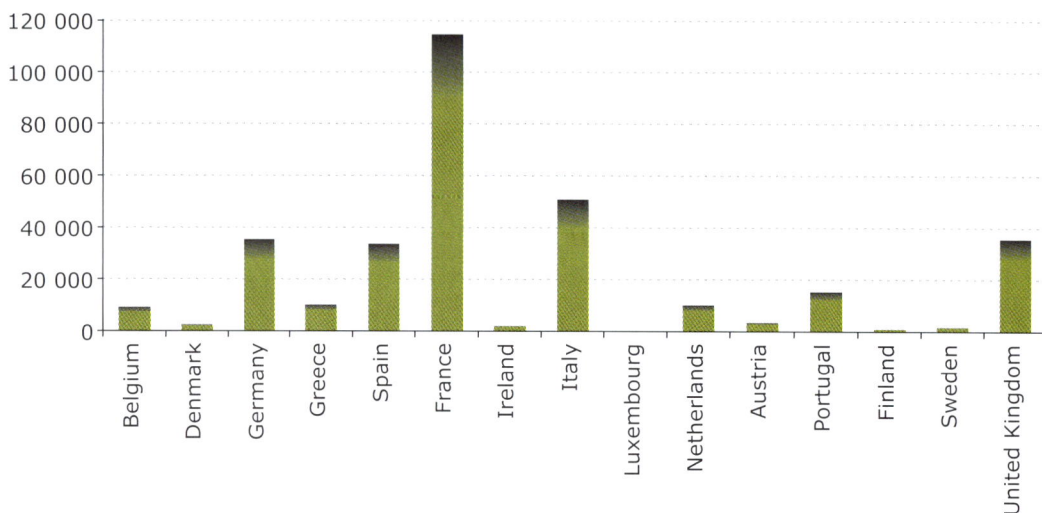

Total sales of pesticides are the sum of all sold fungicides, insecticides and other pesticides.

Commercial fertilizer consumed in agriculture in 1999
Total of nitrogen (N), phosphate (P205) and potash (K20);
metric tonnes of plant nutrient

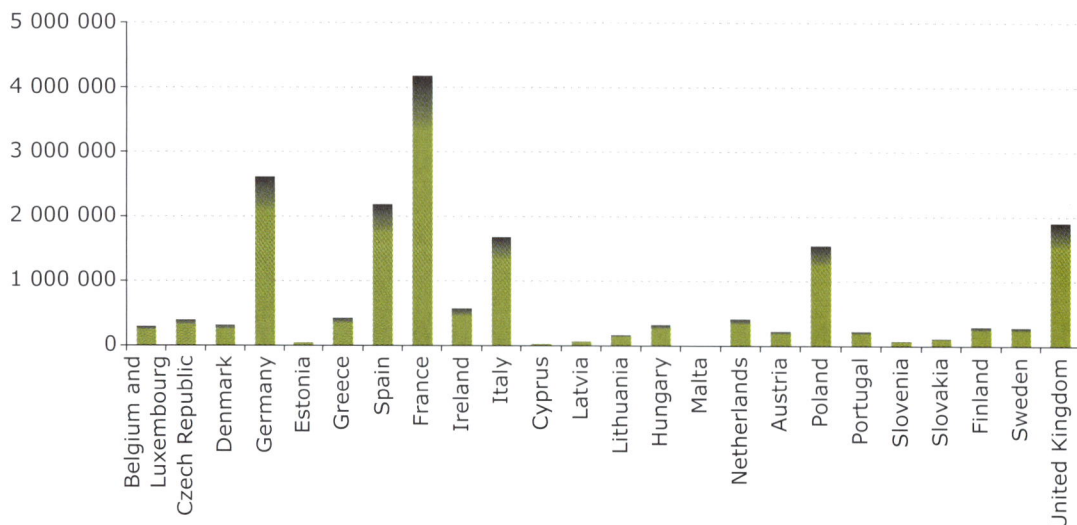

Source: FAO

Science and technology

5

Research and development

Research and development: an engine of growth

Research and development (R&D) is a driving force behind economic growth, job creation, innovation of new products and increasing quality of products in general, as well as improvements in healthcare and environmental protection. At the Lisbon Summit in March 2000, the European Council set a clear strategic objective for Europe in the next decade: to make the EU the most competitive and dynamic knowledge-based economy in the world.

Eurostat supports this ambitious goal with its reliable and relevant statistical information on R&D and innovation as well as on science and technology. Eurostat calculates a number of indicators and provides data for deeper analytical studies. Most indicators are calculated annually and are available at national and regional level (for most of the countries at NUTS 2 level). Depending on the indicator, data are available not only for the Member States of the European Union but also for other members of the European Economic Area, candidate countries, Japan or the United States.

Inputs into R&D

Data on R&D expenditure and personnel as well as on government budget appropriations or outlays for research and development (Gbaord) are mainly collected every year from the national statistical offices.

R&D expenditure is a 'priority indicator' for the effort devoted to R&D. The basic measure is 'intramural expenditures', i.e. all expenditures for R&D performed within a statistical unit or sector of the economy, whatever the source of funds. Among the several indicators available, R&D intensity (i.e. R&D expenditure as a percentage of GDP) is the most recommended for international comparisons and is very significant for comparing the countries' R&D efforts.

R&D intensity for EU-15 showed a decreasing trend during the 1990s, but it stabilised towards the end of the decade. When compared

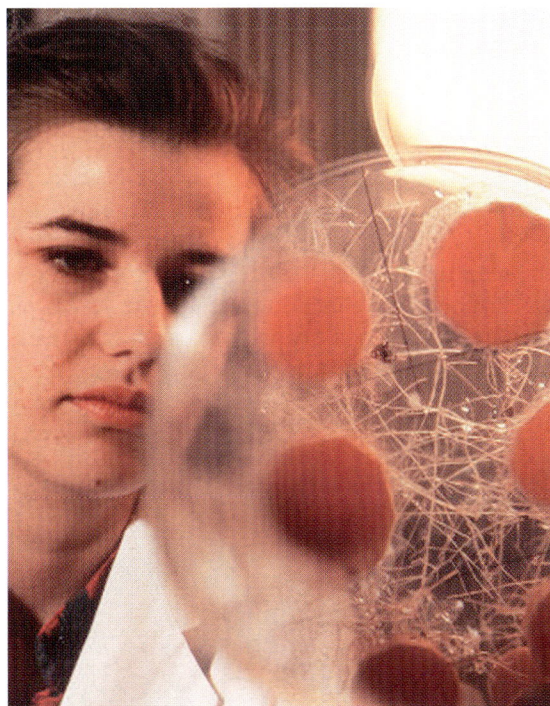

5

with the United States and Japan, the EU lags behind, but this is mainly due to the differences observed in the business enterprise sector. Within the EU, R&D intensity is highest in Finland and Sweden, which outperform countries with the highest R&D expenditure in terms of volume (Germany, France and the United Kingdom). Portugal, Denmark and Ireland show the highest real growth rate in R&D expenditure.

In terms of human resources, data on scientific and technical R&D personnel provide indicators for useful international comparisons of resources devoted to R&D. For statistical purposes, indicators on R&D personnel are compiled in terms of persons, i.e. head count (HC), in full-time equivalent (FTE) or person-years and by gender. At the EU level, R&D personnel in HC as a proportion of the labour force has seen a modest increase over the last decade, with the Nordic countries taking the lead.

Gbaord are the amount governments allocate towards R&D activities. Comparisons of Gbaord across countries give an impression of the relative importance attached to State-funded R&D. Gbaord statistics complement the *ex post* figures on 'government-financed' gross expenditure on research and development (GERD) and, when broken down by socioeconomic objective, underline the domains governments believe to be important for current and future policy action. When measured as a proportion of GDP, Japan has caught up with both the EU and the United States to a significant degree since the end of the 1980s. Data show that the efforts made by governments in R&D activities are clearly converging.

Outputs of R&D

Patents reflect part of a country's inventive activity and show the country's capacity to exploit knowledge and translate it into potential economic gains. In this context, indicators based on patent statistics are widely used as a measure of R&D output and serve to assess the inventive performance of the countries, regions or industries. Patent data published in the Eurostat yearbook are provided by the European Patent Office (EPO) and the United States Patent and Trademark Office (USPTO).

The data from the EPO refer to patent applications filed under the European Patent Convention or under the Patent Cooperation Treaty and designating the EPO for protection. Although not all applications are granted, each one still represents technical effort by the inventor and so is regarded as an appropriate indicator of innovative potential. Germany has the highest number of patenting activities of the EPO total, when measured in absolute values. In relative terms, the country with the highest number of patent applications per million inhabitants is Sweden followed by Finland. These two countries are also leading in high-technology patenting and show a high specialisation in the communication technology field.

Human resources

The importance of high-technology sectors has increased considerably over the last few years and this has had a significant impact on the structure and organisation of employment in Europe. In order to permit analysis of knowledge- and technology-intensive sectors, Eurostat collects data on employment in high-technology and medium-high-technology manufacturing sectors, knowledge-intensive services (KIS), high-technology service sectors, other subsectors and reference sectors (for definitions, see glossary entry total 'High-technology sectors').

Data on employment in high-technology and derived indicators are extracted and built up using data from the Community labour force survey (LFS). Data are available both at the national and regional levels. Within Europe, UK regions and Finland show high employment in high and medium-high technology. In the service sector, Greece appears to be one of the most dynamic regarding employment in other KIS.

Researchers
Full time equivalent; all institutional sectors

	1991	1992	1993	1994	1995	1996	1997	1998	1999	2000	2001
EU-25	:	:	:	:	:	:	:	:	:	:	:
EU-15	739 390(s)	774 743(s)	787 066(s)	814 410(s)	830 565(s)	845 212(s)	851 627(s)	886 053(s)	923 459(s)	954 675(s)	981 209(s)
Euro-zone	570 163(s)	598 294(s)	603 738(s)	621 713(s)	628 571(s)	647 304(s)	650 556(s)	671 083(s)	704 824(s)	741 723(s)	763 369(s)
Belgium	18 104(s)	:	20 839(e)	22 773(e)	23 491(e)	24 477(e)	25 579(e)	28 149(e)	30 219(e)	30 395(er)	32 298(er)
Czech Republic	:	20 084(i)	13 627(i)	13 325(i)	11 935(b)	12 963(i)	12 580(i)	12 566(i)	13 535(i)	13 852	14 987
Denmark	12 049	:	13 611	:	15 955	16 699(bi)	17 511(i)	:	18 439	:	19 453
Germany	241 869(b)	:	229 839	:	231 128(e)	:	235 791	237 712	255 261(e)	257 874(e)	259 597(e)
Estonia	:	:	:	:	:	:	:	2 978	3 002	2 666	2 631
Greece	6 230	:	8 015	:	9 706	:	10 964(r)	:	14 828(i)	:	:
Spain	40 641	41 687	43 368	47 868	47 344	51 632	53 883	60 269	61 568	76 670(e)	80 081
France	112 993(b)	142 198	145 824	148 638	149 824	152 533	152 740	155 006	:	170 628(r)	177 374
Ireland	5 137(s)	5 561(s)	6 425(s)	:	:	:	:	:	8 217(e)	8 516	:
Italy	7 5238	74 422	74 434	75 722	75 536	76 441	:	64 230	64 886	66 110	:
Cyprus	135(i)	147(i)	:	:	:	:	:	236	278	303	333
Latvia	:	:	3 999	3 010	3 072	2 839	2 610	2 557	2 626	3 814(r)	3 497
Lithuania	:	:	:	:	:	7 532	7 800	8 436	7 777	8 075	:
Luxembourg	:	:	:	:	:	:	:	:	:	1 625	:
Hungary	14 471	12 311	11 818	11 752	10 499	10 408(i)	11 154(i)	11 731(i)	12 579(i)	14 406(i)	14 666(i)
Malta	:	:	:	:	:	:	:	:	:	:	:
Netherlands	:	:	32 200(b)	34 200	34 038	34 012	38 055(i)	39 081(i)	40 640	41 896	45 328
Austria	:	:	12 821	:	:	:	:	18 715	:	:	:
Poland	:	41 440(i)	:	47 433	50 426	52 474	55 602	56 179	56 433	55 174	56 918
Portugal	:	:	:	:	11 586	:	13 580	:	15 752	:	17 724(e)
Slovenia	:	:	3 745(i)	4 767(i)	4 897(i)	4 489	4 022	4 285	4 427	4 336	4 497
Slovakia	:	:	:	10 249	9 711	10 010	9 993	10 145	9 204	9 955	9 585
Finland	16 937	:	18 589	:	20 857	:	26 412	30 431	32 677	:	:
Sweden	26 515	:	30 495	:	33 665	:	36 878	:	39 921(i)	:	:
United Kingdom	124 226	135 064	139 183	145 792	152 331(s)	145 863	146 541(s)	158 586(s)	:	:	:
Iceland	688(s)	709(s)	815(s)	846(s)	1 076(s)	890(s)	1 456	1 533	1 577	:	1 869
Norway	13 460	:	14 763	:	15 928	:	17 490	:	18 295	:	19 722
Japan	598 333(i)	622 410(i)	641 083(i)	658 866(i)	673 421(i)	617 365b(i)	625 442(i)	652 845(i)	658 910(i)	647 572(i)	675 898(i)
United States	981 659(i)	:	1 013 772b(i)	:	1 035 995(i)	:	1 159 908(i)	:	1 261 227(i)	:	:

Researchers (RSE) are professionals engaged in the conception or creation of new knowledge, products, processes, methods, and systems, and in managing the projects concerned. Included are managers and administrators engaged in the planning and management of the scientific and technical aspects of a researcher's work as well as postgraduate students engaged in R&D. One FTE may be thought of as one person-year. For instance, a person who normally spends 40 % of his time on R&Dand the rest of it on other work (e.g. lecturing, university administration, guidance) should be counted as only 0.4 FTE — Frascati manual.

5

Research and development personnel in 2001
Share in the labour force in %

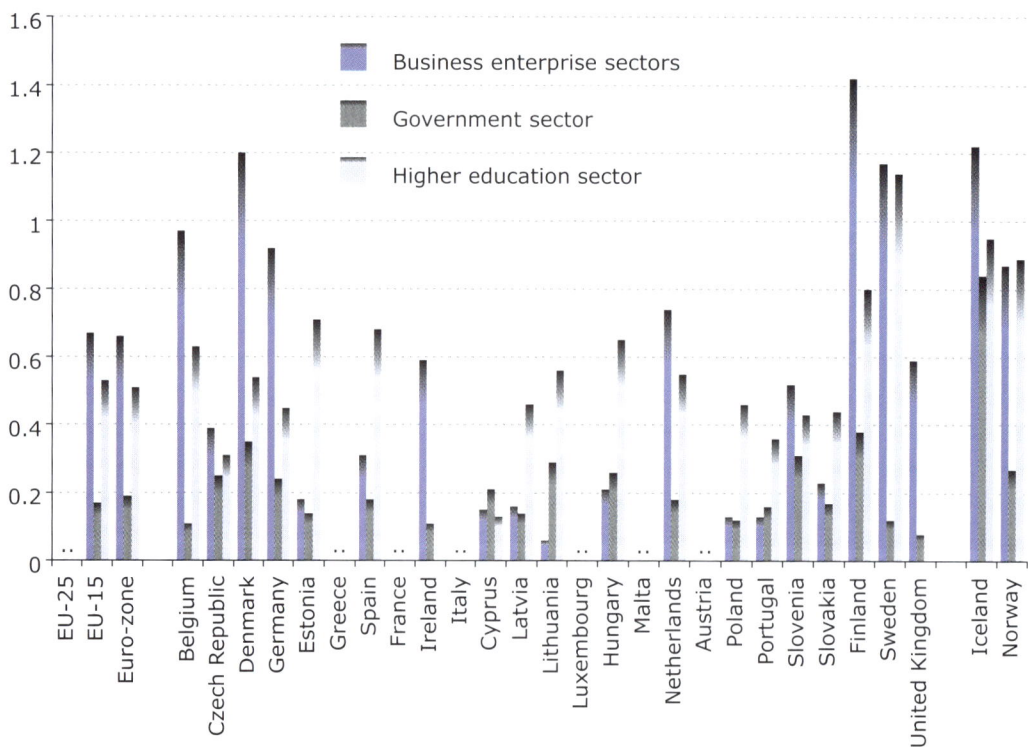

Includes estimated data.

R&D personnel include all persons employed directly on R&D, plus persons supplying direct services to R&D, such as managers, administrative staff and office staff. Head count (HC) data measure the total number of R&D personnel who are mainly or partly employed on R&D. R&D personnel in HC are expressed as a percentage of the labour force (comprises of population aged 15 and over who are employed or unemployed but not inactive).

Government budget appropriations or outlays on R&D
In % of GDP

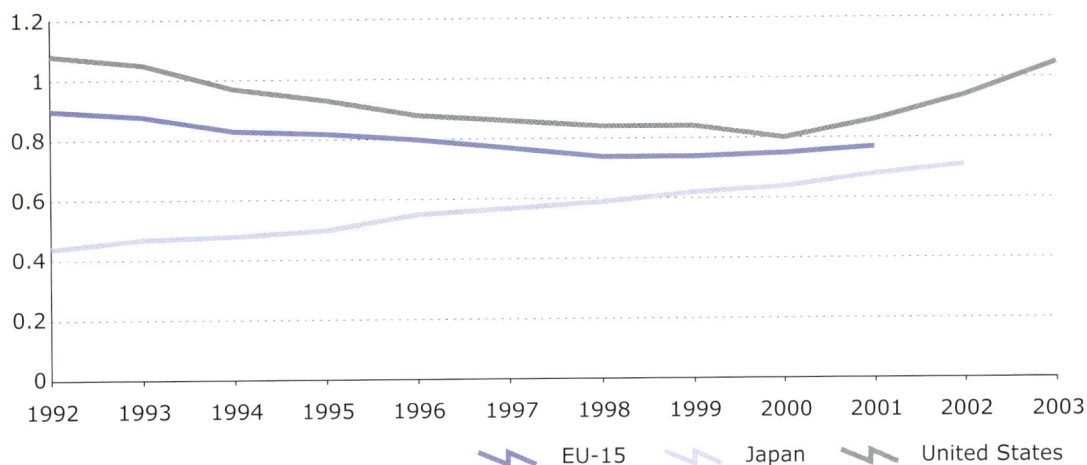

EU-15, Eurozone-12 1995, 1996, 2000, 2001: estimated values; Japan, United States 2002: provisional data; United States: 2003 forecast.

Data on government budget appropriations or outlays on R&D(GBAORD) refer to budget provisions, not to actual expenditure, i.e. GBAORD measures government support for R&D using data collected from budgets. GBAORD are a way of measuring government support to R&Dactivities. GBAORD is expressed as a percentage of GDP.

R&D expenditure in the EU-15, by source of funds
In %

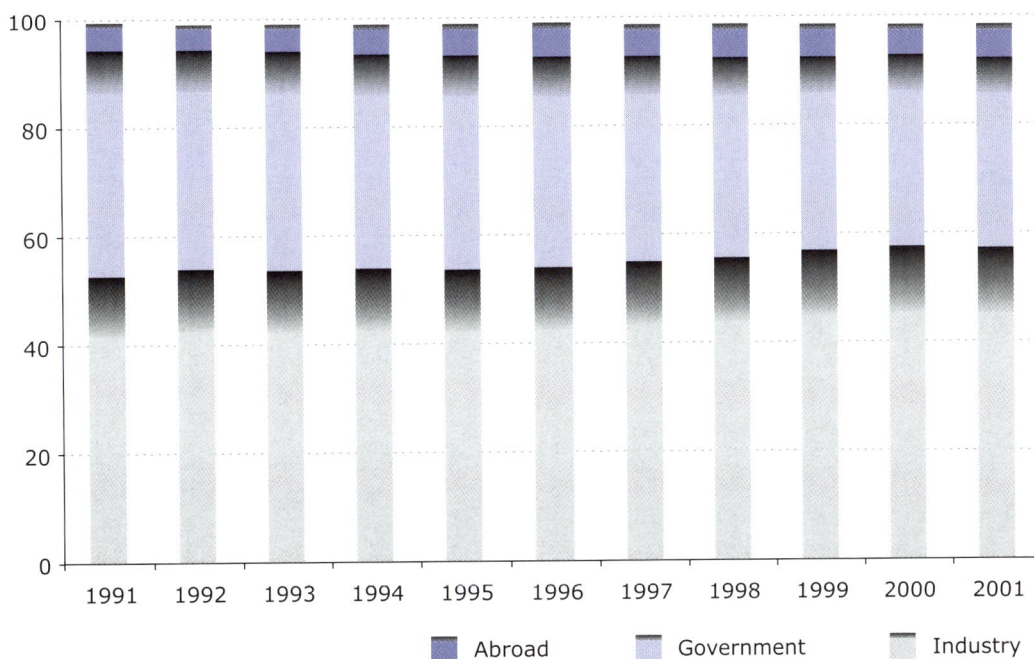

Estimated data.

Source: OECD.

Number of patent applications to the European Patent Office (EPO)
Per million inhabitants

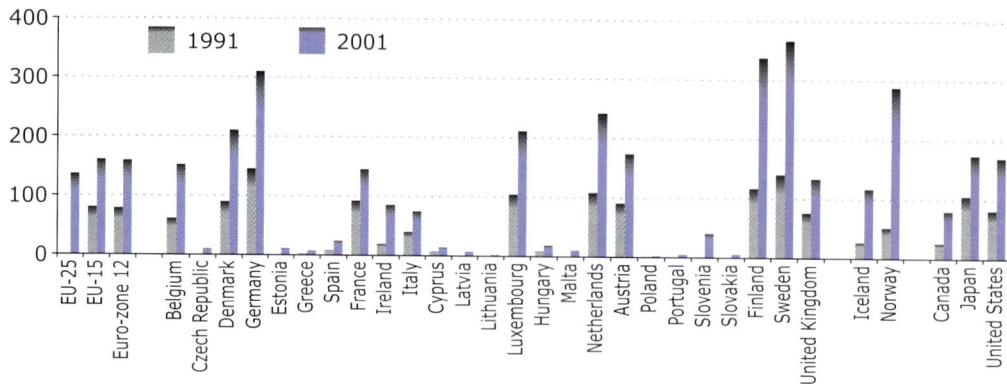

Legend: 1991, 2001

(*) The values for Liechtenstein were 1 171 (1991) and 1 080 (2001).

Includes estimated data.

Data refer to applications filed directly under the European Patent Convention or to applications filed under the Patent Cooperation Treaty and designated to the EPO (Euro-PCT). Patent applications are counted according to the year in which they were filed at the EPO and are broken down according to the International Patent Classification (IPC). They are also broken down according to the inventor's place of residence, using fractional counting if multiple inventors or IPC classes are provided to avoid double counting.

In EU-15, the number of patent applications to the European Patent Office (EPO) almost doubled from 1991 to 2001. Sweden, Finland and Germany reached the highest rates per million inhabitants in 2001 (over 300 patents per 1 million inhabitants). Their rates were double those for Japan and the United States. In many countries, the increases from 1991 to 2001 were more than double, and up to even five times in the case of Norway.

Number of patents granted by the US Patent and Trademark Office (USPTO)
Per million inhabitants

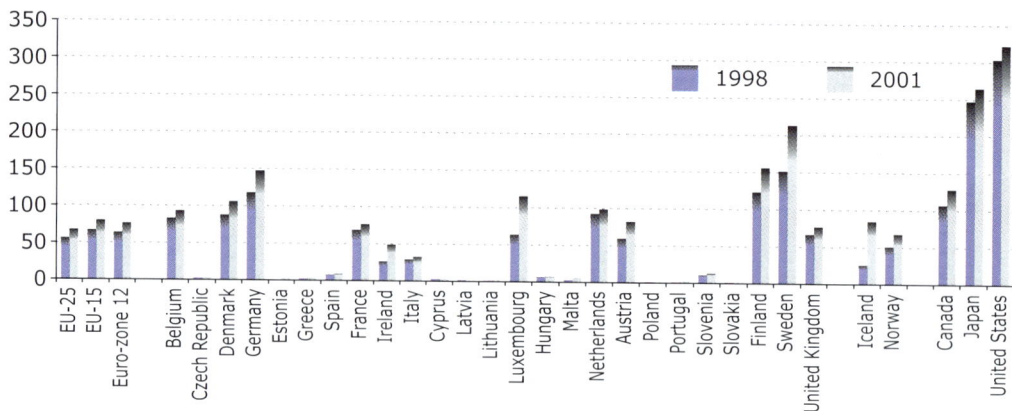

Legend: 1998, 2001

Includes estimated data.

USPTO data refers to patents granted while EPO data refers to patent applications. Data are recorded by year of publication as opposed to the year of filing used for the EPO data. This is because patents in the US (at least in the past) were only published once they were granted. Patents are allocated to the country of the inventor, using fractional counting in the case of multiple inventor countries. The methodology used is not harmonised with that of Eurostat and therefore the comparison between EPO and USPTO patents data should be interpreted with caution.

In 2001, the biggest rates of patents granted by the United States Patent and Trademark Office (expressed in the number of patents to 1 million inhabitants) were reached in the United States, Japan, Sweden, Finland and Germany.

Total European patent applications

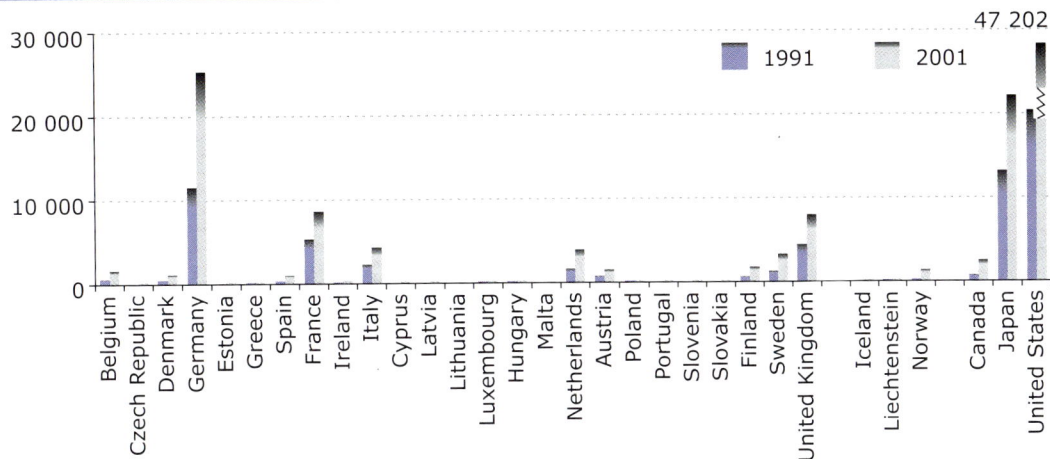

2001: provisional data.

The total European patent applications refer to requests for protection of an invention directed either directly to the European Patent Office (EPO) or filed under the Patent Cooperation Treaty and designating the EPO (Euro-PCT), regardless of whether they are granted or not. The data shows the total number of applications per country.

There were nearly 61 500 patent applications in 2001 in the 25 countries that today form the European Union. The increase in the number of patent applications shows the significant growth in research and development activities in Europe.

European high-technology patents
Per million inhabitants

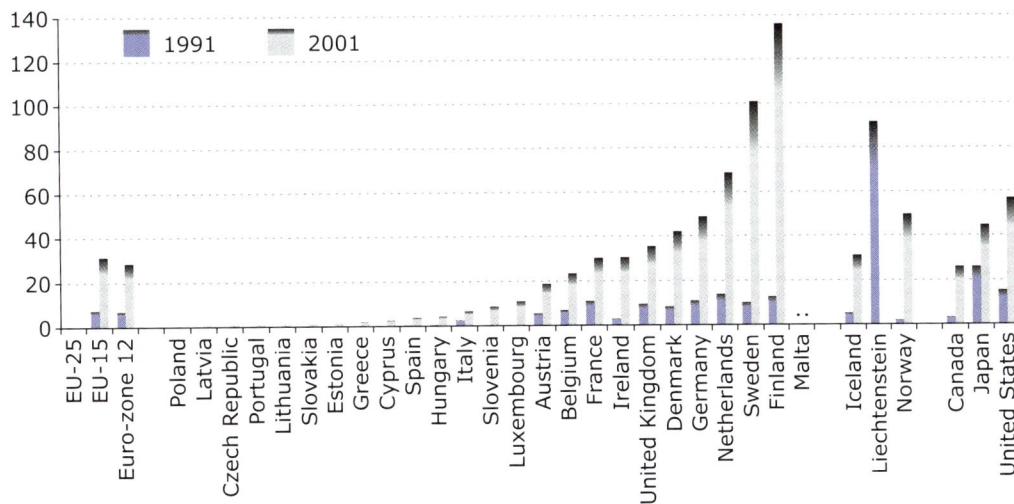

Includes estimated data.

The data refers to the ratio of patent applications made directly to the European Patent Office (EPO) or via the Patent Cooperation Treaty and designating the EPO (Euro-PCT), in the field of high-technology patents per million inhabitants of a country. The definition of high-technology patents uses specific subclasses of the International Patent Classification (IPC).

The rate of patent applications (relative to the population) on high technology reflects the output of the efforts made for research and development. In 2001, the 'top 10' countries for high-technology patents were Finland, Sweden, the Netherlands, the United States, Norway, Germany, Japan, Denmark, the United Kingdom and Iceland.

Total R&D expenditure
In % of GDP

	1992	1993	1994	1995	1996	1997	1998	1999	2000	2001	2002	2003
EU-25	:	:	:	1.86(s)	1.84(s)	1.83(s)	1.83(s)	1.88(s)	1.91(s)	1.93(s)	:	:
EU-15	1.92(s)	1.94(s)	1.91(s)	1.89(s)	1.88(s)	1.87(s)	1.88(s)	1.92(s)	1.95(s)	1.98(s)	1.99(s)	:
Euro-zone	1.86(s)	1.89(s)	1.84(s)	1.83(s)	1.82(s)	1.81(s)	1.82(s)	1.87(s)	1.89(s)	1.91(s)	1.92(s)	:
Belgium	:	1.70(e)	1.69(e)	1.72(er)	1.80(er)	1.87(er)	1.90(er)	1.96(er)	2.04(er)	2.17(er)	:	:
Czech Republic	:	:	:	:	:	:	:	:	1,23	1,22	:	:
Denmark	1.68(e)	1.74	:	1.84	1.85(e)	1.94	2.06(ei)	2.10(r)	2.27(er)	2.4	:	:
Germany	2.40(eir)	2.33(ir)	2.24(eir)	2.25(ir)	2.25(eir)	2.29(r)	2.31(eir)	2.44(r)	2.49(eir)	2.51(r)	2.51(eir)	:
Estonia	:	:	:	:	:	:	0.61	0.75	0.66	0.78	:	:
Greece	:	0.47	:	0.49	:	0.51	:	0.67(e)	:	0.64(e)	:	:
Spain	0.88	0.88	0.81	0.81	0.83(e)	0.82	0.89(e)	0.88	0.94(er)	0.95(r)	:	:
France	2.38	2.4	2.34	2.31	2.3	2.22	2.17	2.18	2.18(b)	2.23	2.20(e)	:
Ireland	1.04(e)	1.17(e)	1.31(e)	1.34(e)	1.32(e)	1.28(e)	1.25(ei)	1.20(e)	1.15	1.17	:	:
Italy	1.18	1.13	1.05	1	1.01	1.05(br)	1.07(r)	1.04(r)	1.07	1.11	:	:
Cyprus	:	:	:	:	:	:	0.23	0.25	0.25	0.27	:	:
Latvia	0.59	0.49	0.42	0.53	0.47	0.42	0.45	0.4	0.48	0.44	:	:
Lithuania	:	:	0.52	0.46	0.52(b)	0.56	0.56	0.52	0.6	0.69	:	:
Luxembourg	:	:	:	:	:	:	:	:	1.71(r)	:	:	:
Hungary	1.05(i)	0.98(i)	0.89(i)	0.73(i)	0.65(i)	0.72(i)	0.68(i)	0.69(i)	0.80(i)	0.95(i)	:	:
Netherlands	1.9	1.93(b)	1.97	1.99	2.03	2.04	1.94	2.02(r)	1.90(r)	1.89(r)	:	:
Austria	1.45(e)	1.47	1.54(ei)	1.56(ei)	1.60(ei)	1.71(ei)	1.78	1.86(ei)	1.84(ei)	1.90(eip)	1.93(eip)	:
Poland	:	:	:	:	:	:	:	0.7	0.66	0.64	0.59	:
Portugal	0.61	:	:	0.57(r)	:	0.62	:	0.75(r)	:	0.85(e)	:	:
Slovenia	1.91	1.60(bi)	1.76(i)	1.61(i)	1.36	1.35	1.4	1.44	1.46	1.57	:	:
Slovakia	:	:	0.9	0.93	0.92	1.09	0.79	0.66	0.65	0.64	0.58	:
Finland	2.13	2.18	2.29	2.28	2.54	2.71	2.88	3.23	3.4	3.41	3.49(f)	:
Sweden	:	2.99	:	3.35	:	3.55	3.62(e)	3.65	:	4.27	:	:
United Kingdom	2.08	2.11	2.06	1.97	1.9	1.82	1.81	1.84	1.84(r)	1.89(r)	1.84(f)	:
Iceland	1.32(i)	1.33	1.38(i)	1.54	:	1.88	2.07	2.38	2.76(e)	3.06	3.09(f)	:
Norway	:	1.72	:	1.7	:	1.64	:	1.65	:	1.6	:	:
Japan	2.89(i)	2.83(i)	2.77(i)	2.90(i)	2.78(bi)	2.84(i)	2.95(i)	2.96(i)	2.99(i)	3.07(i)	:	:
United States	2.62(i)	2.50(i)	2.40(i)	2.49(i)	2.53(i)	2.56(i)	2.59(i)	2.63(i)	2.70(i)	2.72(i)	2.64(ip)	2.59(ip)

The indicator provided is GERD (Gross domestic expenditure on R&D) as a percentage of GDP. 'Research and experimental development (R&D) comprises creative work undertaken on a systematic basis in order to increase the stock of knowledge, including knowledge of man, culture and society and the use of this stock of knowledge to devise new applications' (Frascati manual, 2002 edition, subsection 63). R&D is an activity where there are significant transfers of resources between units, organisations and sectors and it is important to trace the flow of R&D funds.

Total R&D expenditure in 2001
In % of GDP

4.27	3.41	3.07	3.06	2.72	2.51	2.40	2.23	2.17	1.93	1.90	1.89	1.89	1.60	1.57	1.22	1.17	1.11	0.95	0.95	0.85	0.78	0.69	0.64	0.64	0.64	0.44	0.27
Sweden	Finland	Japan	Iceland	United States	Germany	Denmark	France	Belgium	EU-25	Austria	Netherlands	United Kingdom	Norway	Slovenia	Czech Republic	Ireland	Italy	Spain	Hungary	Portugal	Estonia	Lithuania	Greece	Poland	Slovakia	Latvia	Cyprus

EU-25, Belgium, Greece, Austria, Portugal: estimated value.

The indicators provided are GERD (gross domestic expenditure on R&D) as a percentage of GDP, percentage of GERD financed by industry, percentage of GERD financed by government and percentage of GERD financed from abroad. 'Research and experimental development (R&D) comprise creative work undertaken on a systematic basis in order to increase the stock of knowledge, including knowledge of man, culture and society and the use of this stock of knowledge to devise new applications' (Frascati manual, 2002 edition, subsection 63). R&D is an activity where there are significant transfers of resources between units, organisations and sectors and it is important to trace the flow of R&D funds.

Information society

The information society: an opportunity for Europe ...

Information technology is developing vigorously day by day. However, the information society, a society whose wealth and growth are based on its ability to handle information efficiently, is not only a technical phenomenon: it is transforming the way we communicate, the way we do business, and the way we live. The information society holds enormous potential and opportunities for Europe and all of its citizens.

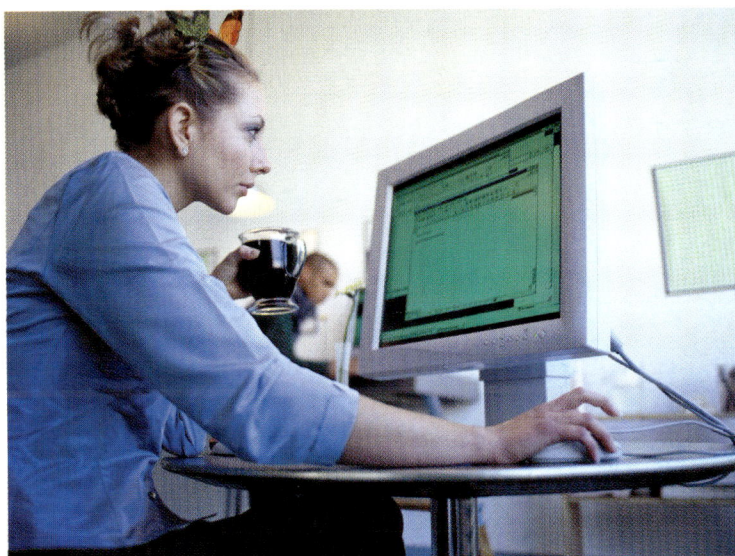

... and a challenge for statisticians

Monitoring the rapid change powered by the Internet and other new means of information and communication is a challenge statisticians are well aware of. They rethink their statistical tools and how best to use them to satisfy the new demands for data concerning all aspects of the information society. They cooperate with the different kinds of data users to identify and mediate the new demands.

The information society in the Eurostat yearbook

The Eurostat yearbook introduced a new section on the information society in its 2000 edition to present basic variables about the phenomenon, especially Internet hosts, Internet users and mobile phones.

— **Internet hosts** are computers connected to the Internet and which provide data and services to other computers. Automated host counts are in many statistics on a country level restricted to country code top-level domains (domain names like '.de', '.uk' or '.fr'). This is also the case for the figures which are shown in this section. Based on registrations, some statistics also attribute generic domain codes (examples are '.com' and '.org') to countries. This results in higher figures than the counting of the country code top-level domains only.

— The **level of Internet access** is reported separately for households and for enterprises.

5

— **Mobile phones** were first introduced in Europe in the early 1980s. Constrained by weight and power requirements, they were at the beginning mainly confined to cars. As mobile phones became lighter, cheaper and technically more advanced, the market started to take off, especially in the second half of the 1990s.

E-commerce
Percentage of enterprises' total turnover from e-commerce in 2003

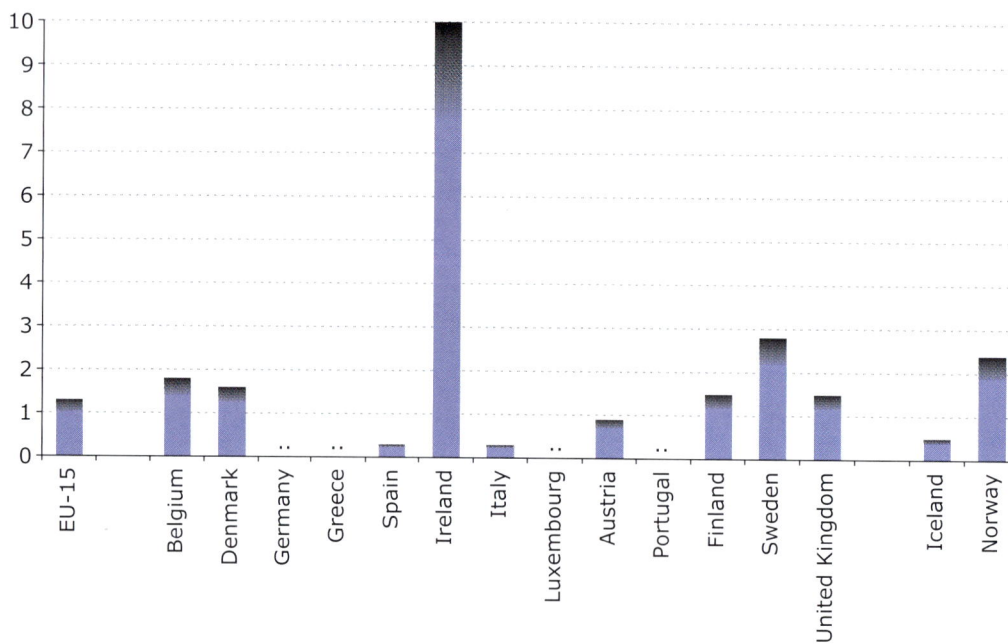

Information comes from the surveys carried out by the National Statistical Institutes on usage of information and communication technologies (ICT) by enterprises. The indicator is calculated as the enterprises' receipts from sales through the Internet as percentage of the total turnover. Sales through other networks are not included, leaving out for instance EDI-based sales. Only enterprises with 10 or more employees are covered.

ICT expenditure: IT expenditure in 2003
In % of GDP

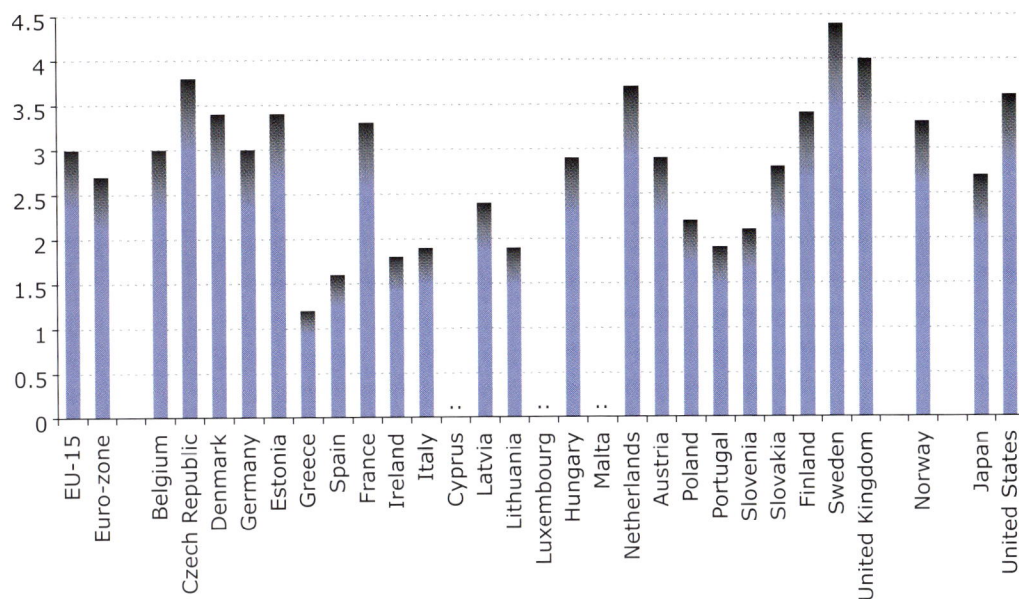

IT expenditure represents annual data on expenditure for IT hardware, equipment, software and other services expressed as a percentage of GDP.

ICT expenditure: Telecommunications expenditure in 2003
In % of GDP

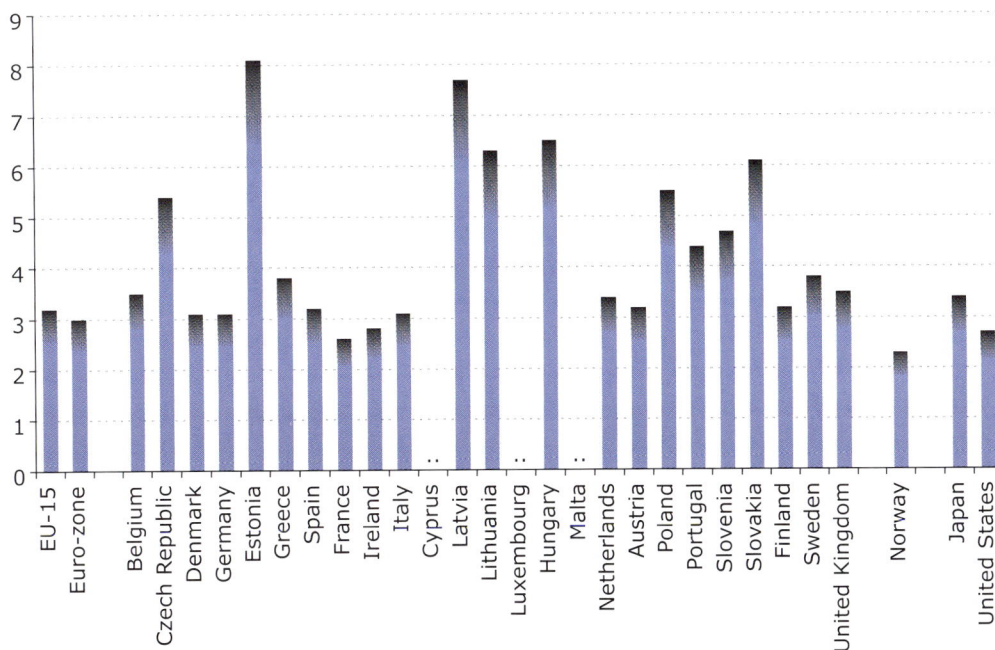

Telecommunication expenditure represents annual data on expenditure for telecommunication hardware, equipment, software and other services as a percentage of GDP.

Internet access of households
In %

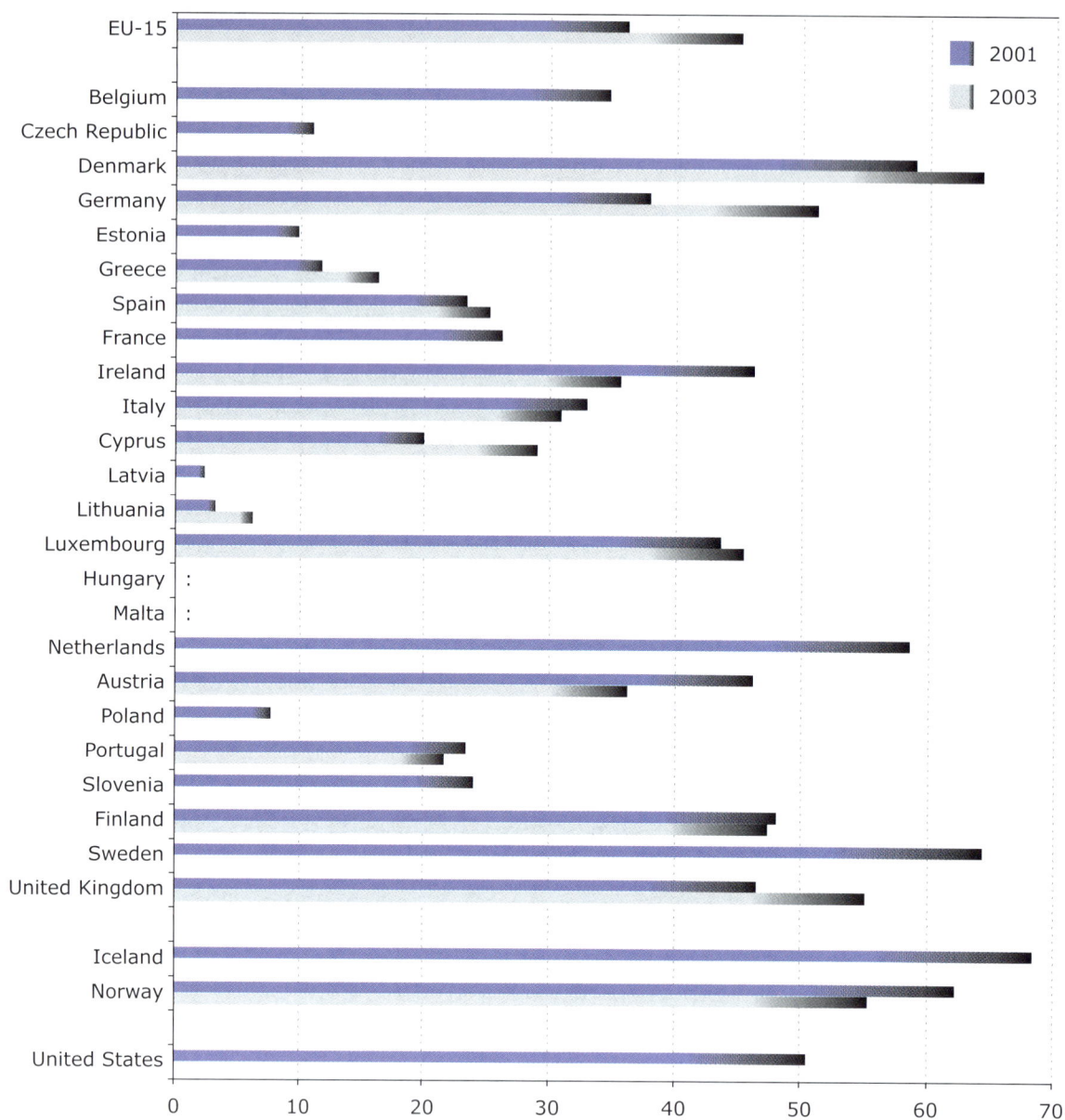

Legend:
- 2001
- 2003

EU-15	
Belgium	
Czech Republic	
Denmark	
Germany	
Estonia	
Greece	
Spain	
France	
Ireland	
Italy	
Cyprus	
Latvia	
Lithuania	
Luxembourg	
Hungary	:
Malta	:
Netherlands	
Austria	
Poland	
Portugal	
Slovenia	
Finland	
Sweden	
United Kingdom	
Iceland	
Norway	
United States	

Percentage of households who have Internet access at home. All forms of Internet use are included. The population considered is equal to or over 15 years.

Access to the Internet has increased for both households and enterprises. In 2003, the level of households' access to the Internet in EU-15 was 45 %. The access of enterprises was higher, reaching in some countries over 90 % of all enterprises (with more than nine employed persons). Thus, the level of Internet access for enterprises in 2003 was 98 % in Finland and Denmark, 95 % in Sweden, 92 % in Belgium and 90 % in Austria. In all the other countries of EU-25 for which data are available, this level was over 60 %.

Level of Internet access: enterprises
In %

EU-15	
Belgium	
Czech Republic	:
Denmark	
Germany	
Estonia	:
Greece	
Spain	
France	
Ireland	
Italy	
Cyprus	
Latvia	
Lithuania	
Luxembourg	
Hungary	:
Malta	:
Netherlands	
Austria	
Poland	
Portugal	
Slovenia	:
Finland	
Sweden	
United Kingdom	
Iceland	
Norway	
United States	

Legend: 2001, 2003

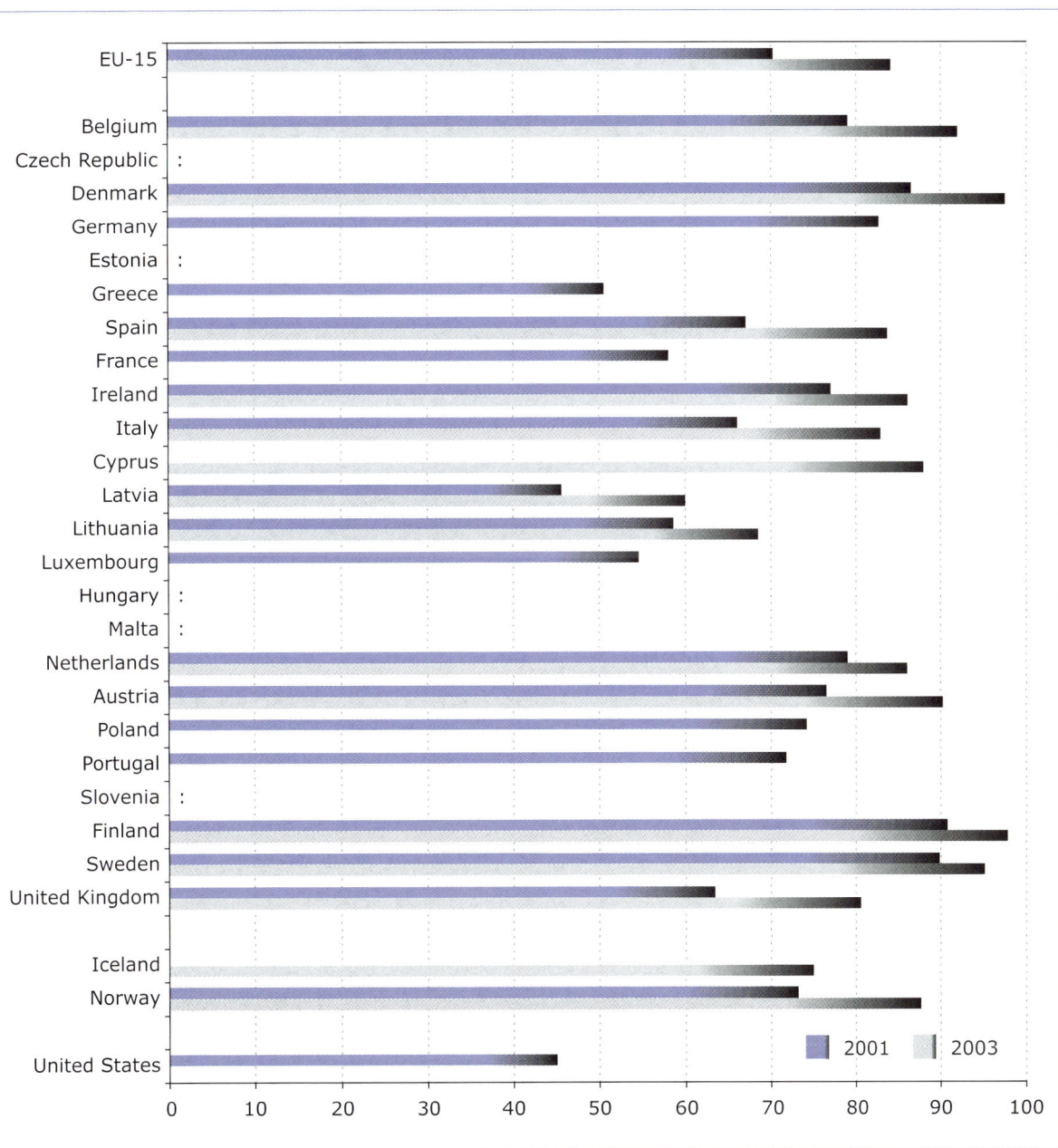

Only enterprises with more than nine persons employed are included. NACE sections D and G to K are covered. The data are provided by national statistical institutes in the frame of the Eurostat survey on ICT usage of enterprises.

Mobile phone subscribers
Per 100 inhabitants

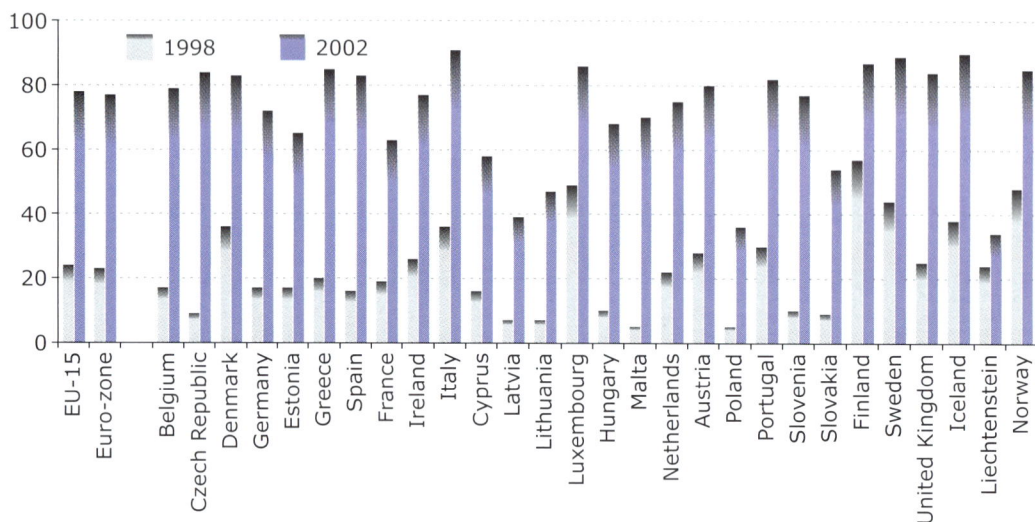

This indicator shows the number of subscriptions to public mobile telecommunication systems using cellular technology related to the population. The total number of mobile subscriptions in the country is divided by the number of inhabitants of the country and multiplied by 100. Active pre-paid cards are treated as subscriptions. One person may have more than one subscription.

From 1991 to 2002, the number of mobile subscribers increased continuously: until 1993, the rate per 100 inhabitants was under 10 in many European countries; in 2002, it often reached over 80. At the top were Italy, Sweden, Finland, Luxembourg and Greece. The number of mobile phone sets in use roughly corresponds to the number of subscriptions.

Prices of telecommunications in 2002
In EUR

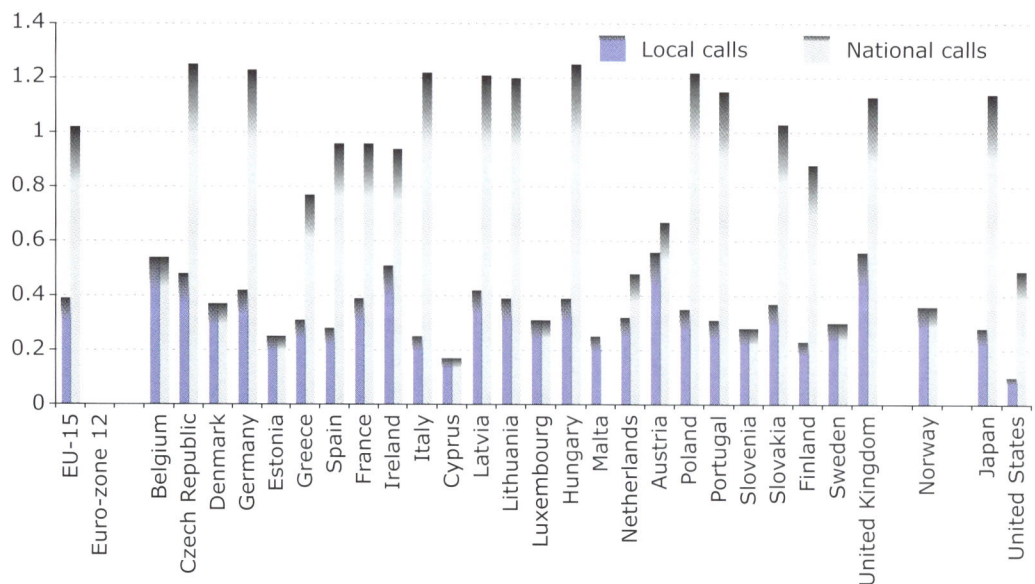

The indicator gives the price in euro of a 10-minute call at 11 am on a weekday (including VAT) for a local call (3 km), respectively a national call (200 km). The prices refer to August each year. Normal tariffs without special rates are used.

Price of telecommunications: calls to the US
In EUR

	1997	1998	1999	2000	2001	2002	2003
EU-15	6.63	4.49	3.48	3.09	2.63	2.22	2.13
Belgium	7.5	6	5.95	5.95	1.84	1.83	1.94
Czech Republic	:	:	:	:	:	3.4	:
Denmark	6.72	5.27	4.73	4.73	2.73	2.73	2.39
Germany	7.41	4.32	2.45	2.45	1.23	1.23	1.23
Estonia	:	:	:	:	:	2.6	:
Greece	7	5.82	5.82	3.26	2.91	2.95	2.95
Spain	6.17	6.08	4.53	4.25	4.25	2.21	1.53
France	6.78	3.44	3.05	2.97	2.97	2.34	2.34
Ireland	4.61	3.68	2.92	2.92	1.91	1.91	1.91
Italy	7.26	4.99	3.63	2.79	2.79	2.24	2.12
Cyprus	:	:	:	:	:	1.7	:
Latvia	:	:	:	:	:	6.9	:
Lithuania	:	:	:	:	:	8.1	:
Luxembourg	7.37	5.67	2.74	2.06	1.44	1.44	1.44
Hungary	:	:	:	:	:	3.8	:
Malta	:	:	:	:	:	12.7	:
Netherlands	8.48	2.77	0.9	0.78	0.78	0.76	0.85
Austria	9.21	5.76	6.08	4.32	4.32	3.77	3.77
Poland	:	:	:	:	:	10.5	:
Portugal	8.25	6.14	4.23	3.68	2.89	2.94	2.94
Slovenia	:	:	:	:	:	1.9	:
Slovakia	:	:	:	:	:	2.7	:
Finland	8.31	7.43	5.65	5.68	4.8	4.84	4.84
Sweden	5.4	4.9	4.9	1.12	1.12	1.12	1.12
United Kingdom	3.92	3.37	3.37	3.37	3.37	3.37	3.37
Norway	5.68	3.48	2.1	1.21	1.18	0.92	0.86
Japan	13.49	15.94	6.07	4.86	4.86	4.86	4.86

The indicator gives the price in euro of a 10-minute call at 11 am on a weekday (including VAT) for an international call (to the United States). The prices refer to August each year. Normal tariffs without special rates are used.

5

Market share of the incumbent in fixed telecommunications in 2002

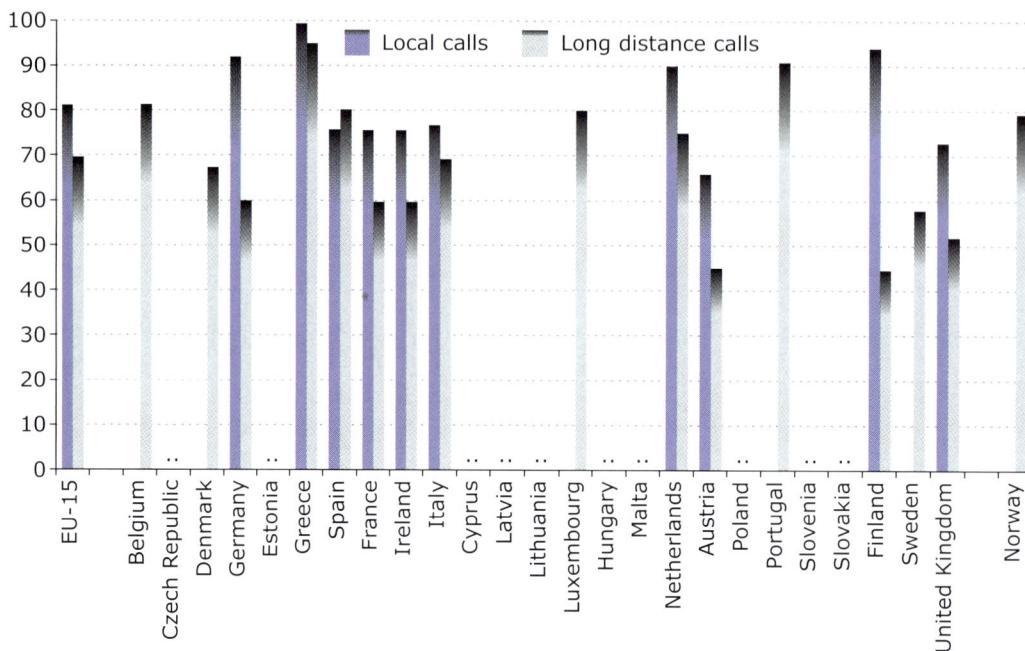

Legend: Local calls, Long distance calls

The incumbent is defined as the enterprise active on the market just before liberalisation. The market share is calculated as the share of the incumbent's retail revenues of the total market. A local call is a call within local networks. A long distance call is a call from one local network to another.

Market share of the incumbent in fixed telecommunications: international calls in 2002

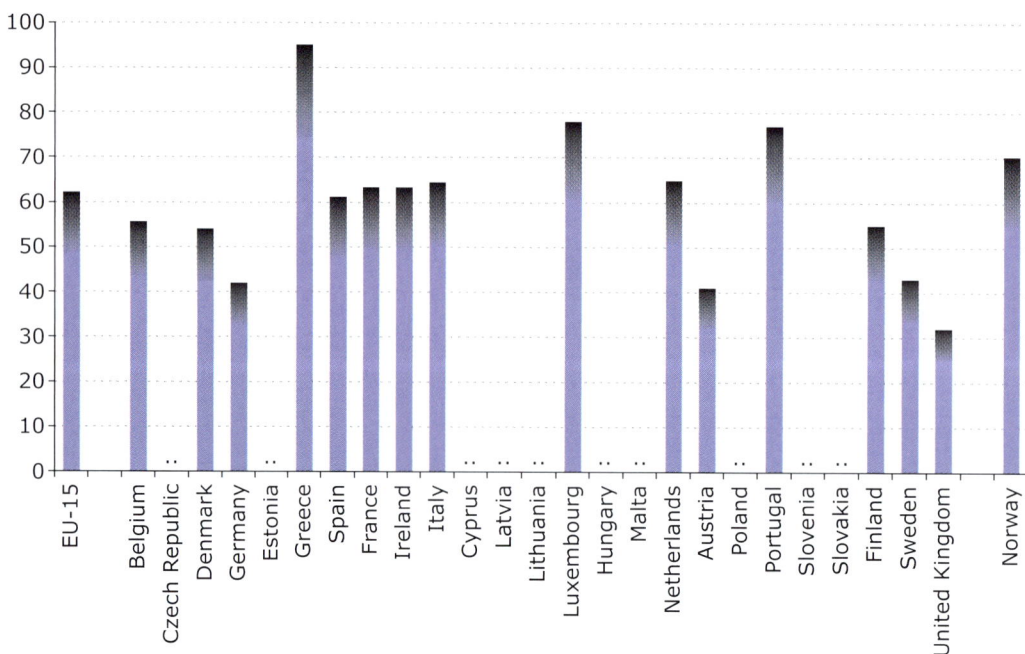

The incumbent is defined as the enterprise active on the market just before liberalisation. The market share is calculated as the share of the incumbent's retail revenues of the total market.

Sectors and enterprises

6

Business structures at a glance

The background for doing business

Eurostat draws a comprehensive picture of the structure of the European business world and thus of the framework for entrepreneurial activity. Its data on business structures show developments in specific activities as well as structural changes of the economy as a whole. Without this information, short-term data on the economic cycle would lack background and be hard to interpret. Enterprises that want to determine their opportunities in a new market or put their performance into perspective use these data, as do business associations, trade unions, market researchers, administrators and politicians.

Production and labour

Structural business statistics describe the economy by observing the activity of units engaged in an economic activity. They answer questions like: How much wealth is created in an activity? How many workforces are needed to create this wealth? How is this activity developing? Is this activity participating in the growth of the economy? Are investments made in this activity?

Principally, the structural information presented in the Eurostat yearbook relates to production or to employment. Among a number of variables describing the input and output sides of business activity, a selection of basic indicators is presented.

— **Turnover** corresponds to the total of all sales (excluding VAT) of goods and services carried out by the enterprises of a sector during the reference year.

— **Gross value added** at factor cost corresponds to the difference between the value of what is produced and intermediate consumption entering the production, corrected for subsidies on production and costs, and assimilated taxes and levies. It can be interpreted as the wealth created by the enterprises of a sector and which is used to remunerate the production factors (capital in the form of the gross operating surplus, and labour in the form of the personnel costs).

— **Personnel costs** are defined as the total amounts paid by the enterprises of a sector to remunerate the work of the enterprises' employees during the reference year. They cover wages and salaries and the social contributions paid by the employers.

— The number of **persons employed** is defined as the total number of persons who work for the enterprises of the sector, whether or not they are paid. This total, however, excludes borrowed staff and agency workers.

The SBS database

The data are taken from the SBS database, Eurostat's reference database on structural business statistics (SBS). It presents the data in absolute values and in the form of some basic ratios that make it possible, for example, to compare levels between countries or to calculate the share of an industry in a total.

A harmonised legal framework

The Council regulation on structural business statistics provides a harmonised legal framework for the annual collection of structural data from businesses in the European Union. It defines the nomenclatures (NACE Rev. 1.1, NUTS) and the statistical units to be used, the coverage (without size threshold), the common deadlines and the quality criteria to be fulfilled.

The regulation covers all market activities (excluding agriculture) normally included in the industry, construction, distributive trades and service sectors (Sections C to K of NACE Rev. 1). In the SBS domain of NewCronos, a much higher level of detail is available than in the Eurostat yearbook.

Value added ([1]) in the EU-25 in 2001
In million EUR

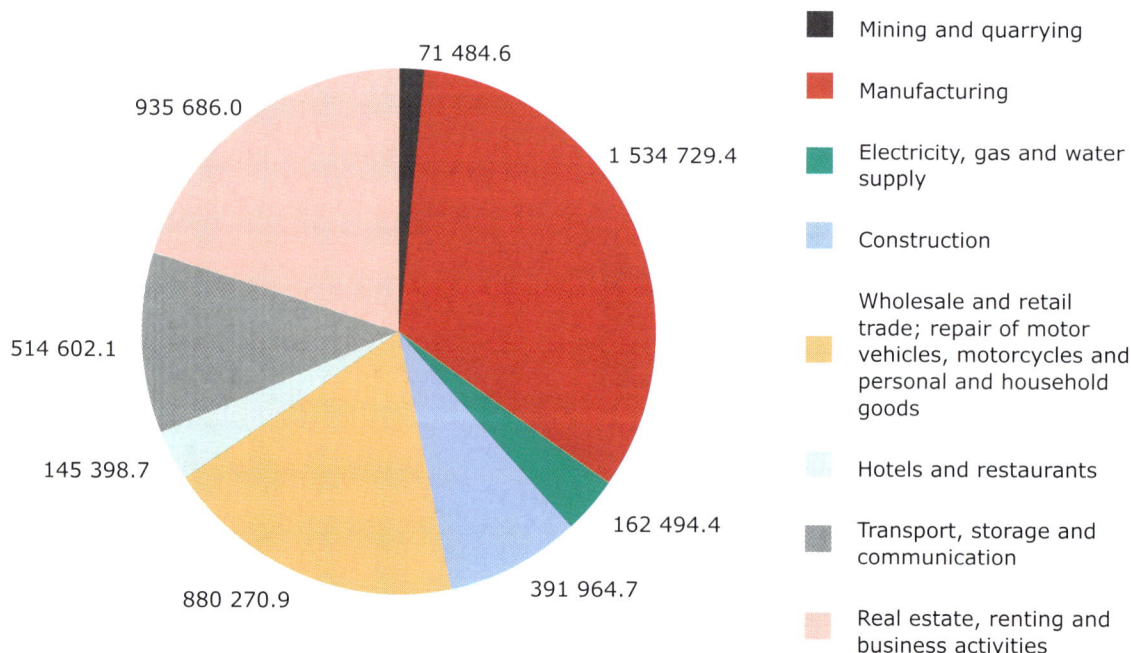

Legend:
- Mining and quarrying
- Manufacturing
- Electricity, gas and water supply
- Construction
- Wholesale and retail trade; repair of motor vehicles, motorcycles and personal and household goods
- Hotels and restaurants
- Transport, storage and communication
- Real estate, renting and business activities

Values: 71 484.6; 1 534 729.4; 935 686.0; 514 602.1; 145 398.7; 880 270.9; 391 964.7; 162 494.4

([1]) At factor cost.

Value added represents the difference between the value of what is produced and intermediate consumption entering the production, less subsidies on production and costs, taxes and levies.

Employed persons in the EU-25 in 2001
In 100

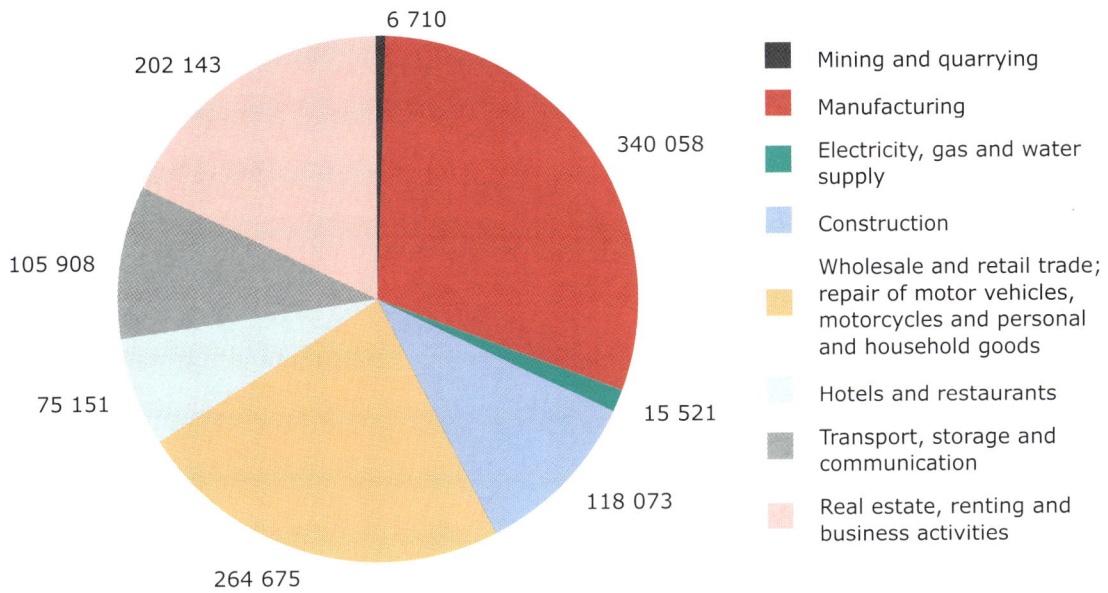

- 6 710
- 202 143
- 340 058
- 105 908
- 75 151
- 15 521
- 118 073
- 264 675

Legend:
- Mining and quarrying
- Manufacturing
- Electricity, gas and water supply
- Construction
- Wholesale and retail trade; repair of motor vehicles, motorcycles and personal and household goods
- Hotels and restaurants
- Transport, storage and communication
- Real estate, renting and business activities

Some results

In 2001 and the 25 countries of today's European Union, about one third of the total value added in industry, construction, distributive trades and services has been generated in manufacturing (33 %) where about 30 % of the employees worked; 18 % of the personnel worked in the sector 'real estate, renting and business activities' that generated 20 % of the value added. The trade and repair business is equally labour intensive with 23 % of the employees generating 19 % of the value added.

Business demography in 1999
Birth and death rates of enterprises in %

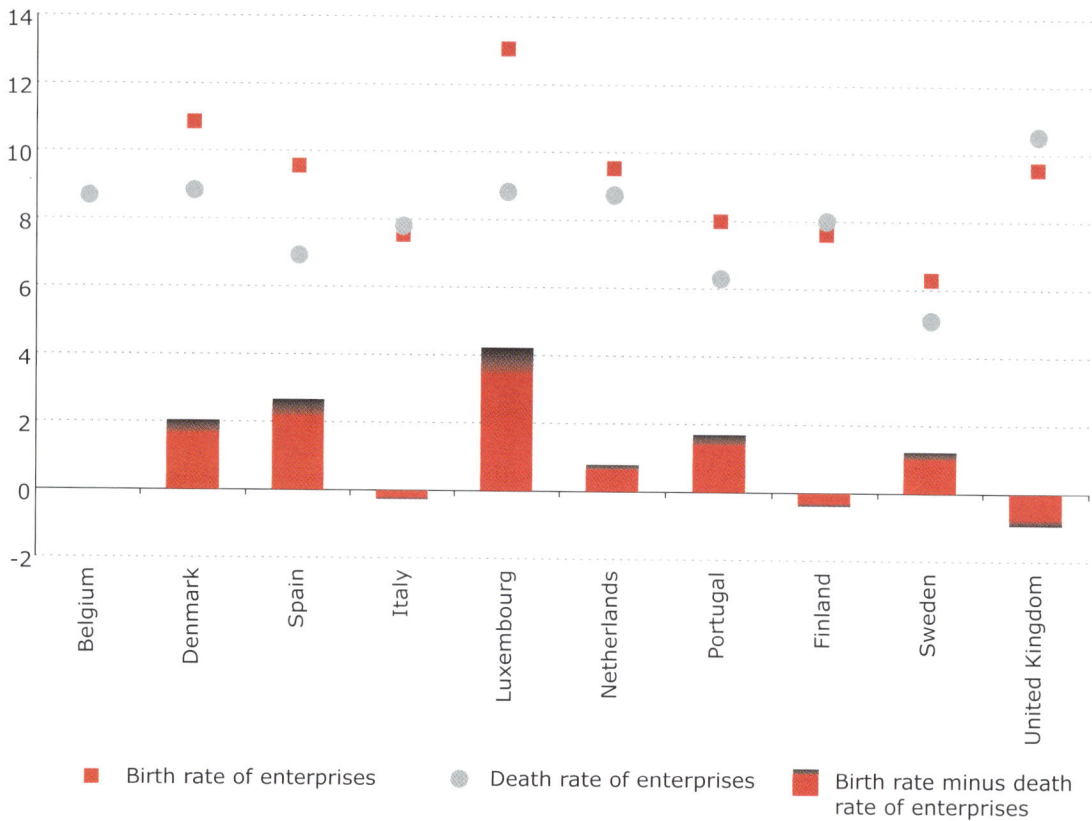

■ Birth rate of enterprises   ● Death rate of enterprises   ■ Birth rate minus death rate of enterprises

No data for Germany, Greece, France, Ireland, Austria.

A birth amounts to the creation of a combination of production factors with the restriction that no other enterprises are involved in the event. Births do not include entries into the population due to mergers, break-ups, split-off or restructuring of a set of enterprises. It does not include entries into a sub-population resulting only from a change of activity. A birth occurs when an enterprise starts from scratch and actually starts activity. An enterprise creation can be considered an enterprise birth if new production factors, in particular new jobs, are created. If a dormant unit is reactivated within two years, this event is not considered a birth.

A death amounts to the dissolution of a combination of production factors with the restriction that no other enterprises are involved in the event. Deaths do not include exits from the population due to mergers, takeovers, break-ups or restructuring of a set of enterprises. It does not include exits from a sub-population resulting only from a change of activity. An enterprise is included in the count of deaths only if it is not reactivated within two years. Equally, a reactivation within two years is not counted as a birth.

6

Eurostat reports data on the business demography, i.e. on the coming into being and the discontinuation of enterprises. The 'newborn' and 'disappearing' enterprises are put in relation to all enterprises that were active during the respective year. For 1999, this measurement was only possible for some countries. However, the results show that behind the absolute number of enterprises there are impressive movements that reflect the innovation and competition within the economies in Europe. The example of the Netherlands demonstrates that the growth in the total number of enterprises of about 0.8 % is a result of about 8.8 % of enterprises closing shop and 9.6 % 'newborn' enterprises more than offsetting this negative effect.

Industry and construction

Share of gross operating surplus in turnover in the EU-25 in 2001
In %

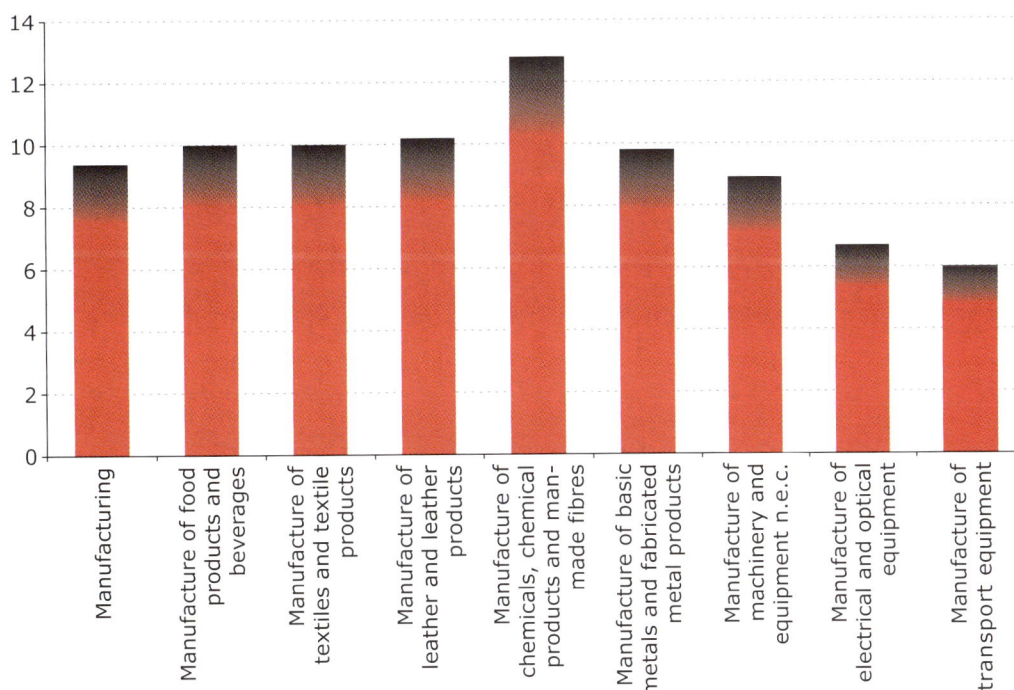

Value added is used to remunerate the production factors: capital in the form of the gross operating surplus, and labour in the form of the personnel costs. The share of the gross operating surplus in the value added varies from sector to sector: The more capital-intensive the sector, the higher the share of gross operating surplus in value added.

Statistics on industry and construction: some indicators

Share of the gross operating surplus in turnover: turnover is used to remunerate the production factors: capital in the form of the gross operating surplus, and labour in the form of the personnel costs. The share of the gross operating surplus in turnover varies from sector to sector: the more capital-intensive the sector, the higher the share of gross operating surplus in turnover. In EU-25 in 2001, the indicator was close to 13 % in the chemical industry, and about 6 % in the manufacture of transport equipment.

6

Share of value added in production in the EU-25 in 2001
In %

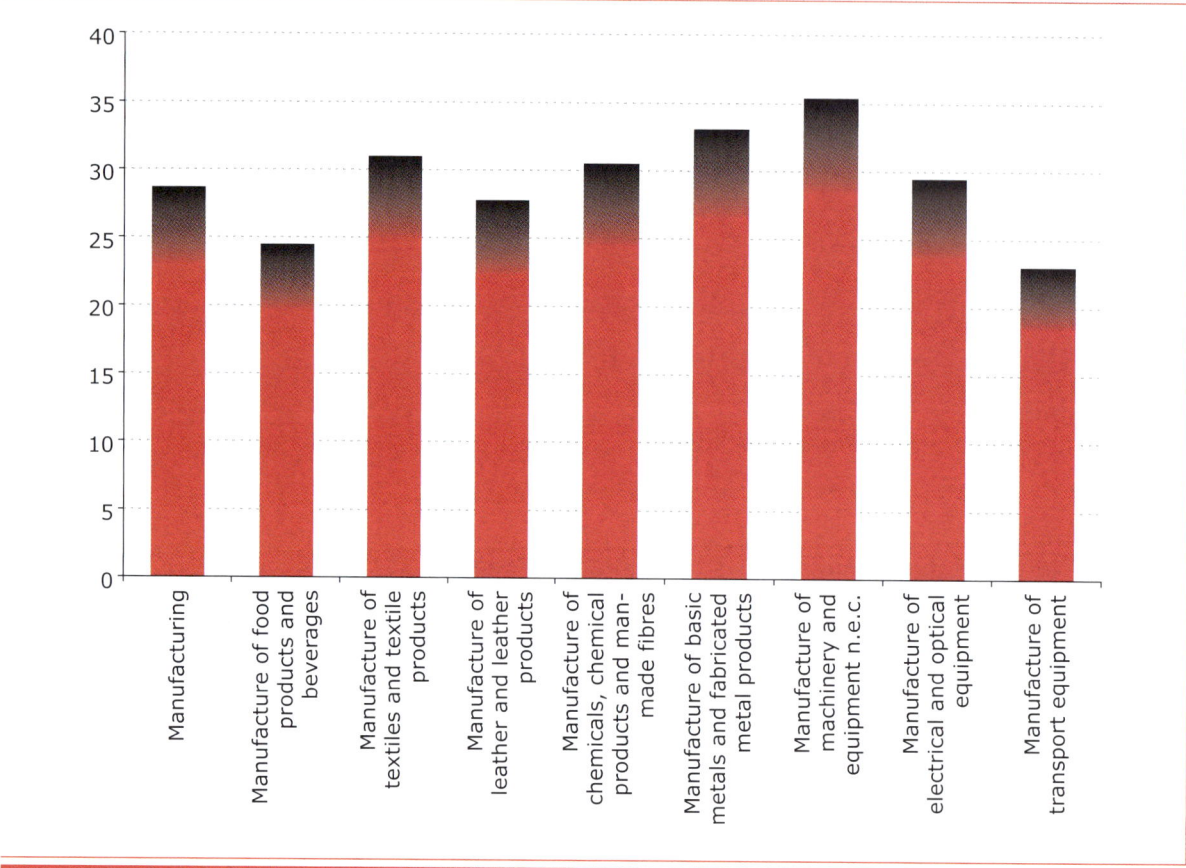

Manufacturing	
Manufacture of food products and beverages	
Manufacture of textiles and textile products	
Manufacture of leather and leather products	
Manufacture of chemicals, chemical products and man-made fibres	
Manufacture of basic metals and fabricated metal products	
Manufacture of machinery and equipment n.e.c.	
Manufacture of electrical and optical equipment	
Manufacture of transport equipment	

1990: estimated values.

The share of value added in production is an indicator of the degree of integration of a sector's enterprises: a low ratio for a particular sector reflects a production process there that makes up for only a small share in the total transformation of the products; this indicates a high interaction of different enterprises. The ratio is rather stable over time; the variation for different activities is more distinct.

Value added in production: this relates the value added to the value of production. It is an indicator of the degree of integration of a sector's enterprises: a low ratio for a particular sector reflects a production process there that makes up for only a small share in the total transformation of the products; this indicates a high interaction of different enterprises. The ratio is rather stable over time (EU-25 in 2001: 28.7 %). The variation for different activities is more distinct: in manufacturing of machinery it stood at 35.4 %, in manufacturing of food and beverage products at 24.5 % and of transport equipment even at 23.0 %.

Distributive trades

Eurostat data

Eurostat provides a wide range of data on:
— Retail trade
— Wholesale trade
— Sale of motor vehicles
— Turnover
— Employment

Structural as well as short-term data

Since 1995, structural business statistics have been collected in the area of distributive trades according to the SBS regulation's harmonised framework. Short-term indicators have been collected at EU level in this area since reference year 1998.

The retail sale of food is carried out either in specialised or non-specialised stores. In EU-15 as a whole, about 86 % of food products are sold in non-specialised stores such as super-markets. This turnover share is lowest in Spain (70 %) and highest in France (93 %).

One of the basic sets of information provided by structural business statistics is on the relative size of industries. This size is measured here in terms of both turnover and employment. While retail trade provides more than half of the jobs in distributive trades, it accounts for less than one third of turnover. This shows that the turnover per capita is lower in retail trade than in distributive trades in general. The opposite situation is found in the highly concentrated productive activity of wholesale trade.

Turnover in retail sale of food 2001, in specialised and non-specialised stores
In million EUR

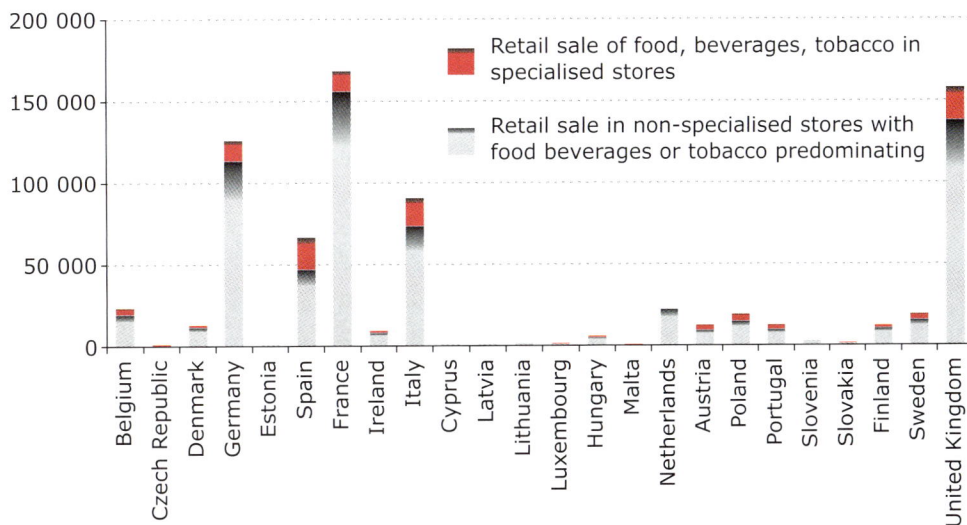

Legend:
- Retail sale of food, beverages, tobacco in specialised stores
- Retail sale in non-specialised stores with food beverages or tobacco predominating

Food products are sold on the retail market, either in non-specialised stores (hypermarkets, supermarkets) or in specialised stores (e.g. fruit and vegetable grocers). A greater proportion of sales in specialised stores is a sign for a more traditional trade pattern.

Shares in total distributive trades in terms of turnover in the EU-25 in 2001
In %

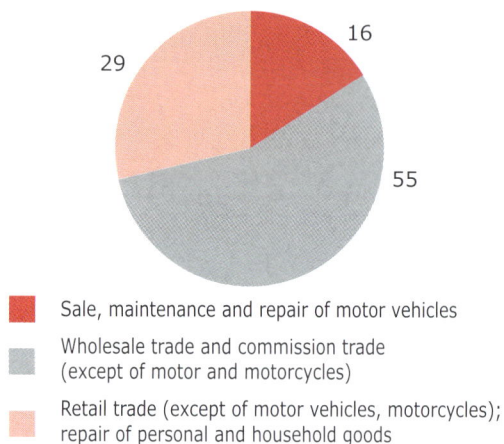

- 16
- 55
- 29

Legend:
- ■ Sale, maintenance and repair of motor vehicles
- ■ Wholesale trade and commission trade (except of motor and motorcycles)
- ■ Retail trade (except of motor vehicles, motorcycles); repair of personal and household goods

Retail sector consists of the wholesale trade, the sale of motor vehicles and the predominant sector of retail trade. Motor trades also comprise maintenance and repair of motor vehicles. Wholesale trade is at the heart of the business to business goods exchange channel and links producers and users in the broad sense. Retail trade includes sales in specialised and non-specialised stores (hypermarkets, supermarkets).

Shares in total distributive trades in terms of employment in the EU-25 in 2001
In %

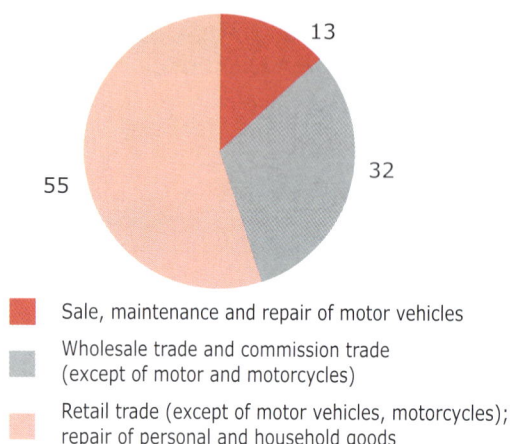

- 13
- 32
- 55

Legend:
- ■ Sale, maintenance and repair of motor vehicles
- ■ Wholesale trade and commission trade (except of motor and motorcycles)
- ■ Retail trade (except of motor vehicles, motorcycles); repair of personal and household goods

Retail sector consists of the wholesale trade, the sale of motor vehicles and the predominant sector of retail trade. Motor trades also comprise maintenance and repair of motor vehicles. Wholesale trade is at the heart of the business to business goods exchange channel and links producers and users in the broad sense. Retail trade includes sales in specialised and non-specialised stores (hypermarkets, supermarkets).

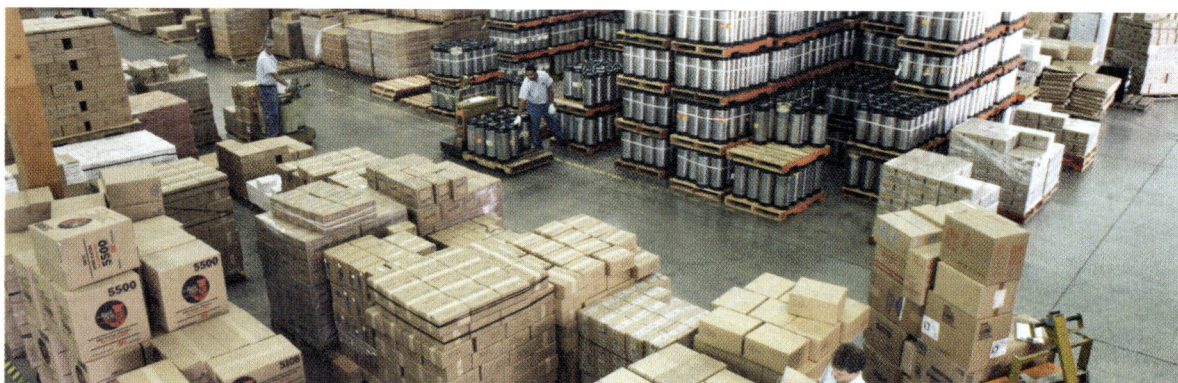

Personnel cost per employee in services in the EU-25 in 2001
In 1 000 ECU/EUR

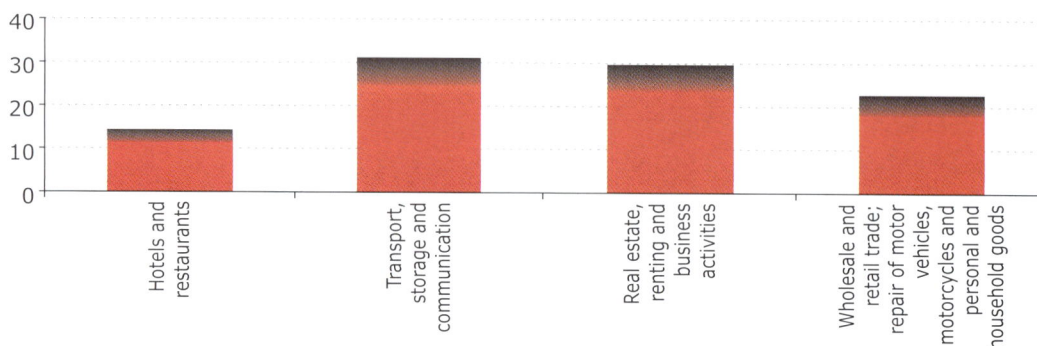

The turnover per head is the average turnover produced by a person working in the considered sector. It serves as a productivity index. The service sector includes sectors with intensive workforce and low productivity (e.g. road freight) and sectors with intensive skilled workforce and high productivity such as communications.

Financial markets

Eurostat data

Eurostat provides a wide range of data on:

— Insurance (life and non-life insurance, reinsurance), credit instituions and pension funds
— Number of enterprises
— Persons employed
— Balance sheet
— Investment
— Pension funds

In the framework of structural business statistics, Eurostat also collects data on credit institutions, insurance services and pension funds. Detailed data on profit and loss accounts, balance-sheet items, geographical breakdowns and insurance products are available. The tables containing figures for the balance-sheet total of credit institutions and the table on the total investments of pension funds give an idea of the relative importance of these institutions.

6

Balance sheet of credit institutions in 2000
1 000 million EUR

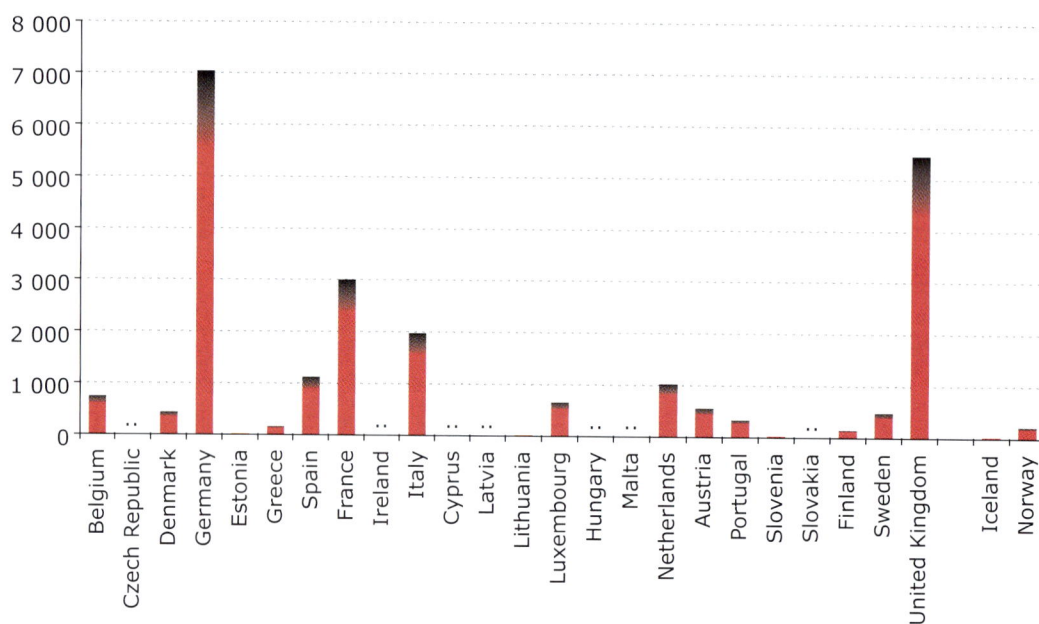

This variable consists of the sum of all items of the assets side or the sum of all items of the liabilities side. This indicator gives an idea of the economic importance of credit institutions.

Interest receivable and similar income of credit institutions in 2000
In million EUR

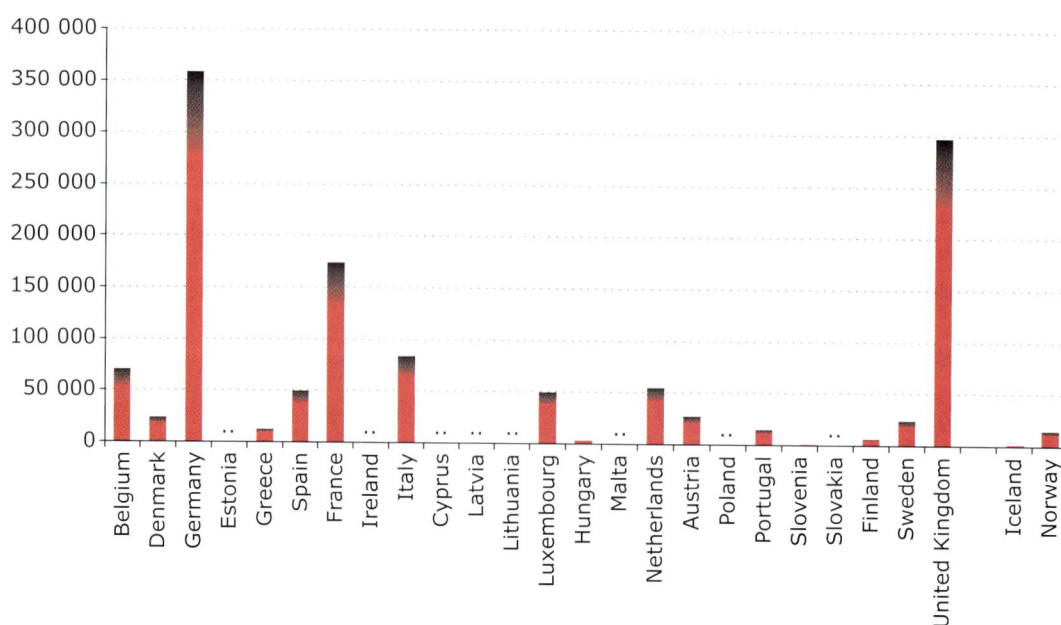

All income received by credit institutions from assets such as loans and advances, treasury bills, fixed income securities. It also includes fees and commissions similar in nature to interest and calculated on a time basis or by reference to the amount of the claim or liability.

Gross premiums written of life and non-life insurance enterprises in 2000
In million EUR

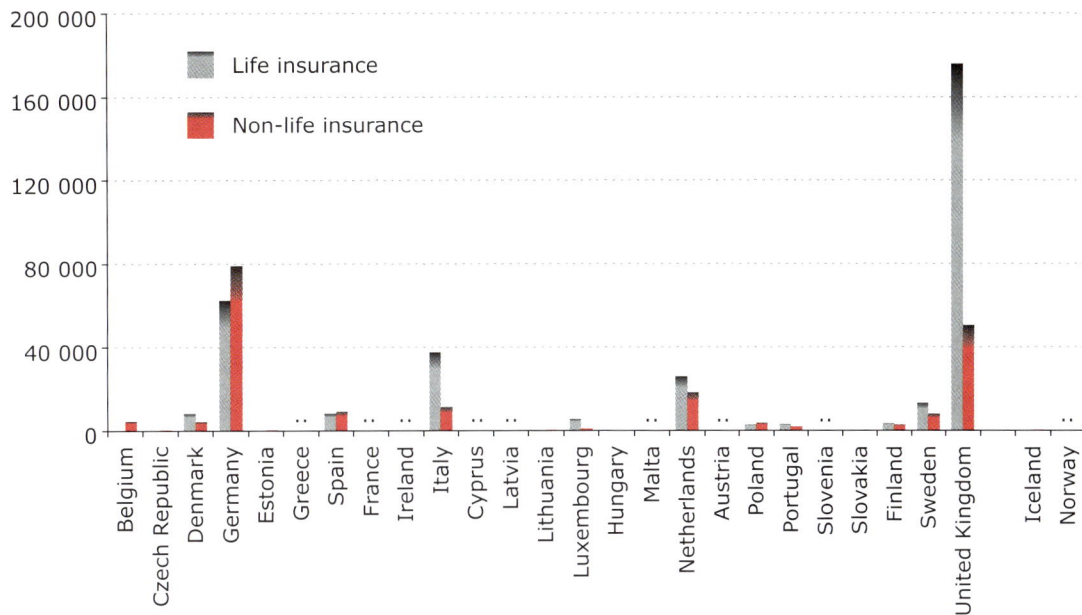

Gross premiums written shall comprise all amounts due during the financial year in respect of insurance contracts regardless of the fact that such amounts may relate in whole or in part to a later financial year, and shall include *inter alia* reinsurance premiums received from other insurance undertakings. The above amounts shall not include the amounts of taxes or charges levied with premiums.

Total investments of pension funds
In million EUR

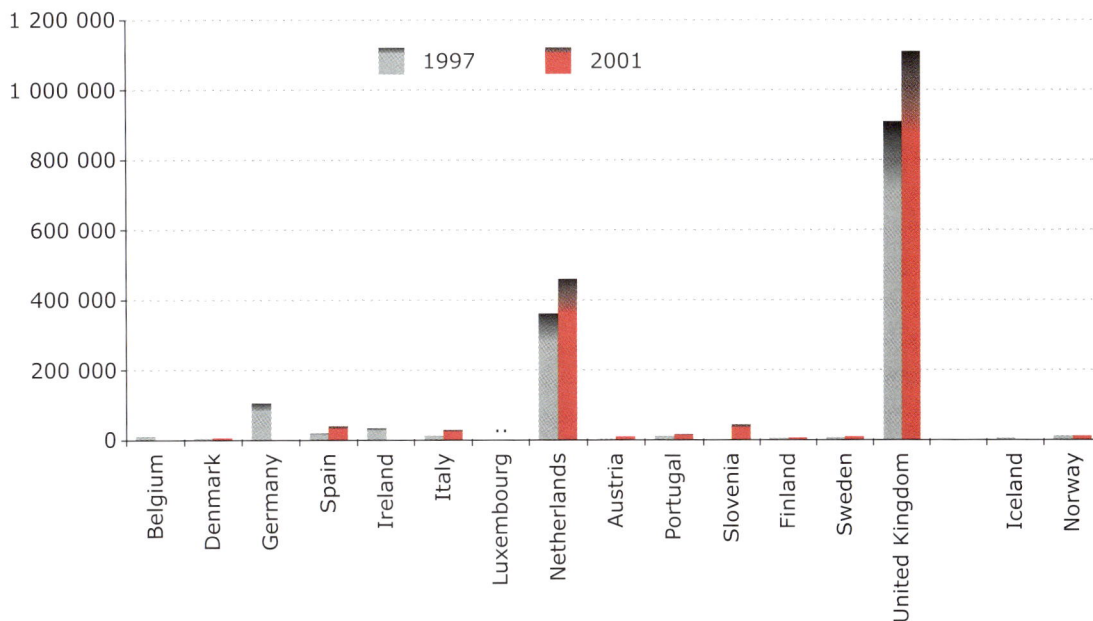

This variable is the sum of the following variables asset items: Land and buildings + investments in affiliated enterprises and participating interests + shares and other variable-yield securities + units in undertakings for collective investment in transferable securities + debt securities and other fixed-income securities + participation in investment pools + loans guaranteed by mortgages and other loans not covered elsewhere + other investments.

Transport

Eurostat data

Eurostat provides a wide range of data on:
— Transport infrastructure
— Transport equipment
— Enterprises and employment in transport
— Passenger transport
— Transport of goods
— Energy consumption and emissions by transport
— Transport safety

A short trip from the past to the future

'Victory is the beautiful bright coloured flower. Transport is the stem without which it could never have blossomed' (Sir Winston Churchill).

The quotation equally characterises the success achieved in increasing the standard of living in Europe and one of the major reasons behind this success: transport.

During the last 100 years, the shares between the modes of transport have changed and the volumes have increased tremendously. Waterways and railways still play an important role, but the dominating mode of transport today is definitely road transport. About 80 % of all tonnage transported (about 45 % of all tonne-kilometres) and of all passenger-kilometres are by road. Air transport is also increasing rapidly. In addition, the number of passenger cars has increased to more than 170 million. The disadvantage of this is that even though fatalities are decreasing, around 50 000 people each year are still killed in road accidents in EU-25.

Transport statistics: spotting the movement

Eurostat's transport statistics describe the most important features of transport in the European Union not only in terms of the quantities of freight and passengers moved and the vehicles and infrastructure used, but also as part of the economy. Transport is not only a necessary support to personal life and economic activity, but also a major service industry: around 4 % of the total EU workforce.

The data collection for this publication as well as for the other Eurostat publications on transport is supported by several legal acts obliging the Member States to report statistical data. In addition to this, there are voluntary agreements to supply additional data. In some cases, outside sources are used.

A transport policy for Europe's citizens

The European Commission's objective for the next 10 years is to focus Europe's transport policy on the demands and needs of its citizens. In adopting the White Paper 'European transport policy for 2010: time to decide', the European Commission places users' needs at the heart of its strategy and proposes 60 measures to meet this challenge. The first of these measures is designed to shift the balance between modes of transport by 2010 by revitalising the railways, promoting maritime and inland waterway transport and linking up the different modes of transport. The European Commission wants to ensure that the development of transport in Europe goes hand in hand with an efficient, high-quality and safe service for citizens. This White Paper and the proposals it contains also constitute the first practical contribution to the sustainable development strategy.

With its new transport policy White Paper, the Commission proposes an action plan aimed at bringing substantial improvements in the quality and efficiency of transport in Europe. It also proposes a strategy designed to gradually break the link between constant transport growth and economic growth in order to reduce the pressure on the environment and prevent

6

Total length of motorways
In km

	1991	1992	1993	1994	1995	1996	1997	1998	1999	2000	2001
EU-25	:	:	:	:	47 497	48 658	50 016	51 796	53 432	54 434	55 641
Belgium	1650	1 667	1 686	1 665	1 666	1 674	1 679	1 682	1 691	1 702	1 727
Czech Republic	:	:	:	:	414	423	485	499	499	499	517
Denmark	653	696	737	786	796	832	855	873	892	953	971
Germany	10 955	11 013	11 080	11 143	11 190	11 246	11 309	11 427	11 515	11 712	11 786
Estonia	:	:	:	:	64	66	68	74	87	93	93
Greece	225	280	330	380	420	470	500	500	500	707	742
Spain	5 235	6 486	6 577	6 485	6 962	7 295	7 750	8 269	8 893	9 049	9 571
France	7 080	7 408	7 614	9 000	8 275	8 596	8 864	9 303	9 626	9 766	9 934
Ireland	32	32	50	56	72	80	94	103	103	103	125
Italy	6 301	6 289	6 401	6 401	6 435	6 465	6 469	6 478	6 478	6 478	6 478
Cyprus	:	:	:	:	168	194	199	204	216	240	257
Latvia	-	-	-	-	-	-	-	-	-	-	-
Lithuania	:	:	:	:	394	404	410	417	417	417	417
Luxembourg	78	95	100	121	115	115	115	115	115	115	115
Hungary	:	:	:	:	335	365	381	448	448	448	448
Malta	-	-	-	-	-	-	-	-	-	-	-
Netherlands	2 118	2 134	2 167	2 200	2 208	2 208	2 336	2 225	2 291	2 289	2 291
Austria	1 532	1 554	1 567	1 589	1 596	1 607	1 613	1 613	1 634	1 633	1 645
Poland	:	:	:	:	246	258	264	268	317	358	398
Portugal	474	520	579	587	687	710	797	1 252	1 441	1 482	1 659
Slovenia	:	:	:	:	293	310	330	369	399	427	435
Slovakia	:	:	:	:	198	215	219	292	295	296	296
Finland	249	318	337	388	394	431	444	473	512	549	602
Sweden	968	1 005	1 061	1 142	1 262	1 350	1 423	1 439	1 484	1 506	1 529
United Kingdom	3 211	3 246	3 252	3 286	3 307	3 344	3 412	3 473	3 579	3 612	3 605
Iceland	-	-	-	-	-	-	-	-	-	-	-
Liechtenstein	-	-	-	-	-	-	-	-	-	-	-
Norway	:	:	:	94	107	106	109	128	144	143	173
Canada	15 983	16 571	:	:	16 571	:	:	:	:	:	:
Japan	:	5 054	5 410	5 568	5 700	5 900	:	:	:	:	:
United States	85 258	86 818	87 447	8 814	88 035	88 588	88 704	88 892	89 232	89 426	:

Source: Eurostat/Energy and Transport DG

6

congestion while maintaining the EU's economic competitiveness.

Although motorways constitute only a small part of the entire road network, their length has more than tripled over the last 30 years. In 2001, the most extensive motorway network within EU-25 could be found in Germany, followed by France and Spain.

Total length of railway lines
In km

	1991	1992	1993	1994	1995	1996	1997	1998	1999	2000	2001
EU-25	:	:	:	:	207 894	206 418	203 716	202 982	202 473	201 010	199 147
EU-15	159 521	157 912	155 876	156 764	160 450	159 044	157 291	159 784	156 542	156 353	:
Belgium	3 466	3 432	3 410	3 396	3 368	3 380	3 422	3 470	3 472	3 471	3 454
Czech Republic	:	:	:	:	9 430	9 430	9 430	9 430	9 444	9 444	9 523
Denmark	2 344	2 344	2 349	2 349	2 349	2 349	2 248	2 264	2 756	2 768	2 768
Germany	41 113	40 815	40 397	41 401	41 718	40 826	38 385	38 126	37 525	36 588	35 986
Estonia	:	:	:	:	1 021	1 020	1 018	968	968	968	967
Greece	2 484	2 484	2 474	2 474	2 474	2 474	2 503	2 299	2 299	2 385	2 377
Spain	12 570	13 041	12 601	12 646	12 280	12 284	12 303	12 303	12 319	12 310	12 310
France	33 990	33 555	32 579	32 275	31 940	31 852	31 821	31 770	31 735	31 397	31 385
Ireland	1 944	1 944	1 944	1 944	1 945	1 954	1 908	1 909	1 919	1 919	1 919
Italy	16 066	16 112	15 942	16 002	16 005	16 014	16 030	16 080	16 092	16 147	16 035
Cyprus	-	-	-	-	-	-	-	-	-	-	-
Latvia	:	:	:	:	2 413	2 413	2 413	2 413	2 413	2 413	2 413
Lithuania	:	:	:	:	2 002	1 997	1 997	1 997	1 905	1 905	1 696
Luxembourg	271	275	275	275	275	274	274	274	274	274	274
Hungary	:	:	:	:	7 632	7 619	7 593	7 642	7 651	7 668	7 680
Malta	-	-	-	-	-	-	-	-	-	-	-
Netherlands	2 780	2 753	2 757	2 757	2 813	2 813	2 805	2 808	2 808	2 802	2 809
Austria	5 623	5 605	5 600	5 636	5 672	5 672	5 672	5 643	5 618	5 563	5 980
Poland	:	:	:	:	23 986	23 420	23 328	23 210	22 891	22 560	21 119
Portugal	3 117	3 054	3 063	3 070	3 065	3 071	3 038	2 794	2 814	2 814	2 814
Slovenia	:	:	:	:	1 201	1 201	1 201	1 201	1 201	1 201	1 229
Slovakia	:	:	:	:	3 665	3 673	3 673	3 665	3 665	3 665	3 665
Finland	5 874	5 874	5 885	5 880	5 859	5 860	5 865	5 867	5 836	5 854	5 850
Sweden	10 970	9 781	9 746	9 661	9 782	9 821	9 798	9 855	9 884	9 900	9 900
United Kingdom	16 909	16 843	16 854	16 998	16 999	17 001	16 991	16 994	16 984	16 994	16 994
Iceland	-	-	-	-	-	-	-	-	-	-	-
Liechtenstein	19	19	19	19	19	19	19	19	19	19	19
Norway	4 027	4 027	4 023	4 023	4 023	4 021	4 021	4 021	4 021	4 179	4 178
Canada	85 563	85 191	84 648	83 351	90 326	:	:	:	:	:	:
Japan	:	30 201	30 190	30 178	30 178	:	:	:	:	:	:
United States	187 691	:	177 712	175 953	174 234	170 304	164 426	161 917	160 082	159 792	:

Source: Eurostat/Energy and Transport DG

During the last decade, the transport infrastructures in the European Union have been extended for all inland transport modes, with the exception of the length of railway lines and inland waterways which has decreased slightly.

Passenger cars in 2001
Per 1 000 inhabitants

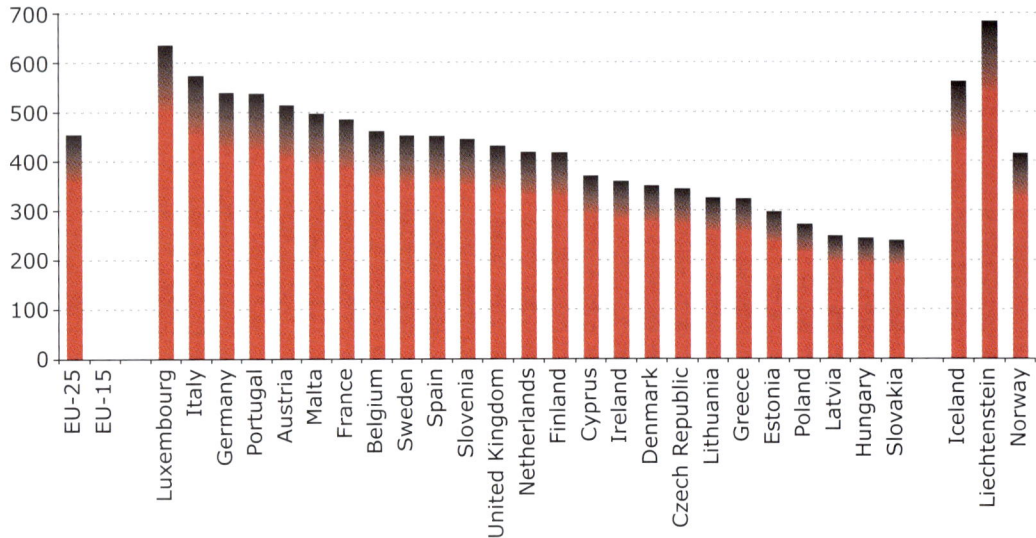

Source: Eurostat/Energy and Transport DG

The car density in the EU has doubled in the last 25 years to reach 454 cars per 1 000 inhabitants in the 25 countries of today's EU in 2001. It is much below the car density in the United States. The number of passenger cars per 1 000 inhabitants has sometimes been interpreted as an indicator for the standard of living. On the flip side of the coin are the negative impact on the environment and the close to 50 000 persons killed each year in road accidents in the EU-25.

Passenger car transport in the EU-15
In million passenger-km

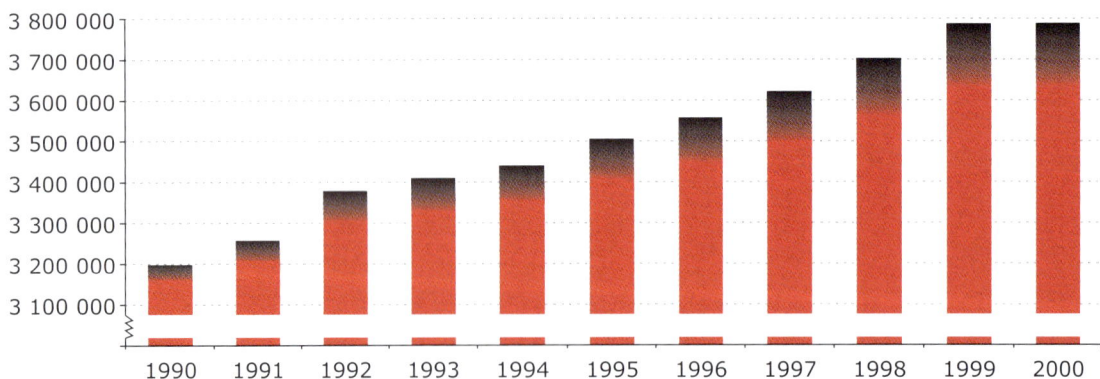

Source: Eurostat/Energy and Transport DG

The increased mobility demand has mainly been satisfied by passenger cars, used for roughly three quarters of all trips.

Rail transport of passengers in the EU-25
In million passenger-km

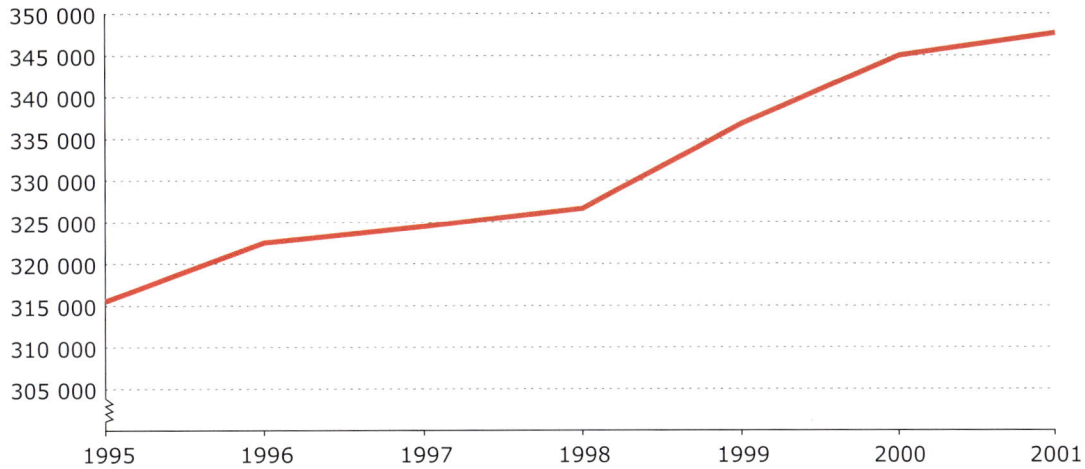

Source: Eurostat/Energy and Transport DG

Compared with the other modes, the transport performance of rail has improved at a modest pace. Since the early 1990s, growth has been slow in most countries, and in some a decrease has been observed. Still, the EU average of kilometres travelled per person per day is above two. The fact that the increase was in spite of a shrinking network and less rolling stock indicates increased efficiency.

Bus transport of passengers in the EU-15
In million passenger-km

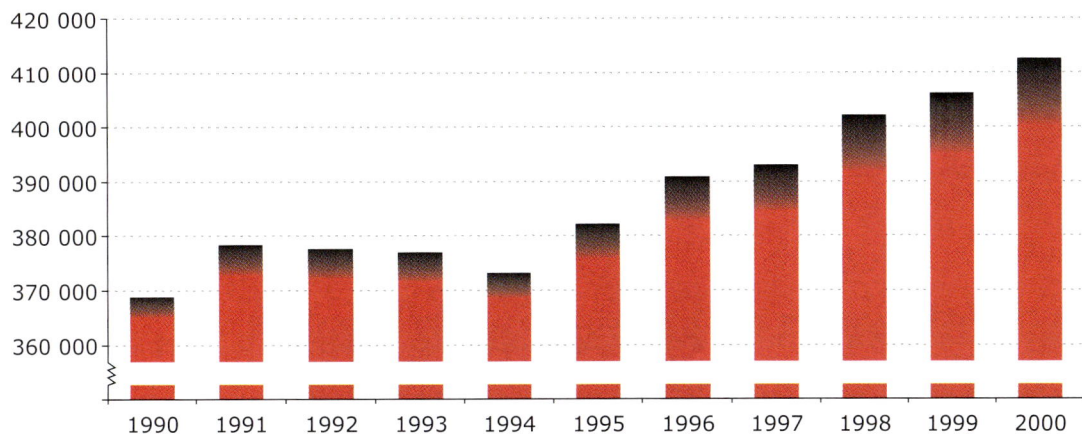

Source: Eurostat/Energy and Transport DG

6

Between 1970 and 2000, the average transport by bus and coach in EU-15 increased by around 50 %, reaching a total of more than 412 billion passenger-kilometres. With more than 94 billion passenger-kilometres, Italy has the highest figure in the EU in absolute terms. However, the populations of Denmark, Luxembourg and Greece travel most by bus and coach in EU-15, with between 5.5 and 6 km per person per day.

Goods transport in the EU-15 in 2000
In million tkm

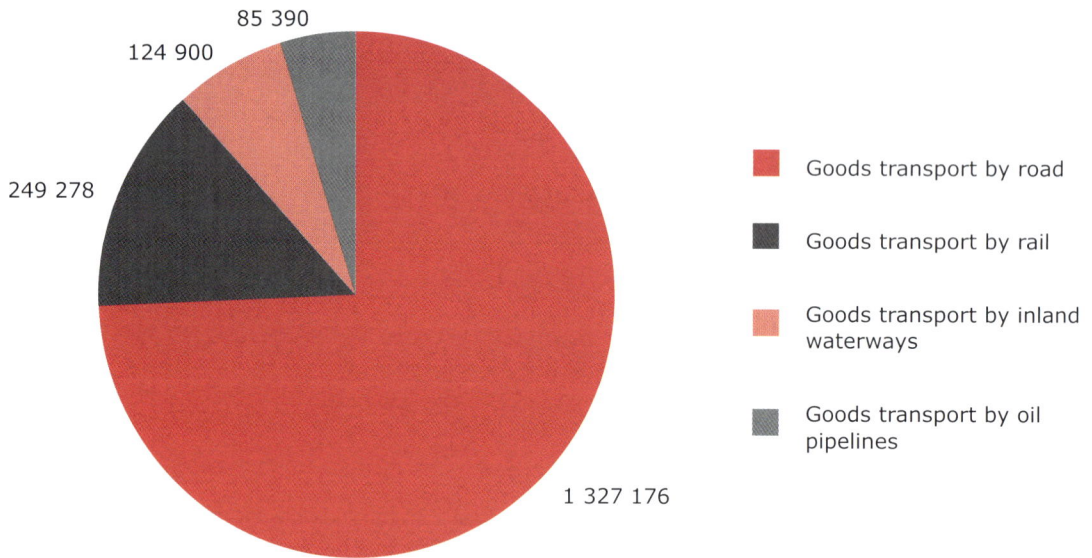

85 390

124 900

249 278

1 327 176

- Goods transport by road
- Goods transport by rail
- Goods transport by inland waterways
- Goods transport by oil pipelines

Source: Eurostat/Energy and Transport DG

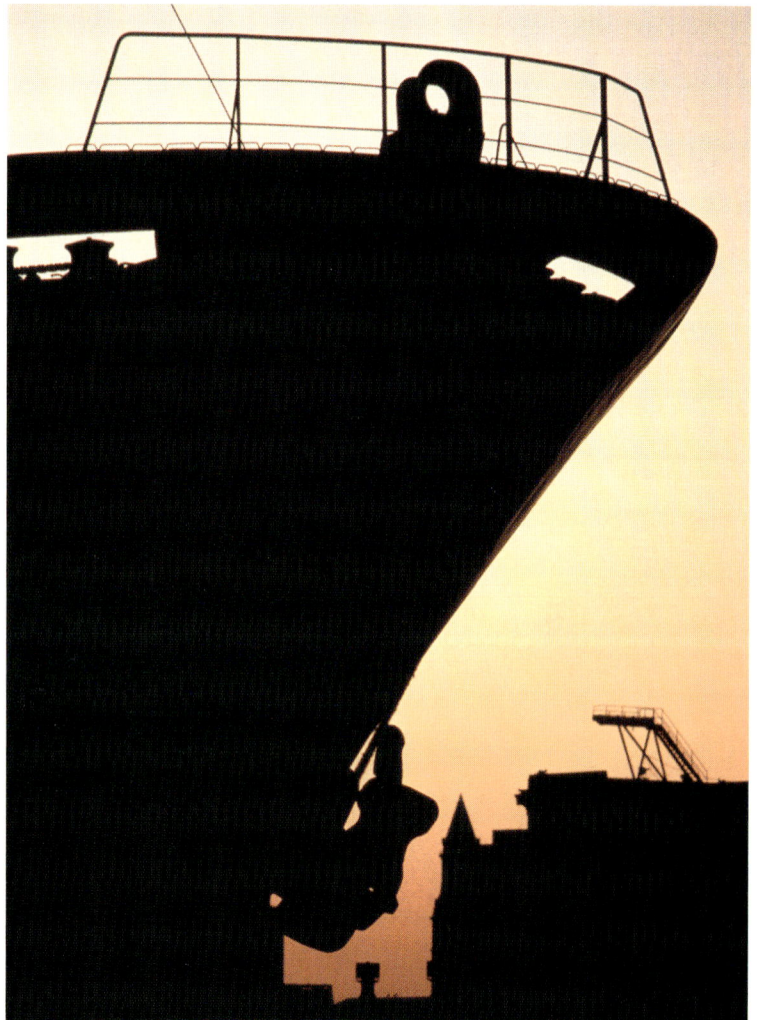

6

Sea transport of goods
In million tonnes

	1997	1998	1999	2000	2001
EU-25	3 071	3 147	3 135	3 167	3 219
EU-15	2 911	2 984	2 969	:	:
Belgium	162	171	166	179	174
Czech Republic	-	-	-	-	-
Denmark	124	105	97	97	94
Germany	213	217	222	243	246
Estonia	23	27	34	40	41
Greece	101	111	113	128	113
Spain	271	280	296	235	315
France	305	319	315	337	318
Ireland	36	40	43	45	46
Italy	459	476	463	447	445
Cyprus	7	6	6	7	7
Latvia	51	52	49	52	57
Lithuania	16	15	16	23	22
Luxembourg	-	-	-	-	-
Hungary	-	-	-	-	-
Malta	3	4	4	4	7
Netherlands	402	405	396	406	406
Austria	-	-	-	-	-
Poland	51	51	50	48	48
Portugal	55	58	59	56	56
Slovenia	7	8	8	9	9
Slovakia	-	-	-	-	-
Finland	75	77	77	81	96
Sweden	150	156	156	159	153
United Kingdom	558	568	565	573	566
Iceland	5(e)	:	:	:	:
Liechtenstein	-	-	-	-	-
Norway	270(e)	:	:	:	:

Source: Eurostat/Energy and Transport DG

Given that tonne-kilometre figures are not available, the performance of sea transport of goods is not easily comparable to those of the other modes. However, the data still show the total volume of goods handled in all the major maritime ports of the EU. The total volume of goods handled in 2001 can be estimated at over 3 200 million tonnes of goods. A large part of the increase over the years can be attributed to the increase in the import of oil and oil products.

6

Air transport of goods
In 1 000 tonnes

	1997	1998	1999	2000	2001	2002
Belgium	518	585	:	:	584	:
Czech Republic	:	:	:	:	36	34
Denmark	:	:	:	:	12	10
Germany	2 019	1 948	2 054(b)	2 554	2 441	2 525
Estonia	:	:	:	:	5	4
Greece	106	101	105(b)	156	:	:
Spain	309	309	340(b)	479	577	564
France	1 025	1 030	1 034(b)	1 282	1 535	1 643
Ireland	70	59	66(b)	86	79	49
Italy	454	446	413(b)	551	:	506
Cyprus	:	:	:	:	32	31
Latvia	:	:	:	:	5	7
Lithuania	:	:	:	:	15	14
Luxembourg	340	383	448(b)	501	510	550
Hungary	:	:	:	:	45	46
Malta	:	:	:	:	12e	12
Netherlands	1 163	1 174	1 182(b)	1 268	1 217	1 279
Austria	109	111	122(b)	130	115	127
Poland	:	:	:	:	43	:
Portugal	105e	:	:	178	152	149
Slovenia	:	:	:	:	7	7
Slovakia	:	:	:	:	5	7
Finland	92	94	88(b)	111	96	96
Sweden	227e	:	:	:	:	:
United Kingdom	1847	1 990	2 091(b)	2 336	2 153	2 203
Iceland	4e	:	:	:	:	:
Liechtenstein	-	-	-	-	-	-
Norway	44	47	46	133	127	:

Source: Eurostat/Energy and Transport DG

Compared with maritime transport, the volumes of freight and mail transport by air are obviously low. However, even though the volumes are small compared with the other modes of transport, the average value of air-transported goods is mostly much higher than for the other modes of transport. EU air transport has increased substantially.

Worldwide commercial space launches

	1991	1992	1993	1994	1995	1996	1997	1998	1999	2000	2001
Total	12	14	11	15	23	24	38	41	39	35	16
United States	6	6	5	5	12	11	17	22	15	7	3
European Space Agency	6	6	6	8	8	9	11	9	8	12	8
Russian Federation	-	-	-	-	-	2	7	5	13	13	3
China	-	2	-	2	3	2	3	4	1	-	-
Ukraine	-	-	-	-	-	-	-	1	-	-	-
Sea launches	-	-	-	-	-	-	-	-	2	3	2

Source: US Department of Transportation

The data Eurostat presents for worldwide commercial space launches give an overview of the commercial international competed (non-captive), satellite launches in the medium-to-large vehicle class. This means that several launches are not counted. According to the US National Aeronautics and Space Administration (NASA), there were altogether 70 successful launches in 1999, compared with the 39 commercial launches listed here. Nevertheless, the data give an idea of Europe's role in the space industry.

Tourism

Europe: top tourism region in a competitive world

Europe remains the major tourism region in the world; its tourism has developed dynamically over the past few years. As worldwide competition to attract tourists intensifies, the awareness of the role of tourism increases. Tourism has an impact on the economy and employment, and also has social and environmental implications. This creates the need for statistics which are harmonised, available at regular intervals and sufficiently detailed.

What is tourism and how to measure it?

Tourism can be defined as the activities serving persons travelling to and staying in places outside their usual environment for not more than one consecutive year, for leisure or business purposes. On the supply side, tourism relies on enterprises from a variety of sectors, which can be summarised as the provision of accommodation, food and drink, transport facilities and services, and entertainment.

Accommodation services are covered by two NACE groups: 55.1 which includes the provision of lodging in hotels, motels and inns, excluding the rental of long-stay accommodation and time-share operations, and 55.2 which covers campsites and other short-stay accommodation, including self-catering holiday chalets or cottages.

Travel services are carried out by enterprises that are engaged in arranging transport, accommodation and catering on behalf of travellers. NACE group 63.3 encompasses enterprises furnishing: travel information; advice and planning; made-to-measure tours; accommodation and transportation for travellers and tourists; tickets; the sale of packaged tours; and the activities of tour operators and tourist guides.

6

Accommodation establishments in 2002

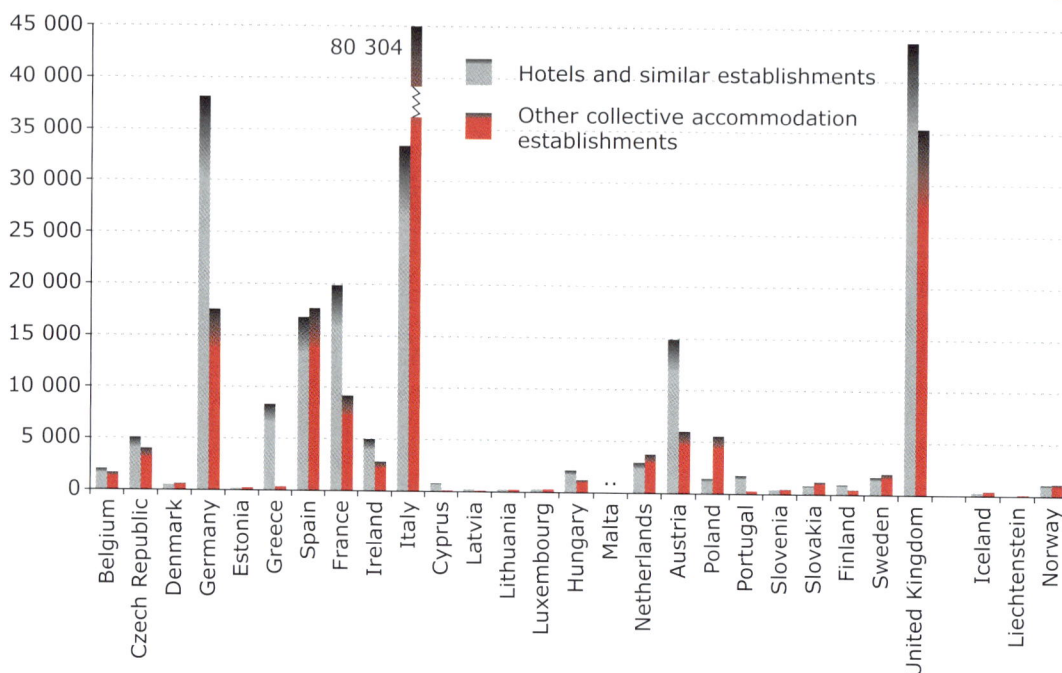

Legend:
- Hotels and similar establishments
- Other collective accommodation establishments

80 304

The number of bed places in an establishment is the number of persons who can stay overnight in the beds set up in the establishment, ignoring any extra beds that may have been set up on customer request. Other collective accommodation establishments include holiday dwellings, tourist campsites, youth hostels, tourist dormitories, group accommodation, school dormitories and other similar accommodation.

Number of bed places in hotels and similar establishments in the EU-15
In 1 000

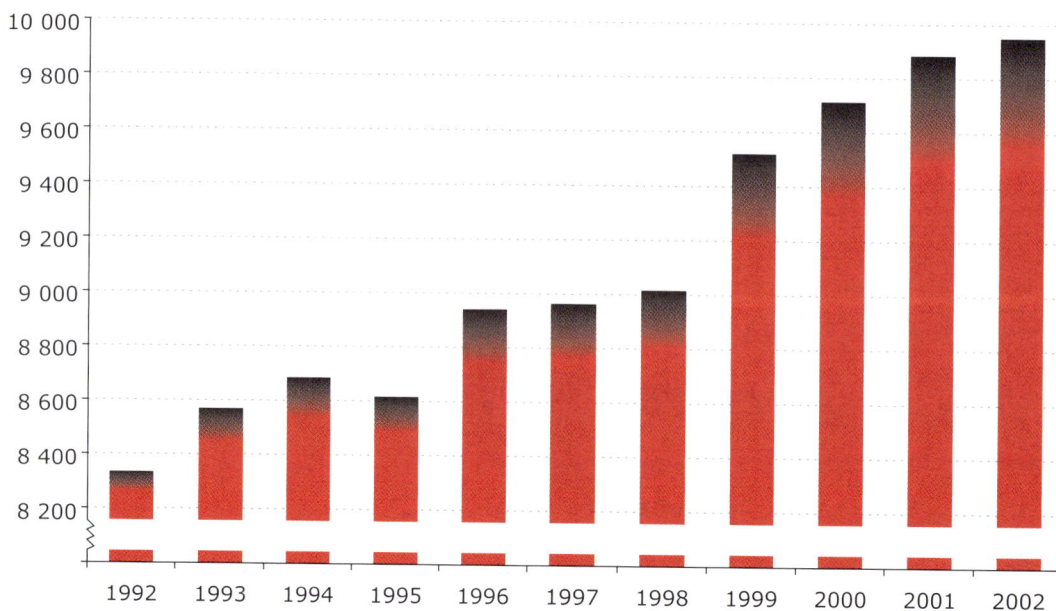

1992, 1993: estimates

Tourists
In 1 000

	1994	1995	1996	1997	1998	1999	2000	2001	2002
Belgium	:	:	5 216	:	4 364	3 430	:	3 517	3 476
Denmark	:	:	3 180	2 944	2 706	2 903	3 307	2 711	2 671
Germany	:	:	:	56 700	62 800	50 700	53 490	55 236	46 665(p)
Estonia	:	:	:	:	:	:	:	:	295
Greece	3 334	3 449	6 878	5 813	5 160	2 320	:	:	:
Spain	:	:	:	:	:	21 658	27 988	15 930	17 825
France	:	:	:	29 088	29 011	28 992	28 556	28 573	:
Ireland	:	:	:	:	2 291	:	:	:	27 569
Italy	:	:	:	22 719	21 965	21 508	22 834	23 730	24 199
Luxembourg	:	:	:	340	387	396	412	425	430
Netherlands	:	:	:	:	8 801	8 835	8 768	8 841	8 892
Austria	:	:	3 116	:	3 132	3 214	3 605	3 479	3 104
Portugal	:	:	:	:	:	2 657	2 626	2 863	2 875
Finland	2 114	2 066	1 970	2 241	2 114	2 156	2 216	2 297	2 308
Sweden	:	:	:	5 624	:	:	:	:	:
United Kingdom	:	:	27 540	28 070	35 410	29 010	21 609	21 703	30 690
Norway	:	:	:	:	:	2 551	2 525	2 568	2 527

Number of visitors (residents) who stay at least one night in a collective or private accommodation in the place/country visited.

Nights spent in hotels and similar establishments: Nights spent by residents
In 1 000

	1992	1993	1994	1995	1996	1997	1998	1999	2000	2001	2002	2003
EU-15	:	:	:	587 164	587 074	601 624	608 823	660 744	733 539	:	:	:
Euro-zone	:	:	:	468 230	467 128	474 129	494 718	533 658	559 698	:	:	:
Belgium	2 593	2 648	2861	3 054	3 140	3 338	3 498	3 652	4 045	4 057	4 091	4 062(p)
Czech Republic	3 773	4 103	5386	6 952	9 908	10 737	9 919	10 608	12 358	8 515(p)	10 476(p)	9 779(p)
Denmark	5 378	5 655	6038	3 908	4 200	4 171	4 339	4 417	4 599	4 589	4 743	4 631
Germany	146 118	142 491	141307	145 147	144 747	144 497	147 274	154 419	163 429	164 197	157 391	156 673(p)
Estonia	:	188	282	325	292	333	413	439	459	489	450	536(p)
Greece	12 001	11 931	11701	11 908	12 178	13 609	13 029	13 477	13 656	:	:	:
Spain	54 363	54 971	56876	58 281	58 043	61 298	66 552	81 504	83 382	85 261	86 549	91 037(p)
France	91 604	90 160	89501	90 349	90 721	92 666	96 696	108 774	114 059	115 576	114 454	115 559(p)
Ireland	:	:	:	6 698	5 647	5 583	6 667	6 938	6 786	7 792	7 395(s)	:
Italy	129 000	122 000	124943	123 467	122 918	122 223	126 178	128 238	136 392	138 559	133 295	134 708(p)
Cyprus	294	391	356	346	480	524	570	585	597	727	868	:
Latvia	:	:	:	600	544	580	551	583	669	638	674	666(p)
Lithuania	:	371	363	331	293	322	364	319	303	293	331	:
Luxembourg	105	118	97	89	91	83	81	67	67	72	78	80
Hungary	:	3 213	3853	3 972	4 135	4 334	4 714	5 196	5 479	5 321	5 574	:
Malta	:	:	:	:	:	:	:	:	:	:	:	:
Netherlands	6 787	7 640	7912	8 798	9 074	10 739	12 622	13 829	14 027	13 608	13 593	:
Austria	16 162	15 954	16090	16 302	15 892	16 088	16 491	17 241	18 031	18 468	18 356	18 667
Poland	5 097	:	:	4 038	4 633	9 359	10 169	7 674	9 353	8 297	8 382	8 813(p)
Portugal	7 437	7 424	7361	7 580	8 101	8 499	9 164	9 397	9 693	9 985	9 983	10 409(p)
Slovenia	1 844	2 016	2019	2 066	2 004	1 787	1 728	1 852	1 860	1 715	1 714	1 725
Slovakia	1 713	1 460	2038	2 180	3 103	2 205	2 830	2 997	2 843	2 953	3 953	3 796(p)
Finland	7 539	7 686	7943	8 464	8 755	9 115	9 494	9 600	9 786	9 882	9 552	9 511(p)
Sweden	11 345	11 890	13898	14 771	14 668	14 815	15 643	16 192	16 586	16 737	16 143	16 253(p)
United Kingdom	77 978	73 407	81381	88 346	88 900	94 900	81 093	93 000	139 000	104 420	130 560	126 780(p)
Iceland	226	217	229	246	260	290	309	321	291	274	290	:
Liechtenstein	1	1	1	1	2	3	3	3	3	3	2	:
Norway	9 023	9 447	9643	9 862	10 261	10 680	11 252	11 319	11 398	11 599	11 482	11 262

A night spent by a resident or a non-resident person (overnight stay) is each night that a guest actually spends (sleeps or stays) or is registered (his/her physical presence there is not necessary) in a hotel or similar establishment.

6

Nights spent in hotels and similar establishments: Nights spent by non-residents
In 1 000

	1992	1993	1994	1995	1996	1997	1998	1999	2000	2001	2002	2003
EU-15	:	:	494 067	477 215	481 892	500 542	516 665	567 992	582 767	:	:	:
Euro-zone	:	:	365 962	376 451	380 873	393 418	413 575	462 139	478 367	:	:	:
Belgium	7 415	7 324	7 879	7 900	8 695	9 267	9 483	9 749	10 184	10 011	10 410	10 176(p)
Czech Republic	4 815	5 562	6 597	8 386	10 858	11 726	11 547	11 921	12 811	13 647(p)	13 327(p)	13 688(p)
Denmark	6 178	5 913	5 932	4 146	4 473	4 505	4 462	4 350	4 611	4 551	4 483	4507
Germany	28 378	26 069	26 368	27 184	27 435	28 608	29 735	30 913	34 641	32 876	32 580	33 294(p)
Estonia	:	506	573	608	693	835	926	1 045	1 253	1 423	1 887	2 027(p)
Greece	36 900	36 547	40 331	37 474	35 102	40 220	38 354	41 408	41 979	:	:	:
Spain	77 341	83 132	97 792	101 000	100 000	105 435	111 803	149 036	143 762	143 421	136 122	13 6834(p)
France	59 635	55 454	57 143	54 339	54 994	60 624	66 330	71 768	77 014	75 652	77 602	69 338(p)
Ireland	9 333	9 556	10 018	11 348	12 978	13 220	13 712	14 327	17 374	17 475	17 321	:
Italy	63 415	64 574	76 173	84 566	87 905	85 377	87 192	90 236	97 221	100 322	97 837	93 567(p)
Cyprus	14 114	12 192	14 265	14 181	12 689	13 148	14 430	16 110	16 790	18 066	15 235	:
Latvia	:	:	637	662	675	744	725	718	691	837	:	954(p)
Lithuania	:	714	474	418	492	536	639	600	579	672	719	:
Luxembourg	1 007	1 065	1 017	1 051	947	1 026	1 089	1 163	1 196	1 174	1 167	1 144
Hungary	:	6 387	6 887	6 894	7 449	7 619	7 714	7 539	8 062	8 405	8 260	:
Malta	8 030	8 230	8 600	7 632	7 328	7 694	8 079	8 235	7 016	7 475	:	:
Netherlands	8 424	7 973	8 733	9 581	9 923	12 444	14 262	15 224	15 695	14 955	14 922	:
Austria	64 189	61 996	59 126	56 198	55 126	53 396	53 503	53 123	53 617	54 086	55 167	55 200
Poland	4 581	:	:	3 161	3 391	5 595	5 325	3 973	4 945	4 918	4 999	5 450(p)
Portugal	17 877	16 176	18 785	20 357	19 962	20 851	23 241	23 331	24 102	23 578	22 437	23 349(p)
Slovenia	1 697	1 706	2 089	2 059	2 167	2 500	2 478	2 267	2 758	2 879	3 049	3 166
Slovakia	884	1 327	1 836	2 340	2 446	2 144	2 401	2 557	2 761	3 101	3 572	3 560(p)
Finland	2 243	2 503	2 928	2 926	2 907	3 171	3 226	3 271	3 562	3 675	3 721	3 707(p)
Sweden	2 804	2 984	3 320	3 694	3 930	4 051	4 409	4 516	4 679	4 927	4 868	4 847(p)
United Kingdom	66 284	71 033	78 522	55 451	57 514	58 347	55 865	55 580	53 131	49 781	48 377	51 704(p)
Iceland	437	444	516	598	636	702	791	862	895	907	970	:
Liechtenstein	147	133	128	127	118	117	120	122	131	120	106	:
Norway	4 275	4 557	5 041	4 985	5 050	5 039	5 168	5 208	4 967	4 817	4 706	4 375

A night spent by a resident or a non-resident person (overnight stay) is each night that a guest actually spends (sleeps or stays) or is registered (his/her physical presence there is not necessary) in a hotel or similar establishment.

Energy

Powering everyday life

Energy is the 'force' behind industry, transport and heating. There is hardly an aspect of daily life which is not in one way or another accompanied by the use of energy. Energy shortages and fluctuations of its price have repercussions in the whole economy. How we use energy has a significant impact on the state of the environment. For these reasons, energy policy is one of the priorities of the European Union.

The major challenges with which the Union is confronted in the energy field are:

— the significant dependence on outside supplies, as the European Union is producing only about half of the energy it consumes (security of supplies);

— the growing need to ensure competitive energy prices in the context of the globalisation of economies, notably by means of liberalisation of the electricity and gas markets and the development of the trans-European energy networks (liberalisation of network industries);

— the pressing need to make the energy sector more compatible with environmental objectives, particularly in the light of the commitments made by the European Union under the Kyoto Protocol (climate change).

Energy monitoring

In order to meet the increasing requirements of energy monitoring and to quantify the components that are influencing energy policies, Eurostat has developed a coherent and harmonised system of energy statistics.

The Eurostat yearbook presents a representative selection of tables and graphs that give an insight into the broad spectrum of energy statistics.

Data coverage in the Eurostat yearbook

In general, annual data collections cover the full spectrum of the 25 Member States of the

6

European Union, the European Economic Area countries Iceland and Norway, and the candidate countries Bulgaria, Romania and Turkey, with time series reaching back to 1985 (for some new Member States and candidate countries only back to 1990).

The same geographical coverage applies to monthly quantities data.

Total production of primary energy
In 1 000 toe

	1990	1991	1992	1993	1994	1995	1996	1997	1998	1999	2000	2001
EU-25	874 199	867 633	858 721	865 621	875 301	891 770	921 990	912 762	892 473	899 809	891 762	892 826
EU-15	705 353	705 923	700 817	707 200	720 409	734 696	760 426	754 225	748 021	762 043	756 118	753 890
Euro-zone	451 168	442 869	438 399	436 234	426 658	428 806	439 671	430 474	415 696	418 803	420 123	435 284
Belgium	11 971	11 753	11 531	10 948	10 706	10 939	11 275	12 552	12 033	13 274	13 065	12 637
Czech Republic	38 321	36 301	35 538	35 017	32 475	31 477	32 184	32 308	30 421	27 619	29 452	30 090
Denmark	10 673	12 524	13 527	14 500	15 218	15 741	17 689	20 172	20 322	23 697	27 607	27 025
Germany	185 839	164 921	159 669	148 137	141 338	140 233	138 328	138 377	131 597	134 535	132 095	131 363
Estonia	5 470	4 825	4 515	3 346	3 476	3 350	3 720	3 632	3 243	2 976	3 168	3 420
Greece	9 152	9 060	8 972	8 797	9 146	9 702	10 136	9 924	10 038	9 463	9 946	9 942
Spain	33 648	33 347	32 293	32 156	31 903	31 207	31 962	30 651	31 289	30 305	31 245	32 860
France	107 996	114 387	114 777	121 873	119 324	122 699	125 632	123 910	120 716	122 845	130 561	131 293
Ireland	3 474	3 294	3 082	3 470	3 628	4 256	3 614	2 843	2 479	2 611	2 111	1 730
Italy	25 463	26 096	27 313	28 378	29 617	29 273	30 137	30 220	30 058	28 914	26 780	25 649
Cyprus	6	6	6	5	12	12	11	9	9	44	45	44
Latvia	437	341	298	314	373	318	238	332	383	1 497	1 259	1 718
Lithuania	4 482	4 526	3 982	3 363	2 202	3 288	3 834	3 387	4 434	3 482	3 161	4 118
Luxembourg	47	46	48	47	51	47	40	47	50	46	57	50
Hungary	13 638	13 390	12 834	12 633	12 380	12 844	12 632	12 281	11 467	11 378	11 127	10 751
Malta	-	-	-	-	-	-	-	-	-	-	-	-
Netherlands	60 257	67 117	67 054	68 209	66 111	65 909	73 717	65 520	62 684	59 209	56 912	60 634
Austria	7 928	8 150	8 325	8 566	8 173	8 492	8 370	8 502	8 629	9 255	9 380	10 165
Poland	98 460	94 699	93 328	96 359	96 086	97 990	101 318	99 081	86 775	82 829	78 441	79 362
Portugal	2 808	2 774	2 302	2 629	2 819	2 602	3 157	3 045	3 036	2 656	3 109	3 895
Slovenia	2 902	2 928	3 038	2 870	2 968	3 020	2 963	2 962	3 036	2 861	3 036	3 105
Slovakia	5 130	4 694	4 365	4 513	4 919	4 776	4 663	4 546	4 683	5 078	5 953	6 327
Finland	11 737	10 984	12 005	11 821	12 989	13 150	13 440	14 805	13 125	15 153	14 809	15 065
Sweden	29 723	31 476	29 252	29 129	30 907	31 512	31 637	32 170	33 178	33 257	30 144	33 685
United Kingdom	204 637	209 994	210 666	218 540	238 480	248 934	261 292	261 484	268 787	276 823	268 299	257 896
Iceland	1 456	1 359	1 369	1 404	1 369	1 390	1 616	1 682	1 814	2 191	2 306	2 451
Norway	120 053	130 405	146 355	154 070	170 114	181 635	207 610	212 181	206 141	209 145	224 491	227 959

Any kind of extraction of energy products from natural sources to a usable form is called primary production. Primary production takes place when the natural sources are exploited, for example in coal mines, crude oil fields, hydro power plants or fabrication of biofuels. Transformation of energy from one form to another, like electricity or heat generation in thermal power plants or coke production in coke ovens is not primary production.

Net imports of primary energy
In 1 000 toe

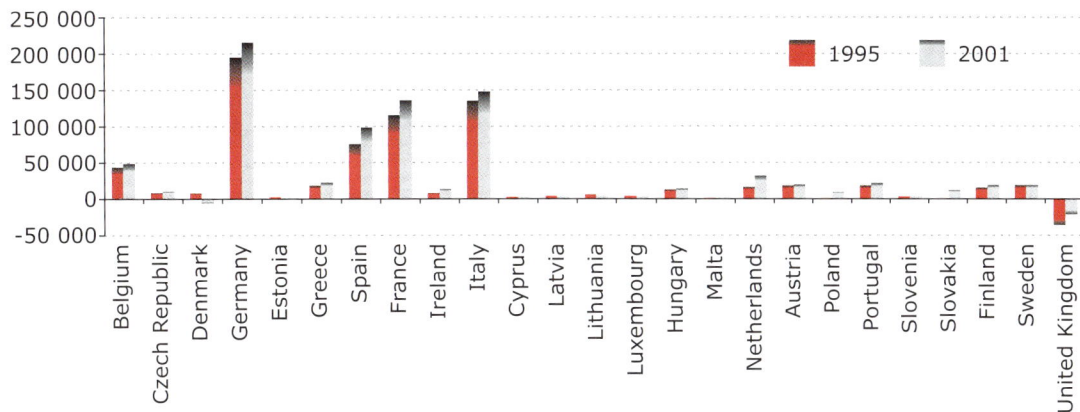

Net imports are calculated as imports minus exports. Imports represent all entries into the national territory excluding transit quantities (notably via gas and oil pipelines); electrical energy is an exception and its transit is always recorded under foreign trade. Exports similarly cover all quantities exported from the national territory.

Norway was a net exporter of primary energy: 157 Mio toe (1995); 202 Mio toe (2001).

Energy intensity of the economy in 2001
In kgoe per 1 000 EUR

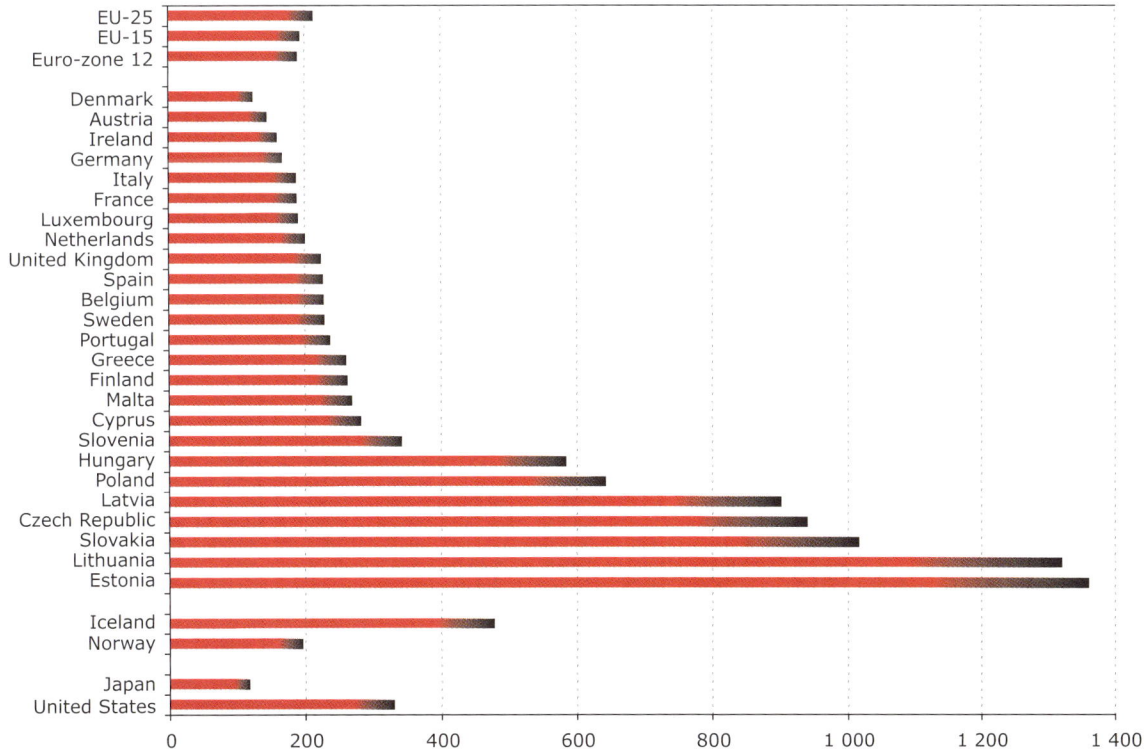

EU-25, EU-15, Euro-zone-12, Germany, Spain, Italy, the Netherlands: provisional data.

This indicator is the ratio between the gross inland consumption of energy and the gross domestic product (GDP) for a given calendar year. It measures the energy consumption of an economy and its overall energy efficiency. The gross inland consumption of energy is calculated as the sum of the gross inland consumption of five energy types: coal, electricity, oil, natural gas and renewable energy sources. The GDP figures are taken at constant prices to avoid the impact of the inflation, base year 1995 (ESA 95). The energy intensity ratio is determined by dividing the gross inland consumption by the GDP. Since gross inland consumption is measured in kgoe (kilogram of oil equivalent) and GDP in 1 000 EUR, this ratio is measured in kgoe per 1 000 EUR.

Share of electricity form renewables
Including indicative targets for 2010; in %

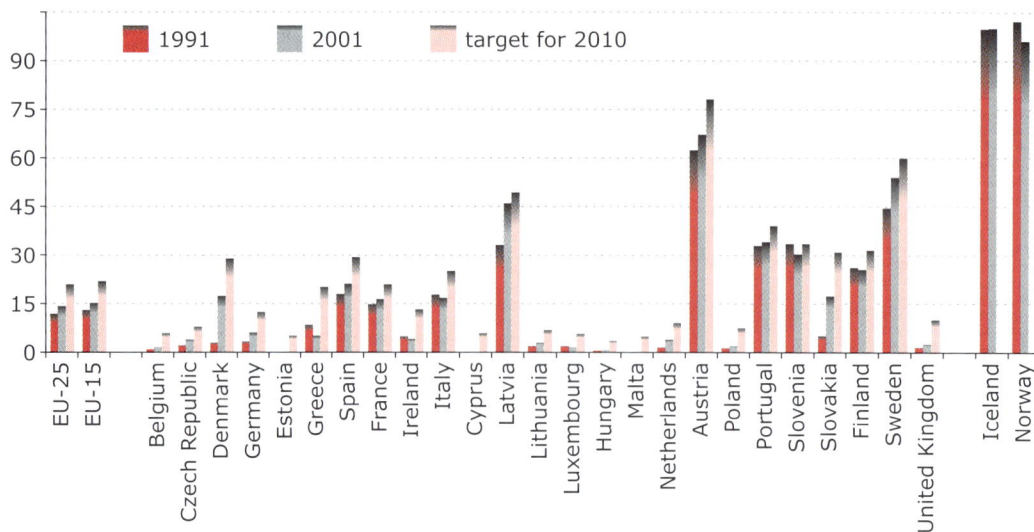

This indicator is the ratio between the electricity produced from renewable energy sources and the gross national electricity consumption for a given calendar year. It measures the contribution of electricity produced from renewable energy sources to the national electricity consumption. Electricity produced from renewable energy sources comprises the electricity generation from hydro plants (excluding pumping), wind, solar, geothermal and electricity from biomass/wastes. Gross national electricity consumption comprises the total gross national electricity generation from all fuels (including autoproduction), plus electricity imports, minus exports.

Renewable energy primary production: biomass, hydro, geothermal, wind and solar energy in the EU-25
In 1 000 toe

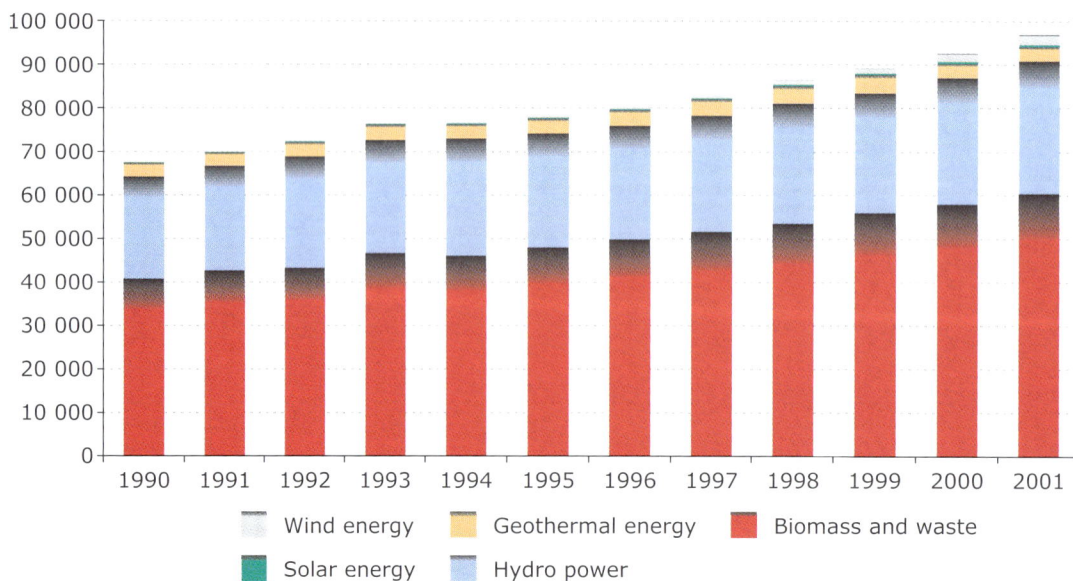

Primary production: biomass; hydro (the electricity generated in pumped storage plants is not included); geothermal; wind; solar energy.

Total gross electricity generation
In GWh

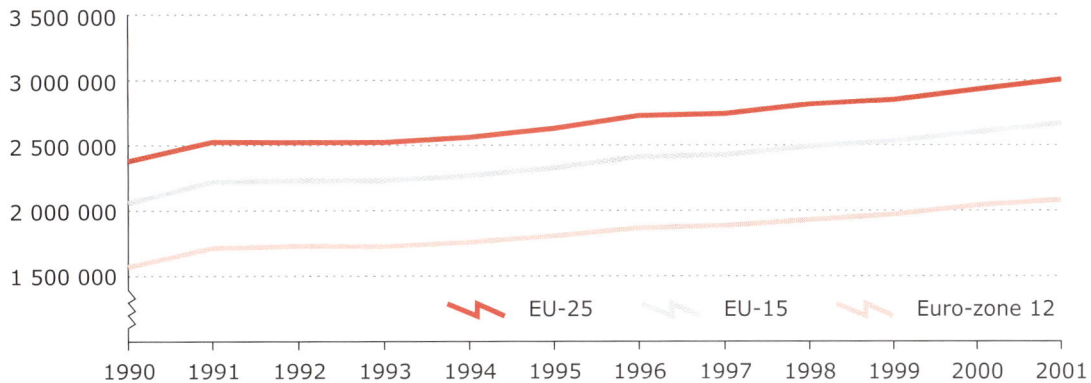

Total gross electricity generation covers gross electricity generation in all types of power plants. The gross electricity generation at the plant level is defined as the electricity measured at the outlet of the main transformers, i.e. the consumption of electricity in the plant auxiliaries and in transformers are included.

Market share of the largest generator in the electricity market in 2001
In %

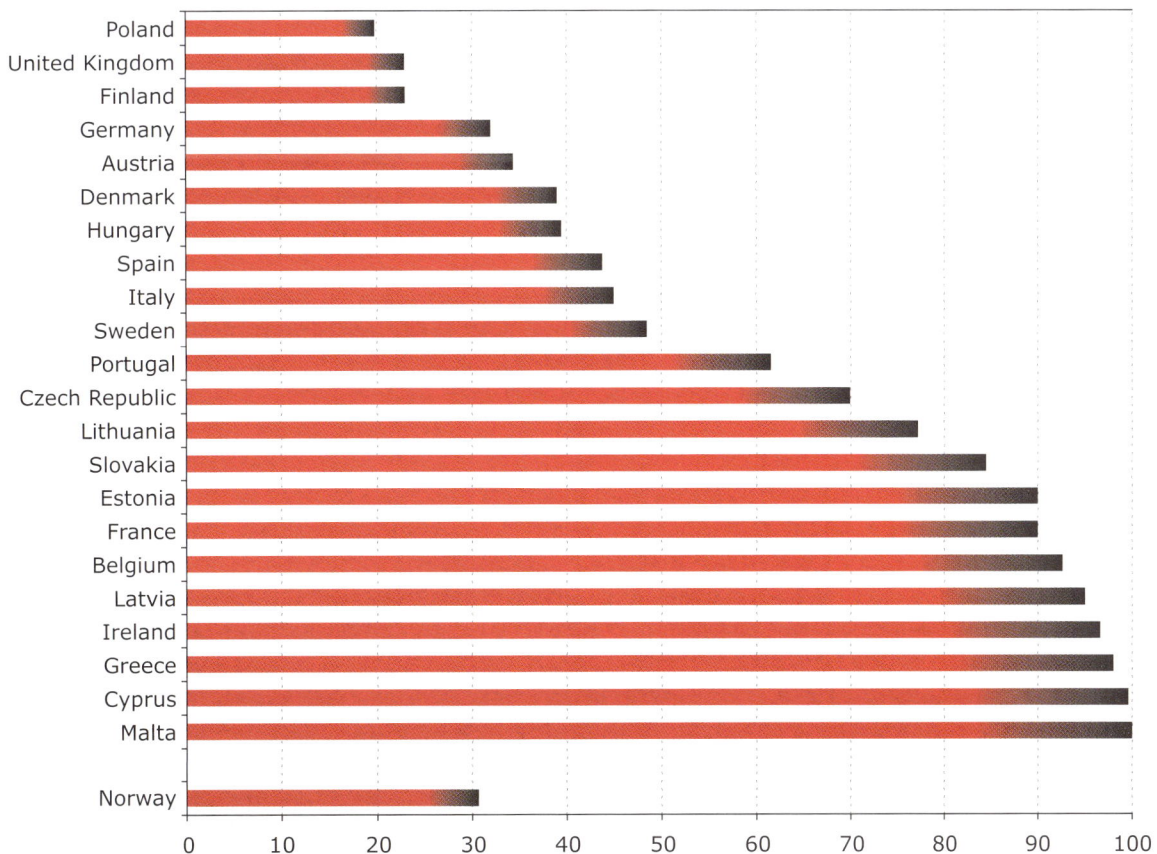

The indicator shows the market share of the largest electricity generator in each country. To calculate this indicator, the total net electricity production during each reference year is taken into account. It means that the electricity used by generators for their own consumption is not taken into account. Then, the net production of each generator during the same year is considered in order to calculate the corresponding market shares. Only the largest market share is reported under this indicator.

6

Prices of premium unleaded gasoline 95 RON, January 2003
In EUR per 1 000 litres

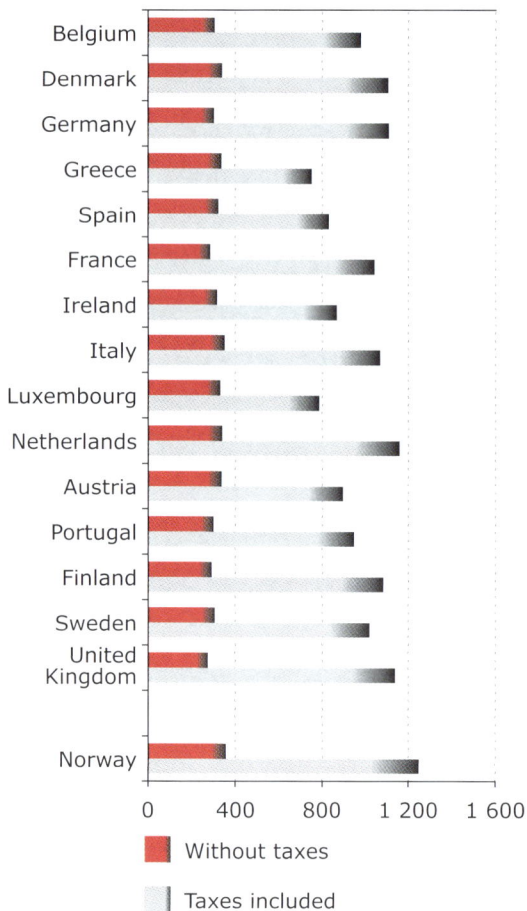

Belgium
Denmark
Germany
Greece
Spain
France
Ireland
Italy
Luxembourg
Netherlands
Austria
Portugal
Finland
Sweden
United Kingdom

Norway

0   400   800   1 200   1 600

■ Without taxes

▨ Taxes included

Prices of diesel oil, January 2003
In EUR per 1 000 litres

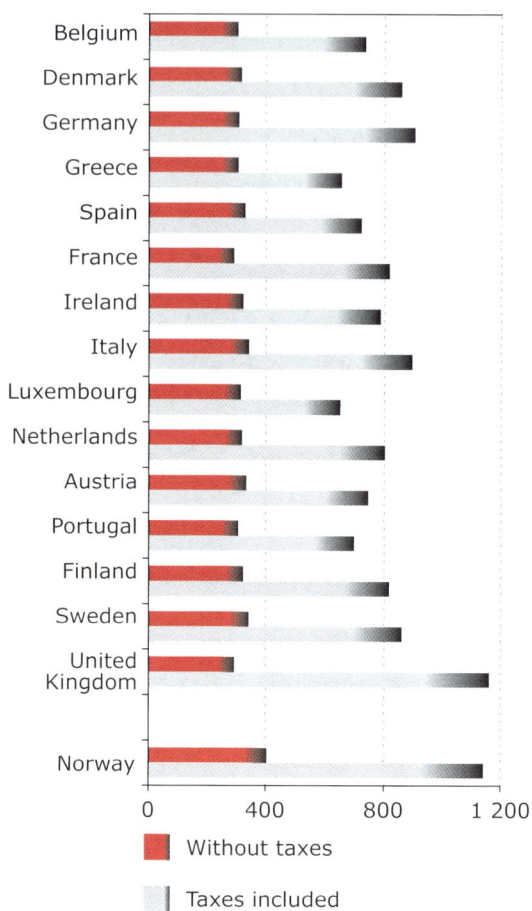

Belgium
Denmark
Germany
Greece
Spain
France
Ireland
Italy
Luxembourg
Netherlands
Austria
Portugal
Finland
Sweden
United Kingdom

Norway

0   400   800   1 200

■ Without taxes

▨ Taxes included

This indicator presents the average unleaded gasoline (Euro-super 95) consumer prices at the pump. The prices are supplied to the Directorate-General of Transport and Energy of the Commission by the Member States as being the most frequently encountered at the 15th of each month.

This indicator presents the average diesel oil consumer prices at the pump. The prices are supplied to the Directorate-General of Transport and Energy of the Commission by the Member States as being the most frequently encountered at the 15th of each month.

6

Electricity prices in EU-15
In EUR/kwh

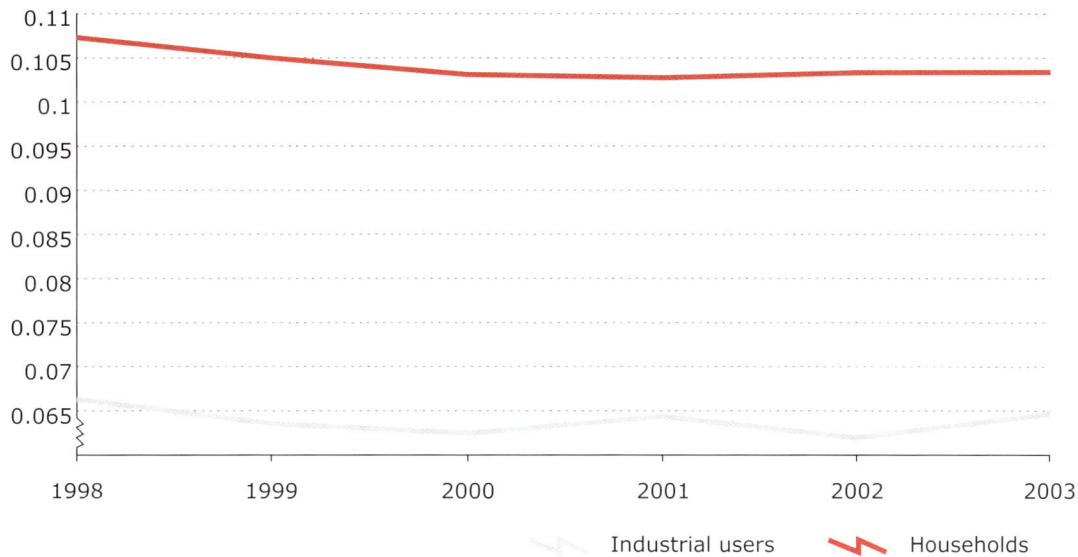

Electricity prices for industrial users: this indicator presents electricity prices charged to final industrial consumers, which are defined as follows: annual consumption of 2 000 MWh, maximum demand of 500 kW and annual load of 4 000 hours. Prices are given in euro (without taxes) per kWh corresponding to prices applicable on 1 January each year. Electricity prices for households: this indicator presents electricity prices charged to final domestic consumers, which are defined as follows: annual consumption of 3 500 kWh of which 1 300 kWh is overnight (standard dwelling of 90m^2). Prices are given in euro (without taxes) per kWh corresponding to prices applicable on 1 January each year.

Gas prices in EU-15
In EUR/kwh

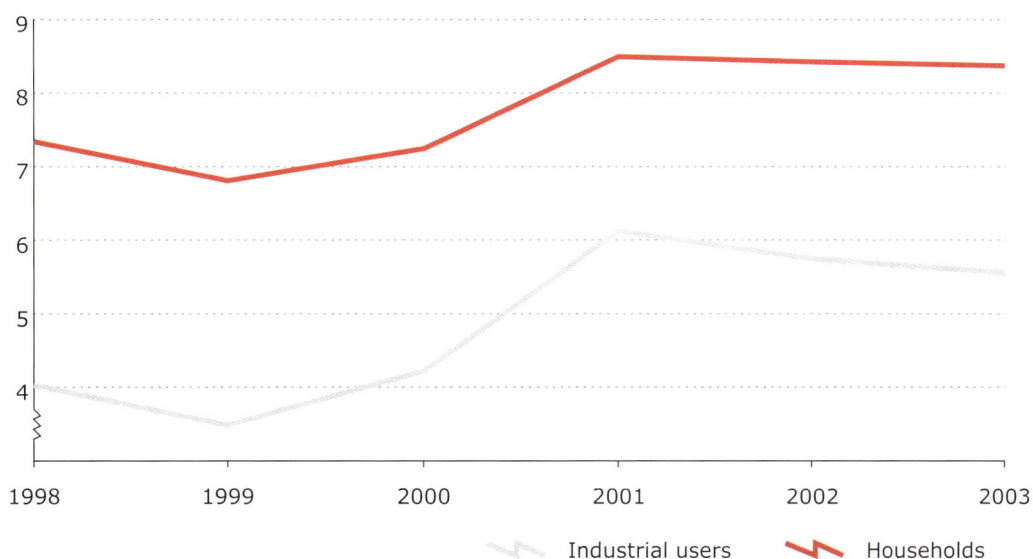

Gas prices for industrial users: this indicator presents the natural gas prices charged to final industrial consumers, which are defined as follows: annual consumption of 41 860 GJ, and load factor of 200 days (1 600 hours). Prices are given in euro (without taxes) per GJ corresponding to prices applicable on 1 January each year. Gas prices for households: this indicator presents the natural gas prices charged to final domestic consumers, which is defined as follows: annual consumption of 83.7 GJ (equipment: cooking, water heating and central heating). Prices are given in euro (without taxes) per GJ corresponding to prices applicable on 1 January each year.

Final energy consumption
In 1 000 toe

	1990	1991	1992	1993	1994	1995	1996	1997	1998	1999	2000	2001
EU-25	1 010 461	1 026 233	1 008 238	1 012 878	1 002 802	1 023 738	1 065 933	1 056 723	1 067 033(p)	1 069 111(p)	1 068 813(p)	1 096 888(p)
EU-15	858 585	879 771	873 496	880 850	874 519	895 915	933 634	926 089	942 185(p)	947 205(p)	950 157(p)	972 739(p)
Euro-zone	662 677	678 932	673 960	676 526	669 547	689 254	716 796	712 211	726 385(p)	729 154(p)	731 734(p)	771 867(p)
Belgium	31 277	33 030	33 769	33 102	33 889	34 489	36 383	36 529	37 092	36 931	36 922	37 211
Czech Republic	36 626	31 835	30 357	27 278	26 168	25 395	25 597	25 550	24 310	23 139	24 079	24 073
Denmark	13 796	14 115	13 990	14 441	14 395	14 729	15 319	14 941	14 984	14 912	14 560	14 992
Germany	227 142	224 161	218 413	219 341	215 457	222 342	230 895	226 131	224 450(p)	219 934(p)	213 270(p)	215 174(p)
Estonia	6 002	5 704	3 587	3 066	3 029	2 648	2 895	2 962	2 609	2 355	2 362	2 516
Greece	14 534	14 701	14 956	15 206	15 349	15 811	16 870	17 257	18 159	18 157	18 508	19 112
Spain	56 647	60 081	59 952	59 365	62 279	63 536	65 259	67 986	71 750	74 378	79411(p)	83 221
France	136 003	142 477	143 103	143 430	137 481	141 243	148 621	145 654	150 829	150760(p)	151 564	158 622
Ireland	7 113	7 096	7 155	7 207	7 795	7 748	8 266	8 658	9 306	9 858	10 463	10 675
Italy	107 096	110 007	110 311	110 446	108 845	113 695	114 401	115 309	118 622	122 998	123 036	125 990
Cyprus	1 271	1 120	1 289	1 303	1 345	1 387	1 436	1 439	1 508	1 575	1 644	1 689
Latvia	3 046	5 363	4 280	3 749	3 324	2 843	3 117	2 930	2 688	2 755	2911(p)	3 640
Lithuania	9 865	9 307	6 098	4 898	4 566	4 357	4 124	4 050	4 450	3 996	3 640	3 778
Luxembourg	3 325	3 561	3 552	3 618	3 551	3 148	3 235	3 224	3 183	3 341	3 544	3 689
Hungary	18 758	17 662	15 389	15 296	15 161	15 161	15 869	15 165	15 274	15 853	15 798	16 388
Malta	332	387	399	423	418	435	505	548	529	551	522(p)	445
Netherlands	42 632	45 566	44 853	46 474	45 761	47 431	51 413	49 103	49 307	48 470	49 745	50 775
Austria	18 599	20 103	19 573	19 757	19 405	20 353	21 982	21 581	22 251	21 864	22 287	24 590
Poland	59 554	60 041	59 015	64 306	61 902	63 414	66 199	65 277	60 377	58 843	55 573	56 196
Portugal	11 208	11 648	12 040	12 172	12 759	13 042	13 863	14 550	15 421	15 982	16 937	18 069
Slovenia	3 368	3 330	3 288	3 577	3 756	3 940	4 359	4 470	4 272	4 352	4 523	4 526
Slovakia	13 053	11 714	11 039	8 132	8 613	8 242	8 198	8 242	8 832	8 486	7 605	10 898
Finland	21 634	21 203	21 238	21 613	22 325	22 227	22 478	23 484	24 172	24 637	24 555	24 739
Sweden	30 514	30 830	30 746	32 406	32 966	33 685	34 621	34 143	34 215	34 065	34 534	33 134
United Kingdom	137 064	141 193	139 844	142 269	142 261	142 436	150 028	147 536	148 443	150 917	150 821	152 746
Iceland	1 602	1 564	1 607	1 662	1 662	1 660	1 726	1 753	1 819	1 953	2 057	2 113
Norway	16 087	15 838	15 717	16 170	16 698	16 854	17 669	17 466	18 187	18 659	18 087	18 561

Final energy consumption includes all energy delivered to the final consumer's door (in the industry, transport, households and other sectors) for all energy uses. It excludes deliveries for transformation and/or own use of the energy producing industries, as well as network losses.

Final energy consumption in the EU-25
In 1 000 toe

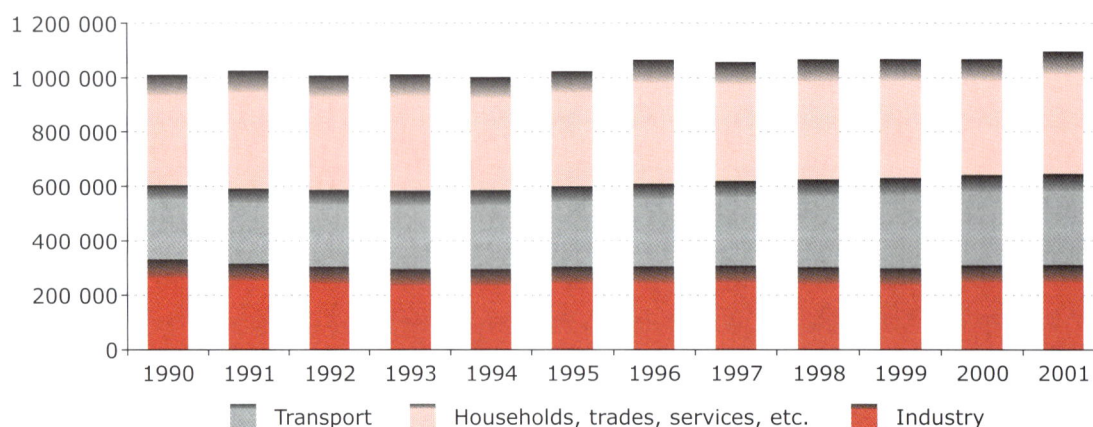

Transport   Households, trades, services, etc.   Industry

Final energy consumption by industry covers all industrial sectors, e.g. iron and steel industry, chemical industry, food, drink and tobacco industry, textile, leather and clothing industry, paper and printing industry, etc., with the exception of transformation and/or own use of the energy producing industries. Final energy consumption by transport covers the consumption of energy products in all types of transportation, i.e. rail, road, international and domestic air transport and inland navigation/coastal shipping, with the exception of maritime shipping. Final energy consumption in households, trades, services, etc. covers all energy products consumed by private households, small-scale industry, crafts, commerce, administrative bodies, services with the exception of transportation, agriculture and fishing.

Agriculture, forestry and fisheries

7

Agriculture

The common agricultural policy (CAP)

The common agricultural policy has had to adapt in order to meet the challenges with which it has been faced over the years: in the early days, it concentrated on securing a fair standard of living for the agricultural community and ensuring security of supply at affordable prices, and then it had to control quantitative imbalances. Now, there is a new approach based on a combination of lowering institutional prices and making compensatory payments.

Data collection

The farm structure survey, carried out about every two years throughout the EU, is devoted to measuring the size (both physical and economic) of holdings. The latest survey from which all figures are available was conducted in 1999/2000.

The survey also supplies information which allows farms to be classified on their type of production. The standard gross margin (SGM) allows different agricultural enterprises to be measured on a common basis. It is basically the difference between the production value and certain costs of production. It is measured for each type of crop and animal production. Specialised farms generate more than two thirds of their SGM from the main categories of field crops, horticulture, permanent crops, grazing livestock or granivores (pigs and poultry). Non-specialised farms or mixed farms generate less than two thirds of their SGM from one of the main categories.

Farm labour is measured in two ways. According to the survey of the structure of agriculture, the labour force includes total employment in agricultural holdings, including work by the farmer and his family. According to the European system of integrated economic accounts (ESA), farm labour means employment in agricultural activities.

Production

Cereals are the main Community agricultural production in volume. Having achieved self-sufficiency, the EU exports a significant part of its cereal harvest. From 1993, the reformed common agricultural policy has been bringing supply into line with demand, combining direct aids to cereal farmers with a compulsory set-aside scheme. The EU is the world's largest wine producer with more than one half of total world production. The main part of the production is consumed in Europe, although exchanges with other continents (particularly America and Asia) are increasing.

Prices

Producer price indices cover sales of crop and animal products (output) from agriculture to the rest of the economy. The share of crop and animal products in total agricultural sales differs between Member States. Purchase price indices cover purchases of means of agricultural production (input). Indices are calculated from farm-gate prices excluding VAT. The agricultural price indices may be deflated using the consumer price index.

Economic accounts for agriculture

Under the new methodology of the economic accounts for agriculture (EAA 97), agricultural output comprises all (agricultural) output sold by agricultural units, held in stock on the farms, or used for further processing by agricultural producers. Furthermore, it includes the intra-unit consumption of crop products used in animal feed, as well as output accounted for by own-account production of fixed capital goods and own final consumption of agricultural units.

Gross value added at basic prices is calculated by deducting intermediate consumption from the output of the agricultural industry (which includes, besides agricultural output, the output of non-agricultural secondary activities which are inseparable from the principal agricultural activity). The agricultural income indicator A is defined as the index of the real income of factors in agriculture, per annual work unit. This indicator corresponds to the real net value added at factor cost of agriculture, per total annual work unit. Net value added at factor cost is calculated by subtracting from gross value added at basic prices the consumption of fixed capital, and adding the value of the (other) subsidies less taxes on production.

Number of agricultural holdings
In 1 000

	1990	1993	1995	1997	2000
EU-15	:	:	7 370	6 989	6 771
Belgium	85	76	71	67	62
Denmark	81	74	69	63	58
Germany	654	606	567	534	472
Greece	850	819	802	821	817
Estonia	1 594	1 384	1 278	1 208	1 287
France	924	801	735	680	664
Ireland	171	159	153	148	142
Italy	2 665	2 488	2 482	2 315	2 154
Luxembourg	4	3	3	3	3
Netherlands	125	120	113	108	102
Austria	:	:	222	210	199
Portugal	599	489	451	417	416
Finland	:	:	101	91	81
Sweden	:	:	89	90	81
United Kingdom	243	243	235	233	233

The smallest farms (less than 1 % of national agricultural activity) do not have to be surveyed.

Regular farm labour force
In 1 000 persons

	1990	1993	1995	1997	2000
EU-15	:	:	15 244	14 757	13 511
Belgium	141	132	122	117	107
Denmark	139	142	141	130	103
Germany	1 776	1 478	1 325	1 231	1 137
Greece	1 543	1 774	1 567	1 596	1 431
Estonia	2 839	2 571	2 543	2 497	2 439
France	1 859	1 610	1 507	1 404	1 320
Ireland	313	320	293	282	258
Italy	5 287	4 762	4 773	4 601	3 964
Luxembourg	9	8	7	7	7
Netherlands	289	290	276	282	276
Austria	:	:	547	513	527
Portugal	1 561	1 263	1 173	1 070	1 064
Finland	:	:	232	224	184
Sweden	:	:	164	169	157
United Kingdom	659	651	572	636	539

The farm labour force includes everyone (over the legal age limit) having provided an agricultural work on and for a holding during the last 12 months. The 'regular' labour force consists of the members of the holder's family working on the holding (the holder included).

Regular farm labour force: women
In 1 000 persons

	1990	1993	1995	1997	2000
EU-15	:	:	5 601	5 436	4 976
Belgium	48	48	44	41	37
Denmark	41	40	38	37	0
Germany	647	534	466	429	416
Greece	648	810	678	698	593
Estonia	900	786	769	757	784
France	658	560	520	476	434
Ireland	93	99	87	81	70
Italy	2 101	1 808	1 838	1 802	1 540
Luxembourg	4	3	3	2	2
Netherlands	86	89	87	94	92
Austria	:	:	230	214	229
Portugal	728	588	548	502	499
Finland	:	:	87	82	66
Sweden	:	:	54	55	51
United Kingdom	199	193	153	168	161

The farm labour force includes everyone (over the legal age limit) having provided an agricultural work on and for a holding during the last 12 months. The 'regular' labour force consists of the members of the holder's family working on the holding (the holder included).

7

Farm holders being a natural person
In 1 000 persons

	1990	1993	1995	1997	2000
EU-15	:	:	7 269	6 869	6 486
Belgium	85	75	70	65	59
Denmark	81	73	68	63	57
Germany	646	600	561	518	440
Greece	850	819	802	821	817
Estonia	1 568	1 354	1 241	1 168	1 236
France	910	786	718	662	538
Ireland	170	159	153	148	141
Italy	2 647	2 475	2 471	2 302	2 138
Luxembourg	4	3	3	3	3
Netherlands	122	116	110	104	95
Austria	:	:	217	206	195
Portugal	594	484	445	411	409
Finland	:	:	101	91	76
Sweden	:	:	83	84	76
United Kingdom	227	228	225	223	206

The farm holder is the legal or physical person taking benefit from the agricultural activity. They are only accounted for as the individual holders and not the holders of group holdings.

Farm holders less than 35 years old
In 1 000 persons

	1990	1993	1995	1997	2000
EU-15	:	:	571	522	528
Belgium	10	9	11	9	7
Denmark	9	7	7	7	5
Germany	101	103	98	86	73
Greece	74	59	49	44	71
Estonia	113	88	77	69	111
France	121	104	92	79	53
Ireland	22	24	21	18	18
Italy	138	133	110	119	111
Luxembourg	0	0	0	0	0
Netherlands	11	12	10	7	6
Austria	:	:	40	35	31
Portugal	40	23	19	15	17
Finland	:	:	16	13	9
Sweden	:	:	7	6	5
United Kingdom	17	15	14	13	11

The farm holder is the legal or physical person taking benefit from the agricultural activity. They are only accounted for as the individual holders and not the holders of group holdings.

Farm holders over 64 years old
In 1 000 persons

	1990	1993	1995	1997	2000
EU-15	:	:	2022	1950	1867
Belgium	17	16	12	12	12
Denmark	16	16	16	13	11
Germany	47	42	42	41	26
Greece	216	241	249	281	253
Estonia	384	364	371	368	347
France	126	116	110	106	97
Ireland	39	32	33	32	28
Italy	851	851	912	828	826
Luxembourg	1	1	1	1	1
Netherlands	19	19	19	20	18
Austria	:	:	21	21	20
Portugal	171	161	157	155	155
Finland	:	:	7	5	5
Sweden	:	:	18	18	16
United Kingdom	50	51	55	50	52

7

Area under cereals
In 1 000 ha

	1993	1994	1995	1996	1997	1998	1999	2000	2001	2002	2003
EU-25	51 719	51 218	51 589	53 220	54 977	54 100	52 126	53 671	53 141	53 242	:
EU-15	35 487	35 167	35 950	37 319	38 476	37 790	36 739	37 722	36 951	37 864	36 830
Euro-zone	28 504	28 201	28 975	29 881	30 850	30 265	29 667	30 453	29 862	30 673	29 860
Belgium	312	309	309	295	301	320	282	314	287	310	308
Czech Republic	1 607	1 660	1 580	1 586	1 686	1 678	1 591	1 650	1 624	1 562	1 460
Denmark	1 438	1 406	1 454	1 545	1 535	1 535	1 497	1 500	1 538	1 528	1 485
Germany	6 224	6 235	6 527	6 707	7 014	7 042	6 635	7 016	7 046	6 941	6 862
Estonia	375	320	304	289	327	354	321	329	274	259	268
Greece	1 360	1 345	1 235	1 318	1 308	1 287	1 283	1 213	1 372	1 303	1 284
Spain	6 426	6 490	6 693	6 767	6 988	6 632	6 696	6 807	6 437	6 728	6 565
France	8 500	8 121	8 246	8 783	9 140	9 153	8 842	9 075	8 936	9 328	8 953
Ireland	285	270	274	293	310	301	290	279	286	299	303
Italy	4 080	4 104	4 225	4 222	4 197	4 068	4 173	4 134	4 133	4 284	4 148
Cyprus	69	64	61	60	43	59	59	51	56	58	58
Latvia	694	486	408	446	483	466	416	420	444	415	429
Lithuania	1 268	1 195	1 027	1 079	1 162	1 108	1 013	980	936	918	864
Luxembourg	30	30	29	30	29	29	28	29	28	29	29
Hungary	2 695	2 884	2 739	2 795	2 954	2 835	2 421	2 764	3 081	2 953	:
Malta	-	-	-	-	-	-	-	-	-	-	-
Netherlands	187	195	199	206	207	211	190	226	236	233	234
Austria	825	821	808	833	848	840	810	830	824	814	810
Poland	8 579	8 481	8 571	8 720	8 899	8 844	8 701	8 814	8 820	8 294	8 163
Portugal	712	681	689	670	703	517	594	578	493	515	454
Slovenia	111	103	100	99	95	95	92	103	105	99	:
Slovakia	835	860	848	828	853	871	774	838	851	820	:
Finland	923	945	978	1 075	1 113	1 152	1 128	1 167	1 156	1 190	1 194
Sweden	1 152	1 172	1 104	1 217	1 268	1 283	1 153	1 208	1 165	1 116	1 145
United Kingdom	3 033	3 043	3 181	3 359	3 515	3 420	3 140	3 348	3 014	3 245	3 056

Area under cereals in EU-25
In 1 000 ha

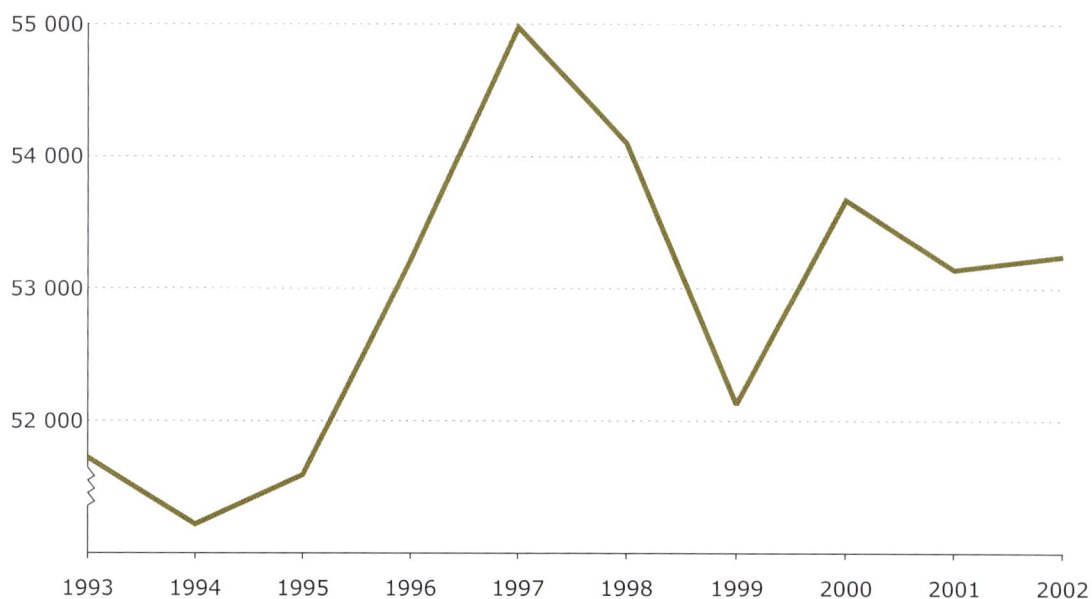

Crop output in EU-15
In million ECU/EUR

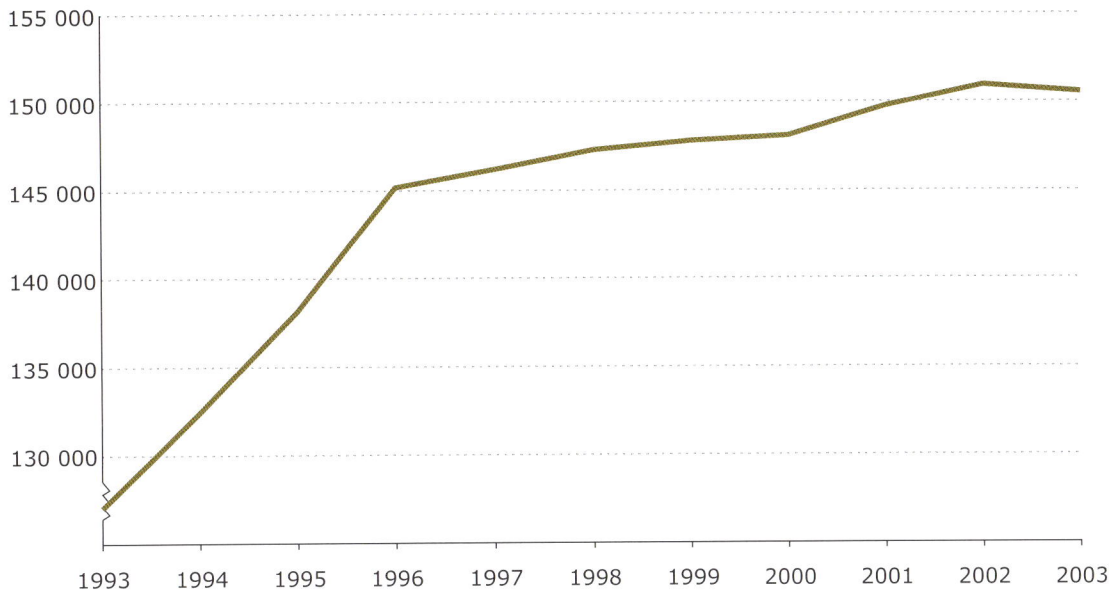

2001: provisional data; 2002, 2003: estimates.

Crop output is valued at basic prices. The basic price is defined as the price received by the producer, after deduction of all taxes on products but including all subsidies on products. The concept of output comprises sales, changes in stocks, and crop products used as animal feedingstuffs for processing and own final use by the producers.

Animal output in EU-15
In million ECU/EUR

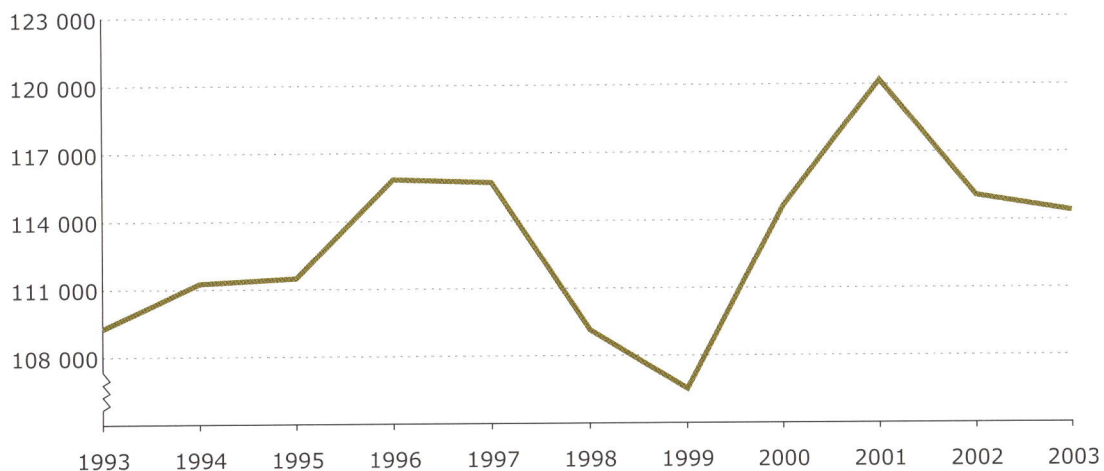

2001: provisional data; 2002, 2003: estimates.

Animal output is valued at basic prices. The basic price is defined as the price received by the producer, after deduction of all taxes on products but including all subsidies on products. The concept of output comprises sales, changes in stocks, and products used for processing and own final use by the producers.

Production of meat in EU-15: pigs
1 000 tonnes

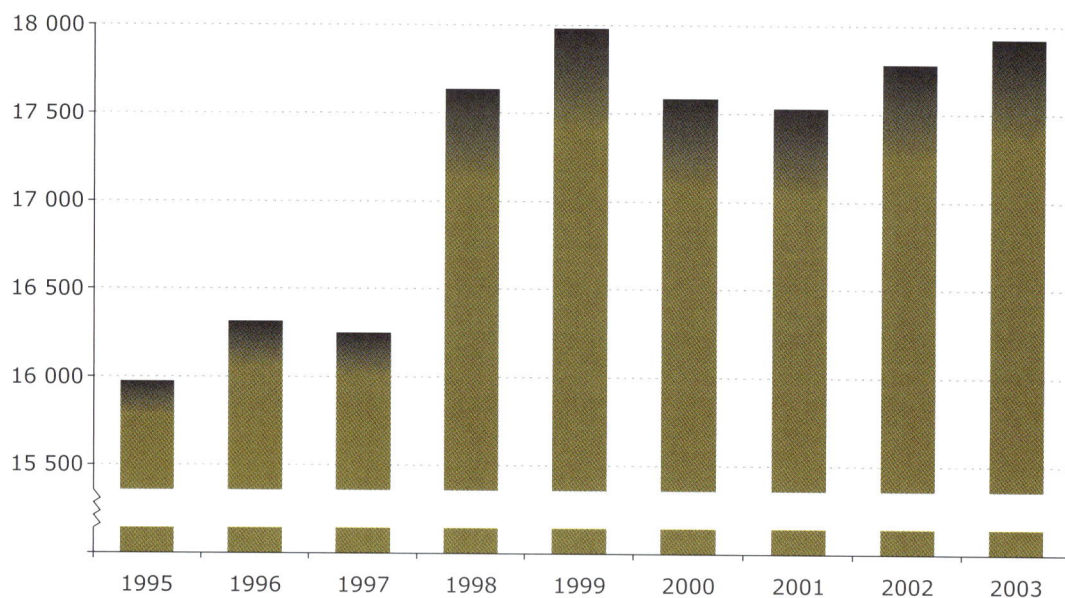

This indicator expresses the total carcass weight of pigs slaughtered in slaughterhouses and on the farm whose meat is declared fit for human consumption.

Production of meat in EU-15: poultry
1 000 tonnes

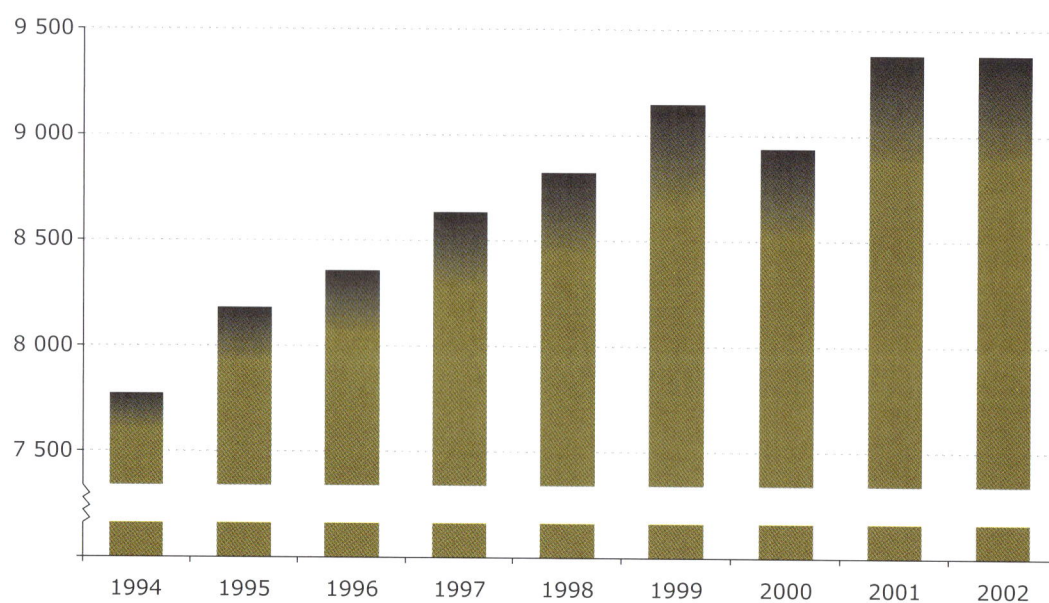

This indicator expresses the total carcass weight of poultry slaughtered whose meat is declared fit for human consumption. The following poultry is included: hens, chickens, ducks, turkeys, guinea fowls and geese. This indicator covers mainly the production of Gallinaceae including broilers.

Production of meat in EU-15: cattle
1 000 tonnes

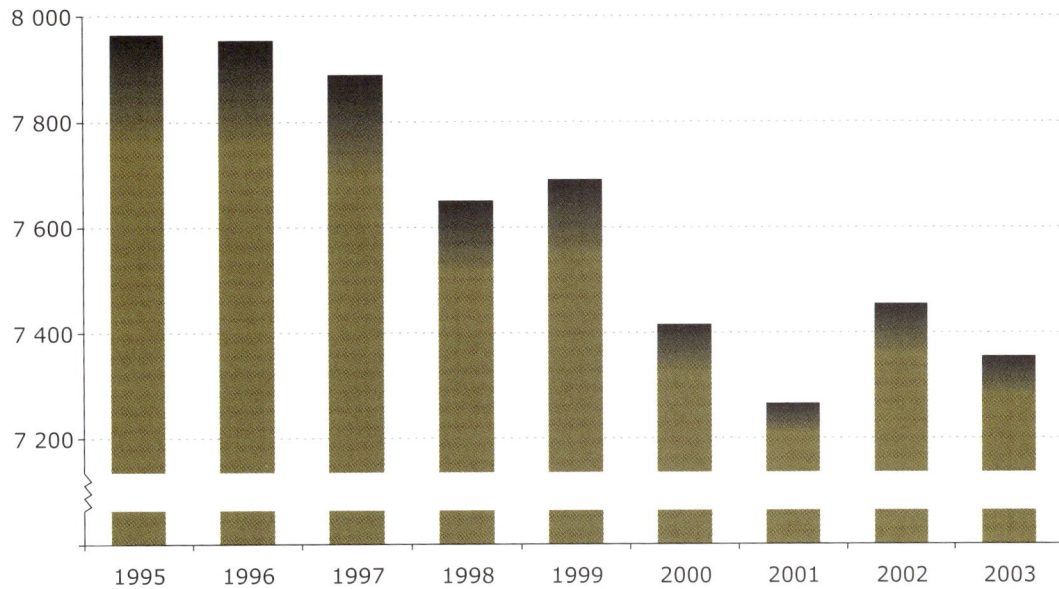

This indicator expresses the carcass weight of bovine animals (calves, bullocks, bulls, heifers and cows) slaughtered in slaughterhouses and on the farm whose meat is declared fit for human consumption.

Collection of cow's milk in EU-15
1 000 tonnes

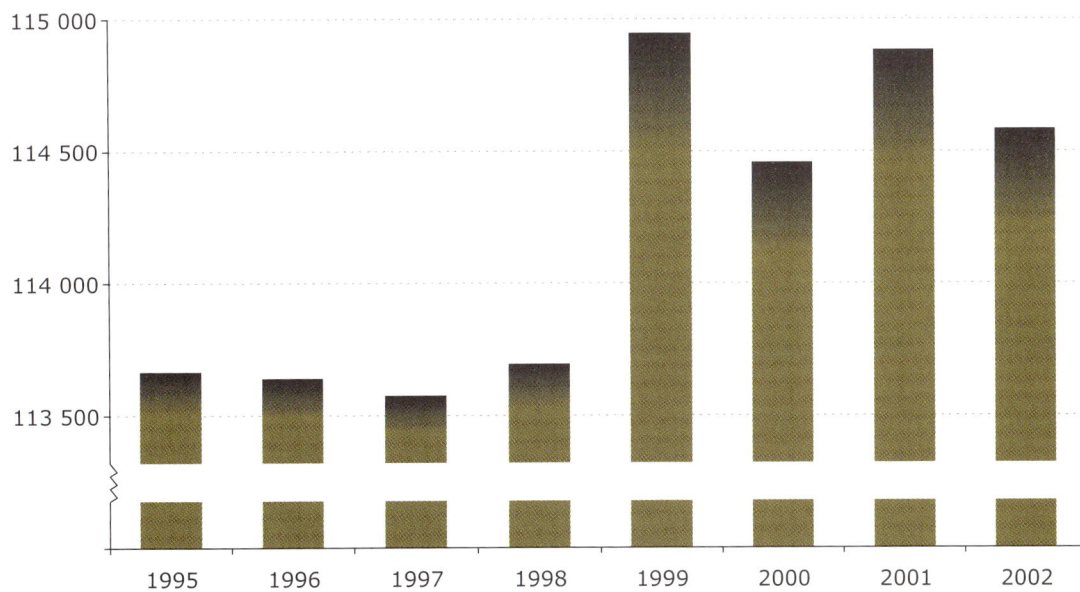

Data cover cow's milk collected on farms by approved dairies. A distinction should be made between 'milk collected by dairies' and 'milk production on the farm'. Milk collection is only part of the total use of milk production on the farm. The other part of the use of milk produced on the farm generally includes domestic consumption, direct sale and cattle feed.

Producer price indices for agricultural production
1995 = 100; deflated

	1993	1994	1995	1996	1997	1998	1999	2000	2001	2002	2003
EU-15	:	:	100	99	96.3	91.5	86.4	87.6	89.8	85.3	:
Euro-zone 12	:	:	100	99.1	97.7	93.6	88.4	89.9	91.7	87.3	:
Belgium	:	:	100	101.4	101.2	94.2	85.4	91.8	91.8	83.7	86.1
Czech Republic	105.3	101.4	100	99.6	94.5	87.3	75.5	79.3	82.7	:	:
Denmark	:	:	100	101.7	99.8	86.6	81.1	88.1	92.4	81.6	76.8
Germany	:	:	100	98.3	97.8	92.5	86.3	90.4	94	86.9	86.1
Estonia	:	:	100	:	:	:	:	:	:	:	:
Greece	:	:	100	99	96	91.1	89.6	90.6	92.9	94.5	99.2
Spain	:	:	100	98.8	93.9	89.8	84.9	85.8	87.2	82.6	82.9
France	:	:	100	97.7	96.7	95.9	92.3	92.2	93.7	87.9	88.4
Ireland	:	:	100	93.4	86.6	84.1	78.6	79.5	79.9	73	69.8
Italy	:	:	100	100.4	99	93.9	88.1	87.9	90.2	89.1	91.3
Cyprus	:	:	100	95.9	100.1	99.1	:	:	:	:	:
Latvia	:	:	100	95.9	84.2	75.3	62.4	65.2	65	70	:
Lithuania	140.4	93.4	100	96.2	83.4	74.2	68.3	64.3	67.8	:	:
Luxembourg	:	:	100	94.3	95.2	94.3	90.7	88.1	88	84	82.5
Hungary	:	:	100	108.3	99.8	89.8	83.8	93.3	89.9	85.2	:
Netherlands	:	:	100	101.5	105.9	98.7	91.2	96	96.6	91.1	91.1
Austria	:	:	100	99.9	101.2	93.3	87.1	91.1	95	88.6	:
Poland	98.1	101.3	100	101.8	97.3	85.7	75.6	79.9	79.1	:	:
Portugal	:	:	100	99.1	97.9	96.9	90.4	92.2	94	86.7	86.8
Slovenia	101.4	100.3	100	102.3	102.5	95.3	89.4	87.3	87.6	:	:
Slovakia	108.9	106.4	100	99.6	99.2	92.7	82.3	78.8	79.1	:	:
Finland	:	:	100	104.1	96.5	93.8	87.8	89.5	91.7	88.1	82.5
Sweden	:	:	100	94.7	91.3	89	87.3	85.1	87.2	83.3	81.8
United Kingdom	98	95.7	100	97.4	83.1	73.5	69.4	67.4	71.8	68.4	73

The indices in this table give information on the trends in the producer prices of agricultural production as a whole. The sub-indices were weighted by the values of sales in 1995. Nominal indices are deflated by means of the harmonised index of consumer prices.

Purchase price indices for means of agricultural production
1995 = 100; deflated

	1993	1994	1995	1996	1997	1998	1999	2000	2001	2002	2003
EU-15	:	:	100	101.8	101.1	96.6	94.1	96.3	97.6	95.7	:
Euro-zone 12	:	:	100	102.1	102	97.8	95.2	97.6	98.5	96.7	:
Belgium	:	:	100	102.1	102.7	98.3	96.6	100.3	100.4	99.3	98
Czech Republic	:	102.4	100	101.1	100.4	90.2	82.7	87.7	88.5	:	:
Denmark	:	:	100	100.9	101.9	99.1	95.5	95.6	99.9	97.3	93.5
Germany	:	:	100	101.6	101.5	98.1	96.9	101.2	102.4	100.9	100.8
Estonia	:	:	100	:	:	:	:	:	:	:	:
Greece	:	:	100	99.7	96.8	94.4	94.1	96.5	95.3	94.3	94.6
Spain	:	:	100	100.9	101.7	99.4	96	97.7	97.5	95.2	93.6
France	:	:	100	101.3	101.5	98.7	97.3	99.6	100.5	99	98.1
Ireland	:	:	100	101.6	99.3	96	95.1	95.7	96.5	94	92.5
Italy	:	:	100	104.6	105.2	97.1	91.4	92.5	94	92.7	92.1
Cyprus	:	:	100	101.7	105.4	99.8	:	:	:	:	:
Latvia	:	:	100	109.5	113.8	111.7	111.1	110.8	109.6	109.9	:
Lithuania	:	:	:	:	:	:	:	:	:	:	:
Luxembourg	:	:	100	100.7	100.3	99	98.8	99.5	100.6	99.5	98.3
Hungary	:	:	100	108.8	106.9	101	100.6	106.2	110.8	107.8	:
Netherlands	:	:	100	103.7	102.3	98.1	95.8	99.2	101.1	98.4	98.1
Austria	:	:	100	100.6	100.8	97.9	97.2	98.4	98.3	96.6	:
Poland	109.4	103.5	100	99	98.9	98.1	100.6	103.8	105	:	:
Portugal	:	:	100	100.1	97	92.3	90.4	91.3	93.8	87.2	87.9
Slovenia	109.8	109.7	100	116	115.5	106.1	101.4	104.8	111.2	:	:
Slovakia	107.3	101.8	100	101	105.3	102.7	96.6	94.2	95.9	:	:
Finland	:	:	100	100.4	101.1	98.4	97	99.6	98.1	96.5	96.7
Sweden	:	:	100	104.3	103.5	100.8	100.3	102.8	105.9	106	105.8
United Kingdom	97.5	95.7	100	98.9	93.6	86.6	84	85.6	88.2	86.7	87.6

The indices in this table give information on the trends in the purchase prices of the means of agricultural production as a whole. The sub-indices were weighted by the values of purchases in 1995. Nominal indices are deflated by means of the harmonised index of consumer prices.

Indicator A of the income from agricultural activity
1995 = 100

	1993	1994	1995	1996	1997	1998	1999	2000	2001	2002	2003
EU-15	85.6	93.9	100.0	103.5	103.9	100.2	100.6	106.5	111.3(p)	105.3(e)	:
Euro-zone 12	86.3	94.8	100.0	104.6	107.2	105.4	105.3	110.1	116.8(e)	111.8(e)	:
Belgium	109.6	111.1	100.0	109.6	113.8	107.5	99.5	108.0	116.9(e)	113.7(e)	125.5(e)
Czech Republic	:	:	:	:	:	:	:	:	:	:	:
Denmark	74.6	85.1	100.0	100.8	97.1	76.3	75.3	91.0	102.3	81.8(e)	73.2(e)
Germany	86.2	92.2	100.0	113.4	116.4	104.6	102.9	126.3	150.7(e)	118.9(e)	1 038 140(e)
Estonia	:	:	:	:	:	:	:	:	:	:	:
Greece	85.2	95.8	100.0	95.2	95.6	95.1	95.4	96.9	100.4	100.0(e)	101.8(e)
Spain	90.0	100.4	100.0	112.3	113.5	106.0	103.4	121.5	123.7(p)	114.4(e)	116.7(e)
France	83.0	94.2	100.0	100.5	104.0	108.6	106.4	105.8	107.5	103.4(e)	104.0(e)
Ireland	89.6	93.5	100.0	102.3	99.9	96.6	92.3	107.7	110.9	103.1(e)	104.5(e)
Italy	85.3	91.1	100.0	105.7	108.3	108.2	116.7	112.5	111.4	109.7(e)	109.1(e)
Cyprus	:	:	:	:	:	:	:	:	:	:	:
Latvia	:	:	:	:	:	:	:	:	:	:	:
Lithuania	:	:	:	:	:	:	:	:	:	:	:
Luxembourg	90.9	88.5	100.0	103.4	95.6	104.3	100.4	100.9	94.6	96.0(e)	96.(e)
Hungary	:	:	:	:	:	:	:	:	:	:	:
Malta	:	:	:	:	:	:	:	:	:	:	:
Netherlands	86.4	97.4	100.0	95.9	103.5	93.0	86.4	87.3	89.6	78.9(e)	80.0(e)
Austria	84.5	91.0	100.0	93.3	83.7	81.0	80.9	88.5	102.3	98.1(e)	92.1(e)
Poland	:	:	:	:	:	:	:	:	:	:	:
Portugal	67.9	91.1	100.0	109.8	104.6	104.9	126.1	109.6	131.0	126.4(e)	128.9(e)
Slovenia	:	:	100.0	89.1	102.9	100.0	93.8	101.1	86.9	114.1(e)	91.8(e)
Slovakia	:	:	100.0	105.1	108.1	95.8	102.2	99.3	113.8	107.5(e)	74.8(e)
Finland	93.7	84.3	100.0	82.8	82.1	65.6	81.4	107.6	109.3(e)	116.6(e)	110.4(e)
Sweden	83.2	83.9	100.0	98.2	104.4	107.0	94.4	105.3	118.0(e)	116.5(e)	113.0(e)
United Kingdom	85.7	91.0	100.0	93.6	72.1	62.6	61.4	58.3	62.4	66.9(e)	79.2(e)

Indicator A corresponds to the deflated (real) net value added at factor cost of agriculture, per total annual work unit. The implicit price index of GDP is used as deflator.

Gross value added at basic prices of the agricultural industry
In million ECU/EUR

	1993	1994	1995	1996	1997	1998	1999	2000	2001	2002	2003
EU-15	124 919.6	132 302.6	136 178.0	143 008.2	143 534.5	141 659.1	139 710.7	144 147.0	148 992.2p	145 064.7(e)	144 629.6(e)
Euro-zone 12	113 316.8	119 968.4	122 687.1	129 110.5	129 711.1	129 156.7	127 587.1	129 998.7	136 171.0(e)	132 193.3(e)	:
Belgium	2 833.1	2 946.1	2 784.4	2 852.1	2 915.3	2 785.3	2 605.9	2 795.6	2 863.6(e)	2 789.7(e)	3 000.7(e)
Czech Republic	:	:	:	:	:	936.8	775.4	867.9	1 064.1	952.5(e)	857.8(e)
Denmark	3 189.5	3 423.9	3 941.9	3 992.8	3 833.3	3 123.8	3 039.6	3 508.7	3 942.6	3 288.4(e)	3 055.6(e)
Germany	14 011.1	14 371.1	15 700.8	16 308.6	16 104.3	15 563.1	15 471.2	17 381.0	19 218.2	16 376.3(e)	14 847.4(e)
Estonia	:	:	:	:	:	174.6	150.1	163.1	183.6	130.4(e)	130.2(e)
Greece	7 089.1	7 945.2	8 389.1	8 181.7	8 456.9	8 169.4	8 387.8	8 243.7	8 500.7	8 513.7(e)	8 722.3(e)
Spain	17 771.5	19 130.9	19 216.7	22 315.2	22 810.9	23 083.5	21 665.1	23 348.7	23 663.0(p)	24 013.4(e)	24 897.4(e)
France	27 148.1	29 572.1	30 910.2	30 889.7	31 059.3	32 122.2	31 664.2	31 661.2	31 874.5	31 606.3(e)	31 207.1(e)
Ireland	3 013.3	3 036.7	3 082.6	3 173.8	3 141.1	2 971.1	2 710.5	2 932.8	2 851.5	2 620.9(e)	2 775.1(e)
Italy	24 229.0	24 471.2	24 020.9	27 478.4	28 533.7	28 431.5	28 877.0	28 219.6	29 258.2	29 127.9(e)	29 241.5(e)
Cyprus	:	:	:	:	:	315.4	326.9	:	:	:	423.2(e)
Latvia	:	:	:	:	:	185.1	164.2	212.1	244.3	255.0(e)	229.4(e)
Lithuania	:	:	322.4	510.2	643.3	476.1	410.3	373.9	324.5(e)	354.8(e)	346.4(e)
Luxembourg	122.1	120.9	135.1	123.3	110.0	124.8	133.4	132.0	129.8	126.6(e)	123.2(e)
Hungary	:	:	:	:	:	2 044.5	1 898.3	1 887.9	2 080.1	2 102.0(e)	1 853.3(e)
Malta	:	:	:	:	:	70.6	70.1	69.0	72.7	71.5(e)	67.8(e)
Netherlands	8 428.5	9 192.1	9 666.8	9 384.8	8 835.2	9 072.3	8 701.9	9 303.0	9 618.0	9 082.0(e)	9 114.4(e)
Austria	3 260.7	3 374.1	3 185.6	2 903.9	2 696.0	2 555.7	2 518.4	2 611.7	2 794.1	2 622.1(e)	2 465.2(e)
Poland	:	:	:	:	:	5 180.3	4 258.0	4 756.5	6 034.8	4 917.2(e)	4 000.6(e)
Portugal	2 051.2	2 513.8	2 700.2	2 858.0	2 592.6	2 467.2	2 864.8	2 690.2	3 165.7	3 264.3(e)	3 419.5(e)
Slovenia	:	:	438.7	411.8	464.6	467.1	439.7	431.2	399.4	494.4(e)	399.2(e)
Slovakia	:	:	533.7	568.7	590.1	483.2	414.8	344.6	440.0	526.6(e)	354.3(e)
Finland	1 998.1	1 969.1	1 698.7	1 580.5	1 535.8	1 104.4	1 278.8	1 519.3	1 561.8	1 634.3(e)	1 497.5(e)
Sweden	1 638.0	1 657.0	1 655.3	1 723.7	1 742.3	1 635.5	1 423.4	1 601.3	1 531.3	1 474.7(e)	1 461.0(e)
United Kingdom	11 397.1	11 952.4	12 275.3	12 145.7	11 863.8	11 005.1	10 887.1	10 809.9	10 813.3	11 146.2(e)	11 266.8(e)

Gross value added at basic prices corresponds to the value of output (at basic prices) less the value of intermediate consumption. The basic price is defined as the price received by the producer, after deduction of all taxes on products but including all subsidies on products. The definition of the agricultural industry is based on Division 01 of NACE Rev. 1.1.

7

Holdings with dairy cows in EU-15
In 1 000

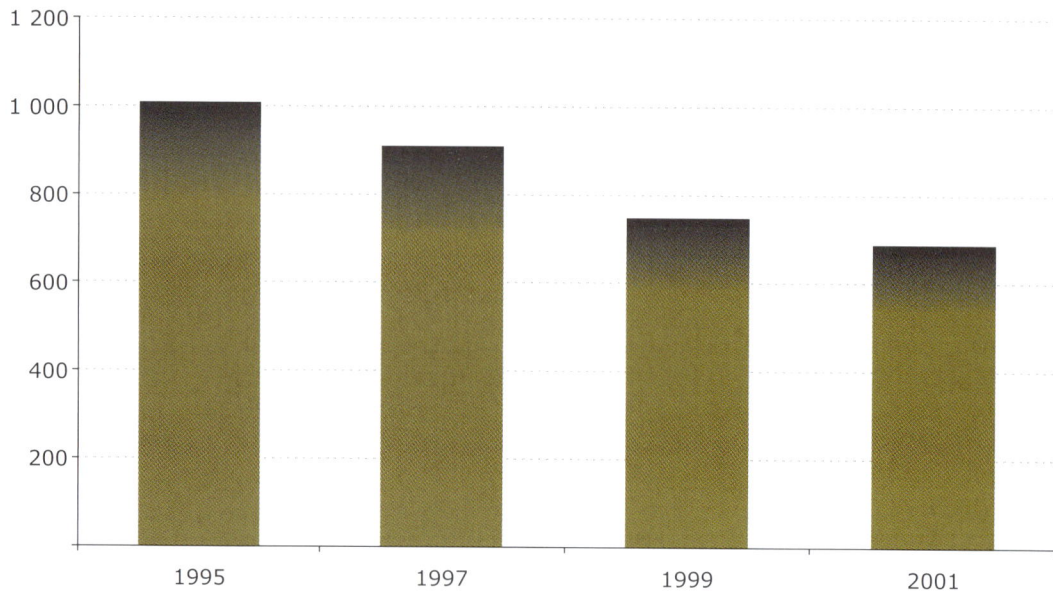

	1995	1997	1999	2001

Number of dairy cows in EU-15
In 1 000

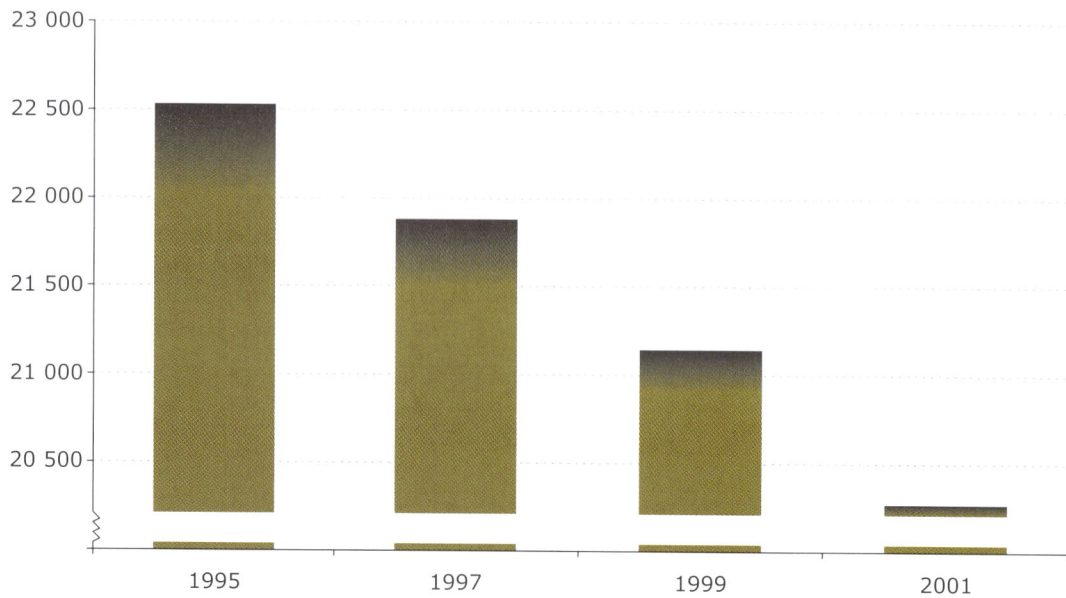

	1995	1997	1999	2001

7

Forestry

European forests

Forests cover around 3 870 million ha, or 29 % of the Earth's land area. The European Union has a total area of forests and other wooded land of 136 million ha accounting for about 36 % of its surface area. Contrary to what is happening in other parts of the world, forest cover in the EU is slowly but steadily increasing at the rate of approximately 0.3 % per year, and forests are present in a huge variety of climatic, geographic, ecological as well socioeconomic conditions. Ecologically, EU forests belong to numerous vegetation zones, ranging from the costal plains to the Alpine zone, while socioeconomic management conditions vary from small family holdings to large estates belonging to vertically integrated companies.

The EU's major objectives in relation to forestry are:
— promotion of the sustainable development of the EU forestry sector as a contribution to rural development and, in particular, to the creation and preservation of jobs in rural areas;
— protection of our natural environment and forest heritage by ensuring the role of forests and forestry in soil protection, erosion control, water regulation, improvement of air quality, carbon sequestration, mitigation and adaptation of climate change effects, and conservation of biodiversity;
— improvement of ecological, economic and socially sustainable forest management within the framework of the internal market, and in line with the Union's international obligations;
— assuring the competitiveness of the EU forest-based industries;
— improvement of forest monitoring instruments in accordance with the requirements of existing environmental agreements;
— increasing the use of sustainably produced wood and other forest products, as environmentally friendly and climate-neutral sources of materials and energy, through encouraging both the certification of sustainable forest management and the labelling of related products;
— promotion of sustainable and equitable forest management as a means of reducing poverty and thus contribute effectively to the EU's development policy.

Data sources

For many years, Eurostat has worked in close cooperation with international organisations in the Intersecretariat Working Group (IWG) on Forest Sector Statistics, with the aim of reducing duplication of work in countries.

The Intersecretariat Working Group brings together Eurostat, the United Nations Economic Commission for Europe (UNECE), the Food and Agriculture Organisation of the United Nations (FAO) and the International Tropical Timber Organisation (ITTO) in collecting forest sector statistics. The Commission's Directorates-General for Agriculture, Enterprise, and the Environment, the European Environment Agency (EEA)

7

and the Organisation for Economic Cooperation and Development (OECD) are also members.

The primary tool for the cooperation is the joint Eurostat/UNECE/FAO/ITTO forest sector questionnaire (JFSQ) on production and trade of roundwood and forest industry products, which is used by all organisations. Each agency collects data from the countries for which it is responsible. The secretariats share the collected data and then use it for their publications. In this framework, Eurostat is responsible for the replies of EU and EFTA Member States.

Total roundwood production
In 1 000 m³

	1997	1998	1999	2000	2001	2002
EU-15	259599	261313	254520	286017	259132	264386
Euro-zone	188 317	190 229	184 584	210 039	186 760	188 065
Belgium	:	:	4 400	4 510	4 215	4 500
Czech Republic	13 491	13 991	14 203	14 441	14 374	14 541
Denmark	1 817	1 538	1 538	2 952	1 613	1 446
Germany	38 207	39 052	37 634	53 710	39 483	42 380
Estonia	5 505	6 061	6 704	8 910	10 200	10 500
Greece	1 783	1 692	2 215	2 245	1 916	1 591
Spain	:	14 875	14 810	14 321	15 131	15 839
France	41 962	42 527	36 008	45 828	39 831	35 900
Ireland	2 180	2 266	2 593	2 673	2 455	2 489
Italy	9 146	9 550	11 138	9 329	8 099	7 789
Cyprus	40	35	36	21	18	15
Latvia	5 149	4 879	14 008	14 304	12 841	13 467
Lithuania	8 922	10 028	4 924	5 500	5 700	6 300
Luxembourg	:	:	260	260	142	140
Hungary	4 251	4 167	5 775	5 902	5 811	5 836
Malta	:	:	0	0	0	0
Netherlands	1 109	1 023	1 044	1 039	865	839
Austria	14 725	14 033	14 083	13 276	13 467	14 845
Poland	21 635	23 107	24 268	26 025	25 016	27 170
Portugal	8 970	8 548	8 978	10 831	8 946	8 742
Slovenia	2 208	2 132	2 068	2 253	2 257	2 283
Slovakia	5 944	5 530	5 795	6 163	5 788	5 765
Finland	51 798	53 660	53 637	54 262	52 210	53 011
Sweden	60 200	60 600	58 700	63 300	63 200	67 500
United Kingdom	7 482	7 254	7 482	7 481	7 559	7 375
Iceland	:	:	:	0	0	0
Norway	8 346	8 172	8 424	8 156	8 996	8 649
Canada	191 178	185 955	193 728	200 326	200 326	200 326
United States	485 880	494 016	497 641	500 174	471 028	477 821

Roundwood production (the term is used as a synonymous term for 'removals') comprise all quantities of wood removed from the forest and other wooded land or other felling site during a certain period of time. It is reported in cubic metres underbark (i.e. excluding bark).

Total paper and paperboard production in 2002
In 1 000 tonnes

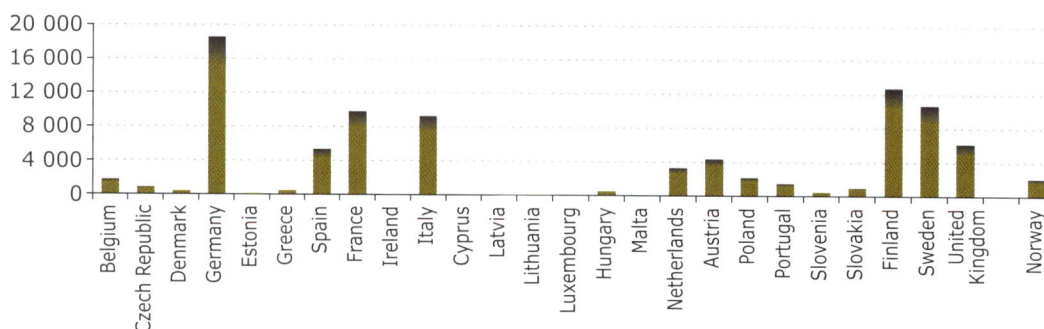

'Paper and paper board' comprises the sum of graphic papers; sanitary and household papers; packaging materials and other paper and paperboard. It excludes manufactured paper products such as boxes, cartons, books and magazines.

Fisheries

Eurostat data

Eurostat provides a wide range of data on:

— Catches by fishing region
— Aquaculture production
— Summary foreign trade in fishery products for all countries
— Supply balance sheets for fishery products
— Fishing fleet
— Landings of fishery products in EU ports
— Employment in the fisheries sector

A common heritage

Fish are a natural, biological, mobile and renewable resource. Fish reproduction takes place without any interference from, or expense to, anyone. The disadvantage, however, is that fish swim around and, in some cases, migrate over wide distances. No one can own fish until they have been captured. Equally, every fish that is taken from the sea is one fewer available to the rest of the catchers. Every fisherman is, therefore, vulnerable to the actions of the others.

This dependence on, and vulnerability to, other people's activities is unavoidable. Fish stocks continue to be regarded as a common resource, part of our common heritage, to be managed collectively. This calls for policies that regulate the amount of fishing, as well as the types of fishing techniques and gear used in fish capture, if this heritage is to be passed to future generations.

The common fisheries policy: fishing the right amount, the right size and the right way

The European Union has a common fisheries policy in order to manage fisheries for the benefit of both fishing communities and consumers, and for the protection of the resources.

Common measures are agreed in four main areas:

— **conservation** — to protect fish resources by regulating the amount of fish taken from the sea, by allowing young fish to reproduce, and by ensuring that measures are respected;

— **structures** — to help the fishing and aquaculture industries adapt their equipment and organisations to the constraints imposed by scarce resources and the market;

— **markets** — to maintain a common organisation of the market in fish products and to match supply and demand for the benefit of both producers and consumers;

— **relations with the outside world** — to set up fisheries agreements and to negotiate at the international level within regional and international fisheries organisations for common conservation measures in deep-sea fisheries.

7

Data collection and concepts

The data are derived from official national sources either directly by Eurostat for the EEA member countries or indirectly through other international organisations for other countries.

The data use internationally-agreed concepts and definitions developed by the Coordinating Working Party on Fishery Statistics, comprising Eurostat and 12 other international organisations with responsibilities in fishery statistics.

Annual catches in 2001
In %; EU-25

8.17 0.96
8.31
10.77
71.8

- North-west Atlantic
- North-east Atlantic
- Eastern central Atlantic
- Mediterranean
- Other fishing regions

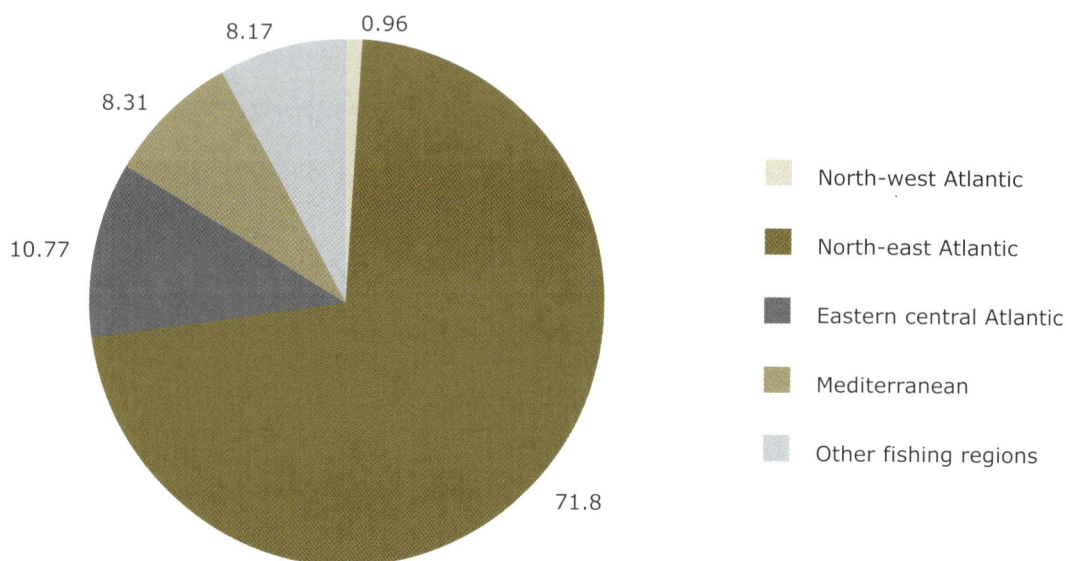

Annual catches in all regions
In 1 000 t live weight; EU-25

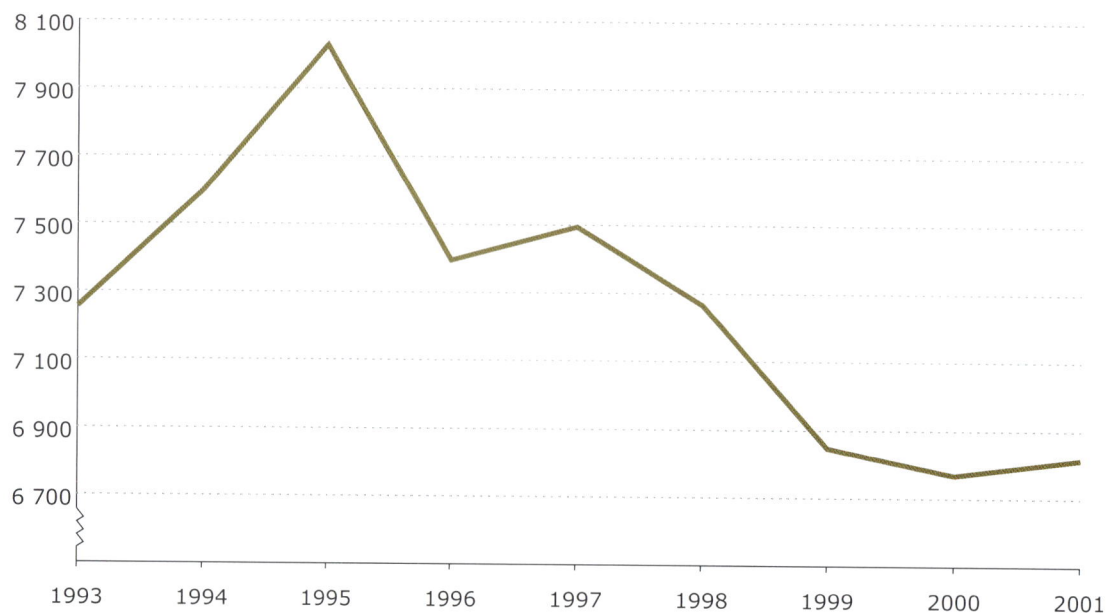

8 100
7 900
7 700
7 500
7 300
7 100
6 900
6 700

1993 1994 1995 1996 1997 1998 1999 2000 2001

Total aquaculture production in the EU-25
In 1 000 t live weight

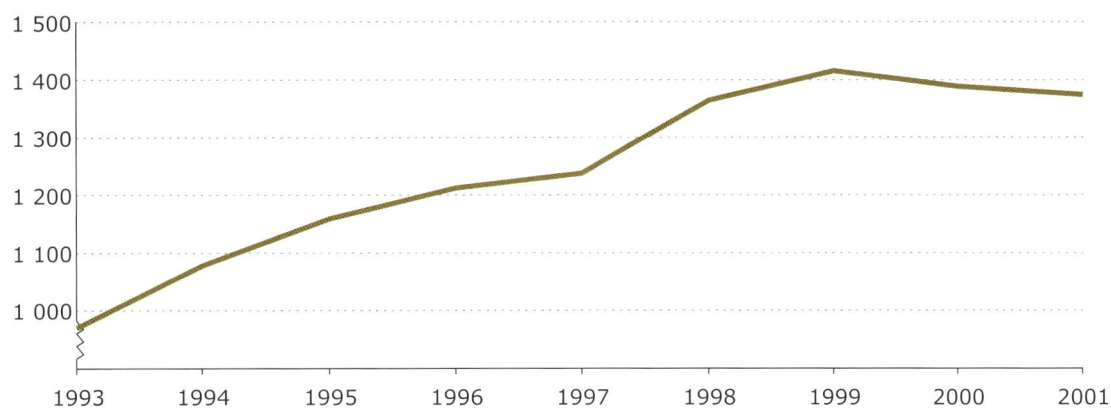

Total aquaculture production
In 1 000 t live weight

	1992	1993	1994	1995	1996	1997	1998	1999	2000	2001	2002
EU-25	:	970	1 078	1 159	1 212	1 238	1 364	1 415	1 388	1 374	:
EU-15	923	915	1 019	1 100	1 151	1 175	1 300	1 343	1 312	1 297	:
Belgium	1	1	1	1	1	1	1	2	2	2	2
Czech Republic	:	20	19	19	18	18	17	19	19	20	:
Denmark	43	40	43	45	42	40	42	43	44	42	38
Germany	97	70	49	64	83	65	73	80	66	53	50
Estonia	1	0	0	0	0	0	0	0	0	0	0
Greece	20	33	33	33	40	49	60	84	95	98	88
Spain	169	126	178	224	232	239	315	321	312	313	264
France	250	277	281	281	286	287	268	265	267	252	250
Ireland	27	30	29	27	35	37	42	44	51	61	:
Italy	170	166	176	215	189	196	209	210	217	221	184
Cyprus	0	0	0	0	1	1	1	1	2	2	2
Latvia	1	0	1	1	0	0	0	0	0	0	0
Lithuania	4	3	2	2	2	2	2	2	2	2	2
Hungary	14	9	10	9	8	9	10	12	13	13	:
Malta	1	1	1	1	2	2	2	2	2	1	1
Netherlands	54	71	109	84	100	98	120	109	75	52	:
Austria	3	3	3	3	3	3	3	3	3	2	2
Poland	30	19	25	25	28	29	30	34	36	35	:
Portugal	6	6	7	5	5	7	8	6	8	8	8
Slovenia	1	1	1	1	1	1	1	1	1	1	1
Slovakia	:	2	2	2	1	1	1	1	1	1	:
Finland	18	18	17	17	18	16	16	15	15	16	15
Sweden	7	6	7	8	8	7	6	6	5	7	6
United Kingdom	57	69	86	94	110	130	137	155	152	171	:
Iceland	3	3	3	3	4	4	4	4	4	4	:
Norway	131	164	218	278	322	368	411	476	491	512	554
Canada	45	52	55	65	72	82	91	113	128	152	:
Japan	1 397	1 359	1 420	1 390	1 349	1 340	1 290	1 315	1 292	1 314	:
United States	414	417	391	413	393	438	445	479	428	461	:

Source: Eurostat/FAO.

Total production of fish, crustaceans, molluscs and other aquatic organisms from aquaculture ('fish-farming'). The data are expressed in the live weight equivalent of the production and is the weight as the product as taken from the water. Thus, for example, in the case of molluscs it includes the shell.

7

Fishing fleet in 2002
Total power in kw

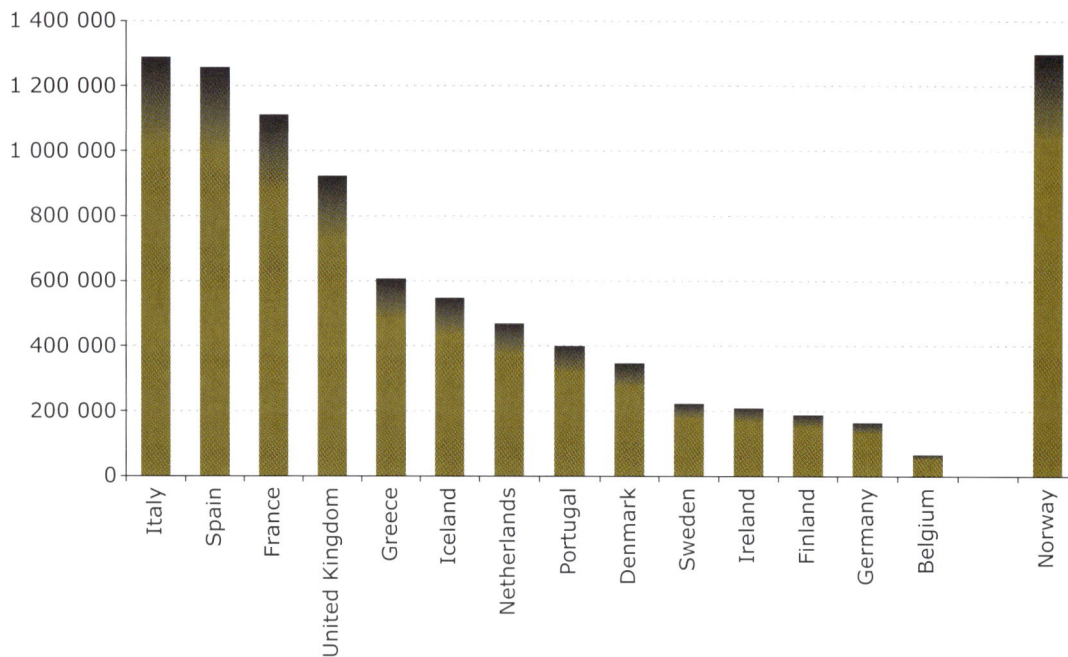

No data for Malta and Slovenia.

Source: Eurostat/Fisheries DG.

The total power, expressed in kilowatts, of the fishing fleets of EU Member States, Iceland and Norway. The EU data are supplied by the Directorate-General for Fisheries from the EU's administrative file of fishing vessels, with the data for Iceland and Norway being supplied to Eurostat directly by the national authorities. In general, the data refer to the fleet size on 31 December of the reference year.

Annexes

8

.

Glossary

Accident at work incidence rate

The incidence rate is defined as the number of accidents at work which occurred during the year per 100 000 persons in employment. To adjust for differences between the Member States in the distribution of the workforce across the risk branches, a standardisation is made giving each branch the same weight at national level as in the European Union total. For Structural indicators, an index of the incidence rate is used as the indicator. The index shows the evolution of the incidence rate in comparison with 1998 (= 100).

Agricultural area (AA) or utilised agricultural area (UAA)

Agricultural area (AA) or utilised agricultural area (UAA) is the area utilised for farming, i.e. categories: arable land, permanent pasture, permanent crops and kitchen gardens.

AIDS case definition

Different case definitions are used in different countries, depending on population factors (number of children or adults, relative occurrence of opportunistic infections) and on the laboratory infrastructure and training available, but the countries participating in the surveillance of AIDS in Europe use a uniform AIDS case definition definitively adopted in 1993. The European definition for AIDS differs from the definition used in the United States in that it does not include CD4+ T-lymphocyte count criteria. The WHO clinical case definition for AIDS is used in countries having limited diagnostic resources.

Annual work unit (AWU)

One annual work unit corresponds to the work performed by one person who is occupied on an agricultural holding on a full-time basis.

'Full-time' means the minimum hours required by the national provisions governing contracts of employment. If these do not indicate the number of hours, then 1 800 hours is taken to be the minimum (225 working days of eight hours each).

Aquaculture

The farming of aquatic organisms including fish, molluscs, crustaceans and aquatic plants. Farming implies some form of intervention in the rearing process to enhance production, such as regular stocking, feeding and protection from predators. Farming also implies individual or corporate ownership of, or rights resulting from contractual arrangements to, the stock being cultivated.

Asylum-seekers

People awaiting a decision on applications for refugee status.

Balance of payments

In the balance-of-payments framework, the balances of the miscellaneous accounts (goods balance, services balance, etc.) are calculated as the difference between exports (credits) and imports (debits). The balance is in surplus when exports are greater than imports, and the balance is in deficit when exports are less than imports.

— Communications services

In the balance-of-payments framework, this item covers two main categories of international communications between residents and non-residents: telecommunications services and postal and courier services.

— Computer and information services

In the balance-of-payments framework, this item covers computer data and news-related service transactions between residents and non-residents.

— Construction services

In the balance-of-payments framework, this item covers work performed on construction projects and installations by employees of an enterprise in locations outside the economic territory of the enterprise. The work is generally performed for a short time period. Goods imported by the enterprise for use in the projects are included in the value of these services rather than under goods.

— Financial services

In the balance-of-payments framework, this item covers financial intermediary and auxiliary services conducted between residents and non-residents.

— Government services, not included elsewhere

In the balance-of-payments framework, this item is a residual category covering all services associated with government sectors or international and regional organisations and not classified under other service sub-items (such as financial services, insurance services, communications services, etc.).

8

— **Income**

In the balance-of-payments framework, income contains two main items: compensation of employees that records wages, salaries and other benefits, in cash or in kind, earned by individuals for work performed for economic units whose place of residence is different from their own; investment income that covers income which a resident entity derives from the ownership of external financial assets and income non-residents derive from their financial assets invested in the compiling economy. This includes interest and dividends on direct, portfolio and other investments.

— **Insurance services**

In the balance-of-payments framework, this item covers the provision of various types of insurance to non-residents by resident insurance enterprises and vice versa.

— **Other business services**

In the balance-of-payments framework, this item includes merchanting and other trade-related services, operational leasing services, and miscellaneous business, professional and technical services.

— **Personal, cultural and recreational services**

In the balance-of-payments framework, this item covers audiovisual and related services and other cultural services provided by residents to non-residents and vice versa.

— **Royalties and licence fees**

In the balance-of-payments framework, this item covers the exchange of payments and receipts between residents and non-residents for the authorised use of intangible, non-produced, non-financial assets and proprietary rights and for the use, through licensing agreements, of produced original prototypes.

Bonds

Securities issued by governments, companies, banks and other institutions. They are normally interest bearing and have a fixed redemption value on a given date.

Business services

These include technical services such as engineering, architecture and technical studies; computer services such as software design and database management; and other professional services such as legal, accounting, consultancy and management.

Catch

Catches of fishery products (fish, molluscs, crustaceans and other aquatic animals, residues and aquatic plants) taken for all purposes (commercial, industrial, recreational and subsistence) by all types and classes of fishing units (fishermen, vessels, gear, etc.) operating both in inland, fresh and brackish water areas, and in inshore, offshore and high-seas fishing areas. The production from aquaculture is excluded. Catch is normally expressed in live weight and derived by the application of conversion factors to the landed or product weight. As such, the catch statistics exclude quantities which are caught but which, for a variety of reasons, are not landed.

Causes of death

Here, these are based on the underlying cause of death, as indicated in Section B of the death certificate. Causes of death are defined on the basis of the World Health Organisation's international classification of diseases, adopted by most countries. Although definitions are harmonised, the statistics may not be fully comparable as classifications may vary when the cause of death is multiple or difficult to evaluate and because of different notification procedures.

Central government

All administrative departments of the State and other central agencies whose responsibilities extend over the whole economic territory, except for the administration of the social security funds.

Communicable diseases

Diseases that cause, or have the potential to cause, significant morbidity and/or mortality across the EU and where the exchange of information may provide early warning of threats to public health. They could also be rare and serious diseases, which would not be recognised at national level and where the pooling of data would allow hypothesis generation from a wider knowledge base and for which effective preventive measures are available with a protective health gain.

Compensation of employees

All remuneration in cash and kind by employers in return for the work done by their employees during the relevant period. The payments cover gross wages and salaries, employers' actual social contributions and imputed social contributions (those directly supplied by the employers to their employees without involving a social security fund, an insurance enterprise or an autonomous pension fund).

Consumption of fixed capital

Value, at current replacement costs, of the reproducible fixed assets used up during an accounting period (usually one year) as a result of normal wear and tear, foreseeable obsolescence and a normal rate of accidental damage. Unforeseen obsolescence, major catastrophes and depletion of natural resources are not included.

Continuing vocational training (CVT)

Training measures or activities financed wholly or partly by enterprises for employees with employment contracts. For the purposes of the European Commission survey, 'employees' means the total number of persons employed, excluding apprentices and trainees.

Continuing vocational training courses

Events designed solely for the purpose of providing continuing vocational training that take place away from the place of work, for example in a classroom or training centre, at which a group of people receive instruction from teachers/tutors/lecturers for a period of time specified in advance by those organising the course.

Convergence criteria

Convergence criteria for European monetary union are as follows:
— price stability;
— government budgetary position;
— exchange rates;
— long-term interest rates.

— Price stability

Member States should have a price performance that is sustainable and an average rate of inflation, observed over the period of one year before the examination, that does not exceed by more than 1.5 percentage points that of, at most, the three best-performing Member States in terms of price stability.

— Government budgetary position

Member States are to avoid situations of 'excessive government deficits', that is to say that their ratio of planned or actual government deficit to GDP should be no more than 3 %, and that their ratio of (general) government debt to GDP should be no more than 60 %, unless the excess over the reference value is only exceptional or temporary or the ratios have declined substantially and continuously.

— Exchange rates

Member States should have respected the normal fluctuation margins of the exchange rate mechanism (ERM) without severe tensions for at least the two years before the examination. In particular, the Member State shall not have devalued its currency's bilateral central rate against any other Member State's currency on its own initiative over the same period.

— Long-term interest rates

Member States should have had an average nominal long-term interest rate over a period of one year before the examination that does not exceed by more than 2 percentage points that of, at most, the three best-performing Member States in terms of price stability.

Crude death rate (CDR)

The crude death rate (CDR) is a weighted average of the age-specific mortality rates. The weighting factor is the age distribution of the population whose mortality experience is being observed. Comparing the CDR from two or more populations is a comparison of a combination of different age-specific death rates and different population structures not reflecting the 'real' mortality differences but including also the effect of the population structure on the total number of deaths and on the crude death rates.

Current taxes on income, wealth, etc.

Current taxes on income and wealth cover all compulsory unrequited payments, in cash or in kind, levied periodically by general government and by the rest of the world on the income and wealth of institutional units, and some periodic taxes which are assessed neither on the income nor the wealth.

Current transfers

Current transfers cover international transactions in which goods, services or financial items are transferred between the residents of one economy and the residents of foreign economies without something of economic value being received in return.

Day-to-day money rate

This usually denotes the rate at which banks lend and borrow among themselves overnight on the interbank market. This rate is a good indicator of the general level of short-term market interest rates. The day-to-day money rate is influenced, among other factors, by the level of central bank interest rates.

Death rate

Deaths per 100 000 inhabitants.

Deaths in road accidents

People killed outright or who died within 30 days as a result of the accident; this is calculated as a standard death rate (SDR).

Direct cost of CVT courses

Costs immediately associated with the provision of continuing vocational training courses: fees and payments to external training

8

providers and training staff; travel and other sundry expenses and subsistence allowances; labour costs for internal training staff wholly or partly engaged in planning, organising and providing the courses; and costs of premises (including training centres) and equipment, together with the costs of materials.

Disease incidence

Incidence is a measure of the number of new cases arising in a population in a given period. Incidence might be expressed as the number of new cases of a disease (or disorder) per 1 000 or 100 000 population in a year. Incidence might refer either to the first onset of a disease (i.e. new cases) or to all episodes.

Disease prevalence

Prevalence is a measure of the number of cases of a given disease existing at a certain time. Prevalence might be expressed as the proportion of a population with a disease at any time in a year. For prevalence statistics from different studies to be comparable, the length of period under consideration must be the same.

Distributive trades

Wholesale businesses, sales agents, retail trade and repair of consumer goods and vehicles.

Dwelling

A room or a suite of rooms and its accessories, lobbies and corridors in a permanent building or a structurally separated part thereof which, by the way it has been built, rebuilt or converted, is designed for habitation by one private household all the year. A dwelling is either a one-family dwelling in a house or an apartment in a block of flats. Dwellings include garages for residential use, even when apart from the habitation or belonging to different owners.

Earnings, gross

Remuneration (wages and salaries) in cash paid directly to the employee before any deductions for income tax and social security contributions paid by the employee.

Earnings, net

Net earnings are calculated from gross earnings by deducting social security contributions and income taxes payable by employees and by adding family allowances if there are children in the family.

ECHP (European Community household panel)

An input-harmonised, longitudinal panel survey using a common set of definitions and directed to a representative sample of private households in each EU Member State, designed to obtain information on income and related social issues by means of personal interviews, which was launched in 1994 and expired in 2001.

Economic territory

The economic territory of a country consists of the geographical territory administered by a government; within the territory, people, goods and capital circulate freely. It also includes the national air space, the territorial waters, the natural deposits in international waters if worked by resident units, the territorial enclaves abroad (own representations, own military bases, etc.) but excludes extra-territorial enclaves (diplomatic representations of foreign countries or of the European Union's institutions, etc.).

Ecu

The former European currency unit may be considered as the cornerstone of the European Monetary System (EMS). It was composed of a basket of currencies (see below). In addition to its official use in the EMS, a private market for the ecu developed, allowing its use in monetary transactions and for denominating financial instruments including bonds. The ecu was replaced by the euro, the new European single currency, on 1 January 1999 at a ratio of 1:1.

Ecu basket

It was defined by specific amounts of 12 currencies of the Member States of the EU. At its inception on 13 March 1979, the ecu was made up of a basket of fixed amounts of the then nine currencies, which was identical at the outset to the European unit of account (EUA). The currency composition of the ecu basket was frozen from November 1993 until the euro was introduced in January 1999. The currencies of Austria, Finland and Sweden did not take part in the composition of the ecu basket because they were only members of the EU from January 1995.

EEA countries

The European Economic Area (EEA) consists of the EU Member States as well as Iceland, Liechtenstein and Norway. In 1989, Jacques Delors, then President of the Commission, proposed a new form of partnership, which was to become the EEA Agreement. The EFTA States, at that time Austria, Finland, Iceland, Liechtenstein, Norway, Sweden and Switzerland, welcomed the ideas; formal negotiations began in June 1990 and the agreement was signed on 2 May 1992 in Oporto. The agreement entered into force on 1 January 1994 and covered the EU and all EFTA countries except for Liechtenstein and Switzerland. Since 1 January 1995, Austria, Finland and Sweden have participated in the EEA as EU Member States. Liechtenstein became a full participant in the EEA on 1 May 1995. The enlargement of the EU had direct bearings on the EEA Agreement, and the 10 acceding countries to the EU applied to become parties to the EEA Agreement in December 2003. Negotiations on enlarging the EEA took place in 2003, and from 1 May 2004 the enlarged EEA has included 28 countries.

Emigrants

People leaving their country of usual residence and effectively taking up residence in another country. According to the 1997 United Nations recommendations on statistics of international migration (Revision 1), such a person is a long-term emigrant if he/she leaves his/her country of previous usual residence for a period of 12 months or more. However, few countries are able to supply statistics based on these definitions. The statistics shown in this volume are generally based on national definitions that may differ greatly from the UN recommendations. Not all countries collect statistics on emigrants, and, in those that do, data sources and the scope of the collection vary.

Employees

Employees are defined as persons who work for a public or private employer and who receive compensation in the form of wages, salaries, fees, gratuities, payment by results or payment in kind; non-conscripted members of the armed forces are also included. An extensive concept of employment is used in international guidelines on labour statistics. Persons in employment as reported by the labour force survey are those who during the reference week did any work for pay or profit for at least one hour, or were not working but had jobs from which they were temporarily absent. Family workers are included.

Employment rate

Persons in employment as a percentage of the population of the same age.

EMS (European Monetary System)

Formally introduced on 13 March 1979, it was operational until 31 December 1998. Its purpose was 'to create a zone of monetary stability in Europe through the implementation of certain exchange rate, credit and resource transfer policies'. The EMS had three components: the ecu, the exchange rate mechanism (ERM) and the credit mechanism. At the end of its existence, the currencies of all EU Member States except Sweden and the United Kingdom were members of the ERM.

EMU (economic and monetary union)

Union of 12 EU Member States which have adopted the single currency, the euro. These countries are officially considered to have fulfilled the convergence criteria. The third stage of EMU began on 1 January 1999, when 11 member currencies were permanently fixed to the euro, joined by the Greek drachma on 1 January 2001. The coins and notes were introduced on 1 January 2002 and national currencies progressively withdrawn.

ERM (exchange rate mechanism)

Part of the European Monetary System aimed at achieving greater exchange rate stability. It had two elements: a parity grid of bilateral central rates and fluctuation bands, and the divergence indicator, which measured the extent to which each currency was deviating from its ecu central rate. It ceased to exist at the start of the third stage of monetary union.

ERM 2

On 1 January 1999, the ERM was replaced by the new exchange rate mechanism, ERM 2. It is aimed at preparing 'pre-in' countries for participation in monetary union, while helping to ensure exchange rate discipline in the EU. The central currency in the system is the euro. At the end of 2000, the currencies of two countries were participating in ERM 2, with fluctuation margins of ± 2.25 % for Denmark and ± 15 % for Greece. Since Greece joined the euro zone on 1 January 2001, Denmark is currently the sole country in the system.

ESA

European system of (integrated economic) accounts, the methodology of national accounts. The new version ESA 95 (the third one) has been gradually introduced since 1999. ESA 95 is fully consistent with the worldwide guidelines on national accounts, the SNA 93.

Esspros

The European system of integrated social protection statistics (Esspros) is built on the concept of social protection. Social protection is defined as the coverage of risks and needs that are precisely defined and that cover all the aspects for social protection: health, disability, old age, family and unemployment. Esspros records the receipts and the expenditure of the various organisations (or schemes) intervening in the field of social protection. The social benefits are broken down by type and functions. The type refers to the form in which the bene-

8

fits are provided: in cash or in kind, for example. The functions gather the needs covered by the benefits: thus income maintenance can be paid in respect of health, but also of disability, old age, maternity or unemployment. The receipts are broken down by type: social contributions, general government contributions and other receipts.

Euro

The third stage of European monetary union began on 1 January 1999 with the introduction of the euro, the European single currency. It replaced the ecu on a 1:1 basis. Since that date, the national currencies of 11 EU Member States (Belgium, Germany, Spain, France, Ireland, Italy, Luxembourg, the Netherlands, Austria, Portugal and Finland) were fixed to the euro at irrevocable conversion rates (see table below). They were joined by Greece on 1 January 2001. The euro existed until the end of 2001 as book money only (cheque, transfer, payment by card) and its use was voluntary (no compulsion — no prohibition). The coins and notes were introduced on 1 January 2002, when use of the euro became compulsory and national currencies progressively withdrawn.

Fixed conversion rates (EUR 1 =)

13.7603 ATS
40.3399 BEF
1.95583 DEM
166.386 ESP
5.94573 FIM
6.55957 FRF
340.750 GRD
0.787564 IEP
1 936.27 ITL
40.3399 LUF
2.20371 NLG
200.482 PTE

The conversion rules of the national currencies to the euro and vice versa are very strict. The official conversion rate with six significant figures has to be used for each conversion without rounding or truncation. To convert into euro, the amount has to be divided by the conversion rate and for the opposite operation the amount has to be multiplied by the rate.

The conversion of a national currency of the euro-zone to another currency of the euro zone has to be done via the euro using the conversion rates.

A conversion in another currency has to be done also via the euro but using the prevailing exchange rate of this currency to the euro.

Euro-zone: EUR-12 (formerly EUR-11)

Countries initially participating in monetary union in January 1999: Belgium, Germany, Spain, France, Ireland, Italy, Luxembourg, the Netherlands, Austria, Portugal and Finland. On 1 January 2001, Greece joined the euro zone. Hence three concepts: EUR-11 (the initial 11 countries), EUR-12 (EUR-11 plus Greece) and the euro zone as a variable concept (EUR-11 until 31 December 2000, EUR-12 from 1 January 2001). Note that the letter 'R' after 'EU' is used to distinguish the euro zone from the European Union (for which the code is just EU).

Eurobarometer

Eurobarometer public opinion surveys have been conducted on behalf of the Directorate-General for Education and Culture of the European Commission each spring and autumn since autumn 1973. Besides general public opinion surveys, the Survey Research Unit of the Directorate-General for Education and Culture organises specific target groups, as well as qualitative (group discussion, in-depth interview) surveys in all Member States of the EU and, occasionally, in non-member countries.

European Patent Office (EPO)

The European Patent Office (EPO) is the executive arm of the European Patent Organisation, an intergovernmental body set up under the European Patent Convention (EPC), which was signed in Munich on 5 October 1973 and which entered into force on 7 October 1977. Members of the European Patent Organisation are the EPC contracting States. The EPO grants European patents for the contracting States to the EPC. The activities of the EPO are supervised by the Organisation's Administrative Council, composed of delegates from the contracting States.

Source: EPO (http:// www.european-patent-office.org).

European Union (EU)

Established on 1 November 1993 when the Maastricht Treaty entered into force. On 31 December 1994, the EU had 12 Member States: Belgium, Denmark, Germany, Greece, Spain, France, Ireland, Italy, Luxembourg, the Netherlands, Portugal and the United Kingdom. From January 1995, the EU had three new Member States: Austria, Finland and Sweden. In May 2004, 10 new Member States joined the EU: the Czech Republic, Estonia, Cyprus, Latvia, Lithuania, Hungary, Malta, Poland, Slovenia and Slovakia.

EU-SILC (EU statistics on income and living conditions)

An output-harmonised data collection tool which replaces the ECHP and which is designed to be the reference source of information on income and related social issues, containing both cross-sectional and longitudinal elements, and placing greater reliance on existing national sources in an attempt to improve timeliness and flexibility.

Exchange rate

The price at which one currency is exchanged for another.

See also 'Convergence criteria'.

External courses

Courses designed and managed by an organisation that is not part of the enterprise, even if they are held in the enterprise.

Extra-EU flows

All transactions between EU countries and countries outside the EU.

Final consumption expenditure

Final consumption expenditure consists of expenditure incurred by resident institutional units on goods or services that are used for the direct satisfaction of individual needs or wants or the collective needs of members of the community.

Foreign direct investment (FDI)

Foreign direct investment (FDI) is the category of international investment within the balance-of-payment accounts that reflects the objective of obtaining a lasting interest by a resident entity in one economy in an enterprise resident in another economy. The lasting interest implies the existence of a long-term relationship between the direct investor and the enterprise, and a significant degree of influence by the investor on the management of the enterprise. Formally defined, a direct investment enterprise is an unincorporated or incorporated enterprise in which a direct investor owns 10 % or more of the ordinary shares or voting power (for an incorporated enterprise) or the equivalent (for an unincorporated enterprise).

FDI flows and positions: through direct investment flows, an investor builds up a foreign direct investment position that features on the international investment position of the economy. This FDI position (or FDI stock) differs from the accumulated flows because of revaluation (changes in prices or exchange rates), and other adjustments like rescheduling or cancellation of loans, debt forgiveness or debt-equity swaps.

Forest

Forest is defined as land with tree crown cover (or equivalent stocking level) of more than 10 % and area of more than 0.5 ha. The trees should be able to reach a minimum height of 5 m at maturity *in situ*.

General government

The general government sector includes all institutional units whose output is intended for individual and collective consumption, and mainly financed by compulsory payments made by units belonging to other sectors, and/or all institutional units principally engaged in the redistribution of national income and wealth. The general government sector is subdivided into four subsectors: central government, State government, local government, and social security funds.

General government debt

Total gross debt at nominal value outstanding at the end of the year and consolidated between and within the subsectors of general government.

See also 'Convergence criteria'.

Government bonds

Official debt instruments issued by governments in order to fund budget deficits and to cover debt which is being redeemed. Government bond yields usually refer to secondary market yields, i.e. derived from the market where securities which are already in circulation are traded.

Government budget appropriations or outlays for research and development

Government budget appropriations or outlays for research and development (Gbaord) are a way of measuring government support to R & D activities and include all appropriations allocated to R & D in central (or federal) government budgets. Provincial (or State) government is only included if the contribution is significant, whereas local government funds are excluded.

Gross domestic product at market prices (GDPmp)

Final result of the production activity of resident producer units. It corresponds to the economy's total output of goods and services, less intermediate consumption.

Gross domestic product in purchasing power standards

Gross domestic product converted into the artificial currency unit PPS (purchasing power standards) through a special conversion rate called PPP (purchasing power parity).

The GDP in PPS represents pure volume after price level differences between countries have been removed by the special conversion rate PPP.

8

Gross fixed capital formation

Gross fixed capital formation (GFCF) consists of resident producers' acquisitions, less disposals, of fixed assets during a given period plus certain additions to the value of non-produced assets realised by the productive activity of producers or institutional units. Fixed assets are tangible or intangible assets produced as outputs from processes of production that are themselves used repeatedly, or continuously, in processes of production for more than one year.

Gross national income (GNI)

Gross national income (GNI) equals gross domestic product plus primary income received (compensation of employees, property income, subsidies) from abroad minus primary income paid (compensation of employees, property income, taxes on production paid to the rest of the world).

Gross national disposable income is derived from GNI by adding current transfers received from the rest of the world and deducting current transfers paid to the rest of the world.

Net national disposable income equals gross national disposable income minus consumption of fixed capital.

The concept of GNI (ESA 95) replaces the one of GNP (gross national product, ESA 79). Both are identical conceptually.

Gross national product (GNP)

See 'Gross national income'.

Gross operating surplus

Gross domestic product at market prices minus compensation of employees paid by resident employers, net taxes (= taxes minus subsidies) on production and imports levied by general government and by the rest of the world, including EU institutions.

The operating surplus corresponds to the income which production units obtain from their own use of their production facilities.

Gross value added at market prices

Final output (at basic prices) minus intermediate consumption (at purchasers' prices). Gross value added can be broken down by industry. For the economy as a whole, it usually makes up more than 90 % of GDP.

High-technology patents

High-technology patents are counted following the criteria established by the trilateral statistical report, where the subsequent technical fields are defined as high technology: computer and automated business equipment; microorganism and genetic engineering; aviation; communications technology; semiconductors; and lasers.

High-technology sectors

The classification of high- and medium-high-technology manufacturing sectors is based on the notion of R&D intensity (ratio of R&D expenditure to GDP). Following this criterion, high-tech manufacturing comprises manufacturing of office machinery and computers, manufacturing of radio, television and communication equipment and apparatus, and manufacturing of medical precision and optical instruments, watches and clocks. Medium-high-tech manufacturing includes the manufacture of chemicals and chemical products, manufacture of machinery and equipment n.e.c., manufacture of electrical machinery and apparatus n.e.c., manufacture of motor vehicles, trailers and semi-trailers, and manufacturing of other transport equipment.

Following a similar logic as for manufacturing, Eurostat defines the following sectors as knowledge-intensive services (KIS): water transport; air transport; post and telecommunications; financial intermediation; insurance and pension funding (except compulsory social security); activities auxiliary to financial intermediation; real estate activities; renting of machinery and equipment without operator and of personal and household goods; computer and related activities; research and development; other business activities; education; health and social work; and recreational, cultural and sporting activities.

Of these sectors, post and telecommunications, computer and related activities, and research and development are considered high-tech services.

Hospital discharges

Discharge is the formal release of an inpatient by an inpatient or acute care institution. The discharge rates are expressed by the number per 100 000 population. Diagnostic chapters (using principal diagnosis) have been defined according to the international classification of diseases, ninth revision, clinical modification (ICD-9-CM).

Household

According to the household budget surveys, household should be defined in terms of having a shared residence and common arrangements. A household comprises either one person living alone or a group of people, not necessarily related, living at the same address with common housekeeping, i.e. sharing at least one meal a day or sharing a living or sitting room.

8

Household consumption

The value of goods and services used for directly meeting human needs.

A household can be composed of a single person or a family.

Household consumption covers expenditure on purchases of goods and services, own consumption such as products from kitchen gardens, and the imputed rent of owner-occupied dwellings (= the rent that the household would pay if it were a tenant).

ICD diagnosis

Diagnoses and procedures associated with hospitalisations are classified in accordance with the ninth revision of the international classification of diseases (ICD-9). This classification is the result of close collaboration among many nations and non-governmental organisations, under the auspices of the World Health Organisation (WHO). Its original use was to classify causes of mortality. Later, it was extended to include diagnoses on morbidity. For example, the clinical modification of the ICD is used in categorising hospital diagnoses. In practice, the ICD has become the international standard diagnostic classification for all general epidemiological, as well as health management, purposes. Most Member States will adopt or are adopting the 10th ICD classification. The diagnostic categories used are based on the principal diagnosis, which is submitted as the first of several possible diagnoses coded on the discharge record. The principal diagnosis represents the 'condition established after study to be chiefly responsible for occasioning the admission of the patient to the hospital for care'.

Immigrants

Persons arriving or returning from abroad to take up residence in the country for a certain period, having previously been resident elsewhere. According to the 1997 United Nations recommendations on statistics of international migration (Revision 1), such a person is a long-term immigrant if he/she stays in his/her country of destination for a period of 12 months or more, having previously been resident elsewhere for 12 months or more. However, few countries are able to supply statistics based on these definitions. The statistics shown in this volume are generally based on national definitions that may differ greatly from the UN recommendations.

Not all countries collect immigration data, and, in those that do, data sources and the scope of the collection vary. A few countries (e.g. France) exclude national citizens from immigration statistics.

Implicit price index, GDP

Indicator of price evolution of all goods and services that make up the GDP.

Inpatient care beds

Beds accommodating patients who are formally admitted (or 'hospitalised') to an institution for treatment and/or care and who stay for a minimum of one night in the hospital or other institution providing inpatient care. Inpatient care is delivered in hospitals, other nursing and residential care facilities or in establishments which are classified according to their focus of care under the ambulatory care industry but perform inpatient care as a secondary activity.

Inactive

People not in the labour force. They are neither employed nor unemployed (International Labour Organisation definitions). Employed persons were those aged 15 years and over (16 years and over in Iceland, Spain, Sweden and the United Kingdom) who during the reference week did any work for pay or profit for at least one hour, or were not working but had jobs from which they were temporarily absent. Family workers are included. For the definition of 'unemployed person', see this entry in the glossary.

Intermediate consumption

Intermediate consumption consists of the value of the goods and services consumed as inputs by a process of production, excluding fixed assets whose consumption is recorded as consumption of fixed capital. The goods and services may be either transformed or used up by the production process.

Internal courses

Courses designed and managed by the enterprise itself, even if held at a location away from the enterprise.

Intra-EU flows

All transactions declared by EU countries with other EU Member States.

ISCED

International standard classification of education, set up by Unesco in 1976.

ISCED 97

The international standard classification of education (ISCED) is an instrument suitable for compiling statistics on education internationally. It covers two cross-classification variables: levels and fields of education with the complementary dimensions of general/vocational/pre-vocational orientation and educational/labour market destination. The current version, ISCED 97 (see

8

http://unescostat.unesco.org/en/pub/pub0.htm), was implemented in EU countries, for the first time, for the collection of data from the school year 1997/98.

The change in the ISCED classification has affected the comparability of chronological series, especially for level 3 (upper secondary education) and for level 5 (tertiary education). ISCED 97 introduced a new level — level 4: post-secondary non-tertiary education (previously included in ISCED levels 3 and 5). ISCED 97 level 6 only relates to Ph.D. or doctoral studies. ISCED 97 distinguishes seven levels of education.

ISCED 97 fields

The classification comprises 25 fields of education (at two-digit level) which can be further refined into three-digit level. The following nine broad groups (at one-digit level) can be distinguished.

0 — General programmes
1 — Education
2 — Humanities and arts
3 — Social sciences, business and law
4 — Science, mathematics and computing
5 — Engineering, manufacturing and construction
6 — Agriculture and veterinary
7 — Health and welfare
8 — Services

ISCED 97 levels

Empirically, ISCED assumes that several criteria exist which can help allocate education programmes to levels of education. Depending on the level and type of education concerned, there is a need to establish a hierarchical ranking system between main and subsidiary criteria (typical entrance qualification, minimum entrance requirement, minimum age, staff qualification, etc.).

0: Pre-primary education
Pre-primary education is defined as the initial stage of organised instruction. It is school- or centre-based and is designed for children aged at least three years.

1: Primary education
This level begins between four and seven years of age, is compulsory in all countries and generally lasts from five to six years.

2: Lower secondary education
It continues the basic programmes of the primary level, although teaching is typically more subject-focused. Usually, the end of this level coincides with the end of compulsory education.

3: Upper secondary education
This level generally begins at the end of compulsory education. The entrance age is typically 15 or 16 years. Entrance qualifications (end of compulsory education) and other minimum entry requirements are usually needed. Instruction is often more subject-oriented than at ISCED level 2. The typical duration of ISCED level 3 varies from two to five years.

4: Post-secondary non-tertiary education
These programmes straddle the boundary between upper secondary and tertiary education. They serve to broaden the knowledge of ISCED level 3 graduates. Typical examples are programmes designed to prepare students for studies at level 5 or programmes designed to prepare students for direct labour market entry.

5: Tertiary education (first stage)
Entry to these programmes normally requires the successful completion of ISCED level 3 or 4. This level includes tertiary programmes with academic orientation (type A) which are largely theoretically based and tertiary programmes with occupation orientation (type B) which are typically shorter than type A programmes and geared for entry into the labour market.

6: Tertiary education (second stage)
This level is reserved for tertiary studies that lead to an advanced research qualification (Ph.D. or doctorate).

Labour costs, direct
See 'Total labour costs'.

Labour costs, indirect
See 'Total labour costs'.

Labour force
People in the labour market, i.e. employed and unemployed people.

Labour force survey (LFS)
A labour force survey is an inquiry directed to households designed to obtain information on the labour market and related issues by means of personal interviews. The EU LFS covers the entire population living in private households and excludes those in collective households such as boarding houses, halls of residence and hospitals. The definitions used are common to all EU countries and are based on international recommendations by the International Labour Office (ILO).

Life expectancy
Average number of years still to live for people of a given age under the prevailing conditions of mortality at successive ages of a given population.

8

Live weight of fishery products

Live weight of fishery products is derived from the landed or product weight by the application of factors and is designed to represent the weight of the fishery product as it was taken from the water and before being subjected to any processing or other operation.

Local government

All types of public administration whose competence extends to only a local part of the economic territory apart from local agencies of social security funds.

Long-term interest rates

Here measured as the yield to redemption on 10-year government bonds.
See also 'Convergence criteria'.

Manufacturing industry

All activities included within Section D of NACE Rev. 1.1 (statistical classification of economic activities in the European Community). Both cottage industry (crafts) and large-scale activity are included. It should be noted that the use of heavy plant or machinery is not exclusive to Section D. It covers industries such as manufacture of non-metallic mineral products; chemicals; man-made fibres; manufacture of metal articles; food, drinks and tobacco; textiles; leather and leather goods; timber and wooden furniture; manufacture of paper and paper products, including printing and publishing; and processing of rubber and plastics. Not included are mining and extraction and building and civil engineering.

Migration, net (including corrections)

The difference between immigration to and emigration from the area. Since most countries either do not have accurate figures on immigration and emigration or have no figures at all, net migration is generally estimated on the basis of the difference between (total) population increase and natural increase between two dates. The statistics on net migration are therefore affected by all the statistical inaccuracies in the two components of this equation, especially population increase.

Mortality rate, crude

Deaths per 1 000 inhabitants.

Mortality, infant

Deaths per 1 000 live-born children aged less than one year.

NACE 70

General industrial classification of economic activities within the European Communities (with regard to data from 1970 to 1990).

NACE Rev. 1.1

NACE Rev. 1.1 is a revision of the general industrial classification of economic activities (with regard to data from 1991 onwards, see annex 'Classification of economic activities in the European Community' below).

National citizens

Persons who are citizens of the country in which they are currently resident.

Non-national citizens

Persons who are not citizens of the country in which they are currently resident.

NUTS

A regulation on the nomenclature of territorial units for statistics was approved by the Commission in 2003 (Regulation (EC) No 1059/2003). The purpose is to provide a single and coherent territorial breakdown for the compilation of EU regional statistics. The current NUTS nomenclature (version 2003) subdivides the territory of the European Union into 84 NUTS 1 regions, 254 NUTS 2 regions and 1 213 NUTS 3 regions. These numbers include NUTS regions defined for the 10 new Member States from 1 May 2004. Please consult RAMON on the Eurostat website for the latest available information (http://europa.eu.int/comm/eurostat/ramon/nuts/splash_regions.html).

Official external reserves

These reserves are held by countries' monetary authorities for the purpose of financing balance-of-payments deficits or for influencing their currency's external value. They are made up of monetary gold, foreign currencies, special drawing rights (SDRs) of the International Monetary Fund (IMF) and reserves held with the IMF.

Paper and paperboard

This is the sum of graphic papers; newsprint; sanitary and household papers; packaging materials and other paper and paperboard. It excludes manufactured paper products such as boxes, cartons, books and magazines, etc.

Population density

Number of inhabitants per square kilometre.

Population increase, natural

Births minus deaths.

Psychiatric care beds

Beds accommodating inpatients for mental health (including substance abuse therapy), but excluding beds for patients who are mentally handicapped if the principal clinical intent is not of a medical nature.

8

Purchasing power parities (PPPs)

Monetary exchange rates should not be used to compare the volumes of income or expenditure because they usually reflect more elements than just price differences (e.g. volumes of financial transactions between currencies, expectations in the foreign exchange markets).

In contrast, purchasing power parities (PPPs) are established to eliminate the differences between the price levels in different countries. Therefore, they truly reflect the differences in the purchasing power, for example, of households. Purchasing power parities are obtained by comparing the price levels for a basket of comparable goods and services that is selected to be representative for consumption patterns in the various countries. Purchasing power parities convert every national monetary unit into a common artificial currency unit, the purchasing power standard (PPS).

PPPs are, at the lowest level, bilateral price relatives between tightly defined individual items (e.g. one loaf of bread in the UK, GBP 1.5, to EUR 2 for it in Germany). Subsequently, these relatives are turned into multilateral relatives and scaled to the EU average and aggregated to more and more complex aggregates (e.g. food) and finally to GDP.

Purchasing power standards (PPS)

The purchasing power standard is an artificial currency unit. One PPS can buy the same amount of goods and services in each country, while, due to different price levels in the countries, different numbers of national currency units are necessary to buy this amount of goods and services.

PPS are derived by dividing any economic aggregate of a country in national currency by its respective PPP (see 'Purchasing power parities').

Real values

Calculated by deflating an economic variable at current prices by the price index of another variable, for example deflating the compensation of employees by the price index of household consumption.

This is typically the case for financial and income flows. For instance, to deflate an income, an appropriate price index is based on a basket of goods and services reflecting how this income is spent.

Refugee

Someone with a well-founded fear of being persecuted for reasons of race, religion, nationality, membership of a particular social group or political opinion (according to Article 1 of the 1951 United Nations Convention relating to the Status of Refugees).

It should be noted that many countries allow applicants for asylum to remain on a temporary or permanent basis even if they are not deemed to be refugees under the 1951 convention definition. For example, asylum applicants may receive a positive response to their application on humanitarian grounds.

Research and development (R & D)

Research and development comprises creative work undertaken on a systematic basis in order to increase the stock of knowledge of man, culture and society, and the use of this stock of knowledge to devise new applications.

Resident producer units

Units whose principal function is the production of goods and services and whose centre of economic interest is on the economic territory of a country.

Roundwood production

Roundwood production (the term is used as a synonymous term for 'removals') comprises all quantities of wood removed from the forest and other wooded land, or other felling site during a certain period of time.

Sawnwood

Sawnwood is wood that has been produced either by sawing lengthways or by a profile-chipping process and that, with a few exceptions, exceeds 5 mm in thickness.

Services

The terms 'service industry(ies)', 'service sector(s)' or simply 'service(s)' are generally used to refer to economic activities covered by Sections G to K and M to O of NACE Rev. 1.1 and the units that carry out those activities.

SMEs

Small and medium-sized enterprises employing fewer than 250 people, according to Commission Recommendation 2003/361/EC adopted on 6 May 2003: enterprise classification with regard to the number of employees, the annual turnover, and the firm's independence. SMEs form the backbone of the EU-25 enterprise culture where over 99 % of businesses employ fewer than 250 people.

Social benefits (other than social transfers in kind)

Social benefits (other than social transfers in kind) are those paid to households by social security funds, other government units, NPISHs (non-profit institutions serving households), employers administering unfunded social insurance schemes, insurance enterprises or other

8

institutional units administering privately funded social insurance schemes.

Social contributions

Social contributions are paid on a compulsory or voluntary basis by the employers, the employees and the self- and non-employed persons. They are of two types: actual and imputed.

Social security funds

Central, State and local institutional units whose principal activity is to provide social benefits, and which fulfil each of the two following criteria: (i) by law or regulation (except regulations concerning government employees), certain groups of the population are obliged to participate in the scheme or to pay contributions; (ii) general government is responsible for the management of the institution in respect of settlement or approval of the contributions and benefits independently of its role as a supervisory body or employer.

Stability and Growth Pact

The Stability and Growth Pact has to be seen against the background of the third stage of economic and monetary union, which began on 1 January 1999. Its aim is to ensure that the Member States continue their budgetary discipline efforts once the single currency has been introduced.

In practical terms, the pact comprises a European Council resolution (adopted at Amsterdam on 17 June 1997) and two Council regulations of 7 July 1997 laying detailed technical arrangements (one on the surveillance of budgetary positions and coordination of economic policies and the other on implementing the excessive deficit procedure).

In the medium term, the Member States undertook to pursue the objective of a balanced or nearly balanced budget and to present the Council and the Commission with a stability programme by 1 March 1999 (the programme then being updated annually). Along the same lines, States not taking part in the third stage of EMU are required to submit a convergence programme.

The Stability and Growth Pact opens the way for the Council to penalise any participating Member State which fails to take appropriate measures to end an excessive deficit. Initially, the penalty would take the form of a non-interest-bearing deposit with the Community, but it could be converted into a fine if the excessive deficit is not corrected within two years.

Standard death rate (SDR)

Death rate of a population of a standard age distribution. As most causes of death vary significantly with people's age and sex, the use of standard death rates improves comparability over time and between countries, as they aim at measuring death rates independently of different age structures of populations. The standard death rates used here are calculated by the World Health Organisation on the basis of a standard European population.

Standard gross margin (SGM)

The gross margin of an agricultural enterprise means the monetary value of gross production from which corresponding specific costs are deducted.

The standard gross margin (SGM) is the value of the gross margin corresponding to the average situation in a given region for each agricultural characteristic.

SGMs are determined on the basis of three-yearly averages. In the 1999/2000 structure survey, the '1996' standard gross margins were calculated from the arithmetic mean for the years 1995, 1996 and 1997.

Gross production is the sum of the values of the principal product(s) and of the secondary product(s). These values are calculated by multiplying production per unit (less any losses) by the farm-gate price, without VAT.

Gross production also includes subsidies linked to products, to area and/or livestock.

State government

Separate institutional units exercising some of the functions of government at a level below that of central government and above that of the governmental institutional units existing at local level, except for the administration of social security funds.

Subsidies

Current unrequited payments which general government or the institutions of the European Union make to resident producers, with the objective of influencing their levels of production, their prices or the remuneration of the factors of production.

Taxes on production and imports

Compulsory, unrequited payments, in cash or in kind, levied by general government, or by the institutions of the EU, in respect of the production and importation of goods and services, the employment of labour, and the ownership or use of land, buildings or other assets used in production.

Tax rate on low-wage earners: tax wedge on labour cost

The tax wedge on labour cost measures the relative tax burden for an employed person with low earnings.

8

Tax rate on low-wage earners: unemployment trap

The unemployment trap measures what percentage of the gross earnings (from moving into employment) is 'taxed away' by the combined effects of the withdrawal of benefits and higher tax and social security contributions.

Total CVT cost

Total expenditure on continuing vocational training courses. This is the sum of direct costs, the labour costs of participants and the balance of contributions to national or regional training funds and receipts from national or other funding arrangements.

Total general government expenditure

According to Commission Regulation (EC) No 1500/2000 of 10 July 2000, total general government expenditure comprises the following ESA 95 categories: intermediate consumption; gross capital formation; compensation of employees; other taxes on production; subsidies payable; property income; current taxes on income, wealth, etc.; social benefits other than social transfers in kind; social transfers in kind related to expenditure on products supplied to households via market producers; other current transfers; adjustment for the change in net equity of households in pension fund reserves; capital transfers payable; and acquisitions less disposals of non-financial non-produced assets.

Total general government revenue

According to Commission Regulation (EC) No 1500/2000 of 10 July 2000, total general government revenue comprises the following ESA 95 categories: market output; output for own final use; payments for the other non-market output; taxes on production and imports; other subsidies on production receivable; property income; current taxes on income, wealth, etc.; social contributions; other current transfers; and capital transfers.

Total health expenditure

Total health expenditure includes: the medical care households receive (ranging from hospitals and physicians to ambulance services and pharmaceutical products), and their health expenses, including cost sharing and the medicines they buy on their own initiative; government-supplied health services (e.g. schools, vaccination campaigns), investment in clinics, laboratories, etc.; administration costs; research and development; industrial medicine, outlays of voluntary organisations, charitable institutions and non-governmental health plans.

Total labour costs

Total expenditure borne by employers in order to employ workers. For presentational purposes, total labour costs can be subdivided into 'direct costs' and 'indirect costs'.

Direct costs include gross wages and salaries in cash (direct remuneration and bonuses) and wages and salaries in kind (company products, housing, company cars, meal vouchers, crèches, etc.). Direct costs are dominated by wages and salaries in cash.

Indirect costs cover employers' actual social contributions (i.e. statutory, collectively agreed, contractual and voluntary social security contributions); employers' imputed social contributions (mostly guaranteed remuneration in the event of sickness or short-time working, plus severance pay and compensation in lieu of notice); vocational training costs; recruitment costs and working clothes provided by the employer; taxes paid by the employer (based on the wages and salaries bill or on employment); minus subsidies received by the employer (intended to refund part or all of the cost of direct remuneration). Indirect costs are dominated by employers' actual social contributions, in particular by employers' statutory social security contributions.

Tourism and travel

On the debit side, there is expenditure by residents staying abroad for less than a year for whatever reason: leisure, work, health or study. The credit side includes the same activities by foreign travellers on the national territory.

Tourist accommodation

This includes all types of accommodation:
Collective tourist accommodation establishments
— Hotels and similar establishments
— Other collective accommodation establishments (holiday dwellings, tourist campsites, marinas, etc.)
— Specialised establishments (health establishments, work and holiday camps, public means of transport and conference centres
Private tourist accommodation
— Rented accommodation
— Other types of private accommodation
NB: Data on private tourist accommodation are not included in Eurostat data.

Tourist accommodation, supply of

This refers to the number of bed places in an establishment where people can stay overnight in permanent beds, discounting any extra beds set up at the customers' request.

8

Turnover

Turnover comprises the totals invoiced by the observation unit during the reference period, and this corresponds to market sales of goods or services supplied to third parties. Turnover includes all duties and taxes on the goods or services invoiced by the unit with the exception of the VAT invoiced by the unit vis-à-vis its customer and other similar deductible taxes directly linked to turnover. It also includes all other charges (transport, packaging, etc.) passed on to the customer, even if these charges are listed separately on the invoice. Reduction in prices, rebates and discounts as well as the value of returned packing must be deducted. Income classified as other operating income, financial income and extraordinary income in company accounts is excluded from turnover. Operating subsidies received from public authorities or the institutions of the European Union are also excluded. For NACE Rev. 1.1 classes 66.01 and 66.03, the corresponding title of this characteristic is 'Gross premiums written'.

Unemployed person

Persons are considered as unemployed if they fulfil three conditions: to be without employment during the reference week; to be available to start work within the next two weeks; and to have actively sought employment at some time during the previous four weeks or who found a job to start later within a period of at most three months. The duration of unemployment is defined as the duration of search for a job or the length of the period since the last job was held (if this period is shorter than the duration of search for a job).

Unemployment rate

The unemployed as a percentage of people in the labour force.

United Nations (UN)

The United Nations (UN) was established on 24 October 1945 by 51 countries committed to preserving peace through international cooperation and collective security. Today, nearly every nation in the world belongs to the UN: membership totals 189 countries. When States become members of the United Nations, they agree to accept the obligations of the UN Charter, an international treaty that sets out basic principles of international relations. According to the Charter, the UN has four purposes: to maintain international peace and security; to develop friendly relations among nations; to cooperate in solving international problems and in promoting respect for human rights; and to be a centre for harmonising the actions of nations.

United States Patent and Trademark Office (USPTO)

The United States Patent and Trademark Office (USPTO) is a non-commercial federal entity and one of 14 bureaux in the Department of Commerce (DOC) of the United States. The mission of the USPTO is to promote industrial and technological progress in the United States and strengthen the national economy by administering the laws relating to patents and trademarks, advising the Secretary of Commerce, the President of the United States, the administration on patent, trademark, and copyright protection and the administration on the trade-related aspects of intellectual property rights.

8

ACP: African, Caribbean and Pacific countries, signatories to the Partnership Agreement (Cotonou Agreement)

Angola, Antigua and Barbuda, Barbados, Belize, Benin, Botswana, Burkina Faso, Burundi, Cameroon, Cape Verde, Central African Republic, Chad, Comoros, Congo, Congo (Democratic Republic of), Cook Islands, Côte d'Ivoire, Cuba, Djibouti, Dominica, Dominican Republic, Equatorial Guinea, Eritrea, Ethiopia, Fiji, Gabon, Ghana, Grenada, Guinea, Guinea-Bissau, Guyana, Haiti, Jamaica, Kenya, Kiribati, Lesotho, Liberia, Madagascar, Malawi, Mali, Marshall Islands, Mauritania, Mauritius, Micronesia (Federated States of), Mozambique, Namibia, Nauru, Niger, Nigeria, Niue, Palau, Papua New Guinea, Rwanda, Saint Kitts and Nevis, Saint Lucia, Saint Vincent and the Grenadines, Samoa, São Tomé and Príncipe, Senegal, Seychelles, Sierra Leone, Solomon Islands, Somalia, South Africa, Sudan, Suriname, Swaziland, Tanzania (United Republic of), The Bahamas, The Gambia, Timor-Leste, Togo, Tonga, Trinidad and Tobago, Tuvalu, Uganda, Vanuatu, Zambia, Zimbabwe.

APEC: Asia-Pacific Economic Cooperation

Australia, Brunei, Canada, Chile, China, Hong Kong, Indonesia, Japan, Korea (Republic of), Malaysia, Mexico, New Zealand, Papua New Guinea, Peru, Philippines, Russian Federation, Singapore, Taiwan, Thailand, United States, Vietnam.

ASEAN: Association of South-East Asian Nations

Brunei, Cambodia, Indonesia, Laos, Malaysia, Myanmar, Philippines, Singapore, Thailand, Vietnam.

Candidate countries

Bulgaria, Romania, Turkey.

CEECs: central and east European countries

Albania, Bosnia and Herzegovina, Bulgaria, Croatia, Former Yugoslav Republic of Macedonia, Romania, Serbia and Montenegro.

CIS: Commonwealth of Independent States

Armenia, Azerbaijan, Belarus, Georgia, Kazakhstan, Kyrgyzstan, Moldova, Russian Federation, Tajikistan, Turkmenistan, Ukraine, Uzbekistan.

DAEs: dynamic Asian economies

Hong Kong, Korea (Republic of), Malaysia, Singapore, Taiwan, Thailand.

EEA: European Economic Area

EU Member States, Iceland, Liechtenstein, Norway.

EFTA: European Free Trade Association

Iceland, Liechtenstein, Norway, Switzerland.

European Union (EU-25), from 1.5.2004

Belgium, Czech Republic, Denmark, Germany, Estonia, Greece, Spain, France, Ireland, Italy, Cyprus, Latvia, Lithuania, Luxembourg, Hungary, Malta, the Netherlands, Austria, Poland, Portugal, Slovenia, Slovakia, Finland, Sweden, United Kingdom.

European Union (EU-15), until 30.4.2004

Belgium, Denmark, Germany, Greece, Spain, France, Ireland, Italy, Luxembourg, the Netherlands, Austria, Portugal, Finland, Sweden, United Kingdom.

Euro-zone

Countries participating in economic and monetary union and having the euro as the single currency. In 2001, these were Belgium, Germany, Greece, Spain, France, Ireland, Italy, Luxembourg, the Netherlands, Austria, Portugal and Finland.

Extra-EU

Other European countries, Africa, America, Asia, Oceania and polar regions, miscellaneous (countries not specified) extra.

Latin American countries

Argentina, Bolivia, Brazil, Chile, Colombia, Costa Rica, Cuba, Dominican Republic, Ecuador, El Salvador, Guatemala, Haiti, Honduras, Mexico, Nicaragua, Panama, Paraguay, Peru, Uruguay, Venezuela.

MEDA: Mediterranean countries in the Euro-Mediterranean partnership (excluding the EU)

Algeria, Egypt, Israel, Jordan, Lebanon, Morocco, Occupied Palestinian Territory, Syria, Tunisia, Turkey.

Mediterranean basin countries (excluding the EU)

Albania, Algeria, Bosnia and Herzegovina, Ceuta, Croatia, Egypt, Former Yugoslav Republic of Macedonia, Gibraltar, Israel, Jordan, Lebanon, Libya, Melilla, Morocco, Occupied Palestinian Territory, Serbia and Montenegro, Syria, Tunisia, Turkey.

Mercosur: Southern Cone Common Market

Argentina, Brazil, Paraguay, Uruguay.

NAFTA: North American Free Trade Agreement

Canada, Mexico, United States.

8

Near and Middle Eastern countries

United Arab Emirates, Armenia, Azerbaijan, Bahrain, Georgia, Israel, Iraq, Iran (Islamic Republic of), Jordan, Kuwait, Lebanon, Oman, Occupied Palestinian Territory, Qatar, Saudi Arabia, Syrian Arab Republic, Yemen.

NICs: newly industrialised Asian countries

Hong Kong, Korea (Republic of), Singapore, Taiwan.

OECD: Organisation for Economic Cooperation and Development (excluding the EU)

Australia, Canada, Christmas Island, Cocos Islands (or Keeling Islands), Heard Island and McDonald Islands, Iceland, Japan, Korea (Republic of), Mexico, New Zealand, Norfolk Island, Norway, Switzerland, Turkey, United States, Virgin Islands (US).

OPEC: Organisation of Petroleum Exporting Countries

Algeria, Indonesia, Iran, Iraq, Kuwait, Libya, Nigeria, Qatar, Saudi Arabia, United Arab Emirates, Venezuela.

SAARC: South Asian Association for Regional Cooperation

Bangladesh, Bhutan, India, Maldives, Nepal, Pakistan, Sri Lanka.

8

A. **Agriculture, hunting and forestry**

B. **Fishing**

C. **Mining and quarrying**
CA. Mining and quarrying of energy-producing materials
CB. Mining and quarrying, except of energy-producing materials

D. **Manufacturing**
DA. Manufacture of food products, beverages and tobacco
DB. Manufacture of textiles and textile products
DC. Manufacture of leather and leather products
DD. Manufacture of wood and wood products
DE. Manufacture of pulp, paper and paper products; publishing and printing
DF. Manufacture of coke, refined petroleum products and nuclear fuel
DG. Manufacture of chemicals, chemical products and man-made fibres
DH. Manufacture of rubber and plastic products
DI. Manufacture of other non-metallic mineral products
DJ. Manufacture of basic metals and fabricated metal products
DK. Manufacture of machinery and equipment n.e.c.
DL. Manufacture of electrical and optical equipment
DM. Manufacture of transport equipment
DN. Manufacturing n.e.c.

E. **Electricity, gas and water supply**

F. **Construction**

G. **Wholesale and retail trade; repair of motor vehicles, motorcycles and personal and household goods**
50. Sale, maintenance and repair of motor vehicles and motorcycles; retail sale of automotive fuel
51. Wholesale trade and commission trade, except of motor vehicles and motorcycles

52. Retail trade, except of motor vehicles and motorcycles; repair of personal and household goods

H. **Hotels and restaurants**

I. **Transport, storage and communication**
60. Land transport; transport via pipelines
61. Water transport
62. Air transport
63. Supporting and auxiliary transport activities; activities of travel agencies
64. Post and telecommunications

J. **Financial intermediation**
65. Financial intermediation, except insurance and pension funding
66. Insurance and pension funding, except compulsory social security
67. Activities auxiliary to financial intermediation

K. **Real estate, renting and business activities**
70. Real estate activities
71. Renting of machinery and equipment without operator and of personal and household goods
72. Computer and related activities
73. Research and development
74. Other business activities

L. **Public administration and defence; compulsory social security**

M. **Education**

N. **Health and social work**

O. **Other community, social and personal service activities**
90. Sewage and refuse disposal, sanitation and similar activities
91. Activities of membership organisations n.e.c.
92. Recreational, cultural and sporting activities
93. Other service activities

P. **Activities of households**

Q. **Extra-territorial organisations and bodies**

This classification is accessible on the Eurostat website:
http://europa.eu.int/comm/eurostat/ramon/ (option 'Classifications').

8

0. Food and live animals

00. Live animals other than animals of Division 03

01. Meat and meat preparations

02. Dairy products and birds' eggs

03. Fish (not marine mammals), crustaceans, molluscs and aquatic invertebrates and preparations thereof

04. Cereals and cereal preparations

05. Vegetables and fruit

06. Sugars, sugar preparations and honey

07. Coffee, tea, cocoa, spices and manufactures thereof

08. Feedingstuffs for animals (not including unmilled cereals)

09. Miscellaneous edible products and preparations

1. Beverages and tobacco

11. Beverages

12. Tobacco and tobacco manufactures

2. Crude materials, inedible, except fuels

21. Hides, skins and fur skins, raw

22. Oilseeds and oleaginous fruits

23. Crude rubber (including synthetic and reclaimed)

24. Cork and wood

25. Pulp and waste paper

26. Textile fibres (other than wool tops and other combed wool), and their wastes (not manufactured into yarn or fabric)

27. Crude fertilisers, other than those of Division 56, and crude minerals (excluding coal, petroleum and precious stones)

28. Metalliferous ores and metal scrap

29. Crude animal and vegetable materials, n.e.s.

3. Mineral fuels, lubricants and related materials

32. Coal, coke and briquettes

33. Petroleum, petroleum products and related materials

34. Gas, natural and manufactured

35. Electric current

4. Animal and vegetable oils, fats and waxes

41. Animal oils and fats

42. Fixed vegetable fats and oils, crude, refined or fractionated

43. Animal or vegetable fats and oils, processed; waxes of animal or vegetable origin; inedible mixtures or preparations of animal or vegetable fats and oils, n.e.s.

5. Chemicals and related products, n.e.s.

51. Organic chemicals

52. Inorganic chemicals

53. Dyeing, tanning and colouring materials

54. Medical and pharmaceutical products

55. Essential oils and resinoids and perfume materials; toilet, polishing and cleaning preparations

56. Fertilisers (other than those of Division 27)

57. Plastics in primary forms

58. Plastics in non-primary forms

59. Chemical materials and products, n.e.s.

6. Manufactured goods classified chiefly by material

60. Complete industrial plant appropriate to Section 6

61. Leather, leather manufacture, n.e.s., and dressed fur skins

62. Rubber manufacture

63. Cork and wood manufacture (excluding furniture)

64. Paper, paperboard and articles of paper pulp, of paper or of paperboard

65. Textile yarn, fabrics, made-up articles, n.e.s., and related products

66. Non-metallic mineral manufactures, n.e.s.

67. Iron and steel

68. Non-ferrous metals

69. Manufacture of metals, n.e.s.

7. Machinery and transport equipment

70. Complete industrial plant appropriate to Section 7

71. Power-generating machinery and equipment

72. Machinery specialised for particular industries

73. Metalworking machinery

74. General industrial machinery and equipment, n.e.s., and machine parts, n.e.s.

75. Office machines and automatic data-processing machines

76. Telecommunications and sound-recording and reproducing apparatus and equipment

77. Electrical machinery, apparatus and appliances, n.e.s., and electrical parts thereof (including non-electrical counterparts, n.e.s., of electrical household-type equipment)

78. Road vehicles (including air-cushion vehicles)

79. Other transport equipment

8

8. Miscellaneous manufactured articles

80. Complete industrial plant appropriate to Section 8

81. Prefabricated buildings; sanitary plumbing, heating and lighting fixtures and fittings, n.e.s.

82. Furniture and parts thereof; bedding, mattresses, mattress supports, cushions and similar stuffed furnishings

83. Travel goods, handbags and similar containers

84. Articles of apparel and clothing accessories

85. Footwear

87. Professional, scientific and controlling instruments and apparatus, n.e.s.

88. Photographic apparatus, equipment and supplies and optical goods, n.e.s.; watches and clocks

89. Miscellaneous manufactured articles, n.e.s.

9. Commodities and transactions not classified elsewhere in the SITC

91. Postal packages not classified according to kind

93. Special transactions and commodities not classified according to kind

94. Complete industrial plant, n.e.s.

96. Coin (other than gold coin) not being legal tender

97. Gold, non-monetary (excluding gold, ores and concentrates)

List of abbreviations and acronyms

Member States

EU-25	the 25 Member States of the European Union
EU-15	the 15 Member States of the European Union until 30.4.2004
euro-zone	EUR-11 (BE, DE, ES, FR, IE, IT, LU, NL, AT, PT, FI) until 31.12.2000 EUR-12 from 1.1.2001
EUR-12	The euro zone with 12 countries participating (BE, DE, EL, ES, FR, IE, IT, LU, NL, AT, PT, FI)
BE	Belgium
CZ	Czech Republic
DK	Denmark
DE	Germany
EE	Estonia
EL	Greece
ES	Spain
FR	France
IE	Ireland
IT	Italy
CY	Cyprus
LV	Latvia
LT	Lithuania
LU	Luxembourg
HU	Hungary
MT	Malta
NL	Netherlands
AT	Austria
PL	Poland
PT	Portugal
SI	Slovenia
SK	Slovakia
FI	Finland
SE	Sweden
UK	United Kingdom

Candidate countries

BG	Bulgaria
RO	Romania
TR	Turkey

Other countries and territories

AF	Afghanistan
AM	Armenia
AR	Argentina
AZ	Azerbaijan
BA	Bosnia and Herzegovina
BR	Brazil
CA	Canada
CD	Democratic Republic of Congo
CH	Switzerland
CN	China
CO	Colombia
CS	Serbia and Montenegro
D-E	territory of the former East Germany
D-W	territory of the former West Germany
DZ	Algeria
GB	Great Britain
HR	Croatia
IN	India
IQ	Iraq
IR	Iran
IS	Iceland
JP	Japan
KR	South Korea
LI	Liechtenstein
LK	Sri Lanka
LY	Libya
NG	Nigeria
NO	Norway
RU	Russian Federation
SA	Saudi Arabia
SG	Singapore
SL	Sierra Leone
SO	Somalia
TW	Taiwan
UA	Ukraine
US	United States of America
ZA	South Africa

Currencies

ECU	European currency unit, data up to 31.12.1998
EUR [1]	euro, data from 1.1.1999 onwards
ATS [1]	Austrian schilling
BEF [1]	Belgian franc
CYP	Cyprus pound
CZK	Czech koruna
DEM [1]	German mark
DKK	Danish crown (krone)
EEK	Estonian kroon
ESP [1]	Spanish peseta
FIM [1]	Finnish markka
FRF [1]	French franc
GBP	pound sterling
GRD [1]	Greek drachma
HUF	forint
IEP [1]	Irish pound (punt)
ITL [1]	Italian lira
LTL	litas
LUF [1]	Luxembourg franc
LVL	lats
MTL	Maltese lira
NLG [1]	Dutch guilder

[1] The euro replaced the ecu (code = ECU) on 1 January 1999. On 1 January 2002, it also replaced 12 Community currencies.

8

PLN	zloty
PTE (¹)	Portuguese escudo
SEK	Swedish crown (krona)
SIT	tolar
SKK	Slovak koruna
BGN	lev
CAD	Canadian dollar
JPY	Japanese yen
ROL	Romanian leu
TRL	Turkish lira
USD	US dollar

Other abbreviations and acronyms

AA	agricultural area
ACP	African, Caribbean and Pacific States party to the Cotonou Agreement
AIDS	acquired immuno-deficiency syndrome
ASEAN	Association of South-East Asian Nations
AWU	annual work unit
BERD	expenditure on R & D in the business enterprise sector
BLEU	Belgo-Luxembourg Economic Union
BMI	body mass index
BOD	biochemical oxygen demand
BSE	bovine spongiform encephalopathy
CAP	common agricultural policy
CCs	candidate countries
CDR	crude death rate
CEECs	central and east European countries
cif	cost, insurance and freight
CIS	Commonwealth of Independent States
COD	chemical oxygen demand
CVT	continual vocational training
CVTS2	continuing vocational training survey
DAEs	dynamic Asian economies
EAGGF	European Agricultural Guidance and Guarantee Fund
ECB	European Central Bank
ECHP	European Community household panel
ECHP-UDB	European Community household panel — user's database
ECSC	European Coal and Steel Community
EEA	European Economic Area (EU + EFTA countries without Switzerland)
EEAICP	European Economic Area index of consumer prices

EFTA	European Free Trade Association (CH, IS, LI, NO)
EICP	European index of consumer prices
EITO	European Information Technology Observatory
EMS	European Monetary System
EPO	European Patent Office
ERDF	European Regional Development Fund
ESA	1. European system of national and regional accounts (ESA 95) 2. European Space Agency
ESF	European Social Fund
Esspros	European system of integrated social protection statistics
EU	European Union
EU-SILC	EU statistics on income and living conditions
Eurostat	the statistical office of the European Communities
Eurydice	information network on education in Europe (http://www.eurydice.org/)
FAO	Food and Agriculture Organisation (UN)
fob	free on board
FTE	full-time equivalent
GBAORD	government budget appropriations or outlays for research and development
GCSE	General Certificate of Secondary Education
GDP	gross domestic product
GERD	gross domestic expenditure on R & D
GHG	greenhouse gases
GNI	gross national income
GNP	gross national product
GT	gross tonnage
GVA	gross value added
HICP	harmonised index of consumer prices
ICT	Institute of Computer Technology/information and communication technology
ILO	International Labour Organisation
IMF	International Monetary Fund
IPI	industrial production index
ISCED	international standard classification of education
ISPO	Information Society Promotion Office
IT	information technology
LFS	labour force survey
LMP	labour market policy
Mercosur	Southern Cone Common Market
MSTI/OECD	main science and technology indicators/Organisation for Economic Cooperation and Development

---

(¹) The euro replaced the ecu (code = ECU) on 1 January 1999. On 1 January 2002, it also replaced 12 Community currencies.

8

MUICP	monetary union index of consumer prices		**SI**	structural indicators
NACE	general industrial classification of economic activities within the European Communities		**SIF**	Statistics in Focus
			SITC Rev. 3	standard industrial trade classification, third revision
NAFTA	North American Free Trade Agreement		**TBFRA**	temperate and boreal forest resources assessment
NHS	National Health Service		**UN**	United Nations
n.e.c.	not elsewhere classified		**Unesco**	United Nations Educational, Scientific and Cultural Organisation
n.e.s.	not elsewhere specified			
NIS	new independent States (of the former Soviet Union)		**UNHCR**	Office of the United Nations High Commissioner for Refugees
NPISHs	non-profit institutions serving households		**USPTO**	United States Patent and Trademark Office
NUTS	nomenclature of territorial units for statistics (Eurostat) (NUTS 1, 2 etc.)		**VAT**	value added tax
			WHO	World Health Organisation

SI structural indicators
SIF Statistics in Focus

OD	overseas departments
OECD	Organisation for Economic Cooperation and Development
OECD-DAC	Organisation for Economic Cooperation and Development - Development Assistance Committee
OPEC	Organisation of Petroleum Exporting Countries
PPP	purchasing power parity
PPS	purchasing power standard
R&D	research and development
RON	research octane number
SDR	standard death rate
SGM	standard gross margin
SDI	sustainable development indicators

Units of measurement

GJ	gigajoule
GWh	gigawatt hour (106 kWh)
ha	hectare
hc	head count
hl	hectolitre
kcal	kilocalorie
kg	kilogram
kgoe	kilogram of oil equivalent
kWh	kilowatt hour
m^3	cubic metre
sq. km/km^2	square kilometre
t	tonne (metric ton)
tkm	tonne-km
toe	tonne of oil equivalent

Directorates-General of the European Commission (incomplete list)

DG	Directorate-General
DG AGRI	Directorate-General for Agriculture
DG AIDCO	EuropeAid Co-operation Office
DG BUDG	Directorate-General for the Budget
DG COMP	Directorate-General for Competition
DG DEV	Directorate-General for Development
DG EAC	Directorate-General for Education and Culture
DG ECFIN	Directorate-General for Economic and Financial Affairs
DG ELARG	Directorate-General for Enlargement
DG EMPL	Directorate-General for Employment and Social Affairs
DG ENTR	Directorate-General for Enterprise
DG ENV	Directorate-General for the Environment
DG ESTAT	Directorate-General Eurostat
DG FISH	Directorate-General for Fisheries
DG INFSO	Directorate-General for the Information Society
DG JAI	Directorate-General for Justice and Home Affairs
DG MARKT	Directorate-General for the Internal Market
DG PRESS	Directorate-General for Press and Communication
DG REGIO	Directorate-General for Regional Policy
DG RELEX	Directorate-General for External Relations
DG RTD	Directorate-General for Research
DG SANCO	Directorate-General for Health and Consumer Protection
DG TAXUD	Directorate-General for Taxation and Customs Union
DG TRADE	Directorate-General for Trade
DG TREN	Directorate-General for Energy and Transport

8

European Commission

Eurostat yearbook 2004 — Data 1992-2002

Luxembourg: Office for Official Publications of the European Communities

2004 — 280 pp. — 21 x 29.7 cm

Theme 1: General statistics
Collection: Panorama of the European Union

ISBN 92-894-4963-2
ISSN 1681-4789

Price (excluding VAT) in Luxembourg: EUR 50

8

How to consult the information on the CD-ROM

1. On successful installation (*) of the CD-ROM, press the 'START' button. A window will appear with the title of the Eurostat yearbook 2004 and the language versions that are available. Click on the chosen language.

2. The following screen lists all the information contained on the CD-ROM. Choose the type of information desired and click on it.

3. Follow the instructions on each of the following screens.

(*) If the programme does not start automatically, please carry out the following steps:
— Open Windows Explorer.
— Double click on the symbol for the CD-ROM drive.
— Double click on **connect.bat** (execute the programme) and follow the installation instructions.

SALES AND SUBSCRIPTIONS

Publications for sale produced by the Office for Official Publications of the European Communities are available from our sales agents throughout the world.

How do I set about obtaining a publication?

Once you have obtained the list of sales agents, contact the sales agent of your choice and place your order.

How do I obtain the list of sales agents?

— Go to the Publications Office website http://publications.eu.int/
— Or apply for a paper copy by fax (352) 2929 42758